History of Brighthelmston

Classics in English Local History

1. *History of Brighthelmston* (1862)
   John Ackerson Erredge

History of Brighthelmston

John Ackerson Erredge

Introduction by John Farrant

BRAMBLETYE BOOKS
FOREST ROW

This edition first published 2005
by Brambletye Books
5 Walhatch Close
Forest Row
East Sussex RH18 5GT
United Kingdom

Brambletye Books is an imprint of Brambletye Publishing

www.brambletye-publishing.co.uk

Printed and bound in the United Kingdom by T.J. International, Padstow, Cornwall.

A CIP catalogue record for this book is available from the British Library.

ISBN 0-9521757-1-1

Contents

Introduction

History of Brighthelmston, or Brighton as I view it and others knew it was the first substantial book devoted wholly to Brighton, past or present. Earlier books on Brighton had been slim guides for visitors, while its history was to be found in volumes with a wider scope. The author, John Ackerson Erredge, was born in the town to a fishing family in 1810 or 1811, worked there as a schoolmaster and then a journalist, and died while the *History* was being published in monthly parts, in 1862.

In this Introduction we piece together Erredge's biography, examine the earlier histories of the town, identify the sources on which he drew for his *History* and, in the context of Brighton's development in his lifetime, speculate as to the audiences for whom he wrote, before noting his successors as historians of Brighton.

The Author

John Erredge was born between November 1810 and April 1811.[1] His parents had married in 1808. Samuel Cynic (or Sinnock) Erredge was from a long-established Brighton family and was a fishermen, probably as an owner of boats, rather than as a working crewman, for he owned a herring deese (smoke-house) and a tan-house. He was a widower, and his first marriage may have been as long before as 1782, so that he had three grown-up children by the time he married again. His second wife Hannah was the daughter of John and Mary Ackerson and was baptised in 1772. The Erredges lived in Kent's Rent, Kent Street, off the west side

1 Aged 51 at death: *Brighton Herald,* 8 Nov. 1862. April 1861 census: aged 50.

of West Street, at the seaward end.[2] The only children of the marriage were twins, John and Ackerson.[3]

Samuel died in 1816 or 1817, having already lost Hannah. John and Ackerson were brought up by their mother's brother, Robert Ackerson (1763-1846) and his wife Jane.[4] For the last few years of her long life - she died at 96 in 1855 - Jane was living with her nephew John, and, we are told, 'was childless; yet many an orphan will long revere her memory.'[5] Robert Ackerson was Samuel's executor and held in trust Samuel's house, deese and tan-house, and the house occupied by Samuel's son Richard, for paying the mortgage, maintaining Ackerson until he was 21 (but, curiously, not John) and his daughter Elizabeth who was presumably unmarried. The will called Robert a bricklayer, but as early as 1800 he was named as a builder, a trade offering many opportunities in early 19th century Brighton.[6] Indeed he had prospered by 1816, as he served the previous year as High Constable for Brighton, and he held other significant local-government offices as a Director and Guardian of the Poor, Overseer of the Poor, Churchwarden (1821) and Assessor for the parish rates. In 1822 he was living at 17 Duke Street.[7]

John was educated at the Revd Dr Henry Stewart Byron's academy, which was still running in 1845 as a boarding school in Air Street. He took up teaching himself, first as an assistant at Dr Byron's academy and then at Mr

2 *Brighton Herald*, 8 Nov. 1862; East Sussex Record Office (hereafter ESRO), Brighton St Nicholas register transcript; W/A 72, p. 800.

3 Ackerson Erredge was aged 40 in the 1851 census, John aged 50 in the 1861 census. I take the baptismal entry (Brighton St Nicholas), 17 Feb. 1815, 'John Ackerson, son of Samuel', as in error for 'John and Ackerson, sons of Samuel'. Both are named in their father's will.

4 *Brighton Herald*, 8 Nov. 1862.

5 J. A. Erredge, *History of Brighthelmston or Brighton as I view it and others knew it* (Brighton: E. Lewis, 1862), 181-2.

6 J. G. Bishop, *A peep into the past: Brighton in the olden time*, People's edn (Brighton: J. G. Bishop, 1892), vi.

7 Erredge, *History*, 25, 55, 181, 300. J. Baxter, *The stranger in Brighton & Baxter's new Brighton directory* (Brighton: J. Baxter & Co., 1822), 32, 38, 39.

Grix's, named in 1845 as Belle Vue Hall in Eastern Road.[8] William Grix was his brother-in-law, perhaps through his wife. She was Mary Ann Bevern whom he married in her home parish of St Anne's Lewes in June 1832. The marriage licence shows that he had adopted Ackerson as his middle name and describes him as a 'school assistant of Brighton'.[9] He later stated that his own school opened in that same year of 1832, and perhaps his marriage was the occasion for his uncle to set John up in his own business. In 1834 his address was in Grenville Place, where Robert Ackerson (by 1843) owned two houses. Between at least 1836 and 1841, the school was at 28 West Street. John and Mary Ann were to have seven children, born between 1834 and 1855, all surviving their father.[10]

Some notion of his teaching can be gleaned from the book which he wrote and which Relfe & Fletcher, the well-known London publishers of schoolbooks, issued in 1840. 'The great bane of Education', Erredge wrote, 'has ever been that the works produced for youth are either too abstruse for their capacity, or too "dry" and uninteresting for their natural cheerfulness, often causing the inherent relish for improvement to subside, from the difficulty or the monotony of the subject; the object; then, of the compiler of this little work has been to blend amusement with instruction, and relieve the tedium unavoidably attendant on some studies.' Its utility, we are assured, has been tested in manuscript in more than one establishment. The small volume of 110 pages with printed board covers is entitled *The student's hand-book of general information* and comprises

8 *Brighton Herald,* 8 Nov. 1862. Dr Byron does not appear in Baxter, *Stranger in Brighton.* Kelly, *The Post Office directory for the six Home Counties* (London, 1845). *Brighton Gazette,* 6 Nov. 1862.

9 E. H. W. Dunkin and E. W. D. Penfold, eds *Calendar of Sussex marriage licences... for the archdeaconry of Lewes, and in the peculiar court of the archbishop of Canterbury for the deanery of South Malling, 1772-1837. Pt. 1 A-L,* Sussex Record Society 25 (Lewes, 1917).

10 W. J. Taylor, *The original Brighton & Hove directory, including Cliftonville* (Brighton, 1854). ESRO, Brighton St Nicholas and Chapel Royal register transcripts; 1861 census. The National Archives, B 3/1642.

nine sections containing some 450 questions and answers.[11] The answers to some questions are supplemented by further explanation in smaller type and by biographical information in footnotes. It is clear that Erredge expected the teacher, rather than each pupil, to have the book, so that learning was by recitation. The sections and typical questions are:

I	Inventions	By whom was the mariner's compass invented?
II	Discoveries	Who discovered galvanism, and what is its use?
III	Origins	Whence the origin of [free]masonry?
IV	Customs and ceremonies	Whence originated the custom of eating goose on Michaelmas day?
V	Institutions	When was the office of poet-laureate first instituted?
VI	Causes	What is the cause of what are called fairy-rings?
VII	Derivations	What is meant by the term deodand?
VIII	Definitions	What is meant by bonfires?
IX	Miscellaneous	How is India rubber made?

Erredge also set up in business as a bookseller and stationer, but these several occupations proved insufficient to yield a livelihood, or he had some financial misfortune of which we have no evidence. For in March 1841 he was declared bankrupt, on the petition of Robert Ackerson of 43 Clarence Place, gentleman. His uncle was the largest creditor, for £266 out of £1134, and was probably the Ackerson joined with Grix for another £150; William Grix was owned £92. Although petitioning by the uncle who had brought him up may seem a hostile act, it was surely intended to be benevolent in the circumstances: if he was going to be bankrupted by debts outside the family, it was better that the process was as far as possible controlled by the family. In the surviving papers, a schedule of expenses

11 Dated 1839 on the cover and 1840 on the title page; the preface is dated 1 October 1839.

runs from 1833 to 1840 and, besides £29 for goodwill of the school, gives annual totals for tent, taxes and houses expenses, the whole amounting to £2704 over eight years. But there is no statement of income. It was as a bookseller and stationer that he was declared bankrupt, because that made him a trader and brought him within the scope of the bankruptcy laws. As a schoolmaster, he was not and would have been an insolvent debtor, liable to indefinite imprisonment if his creditors so wished. Stock in trade, at cost prices, household furniture, glass, linen, etc., were valued at £487 and a share in property bequeathed to his wife at £80, but the distribution to creditors was only £90. The creditors outside the family were Brighton tradesmen, such as bakers, butcher, ironmonger, draper, stonemasons and cabinet maker, and two London publishers, Relfe & Fletcher, and W. F. Rock & Co.[12] Relfe & Fletcher presumably acquired the copyright of *The student's handbook* at this juncture; they were to invite John Quested to revise it for republication in 1860.

Robert Ackerson ensured that the Erredge family, now with three children, could retain a home and continue the school. The school's address later in 1841 was Western Road.[13] In August 1842, when Erredge advertised for a gentleman under the age of 25 to teach French and Latin and to assist generally for £25 a year, it was called the Regent House Academy.[14] In 1845 it was at 43 Clarence Street, Ackerson's own address in 1841 and 1843. He died in early 1846.[15] In 1850 – as a day school – it was at 44 Clarence Place which he had bequeathed to John subject to a £250 mortgage, in 1851 at 7 Clarence Street. John also received under the will half the household goods, excepting the plate

12 The National Archives, B 3/1642.

13 ESRO, Brighton Chapel Royal register transcript.

14 *The Times*, 20 Aug. 1842.

15 Kelly, *Post Office directory*. The National Archives, B 3/1642. ESRO, W/A 82, p. 143.

which passed to the widow, Jane, and 52 London Road for life with a £600 mortgage. [16]

In or about 1852 the family with aunt Jane moved to Cambridge Lodge, 87 London Road.[17] Two years later, the following advertisement appeared in Taylor's *Original Brighton & Hove Directory*:

Established 1832
COMMERCIAL & MATHEMATICAL
ACADEMY.
CAMBRIDGE LODGE, LONDON ROAD,
BRIGHTON, -- CONDUCTED BY
MR. ERREDGE,
Assisted by qualified Masters.

TERMS, INCLUDING THE USE OF BOOKS:
Boarders.............30 guineas per annum
Daily pupils...........6 guineas " "
Payable in advance, quarterly
French, Latin, Drawing, Dance, and Drilling on the usual terms

----

School and Class Rooms
21, MIDDLE STREET, BRIGHTON

So Cambridge Lodge served as a boarding house for the school, while the class rooms were in Middle Street, which was listed in the directory also as the address for the seminary run by Erredge's eldest child, 20-year-old Ada Mary.[18] Aunt Jane Ackerson was presumably subsidising the family. She died in February 1855 and it must be significant that thereafter the only later reference to the school, for day pupils only, is from 1856, at 55 West Street.[19]

Another reason for giving up teaching may have been a gammy leg. Erredge tells us that he would have lost a leg by amputation, but for Mr Henry Harrap's 'rubbing'. The rigours of a boys' school may have been too demanding. Erredge became a journalist - and the family

16 R. Folthorp, *The court guide & general directory for Brighton* (Brighton, 1850), 55, 180. ESRO, W/A 82, p. 143.

17 Folthorp, *Directory* (1852), 92, 167, 276. Erredge, *History*, 182n.

18 Taylor, *Directory*.

19 Erredge, *History*, 182n. Folthorp, *Directory* (1856).

moved to small houses. At the beginning of 1858 the Erredges were living at 1 Wykeham Terrace, but in March moved to 35 West Hill Street. By then another line of business had been added: the production and marketing of Erredge's Brighton Relish. Another move occurred by April 1861, to 16 Sydney Terrace. There the census enumerator, John's 18-year-old son Herbert Edward, an apprentice reporter, listed, besides himself, John, aged 50, journalist, his wife Mary Ann, 48, and their children Ada Mary, 27, governess, Mariann, 12, Walter James, 10 and Frank, 6. Ileen Jane, 24, and Helen Rose, 19 or 20, were away from home. Within a month the house was up for auction, described as in the occupation of a good tenant at the very modest rental of £24. The seven resident members squeezed into back and front sitting rooms, two good bedrooms and, in the basement, kitchen and housekeeper's room - though not required for that purpose by a family of the Erredges' limited means.[20] Late in the following year they were living at 33 Gloucester Street.

One obituary described Erredge as editor of the *Brighton Observer*, but the latter spoke only of his connection with it from the first number in November 1856. Both he and Ebenezer Lewis the founding proprietor in 1862 had offices at the printing works in North Street, and the truth may be that Lewis closely directed the editorial policy, leaving Erredge with the donkey work of proofreading, etc. 'In light and sketchy writing Mr E. was particularly at home,' the *Brighton Herald* recorded, 'and his "To Dieppe and back," his "Nomenclature of Trades and Tradesmen," and other works, are well known and possess genuine wit and humour. His numerous articles in the *Observer* in the same vein were always read with interest.' *The nomenclature of trades and tradesmen in Brighton* had first appeared in the *Observer* over several issues in 1857-8 and was published complete in 1860, with Thomas Clark's *A metrical enumeration of the churches of Brighton, connected with the*

20 Erredge, *History*, 237. ESRO, HOW/106/10.

Establishment, and the names of the officiating clergy.[21] Both today read rather laboured: a verse from Erredge's effort runs:

A Bright jeweller few towns can boast
Or a Thorowgood bootmaker;
Yet here are both, and what is rare
A Brown bread and biscuit baker.
Strong plumbers here are numerous;
Flee-sons are all female:
Absalom don't wear a bob-tail wig
But beer and stout retails.

Erredge was probably responsible for the regular 'Literature', and 'Fine Arts, Music, and the Drama' columns, and also for 'Cullings. Quaint and Quizzical' in the earlier years, containing paragraphs doubtless taken from other newspapers and magazines, for example:

> FORETHOUGHT.- Jane Smith, the other day, went to her uncle Benjamin and asked for the loan for £5; and when the old gentleman enquired when she would repay it, the forward young lady coolly told him he might deduct it when he made his will.[22]

He was attributed with 'Brighton Chit-Chat' which appears occasionally, with the by-line:

While on their way in friendly chat
Now talk of this, and then of that

The article for 24 January 1858, for example, ran for two thirds of a column unrelieved by paragraph breaks, from children returning to Brighton boarding schools after Christmas, through the sending of valentine cards, how railway carriages might be heated, the case for a volunteer fire brigade in the town, to the desirability of donating to charities rather giving to street beggars.

21 Published by E. Lewis, "Observer" Office, King Street, Brighton, 1860; copy in the Brighton History Centre.

22 26 Feb 1858.

The *Brighton Observer, Fashionable Arrival List, and County Intelligencer*, to give its full title, first appeared on 28 November 1856, under the proprietorship of Ebenezer Lewis, from 54 West Street, next door to the last address for Erredge's school. Two years later printing and publication moved to 16 King Street, and in July 1862 to 53a North Street.[23] Its editorial stance was Liberal and it advocated progressive improvements and reforms; its pages gave local information, general news, literary critiques, etc.; and a list of fashionable arrivals. An advertisement of 1862 asserted:[24]

> ...the first established of the local cheap press, and hence, *pater-familias* of the Brighton Newspapers, [it] is the largest circulated of the Brighton press in the town and district, its weekly average being upwards of 5,000, and as an advertising medium is consequently the best.
>
> In addition to the ordinary newspaper intelligence, a considerable space is devoted to the announcement of fashionable arrivals, departures, parties &c., which causes it to be largely patronised in fashionable circles, and among the reading community. It is essentially a family paper, carefully omitting the insertion of matter and advertisements which may have an immoral and indelicate tendency.

The circumstances of Erredge's death were fully recorded in the local press. He left home at about 9.15 on the morning of Wednesday 5 November 1862. He reached the *Brighton Observer* office and was going upstairs to his room when Mr Lewis called him into his back room. For a minute or two they talked, Erredge standing with his hands on Mr Lewis's table. He reeled over, hitting his head on the sideboard. Other staff rushed in, including his son Herbert, assistance was summoned, but he was dead by the time Mr Rugg the surgeon arrived ten minutes later. With added (and inaccurate) melodrama, the Preface to the *History*

23 Erredge, *History*, 343.

24 *The newspaper press directory and advertiser's guide* (London: C. Mitchell & Co., 1862), 41, 139. Few issues of the paper are held locally and the only complete run is in the British Library, but issues for some years are unfit for use, including 1856-7 and 1861.

reads: 'Death came upon him, not stealthily, but in its most awful form. It surprised him literally at the desk. Whilst talking cheerfully to the publisher, the hand of Death was laid upon him, and he fell dead to the ground; —the ink of these pages was still wet whilst the Author was extended on the floor a corpse.' The coroner's inquest that afternoon heard evidence indicative of untreated heart disease, and the immediate cause was identified as sudden rupture of the aorta. At the funeral at the Extra-Mural Cemetery the following Monday, 'a large number of the tradesmen of the town and personal friends of the deceased manifested their respect.'[25] 'We fear', the *Brighton Guardian* reported, 'that his is another instance of the rarity of men of generous disposition leaving their family a sufficient pecuniary provision.' Friends were said to be starting a subscription, and Mr Lewis resigned his interest in the *History*, so that the full profits would go to the family.[26]

The same issue of the *Observer* as reported Erredge's death carried the following advertisement on the front page:

On November 8th will be published Part XI. - price Sixpence
of the
HISTORY OF BRIGHTHEMSTON;
or, Brighton as I View It, and Others Knew It;
being a
COMPLETE HISTORY OF THE TOWN
FROM THE EARLIEST AUTHENTIC DATE
Through its
PROGRESSIVE RISE AND PROSPERITY
TO THE PRESENT TIME
By J. ACKERSON ERREDGE
Author of the "Student's Handbook" &c.
CONTENTS OF PART XI
Chapter XXVIII. - Past and Present Pastimes
Chapter XXIX.- The Historical Street of the town
Chapter XXX.- Institutions, Charities and Endowments.
Published by E. LEWIS, *Observer* Office, 53a North street.
Brighton.
Subscribers' Names received at the *Brighton Observer* Office,
at Messrs Beal and Embling's, booksellers, East Street; and at
Messrs Molyneux's, booksellers, 207 Western road; and Mr Brook,

25 *Brighton Observer*, 7, 14 Nov. 1862.

26 *Brighton Guardian*, 6 Nov. 1862. *Brighton Observer*, 7, 14 Nov. 1862.

bookseller, 109 and 110, Western road.
The work will consist of Thirteen Monthly parts, 32 pp., demy 8vo, in tinted wrapper.

Similar advertisements had appeared weekly since the previous December, appropriately updated as parts appeared. Initially the work was available only to subscribers, and only at the *Observer* office, with the added inducement that the wrappers would not be 'incumbered with advertisements'. The reference to thirteen, rather than twelve, parts appeared only on 31 October and 7 November. A part is dated to each month from December 1861, except August. Part XII was published on 24 December, at the price of 9d, 3d extra as with it came the title page, preface and contents page. Each part comprised two sheets, each folded to sixteen pages and stitched through the margin, with the wrapper glued on top. The stitch holes can be seen in a copy bound up from parts. The openings of chapters did not correspond with parts, so usually a part opened with the tail end of a chapter and the last chapter advertised was incomplete. Mr Swane, jun., at 51 Market Street offered cases for binding at 9d.[27]

The *History* was also issued in 1867 by W. J. Smith, second-hand bookseller in North Street and Brighton antiquarian, with a new title-page giving a different title: *The ancient and modern history of Brighton, with a reprint of "The Booke of all the Auncient Customes, 1580"* and a frontispiece of the Pumphouse at Pool Valley. Probably Smith bought the remaining stock from Lewis and bound up sets, rather than instigated a reprint.[28] Lewis is likely to have broken up the type for reuse.

Erredge's precursors

Erredge's *History* was the first substantial volume to claim to be a history of the town, though it was not the first under

27 Brighton History Centre has nine unbound parts which are numbered No. 3 to No. 5 and No. 7 to No. 12. The chapter numbering went awry in Part XI, and 'The Historical Street of the Town' was, like 'Past and Present Pastimes', numbered XXVIII.

28 This is indicated by stitch holes in the margins.

such a title or of the genre to which it belonged - and from the perspective of what a town history should comprise, it was another 90 years before Brighton gained its first history. All accounts of Brighton before the mid-20th century mix reference to its present condition and character with historical matter, in the manner of a guide book. Indeed the literature on Brighton and most other English towns was more topographical than (in modern terms) historical, and Erredge's subtitle, *Brighton as I view it and others knew it,* acknowledged as much.

Brighton first gained more than passing reference in print, in *Magna Britannia et Hibernia, antiqua et nova.* This finished as a six-volume work, having been published in parts. The Sussex parts appeared between November 1728 and May 1729, and were bound into volume 5, dated 1730. The account of Brighton was written by Richard Haylor of Steyning, a Quaker who died in 1726; it ran to about 1,000 words. He argued for the town's antiquity from the likelihood that Julius Caesar landed here and from Earl Godwin's lordship before the Norman Conquest; referred briefly to Charles II's escape in 1651; and described Elizabethan fortifications, unclear as to what was still visible and what was by tradition. Modern research has broadly substantiated his account of the town's falling population since the Civil War due to decline in the fisheries and erosion by the sea.[29]

Within a generation, Brighton's fortunes revived, as the medical profession, prominent among them Dr Richard Russell of Lewes, recommended sea air, sea bathing and seawater drinking. For this clientele Dr Anthony Relhan (1715-76), who had taken over a large part of Dr Russell's practice at Brighton in 1759, published in 1761 *A short history of Brighthelmstone,* in which he gave an account of the climate, mineral spring, and other advantages of the place

29 The identification of 'Mr Haylor' is based on his writing also about Steyning and on Religious Society of Friends (Quakers) Library, MS Vol. S420, memorandum book of Elizabeth Grover. J. H. Farrant, 'The rise and decline of a south coast seafaring town: Brighton, 1550-1750', *Mariner's Mirror,* 71 (1985). J. H. Farrant, 'The Brighton charity school in the early 18th century', *Sussex Archaeological Collections,* 122 (1984).

as a resort for invalids. While giving some account of the contemporary town, it was distinctly short on history, though Relhan sought to establish that Brighton had been a Roman station by reference to the form of its streets, an urn of 1000 denarii found 'some time ago', and a Roman *via* between Shoreham and Lewes found by an ingenious gentleman. He had consulted the 1580 customs and, among current documentary sources, the custom-house diaries, the poor-rate book and the parish register.

The first substantive history of Brighton appeared in 1795 as an adjunct to the history of the nearby county town, Lewes. Their author is a shadowy figure, unnamed on the volume, Paul Dunvan, of French extraction, usher at the Lewes grammar school and only briefly, it seems, a Lewes resident. He was in the riotous minority at a meeting to launch a Loyal Association against Republicans and Levellers in December 1792 - consistent with the advanced radical views reflected in his writing. He must have been commissioned by the printer William Lee, rather than have offered to Lee the fruits of many years' research. He produced a volume of 555 pages with remarkable speed. The *Ancient and modern history of Lewes and Brighthelmston* was published in twelve 48-page parts, starting in June/July 1792 and finishing in March/April 1795. The last three parts were devoted to Brighton, 122 pages, some 30,000 words. [30] Dismissing Mr Haylor's placing of Caesar's landing place at Brighton, as 'puerile reveries', he acknowledged that little was known before the 11th century and then devoted 20 pages to Earl Godwin, Harold and the Norman Conquest, as Godwin was a lord of Brighton. Nevertheless he introduced the conjecture that the town received a colony of Flemings in the 12th century. He was happy to repeat Haylor's account of the town walls. Charles II's escape and Nicholas Tattersall, who skippered the boat, are treated at length. The Ancient Customs of 1580 and the amendments of 1618 are printed in full. Other primary sources which he clearly consulted were deeds to town

30 J. H. Farrant, *Sussex depicted. Views and descriptions 1600-1800*, Sussex Record Society 85 (Lewes, 2001), 59.

property, Charles Goodwyn's rental of 1665 and the vestry book started in 1682. He outlined the town's depressed state round 1700 and its recovery thanks to the revival of 'the long-lost medical use of sea-water', whereby 'the erection of lodging-houses now became a profitable speculation.' In a useful account of the town's recent development, Dunvan's anti-monarchism allowed only slight mention of the royal patronage the town enjoyed.

Haylor, Relhan and Dunvan provided enough material for historical sections in the guide books which proliferated from around 1800.[31] These were also sufficient for the Revd Thomas Walker Horsfield (1792-1837), minister of the Westgate chapel in Lewes. He followed *The history and antiquities of Lewes and its vicinity* (1824) with a second volume (1827) covering 43 parishes within an eight to ten-mile radius. Though Brighton was the first parish in the volume, it received only nine pages, with Horsfield's assessment that 'to attempt to shew that Brighton, till within the last fifty years, was otherwise than a poor and inconsiderable fishing town, would be little better than a waste of time.' However, five years later the publisher, John Baxter, issued a prospectus for a third uniform volume which would complete a 'History of Sussex'. It was to have three parts:

i. the history of Brighton, past and present
ii. the history and antiquities of the coast of Sussex, with the geology and natural history, the material being arranged by routes for the tourist
iii. those places not comprised under the previous heads, together with whatever may be worthy of notice as to trade, manufactures, agriculture, etc.[32]

31 The way in which these guides created and perpetuated an alternative history of early Brighton, to that in the 'histories' so called, is discussed in S. Berry, 'Myth and reality in the representation of resorts. Brighton and the emergence of the 'Prince and fishing village' myth 1770-1820', *Sussex Archaeological Collections*, 140 (2002).

32 Farrant, *Sussex depicted*, 68-9.

But the project was abandoned, perhaps because almost simultaneously the Revd John Docwra Parry announced *An historical and descriptive account of the coast of Sussex* which appeared in 1833.[33] Rather disarmingly, Parry's opening paragraph records that 'This volume was begun, completed, and published within the space of six months, although it had been meditated for about the same number of preceding ones, which, with one or two brief previous exceptions, forms the whole of the author's acquaintance with the County of Sussex. It has been conducted under every possible discouragement and want of support.' Parry - who came from Bedfordshire - spent some of that time in the libraries of the British Museum and the University of Cambridge, and was not ashamed to share his discoveries at length, like a list of the Royal Navy's ships in James I's reign which, he acknowledged, 'has no local application, but we doubt not there are many to whom it will prove both new and interesting.' Of Brighton interest was Colonel Gunter's account of Charles II's escape through Sussex in 1651, which the British Museum had purchased in 1830, and verbatim extracts from Sir William Burrell's historical notes bequeathed in 1796 and the Revd William Hayley's notes presented by John Fuller in 1820.[34]

Baxter turned to another project, a two-volume History of Sussex in a larger format, again by (or more likely edited by) Horsfield. *The history, antiquities, and topography of the County of Sussex* appeared in two large volumes in 1835, priced, at £4 4s, 'so low as to place it within the reach of a large class of persons to whom other county histories are sealed books.' His marketing was successful, as 1019 subscribers are listed. Brighton was the first parish to be treated, over 53 pages. But his account was

33 On Parry, see C. R. J. Currie and C. P. Lewis, eds *English county histories: a guide* (Stroud: Alan Sutton, 1994), 35.

34 Parry's was the first printed edition of Gunter's account. The authoritative edition, collating three copies, is now W. Matthews, ed. *Charles II's escape from Worcester* (Berkeley & Los Angeles: University of California Press, 1966), 144-64. Hayley's notes are wrongly acknowledged: the sections credited to John Elliot in the Burrell MSS (e.g. pp. 4-6, 325-6) are from British Library, Add. MS. 6343.

heavily reliant on the existing histories and the only significant new material for a local audience was an engraving of the 1538/9 bird's-eye view of Brighton in the British Museum, which had been published in *Archaeologia* in 1832.[35] About a third of the article was devoted to the 'Modern state of the town'.

Erredge's sources

When the final part appeared on Christmas Eve 1862, Erredge's *History* was, at 372 pages, easily the longest book which had been published about Brighton. It contained much information new to historical accounts of the town, but - as is still the case with much local history writing - he was not particularly diligent in citing his sources. From where did he gather his material?

First, he drew on Haylor, Relhan, Dunvan and Parry - more than his references to them indicate. All his references to William Burrell's notes (both acknowledged and unacknowledged) come from Parry. The suggestion (p. 26) that the Ancient Customs of 1580 were taken from a copy held by the vestry clerk is misleading: almost certainly the text is from Dunvan, with only the names and marks from the original. Many of the references to antiquarian writers and early records are probably second-hand, for example 'Skinner' mentioned on page 11 comes from Dunvan, page 433, as do the several references to 'Rowe's MS' and 'Goodwyn's rental' and the letters patent of 1672 granting reversion of Tettersell's captaincy, while for Holinshed's chronicles he relied on Parry and/or Horsfield.[36] Gunter's account of Charles II's escape must

35 The map is now British Library, Cotton Aug. I.i.18, and is attributed to Anthony Anthony in 1538/9. See C. S. Knighton and D. M. Loades, eds *The Anthony roll of Henry VIII's navy : Pepys Library 2991 and British Library additional MS 22047 with related documents,* Occasional publications of the Navy Records Society 2 (Aldershot: Ashgate, 2000).

36 The modern edition of the Ancient Customs is C. Webb and A. E. Wilson, eds *Elizabethan Brighton. The Ancient Customs of Brighthelmston 1580* (Brighton: John Beal, 1952). 'Rowe's MS' is published as J. Rowe, *The book of John Rowe, steward of the manors of*

come from Parry, as also Thomas Pennant's of the fisheries. Several of the 'letters from Brighton' (e.g. pp. 68, 77) can be traced to newspaper extracts in Parry.

Secondly, Erredge did consult some of the early printed guidebooks and tourist literature. They were likely his mainstay for descriptions of the town's amenities around 1800. All the quotations from a diary kept in 1778 and 1779 are in fact taken, not from a manuscript, but from Peregrine Phillips, *A diary kept in an excursion to Littlehampton, near Arundel, and Brighthelmston, in Sussex, in 1778; and also to the latter place in 1779*, 2 vols (London: J. Bew and M. Davenport, 1780). The account of Dr Knox and the Surrey Militia relied much more on the contemporary pamphlet than the footnote to page 93 implies.

Thirdly, he did own a few original documents, though not, it seems, the 'large and valuable accumulation of records connected with the town' as the *Brighton Herald* obituary claimed. The manuscript diary which he quoted for 1805 and 1807 (pp. 71, 72, 186, 191, 202) may be the source also for the extracts from the *Morning Chronicle*, collected by the diarist (pp. 186, 229, 235, 252, 283, 286). The three other items stated as his own were a publican's bill of 1824 to the churchwardens (p. 91), the brief for a horse-thief's prosecution in 1792 (p. 176) and the last letter written by Edward Cooke before his execution for mutiny in 1795 (p. 172). The last two events are treated at great length. It is likely that he was heir to papers accumulated by his uncle during a long business and public life.

Fourthly, he saw material in other private collections, such as Alderman Martin's calendar of races, 1804, and tobacco stopper made from the hanged horse-thief's finger bone (pp. 283, 175), and Mr Cunditt's 1785 play bill (p. 207). Other items had been recently found and doubtless reported in the local press, such as another play bill found on 20 May 1862 (p. 213) and the poster for a concert in 1802, found 'recently' on stripping wallpaper (p. 255). The Bible

Lord Bergavenny, 1597-1622, ed. W. H. Godfrey. Sussex Record Society 34, 1928) (1928). The rental of the manor of Brighton by Charles Goodwyn, 1665, is now ESRO, SAS-C/1.

in the possession of Mr Ade was said to have been thrown to onlookers by the Protestant martyr Deryk Carver as he burned at the stake (p. 122) - but it has since been shown to have been printed at a later date.[37]

Fifthly, Erredge did some fieldwork among the gravestones in the churchyards (pp. 103-14) and recalled from his childhood Phoebe Hassell's visits to Robert Ackerson's house (p. 181).

Sixthly, he consulted some original official records. Most notable was the vestry book, or maybe more correctly the vestry clerk's memorandum book, started in 1682. Until recently this important document for Brighton's history has been known only from Erredge's and, to a lesser extent, Dunvan's quotations. It was rediscovered by W.A. Barron in 1952 during a National Register of Archives survey of the records of Howlett & Clarke. But it was missing when vestry records deposited by the firm with the Sussex Archaeological Society in 1961 were listed, having been 'borrowed' by the Society's museum curator, only to be recovered from his house after his death in 1991.[38] It is now East Sussex Record Office, HOW/34/16. Erredge also drew on the systematic minutes of the vestry surviving from 1789 (e.g., pp. 85, 89; now ESRO, HOW/34/17, 18), and presumably found loose among the parish records the removal order of 1701 and the bastardy bond of 1769 reprinted at pp. 58-60. He seems also to have consulted minutes, since lost, of the Directors and Guardians of the Poor, possibly from as early as 1799 (pp. 55-7).

Finally, he must have made extensive use of local newspapers, the more so for closer to his own day. Not only was he a journalist, but his was the era of broadsheet newspapers with up to eight columns of solid, small, print to the page. Brighton had had its own newspaper since 1806, and the local press had proliferated with the final

37 F. Harrison, 'Deryk Carver's Bible', *Sussex Notes & Queries*, 7 (6) (1938), 72-3.

38 W. A. Barron, 'Gleanings from Sussex archives: Brighton and the smallpox', *Sussex County Magazine*, 26 (1952), 605. See also A. Dale, *Brighton town and Brighton people* (Chichester: Phillimore, 1976), 1-2.

abolition of stamp duty in 1855, heralding the 1d paper, down from 7d. before 1836 when duty took 4d. (then reduced to 1d.). Public affairs were reported with summaries of each speech at local government bodies' meetings and full transcripts of official documents. So, for example, Erredge probably knew of Mr Maynard's report of November 1861 to the Directors and Guardians of the Poor about the digging of the well at Warren Farm (pp. 7-8) from a newspaper rather than straight from an original document.[39]

One advantage of publication in parts was that new material which came to hand during publication could be incorporated. That may explain the uneasy insertion at pages 271-6 (September part) of Thomas Herbert's poem on the Bonfire Night riot in 1817, which more appropriately should have been at page 114 (March part) - someone obviously drew it to Erredge's attention after March. And at page 7 (December 1861) the drivers of the Warren Farm well had not yet hit water, but at page 294 (October) they did in March.

Reviewing Erredge's sources serves as a reminder that the *History* should be read today with a recognition of its limitations. It was written against the clock in monthly instalments. It did not benefit from editing of the whole, to iron out the order, inconsistencies, etc. It was journalistic, not a work of painstaking original scholarship. It was written for a local audience who had to be presented with an easy read.

Erredge's audience

We can only speculate as to why Erredge thought there was a market for his *History*, from which he and Ebenezer Lewis might make a profit. As recently as four years earlier, between April and June 1858, Alfred Hawkins & Co of 33 West Street, Brighton, had announced the imminent publication of part 1 of a 'History of Brighton from the earliest date to the present time, illustrated with lithographs

39 Maynard's report of 13 Jan. appears verbatim in *Brighton Observer*, 19 Jan. 1862.

and wood engravings of the ancient and modern town.' Nothing more is known of the project, so it must have been abandoned for want of subscribers.[40] We do not know whether Erredge and Lewis were foolhardy in proceeding with their venture. The reissue of the volume under a different title from a different publisher may reflect disposal of dead stock as a 'remainder'. In relinquishing his share in the profits to Erredge's family, Lewis may have been giving much - or only a little - away.

To suggest whom they may have identified as their readership, we should review the social structure of Brighton and Hove in 1861. By then, Brighton's prosperity had been founded on its function as a seaside resort for over a century, depending first on the medical profession's recommendation to upper middle class patients, then on royal patronage. The resident population grew during Erredge's lifetime, from some 12,000 in 1811 to 77,700 in 1861 - or from 12,200 to 87,300 including Hove, representing an annual compound growth of over 4%, for 50 years. However much Hove may have striven to differentiate itself from Brighton, it was a suburb, dependent on Brighton for services and for housing its servants. Except for this extension to the west, and the very beginnings of overflow into Preston north of Preston Circus, the built-up area of Brighton was still confined to the ancient parish, bounded today, from the south west corner, by Western Road and Norfolk Road, north to Old Shoreham Road at the junction with Prestonville Road, east along New England Road and Viaduct Road to Ditchling Road, north to Hollingdean Road and east along it, Bear Road and Warren Road, as far as Wilson Avenue, and south across the race course to the sea at Black Rock.

The image and reputation of Brighton had been founded on fashionable visitors who came for the 'season'. The last royal visit to the Royal Pavilion was in 1845, the town being the victim of its own success: now close hemmed by buildings, the Pavilion could not afford Queen Victoria the privacy and comfort she wanted. Nevertheless,

40 *Brighton Observer*, 30 Apr. to 11 June 1858.

the aristocracy continued, until the 1880s, to come to Brighton for a month or two leading up to Christmas, owning or renting the large houses in Kemp Town and Brunswick Town. They were always relatively few in number, but arrivals and departures were noticed in the press and they gave the town that fashionable aura which helped to attract others. The upper-class season was preceded, in the late summer and early autumn, by the middle-class season of holidays for professional and other affluent families, particularly from London. The 1860s was too early for holiday-making by clerks and other white-collar workers, staying in boarding houses, to have had much impact on the town. What was a recent and conspicuous innovation were the day-trippers, or 'excursionists' as they were called at the time. Reduced day-return fares on special trains dated from the mid-1840s and by 1860 as many as 36 trains ran on a summer Sunday to bring thousands of Londoners for ten or so hours by the sea.[41]

These visitors, if they wanted reading matter on the town, were catered for by the guide books of which half a dozen different titles competed for custom. They were not the target audience for a history appearing in twelve monthly parts. That audience included a group which, becoming more numerous from Victorian prosperity, was playing an increasingly important part in Brighton and Hove's development, namely the middle-class resident, often an immigrant to the town, who engaged in a high-status profession, owned a business which did not demand full-time management or lived on an unearned income, whether from inherited wealth or accumulation before retirement or from a pension after public service. Such residents were to be found in Kemp Town and Brunswick Town, but also in smaller but still smart terraced housing near the sea, such as Royal Crescent, Regency Square and Adelaide Crescent. It was for such people that 'villas', detached or semi-detached, were built north of the Level,

41 E. W. Gilbert, *Brighton, Old Ocean's Bauble* (London: Methuen, 1954), 175-6, 186, 205.

on the Montpelier Estate and in Cliftonville, Hove. They would have been a significant part of what Lewis called 'the reading community' in advertising the *Brighton Observer*. They had the leisure and, often being recent arrivals to the area, the inclination to find out about it.[42]

Another important target readership was the group to which Erredge himself belonged. When referring to his role in the Brighton and Hove Regatta of 1853 Erredge wrote of 'a few of the principal tradesmen who were accustomed to meet of an evening in conviviality at the New Ship Inn' - he among them.[43] And at his funeral, 'a large number of the tradesmen of the town and personal friends of the deceased manifested their respect.' 'Tradesman' then had a wider meaning than today, not only someone who practised a trade (or craft), but also someone who was 'in trade', or ran a business - so covering the whole swath of occupations between the professions narrowly defined (law, medicine, the Church) and the employed craftsman, the domestic servants and the unskilled. They must have enjoyed the doggerel verse of *The nomenclature of trades and tradesmen in Brighton*, looking for their own name and laughing at the puns on their friends', neighbours' and business associates' names.

The Brighton tradesmen had good reason to be proud of and confident in their town. They no longer worked in the shadow of a royal patronage which had debased the monarchy. As Erredge put it, referring to the first decade of the century, 'the inhabitants had found that Royalty was the staple article upon which they existed, and they so assimilated their ideas with their position, that their chief fears were that they might by some inadvertence or mischance give the Prince offence, hence His Royal Highness was their chief study' (page 262). From the standpoint of the 1860s he could write of the Prince's 'evil

42 S. Farrant, ed. *The growth of Brighton and Hove 1840-1939*, Occasional Paper 14 (Brighton: University of Sussex Centre for Continuing Education, 1981), ch. 3.

43 Erredge, *History*, 319-21.

propensities', 'his numerous amorous peccadillos' and 'his Royal Pavilion midnight orgies' (pages 265, 270).

Queen Victoria having chosen Osborne on the Isle of Wight as her marine residence, in 1848 H. M. Commissioners of Woods and Forests set about selling the Royal Pavilion; by a narrow margin the Vestry voted that the Town Commissioners should borrow to buy it. Happily in 1862 Erredge could record that the debt was being reduced and the town had an extensive park of its own in its very centre.' He applauded that since 1851 'numerous balls, concerts, and meetings of scientific, benevolent, and other societies have taken place there, and it has now an excellent gallery for paintings, and several rooms have been set aside for the Brighton Museum, an institution that is well deserving of support', while urging that the stables be converted for law courts, public baths and wash-houses (pages 279, 256). The tradesman, his wife and children could now pass an edifying Sunday afternoon where once royalty frolicked.

Not only were Brighton's roles as a resort town diversifying, its economic base was widening, driven above all by the railway. The main line from London had opened in 1841. North of the station, the London, Brighton and South Coast Railway located its principal workshops, and from 1852 locomotives were being built there. The number of its employees in Brighton was around 550-600 in 1851, and probably doubled in the decade following. The impact must have been magnified by contracting to local firms which thereby developed competencies previously supplied from elsewhere and now provided to a wider region than the town itself.[44]

In another way the town had recently grown in status and confidence. In April 1854 the town had been incorporated as a borough. The proposal for incorporation had been controversial and revolved around the application of the Public Health Act 1848 - an inspection under which had revealed high mortality linked to poor sanitation, not a

44 J. A. Sheppard, 'Brighton's railway workers in the 1850s', *Sussex Archaeological Collections*, 139 (2001), 191, 195.

good advertisement for a seaside resort.[45] The matter of drainage was to be a long time in being resolved (and curiously one on which Erredge was silent), but the greater extent and coherence of local government - and the panoply of mayor, aldermen and councillors - must have instilled a civic pride in the tradesmen, whose fortunes were so entwined with the town's prosperity, and made them the more inclined to invest 7s. in a book about it by one of their number.

Erredge's successors

The reissue of the *History* by W. J. Smith in 1867 seems to have been, not a reprint, but disposal of the original printing. Nevertheless it may be a tribute to Erredge, and interest engendered by his book, that in February and March 1871 the Brighton Museum Committee held a series of lectures in the Banqueting Room of the Royal Pavilion, on the history of Brighton. These were given by Alderman Henry Martin who arranged them for publication later that year as *The history of Brighton and environs*. Brighton took 200 pages, the environs 60. The scope and style were similar to Erredge's, though at lesser length and with rather more direct quotation from sources. Martin owned one of the private collections which Erredge had drawn on.

The next significant author on Brighton history was John George Bishop, another journalist, who started as an apprentice at the *Brighton Herald* in 1839 and became its sole proprietor in 1880.[46] He was the author of:

> *Strolls in the Brighton Extra-Mural Cemetery*. First and second series (1864, 1867)
>
> *The Brighton Pavilion and its royal associations. To which is added a Guide to that portion of the edifice open to the public* (1875), which remained the standard guide through thirteen editions down to 1910

45 Dale, *Brighton town*, 236-45. See also M. Whittick, 'A three-headed Cerberus: Brighton and the Health of Towns Bill, 1846', *Sussex Archaeological Collections*, 131 (1993) and S. Farrant, 'The drainage of Brighton: sewerage and outfall provision as an issue in a famous seaside resort *c.* 1840-80', *Sussex Archaeological Collections*, 124 (1986).

46 Bishop, *Brighton in the olden time*, 360.

A peep into the past: Brighton in the olden time, with glances at the present (1880, 1892)
A Peep into the Past: Brighton in 1744-61 (1895)
The Brighton Chain Pier: in memoriam. Its history from 1823 to 1896, with a biographical notice of Sir Samuel Brown, its designer and constructor (1896).

The second, People's, edition of *Brighton in the olden time*, was the largest, most wide-ranging and best known of his books. Bishop concentrated on the period from the mid-18th century and had a regular column for historical articles in the *Herald*. Though similar in presentation to Erredge's, his work was more thorough and systematic, but again heavily reliant on old newspapers. *Brighton in 1744-61* was significant for being an analysis of a rate book recently discovered in the parochial offices - which disappeared from sight again until 1981 (now ESRO, AMS 5889).

The first half of the 20th century saw several books from national publishers on the Regency period, such as Lewis Melville, *Brighton : its history, its follies, and its fashions* (1909) and Osbert Sitwell and Margaret Barton, *Brighton* (1935) which relied heavily on published memoirs and letters. Significant original work began with Henry D. Roberts's edition of *The parish register of Brighton ... 1558-1701* (1932) and his *History of the Royal Pavilion, Brighton: with an account of its original furniture and decoration* (1939), and was followed by Catherine Jamison's article in *Victoria County History of Sussex, 7, Rape of Lewes* (1940) and Antony Dale's *Fashionable Brighton, 1820-1860* (1948). In the early 1950s, Dr A. E. Wilson conducted a Local History class at Brighton Technical College, but its only publication was an edition of the Ancient Customs 1580; it was probably for this class that the 1744-61 ratebook was 'borrowed'. A major landmark was the publication in 1954 of E. W. Gilbert, *Brighton, Old Ocean's Bauble* (reprinted with minor corrections, Bath, 1968, and Hassocks, 1974). Gilbert (1900-73) was an historical geographer of distinction and recently elected professor of geography at Oxford, well able to blend his discipline with social history, making wide and judicious use of the printed primary sources, making *Old Ocean's Bauble* still a good read fifty years on.[47]

Aside from the instances noted, and Roberts and Dale within their limited topics, no one to this point had exploited unpublished, manuscript, sources for Brighton's history. This changed in the 1970s, with several Occasional Papers from the University of Sussex's Centre for Continuing Education, by Sue Farrant (the first two with John Farrant): *Brighton before Dr. Russell* (1976), *Aspects of Brighton before 1800* (1978), *Georgian Brighton 1740-1820* (1980) and *The growth of Brighton and Hove 1840-1939* (1981). Some of the articles published elsewhere extending this work have already been cited.

Lewes
December 2004

John Farrant

47 Ian Scargill, 'Gilbert, Edmund William (1900-1973)', *Oxford Dictionary of National Biography* (Oxford University Press, 2004).

HISTORY

OF

BRIGHTHELMSTON

OR

Brighton as I View it and others Knew it,

WITH A

CHRONOLOGICAL TABLE OF LOCAL EVENTS.

BY JOHN ACKERSON ERREDGE,

(Author of "The Students' Hand Book," &c.)

BRIGHTON:
PRINTED BY E. LEWIS, "OBSERVER" OFFICE, 53A, NORTH STREET.
1862.

PREFACE.

The publication of the History of Brighton had proceeded, with the most gratifying success, through ten monthly numbers, when it was suddenly interrupted by the lamented decease of the Author—Mr. J. A. Erredge. Death came upon him, not stealthily, but in its most awful form. It surprised him literally at the desk. Whilst talking cheerfully to the publisher, the hand of Death was laid upon him, and he fell dead to the ground;—the ink of these pages was still wet whilst the Author was extended on the floor a corpse. So terrible an occurrence for a brief space delayed the publication of the work, but fortunately for the family of the author, the MS. was nearly completed, and his sons were enabled, from the materials left by their lamented father, to compile the few last pages and send the two concluding numbers through the press. The History of Brighton is now completed, and whatever shortcomings may be detected in the two concluding numbers, which had not the advantage of being corrected by the Author, will no doubt be pardoned by a generous public.

CONTENTS.

History of Brighthelmston.

Chapter I.

THE ROMANS AT BRIGHTON.

Although there is no doubt that the vicinity of Brighton at a very remote period was occupied as a Roman military station, it is not the intention of the compiler of this work to date, merely on supposition, the origin of the town, coeval as it might have been with the landing of Julius Cæsar in Britain. The "Magna Britannia," published in 1737, mentions:—"As to the antiquity of this town, there is reason to believe it to have stood a vast tract of time. From the accounts our historians give of it, for some of them speak of it ever since Julius Cæsar's arrival in Britain, and affirm, that this was the place where he landed his legions; (August 26th, 55 B.C.,*) but since others assert his landing to have been at Hastings, we shall not be very positive, yet may justly insist upon it as most probable, because there is good anchorage in the bay here; and besides, there appears on the west side of this town to this day, for near a mile together, vast numbers of men's bones, and some of them of prodigious size, which plainly proves that there has been some warlike engagement near it." As an illustration that what has been transmitted to us orally, especially of remote periods, cannot be relied on, there is told the following tale of "Cæsar's Stile":—Dr. Stukely, or some other antiquarian, was travelling through England, when he heard that on a certain hill there was a stile called Cæsar's Stile. "Ay," said the doctor, "such a road, mentioned in Antoninus, passed near here; and the traditional name confirms the possibility of a Roman camp on this

* Temple Sydney's History of England, published 1772, at Shakespear's Head, No. 17, Paternoster Row, London.

spot." Whilst he was surveying the prospect, a peasant came up, whom the doctor addressed thus—"They call this Cæsar's Stile, my friend, do they not?" "Ees, zur," said the man, "they calls it so arter poor old Bob Cæsar, the carpenter; rest his soul; I holped him to make it, when I was a boy."

The "Burrell MSS." state that:—"There are three Roman castra, or camps, lying in a line over-thwart the Downs from Brighthelmstone to Ditchelling, from south to north. The first, a large one, called the Castle, about a mile from Brighton, eastward, and a mile from the sea, on the summit of a lofty hill commanding the sea-coast; the next, a smaller, called Hollingbury Castle, nearly about the middle of the Downs, also commanding from a lofty hill, by Stanmer, the whole western sea-coast of Sussex; and a third, a large one, called Ditchelling Castle, containing between twelve and fourteen acres, is the highest point of the Downs thereabouts, and commands part of the sea-coast, and all the northern edge of the Downs, and the wild underneath it." A military Roman way was discovered a few years ago, on St. John's Common, and in the enclosed lands adjoining, in the parishes of Keymer and Clayton, fully confirming the opinion of Camden and Stillingfleet that the *Portus Adurni* of the Romans was at Aldrington.* On the west side also of Glynd Bridge, near Lewes, a paved Roman causeway was discovered, lying three feet beneath the turf, upon a bed of silt, or blue clay, twenty feet thick; and near it was found a large brass coin of Antoninus Pius.

By whatever name Brighton was then known, there is no doubt it was a place of some note in the time of the Romans, as it was peculiarly favourable to all the purposes of the fisher and the hunter. Romish coins are still frequently found in its vicinity, and in the year 1750, near the town, an urn was dug up, which contained a thousand *denarii* of different impresses from Antoninus Pius to the Emperor Philip; and since that time there have been

* 4. Jac.—Sir Edward Bellingham held freely to himseif and his heirs lands and tenements in Aldrington, as of the Manor of Atlingworth.—*Rowe's M.S.*, p. 156.—6. Hen. 6. De quarta parte feod. milit. in Athelyngworth in Hundr. de Fyshergate dicunt quod sit in manu Prioris de Lewes et est dec.—*Inq. capt. ap. Lewes*, 6 *Hen.* 6.

found in some of the burghs or barrows to the east of the town, ashes and fragments of human bones, enclosed in urns of Roman manufacture. In preparing the ground for enclosing of the Old Stein, in 1818, several Roman coins were turned up by the workmen, on one of which, round the impression of the head, was the inscription, "IMP. ALEXANDER PIUS, A. V. C.," and on the reverse, "MARS ULTOR," with the initials S. C. between the figure of Mars. The date, however, was illegible. In forming the Race Course to the south of the Stand,—since restored to its original state,—several urns of Roman fabrication were dug up; and since then, to the east of the town, ashes and fragments of human bones have been found enclosed in Roman urns.

Relicts of the ancient Britons, before the time of the Romans in Britain, have at various times been found in the vicinity of Brighton. The most perfect were those discovered in a Barrow in Coney-burrow field, Hove, in January, 1856. In this field was a mound about 20 feet high, situated north of the pathway from Brighton to Hove, about N.N.E. of the church of St. John the Baptist. Some 40 years since, this hillock was covered with furze, and was a burrow for rabbits; but at a more recent date, when the habitations of men became erected contiguous, and the human family extended thither, the colony of rabbits dispersed, and their abode became the rendezvous of rustic games. Our highly respected local antiquarian, Barclay Phillips, Esq., thus describes it, and the incidents connected with it:—

"Rising from a perfectly level plain, and being unconnected with any other hills, it always presented the appearance of an artificial mound, and therefore, when, some years ago, a road was cut through it to the Hove Station of the Brighton and Portsmouth Railway, I was anxious to learn whether any antiquities had been met with; but not any were then found. Now, however, all doubt on the subject has been set at rest, and the hillock proved to be a Barrow, or monumental mound erected over the remains of an ancient British chieftain. Labourers have recently been employed removing the earth of this hill, and last week, on reaching the centre of the mound, about two yards west of the road leading to Hove Station, and about nine feet below the surface, dug out a rude coffin between six and seven feet long. On exposure to the atmosphere the boards immediately crumbled away; but a few of the knots remained, and prove to be of oak. The coffin contained small fragments of bone, some of which I have seen, and the following curious relics:—

"1. An Amber Cup, with a handle on one side. It is hemispherical in shape, rather deep, with a lip turning outwards, and is ornamented merely with a band of fine lines running round the outside about half an inch from the top. From the fact of the rim not being perfectly round, and the band before-mentioned not passing over the space within the handle, and its being marked off at each end with a line seemingly cut across, we may conjecture it to have been made and carved by hand.

"2. Head of a Battle Axe, about five inches long. It is in perfect preservation, and made of some sort of iron-stone, the wooden handle, having of course, long since decayed.

"3. A small Whetstone, with a hole neatly drilled through one end, so that it might be suspended by a thong to the person, and carried about.

"4. A Bronze Spear Head, very much oxidised, and so brittle that it broke into halves as it was being taken out of the ground. Two of the rivets and fragments of the spear handle still remain attached to the lower end of the blade.

"The workmen described the coffin as resting on the natural soil, which is stiff yellow clay, while the mound itself bears every appearance of having been formed of surface earth and rubbish thrown up together. I minutely examined the sections of the hill, and myself picked out several specimens of charred wood, and was informed that such fragments were very abundant.

"The manner of sepulture and all the relics, excepting the spear head, indicate this mound as having been the burial-place of a British chieftain before the time of the Roman invasion;—the spear-head certainly more nearly, though not exactly, resembles those used afterwards. The mound was of the simplest and most ancient form, and therefore I am inclined to think we may reckon it as at least 2000 years old, perhaps more! It has now disappeared. The last clod of that earth which so long covered the bones of a British chieftain was this afternoon carted away; and coffin, bones, and earth have been thrown pell-mell to form the mould of the future rosary of Palmyra square."

At a meeting of the Archæological Society in London, about a month after the opening of this barrow, the cup, &c., were exhibited; when Mr. Kemble and other celebrated antiquaries gave their opinion thus:—"The cup is the only known specimen of so large a size, and the battle axe is superior to any similar object in the British Musum." Mr. Hawkins and Mr. Franks, who have the care of the antiquarian departments, both declared the "find" in this barrow to have been the richest ever known. These rare specimens of local antiquity, through the kindness of Sir Francis Goldsmid, of "The Wick," on whose land they were found, form a prominent feature of the Brighton Museum, at the Royal Pavilion.

Chapter II.

SITUATION, SOIL, GEOLOGY, AND CLIMATE OF BRIGHTON.

Brighton is situated in 50°.55'. N. latitude, and about 3'. W. longitude, on the eastern side of a shallow bay of the south coast. The centre of the town is in a valley, which at the north diverges to Preston in two courses prominently marked by the London road and the Lewes road, Hollingbury Hill intervening. The east and north-west portions of the town are on acclivities, that to the east terminating abruptly at the south in cliffs ranging from 60 to 80 feet in height; and that to the north-west gradually sloping to the sea-shore. The southern front is bold, and commands an extensive view of the British Channel from Beachy Head to Selsea Bill.

The soil to the east and north-west is principally a thick substratum of chalk, covered with a thin layer of earth. The subsoil of the centre is marl and shingle; and to the westward there are large beds of clay of very irregular character. Dr. Mantell, in his valuable work, "The Geology of the South-east of England," says:—"The town of Brighton is situated on an immense accumulation of water-worn materials, which fills up a valley, or hollow, in the chalk. The diluvial deposit is bounded on the north-west by the South Downs; on the east it extends to Rottingdean, and is there terminated by the chalk; on the west it may be traced more or less distinctly to Bignor; on the south it is washed by the sea, and forms a line of cliffs from 70 to 80 feet high; these exhibit a vertical section of the strata, and enable us to ascertain their nature and position."

"The soil of the Downs," says Young in his Agricultural Survey of Sussex, "is subject to considerable variation. On the summit it is usually very shallow, the substratum is chalk, and over that a layer of chalk rubble, and partially rolled chalk flints, with a slight covering of vegetable mould. Along the more elevated ridges there is sometimes merely a covering of flints, upon which the turf grows spontaneously. Advancing down the hills, the soil becomes deeper, and at the bottom is constantly found to be of very sufficient depth for ploughing: here the loam is excellent, generally ten or twelve inches thick, and the chalk rather broken, and mixed with loam in the interstices."

Coombe rock,—a provincial term,—which greatly abounds in and about the eastern part of the town, is geologically known as the Elephant bed; and, according to the same authority, "is composed of broken chalk, with angular fragments of flint, imbedded in a calcareous mass of a yellowish colour, constituting a very hard and coarse conglomerate. It is not stratified, but is merely a confused heap of alluvial materials; where it forms a junction with the shingle bed, a layer of broken shells generally occurs: they are too fragile to extract whole: they appear to belong to the genera modiola, mytilus, nerita, &c. It varies considerably in its appearance and composition, in different parts of its course. In the inferior portion of the mass, the chalk is reduced to very small pieces, which gradually become larger in proportion to their height in the cliff: at length fragments of flint appear; and these increase in size and number as they approach the upper part of the bed, of which they constitute the most considerable portion. These flints are more or less broken, and resemble those of our ploughed lands that have been long exposed to the action of the atmosphere. In some parts of the cliff, irregular masses occur of an extraordinary hardness; these have been produced by an infiltration of crystallised carbonate of lime. Large blocks of this variety may be seen on the shore, opposite to the New Steine, where they have for years resisted the action of the waves. This bed also contains water-worn blocks of siliceous sandstone, and ferruginous breccia. Small nodular masses, composed of carbonate of iron in lenticular crystals, interspersed with brown calcareous spar, have occasionally been found at the depth of ten or twelve feet from the summit of the cliff. The organic remains discovered in this deposit are the bones and teeth of the ox, deer, horse, and of the Asiatic elephant*; these occur but seldom, and are generally

* In April, 1822, a large molar tooth of the Asiatic elephant was discovered in Lower Rock gardens, in a well fifty feet deep; and four very fine and perfect ones were dug up by the workmen employed on the foundation of the walls for the esplanade, at the Chain Pier, in 1831.

more or less waterworn*; but, in some instances, they are quite entire, and cannot have been subject to the action of the waves, The wells in the less elevated parts of the town pass through the calcareous bed, shingle, and sand, in succession; upon reaching the chalk, springs of good water burst forth, and these are said to be influenced by the tides.†

The sinking of the Warren Farm Well, at the Industrial Schools, has formed a very interesting subject to geologists, and on the 5th of November, 1861, the Surveyor, Mr. George Maynard, made a report to the Directors and Guardians, as to the state of the well, wherein he "wished it to be understood that he was neither a professor of geology nor an hydraulic engineer." It stated that the work was commenced on the 22nd March, 1858, and had been continued since without intermission:—"In sinking the well (says Mr. Maynard), I have found that the different strata perforated have been thicker than is generally set forth by professors of, or writers upon geology, proving that the dip of the strata is greater at this particular spot than is commonly found elsewhere, especially the gault, which is now being perforated. I have ascertained that the shanklin, or lower green sand, forming the bottom portion of the glaucomic strata, appear on the surface at Henfield, and continue near the base of the Downs as far as Albourne, thus proving, from the depth attained, that a considerable vale is formed in the strata between Henfield and Beachy Head. The well at the Industrial Schools lies nearly in a direct line, and not far from the centre in distance, between Henfield and the point at Beachy Head, at the base of which water is continually flowing between the malm and gault strata. Hence arises the fact of the gault stratum being so much thicker than was contemplated; but if the shanklin, or lower green sand is reached and penetrated, there

* I have (says Mantell) specimens of the teeth, found in a well fifty yards inland, at the depth of forty-six feet, in the *Coombe Rock*, and immediately above the bed of shingle.

† Some wells at Tetney (a village on the coast of Lincolnshire) that are sunk in the chalk, are also affected by the tide; the wells overflowing with a greater flux at the time of high water, and particularly at spring tides; showing that the water in the chalk communicates with the sea."—*Geolog. Trans.* vol. iii. p. 394.

is little doubt an ample and continuous supply of water will be obtained, which in all probability will run up to the level of the land at Henfield (from whence the supply will originate), or above the bottom pump in the well. I have tested the quality of the stratum now being penetrated, and feel pursuaded that if water is obtained it will be of a good quality. I have already reported my interview with Sir Roderick Murchison and other professors of geology, at the Institute of Practical Geology, in Jermyn Street, London, at which meeting I was encouraged to hope that water would be obtained at a depth not far distant from that which the well has already been sunk; they, at the same time, expressing their surprise that the shanklin sand had not been reached before, and also kindly giving me valuable information how to proceed when that stratum was penetrated. The stratum in which the men are at work at this present time is very soft, so much so that if boring was determined on, it would be requisite to insert iron pipes, which, in my opinion, would be more expensive than the present mode of digging and steining. The depth of the well now attained is 1,080 feet."

Few organic remains have been found near Brighton. Dr. Mantell mentions but a fragment of a bone resembling the femur, and a grinder of a large size, decidedly the latter that of an Asiatic elephant, in the brick-loam at Hove; the jaw of a whale in the shingle bed; the antlers and bones of the red deer in a bed of loam, in sinking a well near the cavalry barracks; the remains of a deer in the diluvium at Copperas Gap, by the Rev. H. Hoper; and similar remains in digging a well near the Western Road.

With respect to climate, medical men, who have made it their study, have divided the town into three districts. In 1845, Dr. Wigan, then in medical practice in the town, published an elaborate treatise, "Brighton and its Three Climates," and in 1859, Dr. Kebbell, Physician to the Sussex County Hospital, produced his valuable book, "The Climate of Brighton." The former considers the north-west part of the town the most salubrious, as it is exempt from the keen easterly winds, and is generally free from the fogs and smoke of the central district. It is free, too, of the marine exhalations to which that district is subject. The air of the east division is bracing, and likewise exempt from the saline particles which impregnate the atmosphere of the lower part of the town, a district which differs but little from any inland town in a low situation, and possesses none of the quality called bracing. Fogs, night and morning, frequently hang about the middle district, which may be termed the business quarter of the town.

Dr. Kebbell says:—"Brighton, in respect of temperature and the sensation of cold, offers great variety of climate according as the situations are more or less elevated, sheltered, or exposed. The observations of myself and others go to prove, that the elevated portions of the Montpelier districts, in the neighbourhood of All Saints' Church, are decidedly the coldest, being exposed to the full effects of the strong currents of air from the Downs. After this come the north-eastern districts, including the upper part of the Marine Parade, Kemp Town, and the portions of the town behind them on the north side of the Bristol Road, which are also very much exposed to the cold winds and draughts from the downs. The central parts of the town, from the Old Steine to St. Peter's Church, are the most sheltered from the winds; both by the downs behind, which protect them from the north-east winds; and by the buildings in front which break the force of the south-west winds; but being on a level surface and enclosed between hills, it is damper than any other part of the town; and I have noticed that in the autumn and winter, the night mists return earlier in the afternoon, and are dispersed later in the morning, than is the case in the more elevated and exposed districts. The low level or valley of the King's Road, though exposed to the full force of the south-west winds, is still more sheltered from the cold north-east winds by the great mass of buildings and the hills behind, and is decidedly the warmest and mildest part of the town, offering a very marked contrast to the cold elevated part of the Montpelier district. Sir James Clark speaks of the West cliff as being 'somewhat damp,'* but I am at a loss to conceive how this can be so, taking into consideration its sloping surface, the general porous character of the soil, together with its direct exposure to the

* Clark on Climate, p. 219.

rays of the sun. In point of warmth, the first half or third of the Marine Parade ranks next to the valley of the King's Road. Further east, towards Kemp Town, the air becomes colder and more bracing, and the draughts from the downs are more keenly felt. The parts of the town between the Western Road, and the line of Upper North Street and Montpelier Terrace, occupy, in point of climate, an intermediate position between the valley of the King's Road, and the cold and exposed portion of the Montpelier district.

* * * * * *

I cannot conceive any place enjoying greater natural advantages than Brighton, and it is incumbent on those who think it unhealthy to state from what source the insalubrity can have its origin, always excepting those artificial and preventable causes of disease which it creates within itself. For upwards of half the year the inhabitants breathe an atmosphere which has traversed the surface of several thousand miles of the great Atlantic Ocean. This at all events must be entirely free from all sources of disease. The staple of the land upon which the town stands, and for several miles round, is composed of chalk and sand, intermixed with flints, with the dip of the strata towards the sea, which, with the absence of any dense foliage in the surrounding district, has the effect of rendering the atmosphere of the place remarkably dry aud bracing. Neither is there any low-lying marsh land, where the fresh and sea water mix and infect the atmosphere, or exposure of mud at the mouths of rivers at low tide, or, in fact, any source of malaria whatever within any distance of the town, which can possibly to any appreciable or injurious extent affect its atmosphere. The winds from the land side, therefore, are probably almost, if not entirely, as healthy as those from the sea. Brighton has also no tidal harbour, nor any exposure of mud at low tide containing decaying vegetable matter, which at many sea-side places, and some much frequented by the public, is not only very offensive, but very injurious to the health."*

---

* The "Climate of Brighton," by William Kebbell, M.D., Physician to the Sussex County Hospital.

CHAPTER III.

THE ETYMOLOGY AND EARLY HISTORY OF BRIGHTON.

The obscurity respecting the etymology of Brighton, or more properly speaking Brighthelmston, is much to be regretted. In the Domesday Book it is written *Brighthelmstun*, evidently derived from *Brighthelm*, the name of some person of eminence, to whom it belonged, and *tun* the Saxon of town or dwelling. Bailey says that the name was given to the town by *St. Brighthelm*, a Saxon. Skinner says the town was so named from *Brighthelm*, a canonised bishop of Fontenoy, who lived about the middle of the 10th century. Stillingfleet and other authorities state that a Saxon bishop of that name resided here during the Heptarchy, and his name was given to the town. The last opinion is most to be relied on, as, when Ella and his three sons—Cimen, Wiencing, and Cisa,—landed in Sussex, at Shoreham, in 447, Bishop *Brighthelm* accompanied them; and one of his successors resided at Aldrington, the *Portus Adurni*, or port of the river Adur, (where, near Fishersgate, till within the last forty years, was the entrance to the harbour from the sea),* and held a considerable portion of the land thereabout until 693, when he was killed in battle; but where the battle was fought no mention is made.

Dr. Relhan says:—"The light sometimes obtained in these dark matters from a similitude of sounds in the ancient and modern names of places, is not to be had in assisting the present conjecture. Its ancient one, as far as I can learn, is no way discoverable: and its modern one may be owing either to this town's belonging formerly to, or being countenanced in a particular manner, by a Bishop Brighthelm, who during the former government of the island, lived in this neighbourhood: or perhaps may be deduced from the ships of this town having their helms better ornamented than those of their neighbouring ones."

---

* The harbour's new mouth was opened on the 25th of January, 1819.

The earliest record of the modern name, Brighton, is to be found in the Burrell MSS. :—

"17. Henry IV. Thomas Seynt Clare holds the manor of Brighton with lands and messuages in the same."

The following is quoted from the same authority —

"2. Mary. The queen on the 27th day of Nov. let to farm to William May, valet of the kitchen, the manor of Brightelston with all its appurtenances for 21 years, from the feast of St. Michæl last past, for the annual rent of 6*l* 13*s* 4d."

Mr. James Charles Michell, who re-published Dr. Relhan's "Short History of Brighthelmston, in 1761," mentions it to be met with in the terrier to the tenantry land, dated 1660.

Domesday book states that two of the three manors of Brighthelmston had been held by Edward the Confessor; but it has been aptly observed, that, notwithstanding, they might not have belonged to that prince; for the Normans, who denounced Harold the Second as an usurper, invariably substituted the name of Edward, when jurors were empannelled, in order to make an accurate return of the several manors within their respective hundreds, putting down that of Harold, as the statutes of the republican parliament of the 17th century are all references to Charles II. It is therefore fair to presume that the whole, or most of the town and parish belonged to the ancestors of Earl Godwin many generations prior to the Conquest, if not ever since the establishment of the Saxon power in this part of the island. They were styled *Thanes*, or noblemen of considerable possessions.

The only *Thane* whose name, qualities, and achievements have been made known to us, was Ulnoth or Wolnoth, the father of Earl Godwin and lord of the manor of Brighthelmston. This nobleman was appointed by Ethelred II. to direct the equipment of, and afterwards to command, the ships sent by the county of Sussex in 1008, as its quota towards the national fleet which the king was then collecting to oppose the Danes, who were come a second time to levy contributions on England. Godwin, his son and successor to the manor, was banished by order of Edward, who took it with other possessions. He regained them by force, and retained them till 17th of April, 1053, when he was suddenly taken ill while dining at Winchester, where the court of Edward was then held, and died four days afterwards.

Earl Godwin was succeeded in two of the chief manors by his son Harold, who, upon the death of Edward, in 1065, was chosen king: but, from some secret arrangements between the king and William, duke of Normandy, the latter made a claim which he asserted by force of arms. He landed at Pevensey. Harold at the time was at Stanford Bridge, near York, where he had defeated Toston, his unnatural brother, and Harold Harfager, the king of Norway; and hearing of William's arrival, he immediately proceeded southward, and with the addition of some levies hastily collected at Brighthelmston and his other manors in Sussex, encamped within nine miles of the invader. On the 14th of October, 1066, he joined battle with the Normans, and after performing all that valour and judgment could do against a brave enemy, he closed his life in the field of battle, near Hastings, having been pierced in the brain with an arrow.

Harold's possessions at Brighthelmston having fallen into the hands of William the Conqueror, the town was conferred on his son-in-law, one of his generals, William, Lord de Warren, in Normandy, who was created Earl of Surrey.

In 1081, when the survey of Sussex was made by commissioners under order from William the Conqueror, the manor of Brighton— Brighthelmston-Michelham, —had attached to it four *hagæ*, or tenements, in the town of Lewes, for which a sum of twelve pounds a-year was paid. These *hagæ* were places of resort for protection in seasons of danger from feuds between neighbouring heptarchs, or from the ravages of the Danes, Lewes being the fortified borough under the lord of the barony, then William de Warren. The manor of Brighthelmston-Michelham was held of the king by three Aloarii, or joint tenants of the same manor, who owed no suit or service to any superior, but "might go where they pleased," that is, in the feudal language of Domesday, were attached to no lord in a *seignoral*, but to the king alone in a civil capacity. This manor defended itself for six hides, and one yardland. One of the tenants had an *aula*, or manor-house on his part. The shares of the two others were used by *villeins*, or slaves. The whole formed but one manor, and contained five ploughlands of arable. After the conquest, this manor was held by one Widard, under William de Warren. He had one ploughland and a half in his demesne, or immediate possession; and fourteen *villeins*, and twenty-one *bordars*, or *bordarii*, occupiers of cottages, used the three other ploughlands and a half. It also contained seven acres of meadow, and wood enough to afford *pannage*, or mast and acorns for twenty-one hogs belonging to the *villeins* of the manor, three of which the lord was, by the general custom of the county, entitled to. Lady Amhurst is the present lady of this manor.

The manor of Brighthelmston-Lewes was held after the Conquest, by Radulphus, a Norman adventurer, under William de Warren, and defended itself for five hides and a half of land. Radulphus held in demesne half a carucate, or ploughland, the whole arable land of the manor being three carucates. Eighteen *villeins* and nine bordars used the rest of the arable land, for the cultivation of which, and the lord's half carucate, they had three ploughs, and one *servus*, or *villein en gross*, under them. The "gablum," or customary rent of this maritime manor, was four thousand herrings or mackerel. To this day, if demanded, the fishermen of Brighton pay to this manor six mackerel for each boat, every time they return from mackerel fishing. The fish thus paid is called "Reve," or more properly "Reves," which signifies rent or tithes, from the Saxon verb, *resian*, to exact. When the Reve Inn, Upper Edward Street, was first opened, the sign represented the lord's reve on horseback, Murrell,—who at that time held the New England farm, the site of the present railway works and land contiguous,—receiving of a Brighton fisherman six mackerel. In 1081 the manor was worth £12 a year. Mr. Charles Scrase Dickens and Mr. Thomas Wisden are the present lords of this manor.

The manor of Atlingworth was held after the Conquest, by William de Watteville, under William de Warren. He used one ploughland in demesne, and thirteen *villeins* and eleven *bordars* used the other. The church stood in this manor, which was, at the grand survey, valued at £12 a year. In the reign of Stephen,

Ralph de Cheney was in possession of this manor, and he gave the Priory at Lewes the advowson of the church, together with all his lands in the parish; and in process of time the whole manor became the property of the Priory. Mr. Somers Clarke is the present lord, and Mrs. Penelope McWhinnie is the present lady of this manor. By a decree of the High Court of Chancery, made on the 21st day of October, 1760, a partition of this manor of Brighthelmston was made between Thomas Friend and Bodycombe Sparrow, the then proprietors of it, and the present lords accordingly possess the soil of it in distinct moieties. In 1771, October 7th, Charles Scrase bought (Henry) Sparrow's moiety.

"Atlingworth, Adelingworth, Ablingworth, Athelingworth, or Addlingworth (Tower Records, No. 50,) manor lies in the parishes of Brighthelmston and Lewes; it is the paramount manor, and extends over the Hoddown (Lord Pelham's estate), formerly a Warren."—*Burrell MSS.*

Besides the three principal manors, there are within the town and parish two other small manors, viz., Peakes and Harecourt; as also parcels or members of the manors of Old Shoreham, *alias* Vetus Shoreham, *alias* Rusper, and Portslade; but the boundaries of them are at the present day very undefined. Mr. Harry Colvill Bridger is the present lord of the manor of Old Shoreham.

Chapter IV.

AFTER THE CONQUEST, TO 1513.

It is highly probable, from the surnames of some of the most ancient families in the town of Brighthelmston, the phrases, and the pronunciation of the old natives, and some peculiar customs of the people, that the town had, at some distant period, received a colony of Flemings. This might have happened soon after the conquest, as a great inundation of the sea took place in Flanders about that period; and such of the unfortunate inhabitants of the deluged country as wanted new habitations, could not have anywhere applied with a greater likelihood of success than in England, as Matilda, queen of William the Conqueror, was their countrywoman, being daughter of Baldwin, Earl of Flanders.

Being thus settled in Brighthelmston, the Flemings were led by habits and situation, to direct their chief attention to the fishery of the Channel. Besides obtaining a plentiful supply of fresh fish of the best kind and quality for themselves and their inland neighbours, they, every season, cured a great number of herrings, and exported them to various parts of the continent, where the abstinence of Lent, the vigils, and other meagre days, insured them a constant market. There is no doubt, but, from time to time, additions were made to this foreign colony, from Spain, France, and Holland, as the names of some of the oldest families of the town verify; namely, Mighell (Miguel), Gunn (Juan), Jasper (Gaspard), Jeffery (Geoffrey), Gillam (Guillaume), &c.

The inhabitants were now classed into landsmen and seamen, or mariners, and they profited respectively by the advantages of their situation. The former, whose dwellings were on the cliff and part of the gentle acclivity behind it, drew health and competence from the fertile soil; while the latter, who resided in two streets beneath the cliff, found a bountiful source of subsistence and profit at the bottom of the sea. In process of time, the mariners and their families, principally descendants from the new comers, the Flemings, had increased in numbers so far as to compose more than two-thirds of the population of the town, and they had a proportionate share of the offices and internal regulation of the parish.

The Flemish, on their arrival, though received in all probability as vassals, found their condition an improvement on the general state-*villeinage;* aad the indulgence shown to foreigners was eventually extended to the natives; and the disfranchised landholders gradually emerged from the most abject state of feudal dependance, to one less precarious, that of tenants by copy of court roll. Once registered on the rolls of a manor, with the consent of the lord or his steward, their title became indefeasible and descendible to their heirs, except in case of neglect or violation of the definite and recorded duties of their tenure. Thus settled, the husbandmen of Brighthelmston had every inducement to marriage, and they toiled with pleasure in their patrimonial field. The mariner also, freed from feudal caprice, braved the dangers of the deep, not only for his subsistence, but as a future provision for his family; and transmitted to his posterity, controlled by manorial custom, his ship or boat, his cottage, his capstan and garden, and other monuments of his paternal solicitude and iudustry. The town being, as now, a member of the port of Shoreham,—all boats of the town register at Shoreham,—was obliged to furnish some seamen for the royal navy; and no other tax or service was imposed upon the inhabitants, till the levying of a poll-tax in the reign of Edward III.

In 1313 Brighthelmston had become so considerable as to need the public accommodation of a market; and John, the eighth and last Earl de Warren, obtained a charter of Edward III. for holding a market every Thursday.

The mariners about this time, in the Lower Town, or under Cliff, increasing in number and property, extended their habitations to the Upper Town, and began two streets westward of the Stein, named from their situations, East Street and West Street, forming the inhabited limits of the town in those directions. After East Street and West street had been continued some considerable way towards the north, the landsmen, who were also becoming numerous, found it necessary to build intermediate streets, parallel to those already constructed; and the proprietor of the north *laines*, finding it more convenient to have their barns, and finally, their own dwellings and the cottages for their workmon, at that extremity of the town, formed North Street.

Most of the ground now occupied by Black Lion street and Ship street, and the intermediate space, are, in all the Court Rolls, called the Hempshares; and were, even after East street and West street were built, plots or gardens for the production of hemp, for the use of the fishermen of the town. The name of the ropemaker who constructed all the cordage for the supply of the fishery, was Anthony Smith, who, in 1670 suffered great persecution from Captain Nicholas Tattersal, a personage who assumed great power when basking in the smiles of royalty, consequent upon his effecting the escape of Charles II. to France. Smith was more especially the object of his malignity, from having been the occupier of the house, in West street, where the king sojourned preparatory to his flight; he happening to recognise His Majesty, yet having too much loyalty to betray him. Jealousy actuated him; as he was desirous of claiming all the honour in the royal escape. He in consequence kept all the merits, which were really due to Smith, in the background, and took all the honour to himself, and the reward to. In process of time, as the population increased, and the sea made encroachments on the lower town, two streets were erected on the site of the hemp-shares or gardens. In the most eastern street of these, with one front to the High street,—that which passed along the verge of the Cliff,—stood an Inn, with a Black Lion for its sign; and in the other there was an Inn, with a Ship for its sign. The two streets of the hemp-shares were soon distinguished by the two signs, and are the present Black-Lion street and Ship street. The Black-Lion Inn on the east side of the street, was converted into a private residence about the beginning of the present century. The Ship, the oldest tavern in the town, is now, and has been since 1650, known as the Old Ship, to distinguish it from the New Ship, a more recent erection. Besides the hemp-shares, the ground to the west of the town, which was afterwards brick-yards, and is now termed the Brunswick Square and Terrace district, was devoted to the growing of flax for the use of the fishermen.

The prosperity of the town received a check about the middle of the fourteenth century, from the ambitious projects of Edward III. against France, which exposed this and other fishing towns of the southern coast to the occasional retaliation of that kingdom. The inhabitants' boats were taken, and their fishery frequently interrupted. In 1377 the French burnt and plundered most of the towns from Portsmouth to Hastings; but no particular injury to the town is recorded of Brighton, at that period. When, however, there was the least appearance of danger, the coast Watch and Ward, called in the king's mandate *Vigiliæ minutæ*, were called into service. Their duties were nocturnal, and seldom exacted, unless an immediate descent was apprehended. The watch consisted of men at arms, and *hobilers* or *hoblers*, who were a sort of light cavalry that were bound to perform the service by the nature of their tenure. They were dressed in jackets called hobils, and were mounted on swift horses. The bold stand made against the French, in 1377, when they landed at Rottingdean, was principally by the watch and ward-keepers of the coast, which had been divided into districts, entrusted to the care of some baron, or religious house, by certain commissioners, called Rectores Commitatus. In the annals of the Prior of Lewes, and the Abbot of Battle, we find that those personages were several times placed at the head of an armed power, to oppose actual or threatened invasion. Certain borough hundreds were also obliged, under pain of forfeiture or other penalty, to keep the beacons in proper condition, and to fire them at the approach of an enemy, in order to alarm and assemble the inhabitants in the Weald.

From the constant alarm of the people and the ruin of war, Brighthelmston generally experienced a considerable share of the public distress; as, besides contributing some of its best mariners for manning the royal fleet, the town was deprived of its trade and fishery. In 1512, in consequence of war being declared by Henry VIII. against Louis XII., all the maritime industry of Brighthelmston suffered, and its buildings were threatened with plunder and conflagration. At this time, Sir Edward Howard, the English Admiral, having made several successful attempts on the coast of Brittany, and being joined by a squadron of ships commanded by Sir Thomas Knivet, went in pursuit of the French fleet, under the command of Admiral Primauget, Knight of Rhodes; the real intention being to destroy the town of Brest. The French fleet, consisting of thirty-nine ships, was in the harbour of Brest. Howard, having been misled by the information and advice of a Spanish Knight, named Caroz, as to the strength of Primauget's force, entered the bay under the fire of two strong batteries, which commanded the entrance, with only a barge and three galleys, and took possession himself, of the French Admiral's. But the French soon recovered from their panic, the two fleets met, and a furious engagement ensued. At length Primauget's ship was set on fire, and determining not to perish alone, he bore down upon the

English Admiral's, and, grappling with her, both ships soon became involved in the same inevitable destruction. This dreadful scene suspended the action between the other ships; but after some time, the French ship blew up, and in its explosion destroyed the English ship. While the conflict was at its height, and the deck was streaming with the blood of his brave companions, Sir Edward was thrust with a half-pike into the sea and perished.

After this misfortune, the English fleet returned home; and Primauget's being reinforced from Brest, and being animated with his recent success, he sailed for the coast of Sussex, to wreak that vengeance on the inhabitants which was due to Henry alone. He accordingly, in the night time, landed some men, who plundered it of everything valuable that they could remove, set many houses on fire, and wantonly slew many of the inhabitants. The rest flying in terror and confusion different ways, the country became alarmed as far as Lewes and the Weald. * The French re-embarked the next morning, with their booty, before the country people could assemble in any force to annoy them. Sir Thomas Howard, brother of Sir Edward, whom he succeeded, soon after, with Sir John Wallop, made a descent on the coast of Normandy, and desolated no less than twenty-one towns and villages, inhabited by people who never did, and perhaps never wished to do, any injury to their fellow men on this side the Channel. Such is the fortune, and such are the advantages and distinctions of the royal game of war.

Holinshead mentions an attack upon the town by the French, about this time; and there is the probability that he refers to the same invasion, as he terms it a nocturnal visit from some

* The Weald of Sussex is an extensive vale that occupies the centre of the south-eastern part of the county, and, running parallel with the Downs, forms their northern boundary. It was anciently an immense forest (called by the earlier colonists, *Coid Andred*, by the Romans *Silva Anderida*, and by the Saxons *Andreadswald*), which, even in the time of Bede, was a mere retreat for deer and swine: the greater part is now in an excellent state of cultivation. It consists of various beds of clay, sand, and limestone, and is comparatively of low elevation; its breadth is from five to ten miles, and its length from thirty to forty miles; it is estimated to contain 425,000 acres. The surface is intersected by numerous valleys, which generally occur at the outcrop or basseting edges of the harder strata, and form channels for the numerous streams that are tributary to the rivers in their vicinity. The whole tract rises with a gradual sweep from the foot of the Downs, and unites with the higher lands of the Forest Ridge.

French ships, but commanded by Prior Jehan, the high admiral. He says: "but when the people began to gather, by firing the beacons, Prior Jehan sounded his trumpet to call his men aboard, and by that time it was day. The certain archers that kept the watch followed Prior Jehan to the sea, and shot so fast that they beat the galley men from the shore, and wounded many in the fleet: to which Prior Jehan was constrained to wade, and was shot in the face with an arrow, so that he lost one of his eyes, and was like to have died of the hurt, and therefore he offered his image of wax before our Lady at Bullogne, with the English arrow in the face, for a miracle."

According to the Burrell MSS.,* in 1589, strict orders were given for maintaining beacons in all accustomed places, with orders to the watchmen, that if the number of invading ships did not exceed two, they were not to fire the beacons, but to cause larums to be rung from church to church as far as the skirts of the hill reached from the sea shore, and no further; and to send a post to the nearest justices: but if the ships exceeded two, they were to fire both their beacons, which were to be duly answered by the corresponding ones, and thus rouse the "force of the shire." Five discreet householders in the neighbourhood, were assigned to each beacon, one to keep watch constantly. In 1590, the beacon watches were ordered to be discharged till further orders.

CHAPTER V.

ANCIENT AND MODERN GOVERNMENT OF THE TOWN.

When king Alfred divided England into shires, the shires into hundreds, and the hundreds into tithings, tithing men or head-

* The Burrell Manuscripts were compiled by Sir William Burrell, a great antiquarian, who for many years spared neither attention nor expense in collecting and arranging the materials for preparing the antiquities of Sussex; and the county looked for their completion with the utmost solicitude. The death of the worthy Baronet, unfortunately, rendered it incomplete, and the ten folio volumes of his rare and scarce manuscripts were deposited in the British Museum. A tablet, by Flaxman, to the memory of Sir William, adorns the wall of Cuckfield Church.

boroughs—heads of boroughs—were the only guardians of the peace, and dispensers of justice within their respective districts, the original limits being the residences of ten *creorles* or freemen, with their families and slaves. Under the Saxon constitution, Brighton had two headboroughs; a proof that its population, even then, was far from being inconsiderable, These headboroughs sat alternately or together, at the borough court, at which the decenners, or free, or frankpledges (friborgs) as had no causes to be tried there, attended as jurors or sworn assessors to the presiding officer. These free-pledges were the origin of the Society of Twelve, which continued in Brighthelmston to the commencement of the present century.

By the statute of Winchester, 13th Edward I., the borough of Brighthelmston had a constable appointed for itself exclusively, an indication of its respectability at that period. According to Alfred's division, the hundred to which Brighthelmston belonged, contained, besides that borough, those of Ovingdean and Rottingdean, called in Domesday, *Welesmere.* The boroughs of Preston (Prestetune) and Patcham (Patchame), which were originally hundreds of themselves, were, under Edward I., united to the borough of Brighthelmston, and composed a new hundred, called *Wellsbourne,* since corrupted into Whalesbone. The boroughs of Ovingdean and Rottingdean were then united to the small hundred of Falmer, under the name of *Ewensmere.*

Wellsbourne took its name from a stream which till within the last few years ran, in the winter time, nearly the whole length of the hundred. It rose near the upper end of Patcham street, and entered the sea at the Pool,—Pool Valley,—in Brighthelmston. Within the last thirty years it burst out with so large a current as to inundate the Level to the north of the town, and even the greatest part of the Stein. In the spring of 1806 it laid the north of the town under water. After the last inundation, in the winter of 1827-8, a large sewer, called the Northern Drain, was laid down from the northern boundary of the London Road, to the sea, its outlet being in front of the Albion Hotel. The source of this stream or bourne, being the well at Patcham, it had its name from that circumstance, and lent it to the said hundred.

The *leet* or law day, the view of frankpledge for this hundred, was held on Easter Tuesday, when all the officers of the hundred, except the headborough of Patcham, were elected. The Constable of Brighthelmston was always chosen by and out of the Twelve of the town. The headborough, afterwards styled the constable of the borough of Deane or Patcham, was nominated in rotation for that office, according to the particular lands he held within the borough. From and after 1618, by arrangement between the two classes of inhabitants, the fishermen and the landsmen, "Twelve out of the ancientest, gravest, and wysest inhabitants of the town, eight fishermen and four landsmen, were selected for assistants to the conestable in every public cause." The constable was then termed the High Constable, and his twelve assistants were called Headboroughs. The constable of Brighthelmston served at Quarter Sessions, musters, aud other public services for the whole hundred, the constable of the Deane being only his assistant or deputy within the borough of the Deane or Patcham. There was also chosen at the leet or law day for this hundred, which is in the deanery of Lewes, an ale-conner and a searcher or sealer of leather. Since the town became incorporated, in 1854, no headboroughs have been chosen; but Mr James Martin, who was appointed at the last annual Court Leet of the Earl of Abergavenny, by the steward of the Leet, F. H. Gell, Esq., on Easter Tuesday, 1855, continues the High Constable of the Hundred of Whalesbone: his duties however are very trifling, merely consisting of taking charge of the Parish Jury List, and presenting it to the Clerk of the Peace for the County.

The following is a list of the Constables who have served the Hundred as far as the records of them are made in the Town Books, or other proofs are given:—

1589. Henry Gunn.
1597. Thomas Jeffery.
1618. Richard Stoneham.
1660. John Brooker.*
1670. Nicholas Tattersal (Captain).
1683. Richard Harman.
1690. Richard Masters.
1691. Richard Harman, senr.
1692. John Ellgate.
1694. Thomas Stanbridge.
1695. Richard Masters.
1696. Henry May.
1697. George Beach.
1698. Henry Stanbridge.

* To commemorate his appointment he had small copper tokens cast, with "John Brooker, 1660," on them, and "Brighthelmston, J. B.," on the obverse. A specimen of this coin, in the possession of the compiler of this book, is in an excellent state of preservation.

1699. John Woolger.
1700. Thomas Gillam.
1701. Israel Pain.
1702. Jonas Hunn.
1703, Joseph Buckall.
1704. Thomas Ridge.
1705. John Gold.
1706. Jonathan Wegeram.*
1707. William Gillam.
1708. James Friend.
1709. Nicholas Roberts.
1710. Richard Masters.
1711. Thomas Roberts, jun.
1712. Thomas Bewman.
1713. Richard Legate.
1714. John Peircy.
1715. Israel Pain, jun.
1716. Dighton Elgate.
1717. Richard Roggers.
1718. Henry Stanbridge.
1719. Thomas Swan.
1720. Philip Mighell.
1721. William Heaves.
1722. Thomas Scutt.
1723. John Masters.
1724. Nicholas Sanders.
1725. Samuel Dean chosen, but dying, Edward Heath served.
1726. Thomas Simons.
1727. John Tuppen.
1728. William Bradford.
1729. Henry Paine.
1730. Thomas Wood, alias Dine.
1731. William Friend.
1732. Richard Lemmon.
1733. Richard Harman.
1734. Richard Masters.
1744. Hugh Grover.
1745. James Ridge.
1746. James Brooker.
1747. Thomas Sanders.
1748. Richard Mighell.
1749. Israel Paine.
1750. William Grover.
1751. Thomas Roberts.
1752. Philip Mighell.
1753. Thomas Kent.
1754. David Vallance.
1755. Thomas Gillam.
1756. Hugh Saunders.
1757. John Lashmar.
1758. Thomas Measor.
1759. William Buckoll.
1760. Edward Smith.
1761. Richard Tidy.
1762. William Lucas.
1764. John Tuppen.
1765. Henry Beach.
1766. Francis Carter.
1767. William Chapman.
1768. Stephen Poune.
1769. Stephen Flemming.
1770. Beach Roberts.
1771. Harry Stiles.
1772. William Bradford.
1773. Robert Davis.
1774. James Buckoll.
1775. Richard Willett.
1791. Robert Williams.
1792. John Kirby.
1793. Thomas Tilt.
1794. William Wigney.
1795. John Baulcomb.
1796. James Vallance.
1797. William Chapman.
1798. Stephen Gourd.
1799. Richard Lashmar.
1800. Cornelius Paine.
1801. Stephen Wood.
1802. Philip Vallance.
1803. Daniel Hack, who affirmed.
1804. Thomas Newington.
1805. Thomas Saunders.
1806. Thomas Saunders.
1807. William Newbold.
1808. Adam Maiben.
1809. John Mills.
1810. John Hargraves.

* In the Town Book the same name appears written Wigram and Wiggram.

1811. Harry Colbron.
1812. Edward Blaker.
1813. Alexander Baldey.
1814. Robert Ackerson.
1815. William Williams.
1816. George Richardson.
1817. John Williams.
1818. Richard Bodle.
1819. Richard Humber.
1820. John Myrtle.
1821. George Wood.
1822. George Wigney.
1823. William Blaber.
1824. William Boxall.
1825. Samuel Akehurst.
1826. Thomas West.
1827. Edward Hill Creasy.
1828. James Cordy.
1829. Thomas Palmer.
1830. J. G. Sarel.
1831. D. M. Folkard.
1832. Samuel Ridley.
1833. John Poune.
1834. William Hallett.
1835. John Yeates.
1836. John Ade.
1837. T. H. Wright.
1838. John Bradshaw.
1839. Henry Smithers.
1840. William Barnes.
1841. Thomas Fuller.
1842. Edward Humphreys.
1843. Edmundus Burn.
1844. George Chittenden.
1845. Robert Williams.
1846. William Catt.
1847. William Towner.
1848. William Lambert.
1849. George Cheesman, jun.
1850. Charles Smith, who appointed his brother George to serve.
1851. M. D. Scott.
1852. William Beedham.
1853. H. P. Tamplin.
1854. P. R. Wilkinson.
1855. James Martin, who continues to be the High Constable of the Hundred.*

On the 5th of April, 1793, at a Vestry Meeting held at the Town Hall, it was ordered: "That in future the Constable (High) be allowed twelve guineas, to be paid in full, for all expenses during his office, including four guineas for a dinner."

It was customary at the Court Leet, each Easter, to choose a High-Constable Elect, but he was not always appointed at the next Court; as, in 1814, Mr. Ackerson was chosen, although Mr. W. Williams was the elect.

* *Anno* 13 and 14 *Caroli* II., cap. 12, sec. "XV. And whereas the Laws and Statutes for the apprehending of Rogues and Vagabonds have not been duly executed, sometimes for want of Officers, by reason of Lords of Manors do not keep Court-Leets every year for the making of them: Be it therefore enacted by the Authority aforesaid, That in case any Constable, Headborough, or Tythingmen shall dye or go out of the Parish, any two Justices of the Peace may make and swear a new Constable, Headborough, or Tythingman, until the said Lord shall hold a Court, or until next Quarter Sessions, who shall approve of the said Officers so made and sworn as aforesaid, or appoint others, as they shall think fit: And if any Officer shall continue above a year in his or their Office, that then in such case the Justices of Peace in their Quarter Sessions may discharge such Officers, and may put another fit person in his or their place, until the Lord of the said Manor shall hold a Court as aforesaid."

CHAPTER VI.

THE BOOK OF ALL THE "AUNCIENT CUSTOMS."

In consequence of the perpetual jealousies and strife between the fishermen and landsmen, a commission was sent to Brighton, in 1580, to settle every difference, assess the town rates, and arrange the public concerns of the parish. The Earl of Arundel, Lord Buckhurst (Lord of the Manor), Sir Thomas Shirley, of Preston, and Henry Shelley, Esq., were the commissioners. The number of landsmen who at that time paid parochial rates and taxes, was 102; while the number of fishermen amounted to 400. The decision of the commissioners gave satisfaction to all parties till 1618, when a fresh arrangement was entered into The orders and regulations of these two commissions were directed to be "written in two several books of parchment," one of which was to be delivered to the Earl of Arundel and Lord Buckhurst, the other was to "be kepte in a cheaste locked with three locks, in some convenient place in Brighthelmston." Provision was made also for the safe custody of the key of the chest, and for the annual reading of the regulations by the Vicar, "openlye in the presence of all the fishermen and others of the parishioners, contributaries, in some convenient time and place."

The "Book of all the Auncient Customs," is dated 23rd July, in the 32nd year of Queen Elizabeth, 1580; and is kept in its original shape in a spacious box, at the office of Messrs. Attree, Clarke, and Howlett, solicitors, Ship Street. It is in black letter, on parchment, and is in a state of good preservation, although the ink, from age, is very yellow. An engrossed copy in corrected modern authority, is deposited with it, and is as follows:—

In the Manors of Brighthelmston, as Parcel of the Barony of Lewes, the following Feudal Customs, partly of Saxon origin, but established for the most part by the Norman settlers in this country, have, by immemorial usage, governed the Courts there:—

1. The lands of *copyholders* in these manors are descendible, on death, to the youngest son, or to the youngest daughter if there be no son, and so on to the youngest relatives collaterally.[1]

2. The widow of a purchaser of a copyhold estate to which he has been

[1] Veteres Rotuli Curiæ

admitted, or the widow of an heir by descent, though unadmitted, may, after three courts to be holden next after her husband's death, claim her *widow's bench*, and shall be admitted for her life, even though she marry again, she paying the lord a reasonable fine, not exceeding one year's value of the land. But if the husband, even on his death-bed, make a surrender of his copyhold, the widow shall not have her *bench*, nor the widow of a purchaser unadmitted, nor the widow of a tenant in reversion.

3. All the tenants of these manors, except such as were discharged by deed, or held by knight's service, held their lands by *suite of court*, the *copyholder* from three weeks to three weeks, and to be of the homage: the *freeholders* were to appear only twice a-year, viz., at the courts holden at Easter and Michaelmas, where, if they knew of any wrong done to the lord, they were bound by their oath of fealty, to make it known to the court. But they (the *freeholders*) were not to be of the homage, because they performed service at juries at the *barony court*, held from three weeks to three weeks at *Lewes;* from which service the copyholders were exempt. The defaulters at each court were to be *essoyned* (excused) or *assirred* (fined) in proportion to their offence.

4. Surrenders made out of court, and presented at the next general court holden for the manor, are good.

5. The heir in possession of a customary tenement, being above the age of fourteen years, or he or she to whose use any surrender shall be made, being of the like age, not coming into court on or before the third half-yearly proclamation, shall forfeit his or her estate.

6. If a *copyholder* leave an heir under the age of fourteen years, such heir is, during his or her minority, to be committed to the care of the next of kin who is able to answer for the profits of the land, and to whom the land cannot descend. At the age of fourteen years the heir may choose a guardian.

7. *Relief* and *Heriot* were due to the lords of these manors on the death of every freeholder, not discharged by deed, who died seized of an estate of inheritance of soccage tenure.

8. On the death or surrender of a tenant for life, no *heriot* is due, except for a stinted *cottage;* nor of a joint tenant: or if a tenant in fee surrender to one of his heirs, part of his customary tenement, and reserve another part to himself and heirs, no *heriot* is, due, because he is still tenant of the *heriotable* tenement.

9. No more than one *heriot* is, by custom, claimable for any number of tenements in one manor, belonging to the deceased.

10. The *copyholder* was to keep his customary tenement in repair, and for that purpose, may cut down on his copyhold the necessary timber, in case the lord, his steward, woodward, or reeve refuse to assign him any for that purpose.

11. If any tenant, free or customary, alien parcel of his tenement, and the rent be apportioned in court with the lord's or the steward's consent, it concludes with the lord and tenant. Otherwise the lord may distrain any part of the tenement for the whole rent.

12. The heir of every tenant, being fourteen years of age, after the death of his ancestor dying seized of customary lands or tenements, as also a purchaser, upon surrender of such lands either in possession or reversion to his use, coming into the court at or before the third proclamation, and desiring to be admitted, shall have a reasonable fine assessed by the lord or his steward, not exceeding one year's value of the land; which fine the tenant is to pay on his admittance, or shortly after; otherwise he forfeits his estate.

13. If a tenant let to farm his *copyhold* for more than one year and a day at a time, he is to come to the lord's court for license, which the lord is to grant, the tenant paying him *four-pence*, and no more, for every year so granted, with a reservation of the lord's customs, duties, and services. Also the *copyholder*, having

a barn on his copyhold, is to pay the lord *four-pence*, or less, but never more, for every wainload of corn or hay that grows on his said copyhold, and is carried out of the manor with license, or to any freehold within the manor. But the tenant may carry corn or hay from one copyhold to another on the same manor, without license, where the two copyholds have equal estates. But if one be a guardian, or a tenant for life, and another tenant in fee, and any manure be removed from the former estate to the latter, the party, so doing, shall be amerced.

14. If a *copyholder* alien his lands by *deed*, pull down his building without license, or wilfully suffer it to fall, commit any wilful waste, let his tenement for more than one year and a day without license, obstinately refuse to pay his rent, or a reasonable fine upon admittance, or absent himself, without sufficient cause, from the lord's court after lawful summons, or, being there, will not be sworn of the homage, without satisfactory excuse, or carry all his corn from the copyhold, if he have a barn there, he is, for any of these offences, liable to forfeit his estate in the said copyhold.

15. *Strays*, found within any of these manors, and proclaimed according to the statute, after a year and a day are passed, become the property of the lord of that manor, by prescription. Every lord is to maintain a common pound within his manor. But, of latter time, all *strays* within the *rape* and *liberties* of the barony of *Lewes*, have, by consent of the lords, been presented at the *law days* or *leet* holden for the hundred in which the *strays* are found.

16. In each of these manors there was a *Reeve*, who was the lord's immediate officer. His name and institution are both of Saxon origin. The *Thane* who generally presided in person at his own court, had at first no other officer belonging to it than the *Gerefa* or *Reve*, who generally received a settlement on the manor, in consideration of his services; and thus, in most manors, did the office become predial, or attached to some particular lands. In some manors however, it was not confined to one denomination only, but imposed on several of the tenants in rotation, by virtue of their tenure. This officer's duty is to account to the lord or his steward, for all the ancient quit-rents both of freehold and copyhold, and all the heriots that fall due within the manor, together with the fines, leviable amercements, and all the other casual profits within the same. But he is not bound to audit out of the manor, unless the lord will recompense him for his pains; nor even then, unless he chooses it. Being an officer of great antiquity, he is not bound to collect any but *old rents*, which were payable before the eighteenth year of *Edward the First*.

17. The majority of the homagers sworn at the lord's court, for the better preservation of order, have, time beyond all memory of man, with the lord's consent, used to make bye-laws for the establishment of the common good, and for preventing of public annoyances: and such laws made with reasonable penalties and clauses for distress for such penalties, have been immemorially binding and concluding to all tenants of the manor, provided such laws or orders cross not the general laws and statutes of the kingdom.

Though many of the following Customs and Regulations are now become obsolete, they are in general too interesting to be ommitted in the History of the town.

Upon supplication[1] by the ancient fishermen of Brighthelmston, unto the Right Honourable the Lords of the Council, for remedy and redress of certain disorders in their town, touching the annual payment of certain money called a *quarter of a share*, heretofore of ancient time usually paid out of every boat in every

[1] The first Town Book, or *Costumal of Brighthelmston*. In transcribing this book, the spelling is modernized.

fishing voyage, to the churchwardens there, towards the maintenance of their church, and other public charges about the necessary defence of their town; and for a contribution by the rest of the parishioners, not being fishermen, toward the bearing of the said charges to be had and levied: and after commission by the means of the Lord *Buckhurst*, for the purposes aforesaid, obtained from the Lords of her Majesty's Most Honourable Privy Council, unto the Right Honourable Earl of *Arundel*, the said Lord *Buckhurst*, Sir *Thomas Shirley*, Knight, and *Richard Shelley*, Esquire, or to any two of them directed, bearing date the 12th day of February, *in anno Domini*, 1579, it pleased the said Lord *Buckhurst* and Sir *Thomas Shirley*, by authority thereof, to will and command certain of the said ancient fishermen to set down in writing their ancient customs and orders, concerning the true making, payment, and employing of the said *quarter share*, and the certainty thereof; which they, the said ancient fishermen, being assembled together, have done accordingly in manner and form here following.

The Ancient Custom used for TUCKNET FARE.—"*Imprimis*, there have used, time out of mind, between February and April yearly, certain small boats called *Tuckers*, to go to sea upon the coast for plaice, of the burden of three tons or thereabouts. Every of these boats have used eight or nine men, or thereabouts, and two nets. Every man hath used to take for his body in this voyage, a share. The boat, the nets and necessaries thereto belonging, hath used to take four shares: and besides, one other share hath been used to be made, whereof half is due to the Vicar, a quarter to the master, and the other quarter to the Churchwardens, for the use of the town: so that every boat in this voyage, having eight men, taking a share a man, maketh thirteen shares, viz., for eight men eight shares; for the boat, the nets, and necessaries, four shares; and for the Vicar, the town, and the master, one share; and if there be more or less men, then the shares are more or less in number, according to the number of the men proportionably."

The Ancient Custom used in SHOTNET FARE.—"*Item*, there have yearly, time out of mind, from April to June, used to go to sea for mackarel, other boats called *shotters*, of diverse burdens between six tons and twenty-six tons. Every boat of the burden of six tons, and not above ten tons, hath used to take two shares; and above ten tons, and under eighteen tons, two shares and a half; and from eighteen tons to the biggest, three shares. Every man having above four nets going to sea in this voyage, hath used to take for his body, half a share, and not above; and every other man hath used to take for his body, a share, and not above: and the nets have accustomably contained in length between thirty and twenty-four fathoms, and in deepness two *ranns*, every *rann* fifty *moxes* deep, whereof every four nets have used to take a share; so that every boat in this voyage, taking two shares and a half, having ten men, taking a share a man, and having four score nets, maketh thirty-three shares and a half, viz., for four score nets twenty shares; for ten men, ten shares; for the boat, two shares and a half; for the Vicar, the town, and the master, one share; and if there be more or less men, or the boat be lesser or bigger of burden, or have less or more number of nets, then the shares are more or less in number, according to the proportion of the boat, men and nets."

The Ancient Custom used in SCARBOROUGH FARE.—"Item. There have, since the memory of man, yearly, from June to September, other boats of divers burden between eighteen and forty tons, used a voyage to *Scarborough* to fish for cod (being about forty years agon). Every boat in this voyage, of the burden of eighteen tons, and not above twenty-eight tons, hath used to take four shares; and from twenty-eight to the biggest, five shares. Every man in the biggest sort of these boats, bringing with him a line, a lead, four lines of hooks, and two norward nets, containing twenty-four yards in length, or thereabouts, hath used to take for his body, and the necessaries aforesaid, one share: and in the smallest sort, every man bringing with him two lines, two leads, and one *heak*,[1] containing twenty-eight yards in length, and five ranns in deepness, hath used to take a share and a half; and having two lines, two leads, and two *heaks*, of the length and deepness aforesaid, two shares: so that every boat in this voyage taking four shares, having twelve men, taking two shares a man, maketh in number twenty-nine shares, viz., for the boat, four shares; for twelve men, twenty-four shares; for the vicar, the town, and the master, one share: and the number of shares is varied more or less according to the number of men and nets, or the bigness of the boat, according to the proportion of this example."

The Ancient Custom used in YARMOUTH FARE.—"Item. There have yearly, time out of mind, from September unto November, used to go to *Yarmouth* to fish for herrings, other boats of divers burden, between fifteen tons and forty tons; every boat of the burden of fifteen tons and not above twenty-four tons, taking three shares; and every boat of twenty-four tons and not above thirty tons, taking three shares and a half; and from thirty to the biggest, taking four shares. Every man in this voyage used to take for his body half-a-share: and these boats have used two sorts of nets, the one sort called *flews*, alias *heaks*, containing between thirty and twenty-four fathoms in length, and in deepness four ranns, every rann fifty *moxes*[2] deep, every three of these nets taking a share; the other sort, called norward nets, containing between fifteen and ten fathoms in length, and in deepness five ranns, every rann fifty moxes deep; every four of these nets taking a share: so that every boat in this voyage, taking three shares and a half, having twelve men, taking a share a man, and having thirty-six flews, alias heaks, and thirty-two norward nets, every four norward nets taking a share, maketh thirty shares in the whole number, and one half-share, viz., for the boat, three shares and a half; for twelve men, six shares; for thirty-six flews, twelve shares; for thirty-two norward nets, eight shares; for the vicar, the town, and the master, one share; and if there be more or less number of men and nets, or if the boat be bigger or lesser, then the shares are more or less in number, according to that proportion."

The Ancient Custom used in COCK FARE.—"Item. There have, time out of mind, between October and the midst of December, used to go to sea upon the coast for herrings, certain small boats called *cocks*[3] of burden, between two and six tons. Every of these boats having a mast and a sail, hath used to take a share and a half; and the other, without mast or sail, have taken a share. These boats have used two sorts of nets, the one called *cock heaks*, containing between thirty and twenty-four fathoms in length, and two ranns in deepness, and the other called *flews*, containing the length aforesaid, and three ranns in deepness. These two sorts of nets have used to take for three nets a share, one with another; so that a boat in this voyage taking a share and a half, having six men, and twenty-four nets, maketh ten shares and a half, viz., for the boat, one share and a half; for six men, six shares; for twenty-four nets, eight shares; and for the Vicar, the town, and the master, one share; and so the shares do vary, more or less in number, according to the bigness of the boat, and the number of men and nets."

The Ancient Custom used in FLEW FARE.—"Item. There have, time out of mind, between the beginning of November and the end of December, used to go to the sea for herrings, other boats, called *flewers*, of divers burden, between eight tons and twenty tons, the biggest boat taking three shares, the smallest two shares.

---

[1] *Heak* is still used in *Yorkshire* for a certain net used in the river *Ouse*.

[2] *Moxes* we may suppose to be a corruption from the Dutch word *maeschen*, mashes, and *fare* from *fahre*, in the same language. Indeed, most of the other technical words in the Town Books are derived from the Teutonic, and were apparently introduced by the Flemish emigrants who are supposed to have settled at Brighthelmston.

[3] Cock, from the Teutonic *cogge*, a small boat.

Every man having above three nets going to sea in this voyage, hath used to take for his body half a share, and every other man a share, and none above. These boats have used one sort of nets, called flews, containing between thirty and twenty-four fathoms in length, and three ranns in deepness, every rann fifty moxes deep, every three nets taking a share: so that every boat taking three shares, having eight men, taking half a share a man, and having thirty-nine nets, maketh twenty-one shares, viz., for the boat, three shares; for eight men, four shares; for thirty-nine nets, thirteen shares; and one share for the vicar, the town, and the master, or more or less shares according to the number of men and nets, and the bigness of the boat."

The Ancient Custom used in HARBOUR FARE.—"Item. There have used, time out of mind, another sort of boats to go to sea in summer time, with harbour hooks for *conger*, every boat containing eight tons or thereabouts, and taking for every boat two shares; and every man having four lines of hooks, every line containing fifty fathoms, taketh a share; and twelve lines of hooks without a man taketh a share. So that a boat having twelve men taking a share a man, and twelve lines of hooks without men, maketh in number fifteen shares, viz., for the boat, two shares; for twelve men, twelve shares; for twelve lines of hooks, one share; and one share for the vicar, the town, and the master, or more or less number of shares according to the number of men and hooks."

The Ancient Custom used in DRAWNET FARE.—"Item. There have used, time out of mind, in the months of May and June, yearly, certain small *cocks*, of the burden of three tons, or thereabouts, to draw mackarel by the shore, whereof the boat and the net take one half, the other half is divided by shares unto the men, to every man a share; and one share is also thereof made for the vicar, the town, and the master: so that if there be ten men, then they make eleven shares, viz., ten men, ten shares; and one share for the vicar, the town, and the master; and if there be more men, then they make more shares."

The Ancient Custom for Payment and Employing the QUARTER SHARE.—"*Item*, The master of every boat at *Brighthelmston*, at *St. Stephen's Day*, next after his return from any fishing voyage, wheresoever or whensoever it was begun, had, or continued, hath used to divide and pay out of the whole profits of the said boat, without diminution or deduction to any stranger going in the said boat, to be made, the said *quarter share* unto the Churchwardens of *Brighthelmston* for the time being, and half a share to the vicar there for the time being, and the other he hath for his own use."—"*Item*. The master of every boat of *Brighthelmston* had, time out of mind, used to take up and pay out of the whole profits of every voyage, whether the rest of his companions be of *Brighthelmston*, or strangers of other parishes, the said whole share for the vicar, the town, and himself, without any deduction thereof unto any other town or parish, or the parson, vicar, or proprietary thereof, to be made: and if the master, or any of his company, have been of *Brighthelmston*, and the boat belonging to any other place, then the said master also hath used to make in the said boat the aforesaid share, whereof he hath had a quarter to himself, and of the other three quarters for the town and vicar of *Brighthelmston*, he hath used to have proportionably, according to the number of men and nets which he used and had out of *Brighthelmston* in the voyage."—"*Item*. The said wardens used to employ the said quarter share, especially upon building of forts and walls towards the sea, for the defence of the said town, and for provision of shot and powder, and other furniture for that purpose; and entertainment of soldiers in time of wars, and other public service of the prince, and maintenance of the parish church. Whereupon, to the intent that the said annual payment, or quarter share, for the better defence and maintenance of the said town, may, in time to come, justly and truly, without fraud, be both made, yielded, and paid; and also preserved, kept, and employed, according to their ancient custom; as also for the avoiding of all such controversies as heretofore have commonly happened between the said fishermen, touching the just and equal division of their fish in every boat in every voyage, and the profits and charges thereof, the said Lord *Buckhurst* and *Richard Shelley*, Esq. having the said fishermen before them at *Brighthelmston*, the 23rd day of July, *anno Domini*, 1580, have, by authority aforesaid, and with the consent of the said fishermen, devised and set down to writing, certain orders to be hereafter for ever used and kept by all the fishermen and inhabitants of the said town of *Brighthelmston*, in manner and form following:

Orders for LENGTH OF NETS.—" *Imprimis.* None shall have any norward net under twenty yards long by the uppermost rann, nor any such net in a boat of thirty tons or upwards, under five ranns in deepness, every rann fifty moxes deep or thereabouts; nor in any other boat any norward net under four ranns deep, at any time after the first day of August, in the year of our Lord, one thousand five hundred four score and one, under pain to forfeit for every net under the said sizes, six shillings."—" *Item.* Whoever shall have *flew* alias *heak*, under twenty-eight yards in length by the uppermost rann, and four ranns in deepness, every rann fifty moxes deep or thereabouts, at any time after the first day of August, in the year of our Lord one thousand five hundred four score and one, shall forfeit for every such *flew* ten shillings."—" *Item.* Whosoever shall have any *shortnet* under twenty-eight yards in length, by the uppermost rann, and two ranns in deepness, every rann fifty moxes deep, or thereabouts, at any time after the first day of April next ensuing, shall forfeit for every such net three shillings and fourpence: and whosoever shall have any cocksheak under twenty-eight yards in length by the uppermost rann, and two ranns in deepness, at any time after the first day of October, in *anno Domini*, one thousand five hundred four score and one, shall forfeit for every such net three shillings and fourpence. *Provided* always that none of the forfeitures before mentioned shall, at any time, extend to any norward net, flew, shortnet, or cocksheak spoiled in length at sea, and newly brought home from any voyage; so that the said net or nets so spoiled be made of the several lengths and deepness in the former orders mentioned, before they be occupied again in any voyage."—" *Item.* The constable, the churchwardens, being sea-faring men, or any twoof them, shall, four times a-year, if they shall think it needful, search, view, and measure the length and deepness of any man's nets in *Brighthelmston*, and he that shall let *(hinder)* them or any of them so to do, the party for every time so letting shall forfeit twenty shillings."

Orders for SHARES *for* MEN.—"*Imprimis.* No man having gone to sea in *Shotnet fare*, above six nets, or in *Yarmouth fare*, or *Flew fare*, above six norward nets, or four flews, alias heaks, and a half, shall take any more than half a share for his body, in any of the said voyages, upon pain to forfeit for every time so doing, ten shillings."—" *Item.* Whoever shall give to any person having in *Shotnet fare* above six nets, or in *Yarmouth fare* or *Flew fare*, above six norward nets, or above four flews and a half, any more than half a share, shall forfeit for every time so doing, ten shillings."—*Item.* That no man shall take or give any more than a share for a man's body in *Shotnet fare*, *Yarmouth fare*, *Cock fare*, *or Flew fare*, upon pain to forfeit, either of them, for every time so doing, twenty shillings."—" *Item.* That no man shall give to any stranger, not dwelling in *Brighthelmston*, any more than a share for his travel in any voyage, upon pain of forfeiting for any time so doing, twenty shillings."—" *Item.* That none shall give to any stranger, any share, or part of share, in any other boat but only in the same boat where the said party is placed, upon pain of forfeiture of twenty shillings for every time so doing."—*Item.* That no man shall hire any person at the first shipping, to go for wages in any voyage except *Scarborough* voyage, upon pain to forfeit for every time so doing, ten shillings."—" *Item.* That no man being entertained by any boat, or by any man, unto any voyage, shall place himself in any other boat, or with any other man, upon pain of forfeiting, as well by the party so entertained, as by him that shall entertain any such person, for every time so doing, twenty shillings."—"*Item.* That no man going to *Scarborough* in a bark going with ground hooks, having a line, a lead, four lines of hooks, two norward nets, and one heak of five ranns deep, shall take for his body, and all the said necessaries, any more than two shares; and if any man bring any more nets than is before mentioned, and do fish with them in the said voyage, then he shall be allowed for the same nets after the rate of two norward nets, and a heak to a share; and whosoever shall give or take anything contrary to this order, shall forfeit for every time so doing, ten shillings."—"*Item.* That no man going to *Scarborough* in a boat with a drove sail, having two lines, two leads, and one heak of twenty-one yards in length, and five ranns in deepness, shall take any more than a share and a half for his body, and the necessaries aforesaid; and if he have two lines, two leads, and two heaks, then he shall take two shares, and not above; and if he bring more nets, then he shall be allowed after the rate of his nets according to the proportion of four nets to a share, and every heak to be allowed for two nets; and what person soever, shall give or take anything in this voyage contrary to this order, shall forfeit for every time so doing, twenty shillings."—"*Item.* It shall be lawful for the owner and master of every boat or bark going to *Scarborough*, at the return of every such boat or bark from the said voyage, to take up, before sharing, so much of the fish as, being indifferently prized by the whole company, will pay all the charges that shall be then owing for the said voyage, so that they become chargeable to the creditors; which fish, being so prized and taken, the warden or wardens, and the Vicar or his deputy, paying the same price in ready money, shall have, if they or any of them require it."—"*Item.* If there shall be any stranger master in any boat of *Brighthelmston* in any voyage, then the owner shall take up and pay the half share for the Vicar of *Brighthelmston*, and the quarter share for the town, upon pain of every owner doing the contrary, to forfeit for every such default twenty shillings."—"*Item.* No man shall take or give above a share and a quarter for any man's travel in *Tucknet fare*, upon forfeiture of ten shillings, to be paid by the giver, and also by the taker for every time so doing."—"*Item.* No owner of any tucker or tucknet shall take any more than four shares for the boat, the nets, and the arms, viz., for the boat and the nets, three shares; and for the arms, one share, upon pain to forfeit, for every time so doing, twenty shillings."—"*Item.* No man going to sea with harbours shall take for his body any more than one share, nor for twelve lines of hooks any more than one share; and so for more or less proportionably; and any man that shall take or give anything contrary to this order, shall forfeit for every time so doing, ten shillings."—"*Item.* To the intent the said quarter share may hereafter be truly paid without fraud or guile, every owner and master of every boat, in every voyage, shall call the Vicar, or his deputy or deputies, to all and every their several accounts at the end of every their several voyages, (*Cock fare*, *Tuck fare*, *Harbour fare*, only excepted, for which three one only account by every master and owner at the end of every voyage, shall be made), and in his presence shall make a true and particular account of all their charges, profits, and shares, upon pain for every owner and master, for every time doing the contrary, to forfeit twenty shillings; a note whereof the said Vicar or his deputy shall give in writing unto the wardens yearly, at *St. Stēphen's Day*, upon pain of twenty shillings to be forfeited by the said Vicar."

"*Orders for* HOOKS, *and going to* SEA.—"*Imprimis.* That every line of small hooks shall contain in length nine score yards and not above; and whosoever shall have any line of hooks above the said length, at any time after the first day of August, in *anno Domini* one thousand five hundred four score and one, shall forfeit for every such line, twenty shillings: and that no man shall bring to sea at any time any more than four lines of the aforesaid hooks: and every man shall pay the seventh fish to the boat, of three of his lines, except the master of the boat, and the young men who are called *tacheners;* the which master shall have all the fishing of his four lines, without paying any duty to the boat; and the said *tacheners* shall have for the keeping of the boat, the fishing of every their fourth line without paying any duty to the boat; and whosoever shall do anything contrary to this order, shall forfeit for every time so doing, twenty shillings. And if any boat shall come to mishap through the default of the *tacheners*, that then the said *tacheners* shall pay for the hurt of the same boat, to the value of the same hurt."—"*Item.* Any man that shall lose any small hooks at sea, shall have for every line so lost two shillings, to be paid unto him by the company in equal portions."—"*Item.* If there be four lines or more lost in any boat, then the whole of the fish, except the boat's part, shall be equally divided among the company; and any man that hath lost any of the same hooks, shall be allowed two shillings for every line so lost, to be paid by the whole company in equal portions."—"*Item.* Every man that shall lose any heak, norward net, or shotnet, in any fishing voyage, shall be allowed by the company for every heak so lost, ten shillings; and for every norward net so lost, ten shillings, and for every shotnet so lost, four shillings, and not above." —"*Item.* That no man, being an inhabitant of this town, shall drive with nets for herrings between *Shoreham Haven* and *Beach (Beachy Head)* on any Saturday night or Sunday, until evening prayer be done, upon pain to forfeit for every time so doing, twenty shillings."—"*Item.* That no man shall drive with any tucknet at any time before sun-rising, or after sun-setting, upon pain to forfeit, for every time so doing, ten shillings"—"*Item.* That no man shall go to sea with tucknet to fish for plaice before *Shrove Tuesday* yearly, upon pain of forfeiture of ten shillings for every time so doing."—"*Item.* If there shall at any time any boat of this town be cast away through the default of the master and the company, then the master and his company to be answerable to the owner for the same boat."

"*Orders for the Payment of the* QUARTER SHARE.—"*Imprimis.* Every master of every boat in every voyage shall divide, receive, and take up the said quarter share accordingly, as it hath been used heretofore, and is before ordered, and not otherwise; and the same shall well and truly pay yearly, upon the feast of *St. Stephen*, to the Churchwardens for the time being, in the place where it has been accustomably paid in former times: and if any master in any boat, in any voyage, shall not divide and take up as aforesaid, or shall detain the said quarter share, and not pay the same unto the Churchwardens at the end of every voyage, at the place above-mentioned, before the feast of the *Epiphany* yearly then next following, that then every such master, for every time so doing, shall forfeit the double value of the same quarter share that he so detained, or not divided, or not taketh up."—"*Item.* If there be in any tucker or cock in the time of *Tucknet Fare* or *Cock Fare*, any more than one master during the voyage, then the owner or first master of any such tucker or cock shall account for and pay the whole quarter share due for all that voyage, and therewithal shall deliver unto the said Churchwardens, a note in writing, of the names of all the other masters in that voyage, upon pain of forfeiting twenty shillings by the owner."

"*Orders for the* CHURCHWARDENS.—"*Imprimis.* There shall be yearly, at the time accustomed, *two* substantial fishermen and *one* such landman, chosen by the consent of the constable, the vicar or curate, and the chief of the town, for Churchwardens."—"*Item.* The same Churchwardens, nor any of them, shall not employ nor disburse any of the money to be kept by the sea-faring and land wardens, to any other use than for the reparation of the church, and for necessary public charges for the town, without the consent of the constable, the vicar or curate, and six substantial men of the parish, first had in writing, of which six, *four* shall be fishermen and *two* landmen, upon pain of paying all sums of money laid out contrary to this order, at and upon the charges of the said wardens."—"*Item.* The same Churchwardens shall yearly, at the time accustomed, yield up a true and perfect account, in writing, of all receipts, reprises, and charges for all that year, and the money then remaining shall then deliver up into the hands of the wardens, their successors, in presence of the constable, the vicar or curate, and the parishioners, upon pain of forfeiting by him or them that shall do the contrary, forty shillings, and shall be chargeable nevertheless with his account before the Commissioners"—"*Item.* Every forfeiture before or hereafter mentioned growing by reason of any matter pertaining to the sea or fishing, shall be paid unto the wardens being fishermen, and every other forfeiture unto the land wardens."—"*Item.* If the Churchwardens shall neglect to demand any of the said forfeitures for the space of six days next after his or their knowledge thereof, then he or they for every time so neglecting, shall pay unto the poor man's box of *Brighthelmston*, three shillings and four pence, or else answer it before the Commissioners."—"*Item.* Whosoever shall not, within five days next after demand in that case by the wardens, or any of them, for the time being, to be made, pay unto the said wardens, or one of them, all such of the said forfeitures as they then from time to time, at any time hereafter, shall have made, then his or their name or names not paying such forfeitures as aforesaid, shall be signified in writing under the hands of the constable, the vicar or curate, and the said wardens, unto the Commissioners, to be bound to appear before the lords of the Council."—"*Item.* That so much of the said quarter share as shall amount to the double value of the contribution (of the landmen) shall be kept employed and accounted for indifferently by all the Churchwardens in such sort as is aforesaid, and the residue of the said quarter share shall be remaining in custody of the sea-wardens, who shall not employ or disburse any part or parcel thereof, but for the common profit of the town, and that only with the consent of the constable, being a fisherman, the vicar, and six other fishermen being of the *Twelve*, in writing first had and obtained, and thereof shall make a true and particular account in writing, in the presence of the said constable, churchwardens, and fishermen, at the time accustomed; and the money remaining shall then yield up unto the sea-wardens, their successors, upon pain to forfeit for every time doing the contrary, the double value of every sum, contrary to this order, employed, not accounted for, or not yielded up as aforesaid, and shall be chargeable also with the same before the commissioners." —"*Item.* The rents, profits, and commodities of the mill and town house, and of all other lands, tenements, and hereditaments which now do belong and appertain, or hereafter shall belong and appertain to the said town of *Brighthelmston*, shall be yearly paid and answered unto the churchwardens; and that the same, and every part thereof, shall and may, from time to time, be disposed, demised, and let out to farm, for the term of seven years at the most, by the said constables and wardens, so as always the same be done to the best profit and commodity of the said town, upon pain that every one therein offending, shall forfeit five pounds, and besides to answer for his offence in that behalf before the said commissioners."—"*Item.* The same churchwardens, shall have in readiness at all times hereafter, in some convenient place in *Brighthelmston*, to be laid up in store, and safely kept, four barrels of powder, and forty round shot, and ten chain shot for every great piece."—"*Item.* There shall be selected by the said commissioners out of the ancientest, gravest, and wisest inhabitants, eight fishermen and four landsmen, for assistants to the constable in every public cause, whereof every one shall be ready, and give his attendance upon the constable as oft as need shall require: and whosoever shall presume to call together any assembly, to the intent to practice or put in use any manner, or device, or art touching the government of the said town, without the privity, consent, and command of the said constable and assistants shall forfeit for every time so doing, forty shillings. And to the intent that the said *Twelve* grave and wise men may have continuance, therefore, upon the death or removing of any one of them, it shall be lawful for the constable, and the residue of the said *Twelve*, or for the most part of them, to choose in supply such other of the said town, as by them, or the more part of them, shall be thought meet, provided that such choice shall be always ratified and allowed by the stewards of the lords of the said town, or by such one of them as shall happen to keep court in the said town, next after such choice made, or otherwise the same choice to be void: and if such choice shall by the said stewards, or by such one of them as shall fortune to be present as aforesaid, be disallowed, until a sufficient man, in the judgment of the said stewards, be chosen."—"*Item.* If any man hath heretofore built, erected, or set up any wall, shed, or any such like thing whatsoever, to the annoyance of the market place, or of the block house there, and shall not, upon warning given him by the constable, or his deputy for the time being, pull down or remove away the same within ten days after such warning given, that then he shall forfeit five pounds, and be further punished by discretion of the commissioners."—"*Item.* Forasmuch, as the town is overcharged with the multitude of poor people, which daily are thought to increase by means of receiving under-tenants, lodging of strangers, and the disorder of tippling-houses, and that the constable cannot, without further assistance, take upon him the whole oversight and charge of all the parts of the town in this behalf, it is thought meet that every one of the *Twelve* shall have assigned upon him some street or circuit near his dwelling-house, where he shall, as deputy to the constable, have special charge for the keeping of good order; and especially to see that the order for the avoidance of under tenants, be duly observed; and that none lodge or keep tippling houses."—"*Item.* All the acts, receipts, reprises, and charges and accounts of the town, shall, from time to time, as they are had, made, and done, be entered into a register book by the clerk for that purpose, by the constable, vicar, and churchwardens for the time being, to be chosen."—"*Item.* The master and owner, or one of them, of every boat, in every voyage, at every sharing and account, without further delay, shall deliver up into the custody of the churchwardens, or one of them, or of one or more indifferently to be deputed or appointed by the said vicar, and churchwardens, the said half-share and quarter-share, without diminution or retention thereof, to be by the said wardens, or him or them so deputed, safely kept until *St. Stephen's Day* yearly then next following, to the use, for the half-share, of the vicar, and for the quarter-share, to the use of the town, upon pain for every owner and master for not delivering up as is aforesaid, to forfeit for every time forty shillings, and to be further punished by the discretion of the commissioners."—"*And whereas* there hath been a controversy of long time between the said fishermen, being the greater part of the parish, and the husbandmen and artificers there, as well for that of the reparations of the church, as all other public charges, which hath been great, as building of forts and walls, provision of shot and powder, and other necessaries for the defence of the town against foreign enemies, have been sustained and borne by the said quarter share of the said fishermen only (except a small annuity or yearly rent of two windmills, whereof one is now utterly decayed); as well for the utter extinguishment of all such controversy and division, as also for the better increase of amity and neighbourly friendship among the said parties, the said Lord *Buckhurst* and Richard *Shelley*, Esquire, have likewise caused to be set down here in writing at the place, and in the day and year aforesaid, the names of all such husbandmen and artificers which are of ability within the said town, and the several sums of money which every of them, by their several consents, have granted yearly to be paid for, and in name of a contribution towards the charges aforesaid."—"Rate of the husbandmen and artificers yearly to be paid on St. Stephen's Day, to the churchwardens, towards the reparations of the church, and other public charges of the town. * * * * * *

There are also in the said town of Brighthelmston, of fishing boats four score in number, and of able mariners four hundred in number, with ten thousand fishing nets, besides many other necessaries belonging to their mystery, all which being matters of great charge, require very great maintenance and reparation, and are like hereafter rather to decay than to increase, by reason the said fishermen are diversly charged and burdened with service of her majesty in sizes, sessions, and other courts and other services, and with musters and setting forth of soldiers, besides their service by sea, properly appertaining unto them, and especially by reason of the great scarcity and dearth of timber and wood now of late years, by means of iron furnaces placed near the Downs, risen from three shillings and four pence a ton, to thirteen shillings and four pence; from two shillings and sixpence a load of wood to seven shillings; and from six shillings and eight pence a load of coal to fourteen shillings; and of billet or tall wood, from two shillings and sixpence the hundred to eight shillings the hundred; and ship board from fifteen shillings the hundred to forty shillings the hundred."—"*Item.* If any owner or lessor of any house within *Brighthelmston*, shall admit any tenant or tenants, under tenant or under tenants, into his said house, except the said tenant or tenants shall, by the opinion of the constable and the churchwardens in writing first to be set down, be thought of sufficient ability to maintain himself and his family without burdening the town, then the said owner or lessor shall forfeit for every month that any such tenant, not being estimated as aforesaid, shall inhabit or dwell in his said house, to the poor man's box, three shillings and four pence."—"*Item.* If any questions, doubt, or ambiguity, shall hereafter happen to arise about any of the said orders, or the pains therein contained, then the same to be expounded and interpreted by the said commissioners, or any of them.

"Signed { "T. BUCKHURST,
"RICHARD SHELLEY."

The signatures of some of the principal inhabitants follow on the next page; but it will be seen by the signs, or characters, affixed to those who could not inscribe their names, that education had made but little progress amongst them, John Slater, Bartholomew Bowredge, Stephen Pyper, William Wollay, Christopher Ingelard, Deryk Carver, and J. Duconde, the younger, being the only persons who could sign their names, and their writing even, is of a most inferior description. The figures in parenthesis correspond with those annexed to the signs as here shown, which are the "his marks" made by the persons signing. The names are:—

Richard Stoneham, constable (1), Thomas Worger (2), John Tuppen (3), Thomas King (4), John Ffrende (5), William Hunn (6), Thomas Brackpell (7), James Plumer (8), Henry Gunn (9), William Stallard (10), John Allen (11), Thomas Hardinge (12), Thomas Gunn (13), Patrick Hacket (14), Nicholas Payne (15), William Frende (16), Richard Turynought (17), Thomas Payne (18), William Dighton (19), Thomas Jackson (20), John Anstye (21), Thomas Harding (22), John Hardinge (23), Thomas Nicholl (24), William Duffell (25), William Payne (26), William Kellaway (27), Richard Coby (28), William Eastwarde (29), Roger Boyse (30), John Coby (31), Bartholomew Bowredge by me, Stephen Pyper, William Wollay, Christopher Ingelard, John Streate (32), Christopher Streate (33), *Mr.* Deryk Carver, Richard Millar (34), John Cooke (35), John Oston (36), John French (37), Roger Hewe (38), John Carver (39), Richard Adroll (40), Francis Morris (41), Edward Bradforde (42), Jo. Browne (43), Thomas Humphreys (44), John Coby (45), John Worger (46), John Eightaker (47), William Broppell (48), John Ffriende, jun. (49), John Bayllye (50), Richard Hardinge (51), Nicholas Good (52), William Body (53), William Heakins (54), Edmund Lock (55), John

Boyse (56), John Shetter (57), John Surredge (58), John Eston (59), John Gillet (60), Thomas Hunn (61), William Tanner (62), John Crovill (63), John Swaine Richard Marchaunte (65), John Duddinge (66), Richard Gunn (67), William a Deine (68), Richard a Deme (69), Jo. a Wood (70), Jo. Smythe (71), John Mellershe (72), John Reggatt (73), J. Duconde, younger.

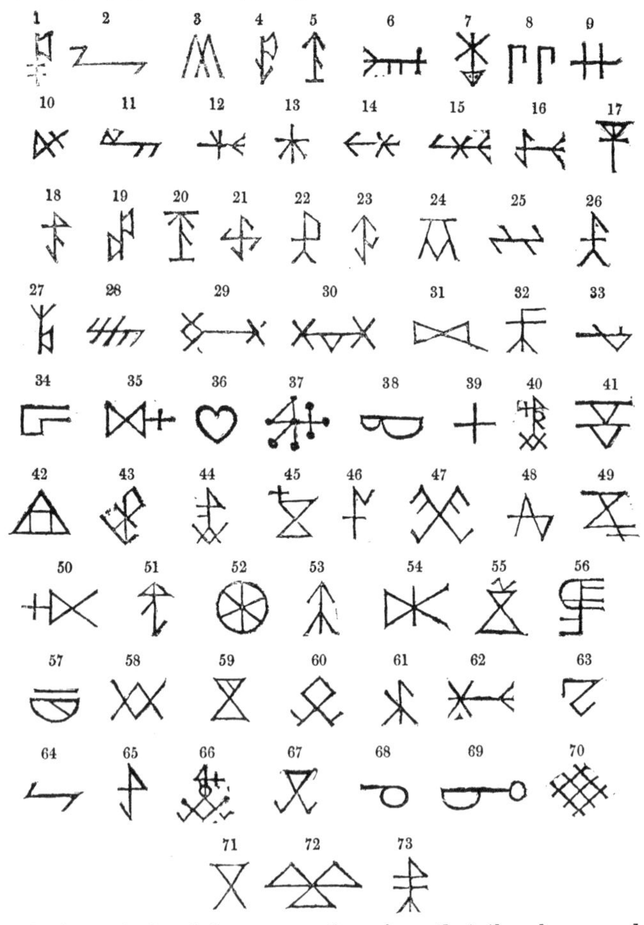

It is conjectured by some antiquarians that the above marks are symbols of the trade or occupation of those who assented to the foregoing recited orders; their opinion being formed from the circumstance of Stoneham, the constable, being a ship carpenter, and attaching a hatchet to his name; and for the same reason the supposition is that Oston, from his sign was a butcher, Good, a wheelwright, and Mellershe a millwright. The rest seem wholly unintelligible.

In the year 1580, Lord *Buckhurst* and Mr. *Shelley* made a new order concerning the penalty falling on the owner or lessor of any house let without the written consent of the constable and churchwardens, which was henceforth to be levied from the under-tenant, as well as from the said owner or lessee.

And in the year 1592, they made another order, which subjected absentees, who owned houses or any other tenements within the parish, to contribute to the public charges of the said parish, in proportion to their possessions there, as if they were residents. In case of contumacious resistance or neglect of the said orders, the constable, or his deputy, and the churchwardens, or any two of them, of which the constable or his deputy being one, were authorised by the above-named commissioners, to imprison such as offended in that particular until they shall be contented to observe and keep the same.

It seems, however, that this commission terminated with the life of Lord Buckhurst, who died in 1608; for we find the inhabitants of *Brighthelmston*, in ten years after, revising and ratifying "the ancient customs heretofore used among and between the fishermen and landsmen" there, "and orders out of the said customs taken and made," without the authority or interference of any superior; and as these customs must be materially directive of the internal polity of the town even at this day, the following copy of them, with a few comments on their immediate relevancy to the present parochial constitution of Brighthelmston, will not be unacceptable to many readers.

"Upon[1] agreement made by and between the ancient fishermen and landmen of the town of Brighthelmston, in the county of Sussex, the second day of February, 1618, for remedy and redress of certain disorders in their said town, as also for the better increase of brotherly love and amity for ever hereafter between the said fishermen and landmen, and for the annual payment of certain money called a *quarter of a share*, heretofore of ancient time usually paid out of every boat in every fishing voyage, to the churchwardens there, towards the maintenance of the church and other public charges about the necessary defence of the town; and of a certain contribution by the rest of the inhabitants, being landmen, towards the bearing of the said charges, to be had and levied; and for the purposes aforesaid the said fishermen and landmen, having met and assembled together, here have set down in writing

[1] Second Town Book, or Costumal of *Brighthelmston*.

their ancient customs and orders concerning the true making, paying, and employing the said quarter share; and also of the paying and employing of the said landmen's contribution, or yearly rate for the uses aforesaid, and for the certainty and true payment thereof in manner and form hereafter following:—

"*The Ancient Custom for Payment and Employing the* QUARTER SHARE.—*Imprimis.* It is concluded and agreed between the said fishermen and landmen, the day and year above mentioned, that they, the said fishermen, shall yearly make as they have done time out of mind, a quarter of a share out of every fishing boat in every fishing voyage; and the same so being made, shall yearly and every year pay, at the end of every voyage, unto the fishermen churchwardens for the time being, without diminution or deduction, the said quarter share, to be by them and the other churchwarden, kept and employed unto the only and proper use of the town in the common town box, until the new constable shall be chosen yearly."—"*Item.* It is agreed between the said landmen and fishermen above said, that the said landmen shall yearly and every year pay and bring unto the said common town-box, in or upon the second day of February, commonly called *Candlemas Day*, yearly, half so much money[1] as the aforesaid quarter share shall amount unto; there to be by all the said churchwardens kept and employed unto the general and public use of the town."—"*Item.* It is further concluded and agreed upon between the said fishermen and the said landmen, that all manner of town charges whatsoever (the king's composition or customary wheat only excepted) shall be taken out of the common town box, whether it be for the maintenance of the church, the communion bread and wine, the maintenance of the lecture, the clerk and sexton's wages, the lights in the fire cage, the paying the king's majesty's oats and coals, and the setting forth of soldiers or sailors, and all manner of other necessary and public town charge shall be taken out of the said common town box, by and with the consent of the constable and churchwardens for the time being, and six other, whereof *four* to be of the sea, two of the land."—"*Item.* It is further ordered by and between the said fishermen and landmen, that if it shall happen that the said quarter share and the land contribution will not at any time amount and countervail the whole charge that shall arise and grow by reason of any extraordinary charge happening, that then the constable and churchwardens, and six other of the said inhabitants shall tax, rate, and cess all the said inhabitants proportionably, every one according to their estate and ability."—"*Item.* It is also agreed between the said fishermen and landmen that the churchwardens, every year, shall collect and gather and bring in unto the common town-box the said quarter share, and the warders for sea causes to collect and gather it; and the land-warden being with one of the sea-wardens shall also yearly, and every year, bring into the said common town-box the rate or taxation of the other inhabitants not being fishermen; which rate or taxation every year ought to amount to half so much as the said quarter of a share doth yearly; and also shall gather, receive, and take up all rents and other land profits belonging to the town, as the rent of the town-house, town mills, and Bartholomews, which, being so received, shall yearly bring into the said town box, there to be kept up to the general use of the town."

"*Orders concerning the* CONSTABLE.—"*Item.* It is further agreed between the said fishermen and landmen, that the constable of the said town shall yearly have for and towards his labour and pains taken in that behalf, and for and towards his charges and expenses, the sum of twenty-five shillings, eight pence, of lawful money of *England*, to be paid unto him out of the said common town-box, and also that every constable, whether he be a landman or a fisherman, shall yearly have, and quietly enjoy, to his own use, without any let, molestation, or trouble, one horse lease."—"*Item.* It is also ordered between the said fishermen and the said landmen,

[1] This was a larger contribution than the landmen had been used to make.

that the two headboroughs of the said town, shall have yearly for their pains and troubles in their office, the sum of five shillings, eight pence, a-piece, to be paid unto them out of the said common town-box; and also shall have and quietly enjoy to their own use, one cow lease, and twenty-five sheep leases, according to the ancient custom."—"*Item.* It is also ordered, that there shall be selected and chosen out of the said ancientest, gravest, and wisest inhabitants, eight fishermen and four landmen, for assistants to the constable in every public cause, whereof every one shall be ready to give his attendance upon the constable as often as need shall require: and whosoever shall presume to call together any assembly to the intent to practice or put in use any manner of device or act touching the government of the said town, without the privilege, consent, and commandment of the said constable and assistants, shall forfeit for every time so doing, forty shillings: and to the intent that the choice of the said *twelve* grave and wise men, may have a continuance, therefore, upon the death or removing of any one of the said *Twelve*, or of the most part of them, to choose in supply such other of the said town as by them, or the most part of them, shall be thought meet, provided always that such choice shall be always ratified and allowed by the stewards of the lords of the said town, at the law day when the constable is chosen, or by such one of them as shall happen to keep such court in the said town, or otherwise the said choice to be void: and if every such choice shall be by the said stewards, or by such one of them as shall fortune to be present as aforesaid, be disallowed, until a sufficient man or such sufficient men, shall be, in the judgment of the same steward, elected and chosen."—"*Item.* For as much as the town is overcharged with the multitude of poor people, which daily are thought to increase by means of receiving under tenants, lodging and harbouring of strangers, and the great disorder of tippling-houses; and that the constable cannot without further assistance, take upon himself the whole oversight and charge of all the parts of the town; in this behalf, it is thought meet that every one of the said *Twelve* shall have assigned unto him some place, street, or circuit of the said town, near about his dwelling house, where he shall, as deputy to the constable, have special charge for the keeping of good order; and especially to see that the order for the avoiding under tenants be duly observed and kept; and that none lodge or keep tippling without license."—*Item.* "For as much as the said inhabitants of the said town of *Brighthelmston*, hath of long time, and yet still are to the making hereof, been over-charged and suppressed by the multitude of poor people, which daily are thought to increase by the means of many ale-house keepers and victuallers which do harbour and receive all comers and goers, to the great hurt and hinderance of the said inhabitants, and doth still sell and keep ale and beer without license, and against the said inhabitants' consent, it is now ordered by the said inhabitants, for the suppressing of the said number of ale-houses and victualling-houses, that from henceforth for ever hereafter none of the said inhabitants whatsoever shall at any time hereafter, draw, sell, or keep any victualling or ale-house within the said town without a letter or testimonial of the said inhabitants, in writing, first had and obtained, by and with the consent of the constable, vicar, or curate, and six other substantial men of the said inhabitants, whereof four to be of the seamen, and two of the landmen in their behalf, to be made unto the Justices of the King's Majesty's Peace, whereby they, and so many of them, and not more, may be lawfully licensed to use the said trade of victualling and ale-house keeping; and also that such a competent number may be by the said Justices of the King's Majesty's Peace (whereof one to be of the quorum), and by and with the consent of the said inhabitants, nominated and appointed: and that none other of the said inhabitants may use or occupy the said trade of victualling or ale-house keeping in the said town, but so many of them as shall be lawfully licensed as is aforesaid, upon pain and peril of every one so doing contrary to the true meaning of this present order, to forfeit for every barrel of beer so drawn, six shillings and eight pence."—"*Item.* If any man hath heretofore builded, erected, or set up any house, wall, pale, shed, or any such like thing whatever; or if any hereafter shall erect, build, or set up any house, wall, shed, pale, or any such like thing whatsoever, to the annoyance of the market-place, or of the block-house there, and shall not, upon warning given him by the constable, or his deputy for the time being, pull down or remove away the same within ten days after such warning given, that then he shall forfeit the sum of five pounds."

"*Orders for Payment of the* QUARTER SHARE.—These being almost literally the same as those presented to, and ratified by, Lord *Buckhurst* and Mr Shelley, in 1580, are purposely omitted; as are also, for the same reason, the Orders for the LENGTH OF NETS in this second book of Customs."

"*Orders concerning the* LANDMEN.—*Item.* It is ordered, that the constable and churchwardens of *Brighthelmston* for the time being, with two or three of the substantial landmen, shall yearly cess, tax, and rate towards the common charge of the town, as well all the landmen, husbandmen, and artificers, and all of the inhabitants having land there; and also all such persons as have lands, tenements, or other yearly profits by land, in the said town, and dwell in other places, according to the quantity of their lands, tenements, and profits, proportionably with the said inhabitants; the which cessment, rate, or taxation, shall be yearly made and set down in writing, under the hands of the said constable, churchwardens, and substantial landmen, before the feast day of *Epiphany*, and shall amount unto half as much as the quarter share shall come unto yearly: and further it is ordered, that such persons as dwell in other places, and have in their own occupation within the said town, lands, tenements, or other yearly profits, shall likewise yearly pay all such sums of money as they, and every of them, in manner and form aforesaid, shall be rated and taxed, upon pain of such forfeitures and punishments as are to be inflicted on the inhabitants of the said town, for not paying such sums of money as they, in like sort, shall be cessed, taxed, or rated."—"*Item.* Whosoever, being a landman, husbandman, artificer, or inhabitant, or every other occupier of land or tenements of and in the said town, that shall not yearly, before the feast day of the *Purification of St. Mary*, pay unto the Churchwardens for the time being, all such sum or sums of money as he or they shall be cessed, rated or taxed, shall for every time so doing, forfeit the double value thereof."—"*Item.* If any owner or lessee of any house in Brighthelmston, admit any tenant or tenants, under-tenant or under-tenants, into his said house, except the said tenant or tenants shall, by the opinion of the constable and the churchwardens in writing first to be set down, be thought of sufficient ability to maintain himself and his family without burdening the town, then the owner and lessee shall, for every month that any such tenant, not being estimated as aforesaid, shall inhabit or dwell in his house, to forfeit unto the use of the poor of the said town, ten shillings."—"*Item.* That whereas it is before ordered, that the owner and lessee of any house in *Brighthelmston*, in case he admitted any under-tenant, without the consent of the constable and churchwardens, first had in writing, shall forfeit monthly during the abode or inhabiting of any such under-tenant not being approved as aforesaid, *monthly*, ten shillings. Now forasmuch as the said penalties cannot conveniently be levied of such owners as are not resident or abiding within the town, and that the town is more burdened and charged with poor than heretofore it hath been, it is now further ordered, that the penalties for every default contrary to the said order, shall be extended in all points as well against the under-tenants, as against the said lessee or owner."

"The orders for the churchwardens in this town book, being in substance the same with those before transcribed from the former, they need not here be repeated.

" The immemorial existence of the above customs in the town of Brighthelmston, is incontestible even at this day: and though some of them be now obsolete on account of the great changes which the town has experienced during the present century, no part of its existing polity can legally run counter to those ancient customs, except upon sanction of an Act of Parliament, or where the right of exercising them has been evidently given up. The commissioners in 1580, only investigated and affixed publicity and order to those customs: and their subsequent orders to the inhabitants, were no more than what a bench of justices may issue at the present day. The independent style of the ancient fishermen and landmen in the second book, seems to be that of men who were conscious of a prescriptive right of legislation in certain matters within their own parish: and the Saxon constitution, whose equitable and benign spirit still feebly pervades what we now call the British Constitution, granted the same right to every parish all over England.

" The custom of choosing three churchwardens annually is still exercised, though the cause of it has ceased to exist for more than half a century past. But the customary existence of twelve assistants and advisers to the constable has ceased, though the occasion for which they were first instituted still remains, nay, increases commensurately with the population of the town. The ancient society of the twelve shall therefore be revived. That such a society did once exist, by custom, cannot be denied: and the mere neglect of a custom for ever so many years is no deseasance of the right to exercise it at any subsequent period. But its revival shall not be for the creation or benefit of a party. Political equality is the birth-right of every Briton; and no civil power can be lawful which emanated not originally from the assent of society, and is invariably exercised for the public good. The Twelve therefore shall be chosen by ballot at a public meeting of all the inhabitants, and every future vacancy in that body filled by public election in the same manner. The gentleman who presides at present at the court leet of the town, there is every reason to suppose, would cheerfully ratify so respectable an election; and the police of so populous a parish would, in future, be managed with signal vigilance, under the inspection of twelve chosen guardians of the public peace and prosperity.

"It was the discontinuance of the ancient society of the Twelve, that made it necessary to appoint commissioners by act of Parliament, in the year 1772, for lighting and cleaning the streets, lanes, and other places within the town of Brighthelmston; as also for removing and preventing nuisances, holding and regulating a daily market there, and building and repairing groynes, in order to render the coast more safe and commodious for vessels to unload and land sea-coal, culm, and other coal, for the use of the town: and in order to enable the said commissioners to accomplish these public and serviceable ends, they are allowed by the act, a duty of sixpence on every chaldron of coal or culm so landed. As it is not unlikely a question may hereafter arise concerning the precincts of the commissioners' power, it may not here be unseasonable to consider how far it extends. As the letter of the act seems to confine it to the limits of the town, the sagacity of litigation may discover that the buildings erected since the year 1772, in the then common fields and environs of Brighthelmston, could not have been in contemplation of the framers of the act, inasmuch as those buildings were not then *in esse*. But as there never were any fixed boundaries to the town, as far as continuous buildings and population reach within the parish, so far, I conceive, shall the town, and consequently the power of the commissioners, be admitted always to extend. Otherwise, indeed, the act would be abortive and absurd. These commissioners were originally sixty-four in number, and constituted of the most respectable inhabitants in the town. Many vacancies by death and removal, have since occurred, and been very properly filled by election among the existing members. Yet I am so fully assured of the evil tendency in general, as well as the injustice of political monopoly of every kind, that I regret the right of election on those occasions had not vested in the inhabitants at large.

"But as the authority of the commissioners exceeds not, except in a few particulars, that of parochial surveyors, the Society of Twelve, if called forth again into existence and exertion, would be of great benefit to the town. In summer, Brighthelmston too frequently becomes the chief receptacle of the vice and dissipation which the sickening metropolis disgorges into our watering places at this season. Its population then is upwards of ten thousand, and only one constable and two headboroughs to preserve the order and safety of the town amidst such a medley. Were there twelve more of the most active and intelligent inhabitants of the town, united with them in directing and strengthening its police, the careful parent would then have less reason to fear the gambler for his son, or the debauchee for his daughter. The constable of Brighthelmston had such a society to assist him when it was but an obscure fishing town: the propriety of reviving the same, at this period of its popularity and splendour, I leave every thinking inhabitant of the place to consider and enforce."—*Dunvan*, 1795.

Chapter VII.

THE TENANTRY LANDS.

Upon the general survey made throughout England, by order of King Alfred, the tenantry land of Brighthelmston, was, like the estates in general, in other parishes of the kingdom, planned and plotted out; and from time to time, down to the present date, the possessions of the different land-owners, have, from various changes in the proprietorship, been re-measured and set out; and such a procedure is termed taking the terrier. Dooms-day Book has it: *Statutum de admensuratione terrarum.* Dooms-day Book is a book that was made by order of William the Conqueror, in which all the estates of the kingdom are registered. It consists of two volumes, which are deposited at Westminster, in the chapter-house; where they may be consulted on paying the fee of 6s. 8d. for a search, and 4d per line for a transcript. It was begun in 1081, and not completed till 1087. There is a copy of it in the library of the dean and chapter of Exeter. One leaf of it was discovered some years since at Nettlecombe, in Somersetshire, a seat of Sir John Trevelyan, Bart., who sent it to the dean and chapter. There is a story extant in connexion with finding this leaf. In a room at Nettlecombe, which was used as a depository for lumber, and furniture and goods not in general use, a square of glass in the window always remained broken; and notwithstanding, from time to time, the window was repaired, the next morning, not only was the glass found to be demolished, but, invariably, three drops of blood stained the sash. It happened on one occasion when the deeds of the estate had to be referred to by the solicitor of the family, Mr. Leigh, that the remarkable incident of the window was mentioned to him; as the family parchments and papers were actually deposited in a strong chest in that very room. Being a person of a superstitious turn of mind, and of antiquarian research, he conceived the idea that amongst the accumulation of musty deeds, there was one which would give the solution to the strange mystery. A general overhauling therefore, of the contents of the old oak chest was made; but nothing of any moment was discovered, save a dingy leaf of some book, which seemed to have no connection whatever with the rest of the papers. This proved to be the long lost and frequently sought for leaf of the Exeter Dooms-day Book. The story continues, that the square of glass was that day repaired; and the next morning not only was it found to be broken, with the three drops of blood sprinkled on the sash, but upon the lid of the old oak chest, having filled its mission, lay dead a pure white dove. Ever after the restored window remained uninjured. On the 3rd day of March, 1738, was made:—"A General Terrier of the several Lands lyeing and being in the Common Laines of Brighthelmston, in the County of Sussex, shewing each person's quantity in Pauls, Eight of which make an Acre; made and agreed unto by several owners and occupiers."

The several Laines are: West Laine, Little Laine, East Laine, Hilly Laine, and North Laine There are besides, portions called White Hawk, and Church Hill. The Laines are set out in measured areas, termed furlongs*, which furlongs are subdivided into irregular portions called paul-pieces, "eight of which make an acre," the tenantry acres varying considerably as to the number of rods they contain, ranging from 35 to 210 rods. Some of these

* Furlong, or Fortylong, from the French *quarante*, forty, a measure of forty perches.

have other pauls running into them; and in such instances, from the shape they thus assume, they are termed "hatchet pieces;" while the extreme pauls of the furlongs in the Laines, are called "headlands."

The Terrier at present used in defining property in the parish, is the "Terrier to the tenantry land in the parish of Brighthelmston, as it was measured and set out in the year MDCCXCII, by Thomas Budgen." Copies of the Terriers, in a book form, are in the hands of several of the solicitors and surveyors in the town, and the proprietors of the tenantry lands. The most concise plan is a map of the whole parish, with elaborate references. For the convenience of cultivation, a Terrier was taken, agreeable to a resolution passed by the principal landholders, at a meeting which was held at the Old Ship, on the 26th day of March, 1776, that by drawing lots the owners of several pauls in different parts af a furlong, might have their lands together in one piece in each furlong. The arrangement did not in the least alter the proprietorship of the several pauls.

The following is the whole content of the Parish, as taken by Mr John Marchant, surveyor, May 12th, 1832:—

WEST LAINE.

	PAULS.	A.	R.	P.	A.	R.	P.
North Butts	76	7	3	12			
Hedge Furlong	146	14	3	10			
The Blacklands	96	11	2	23			
Furlong, near West Fields*	300	29	1	12			
Cliff Butts	101	6	0	0			
Furlong, heading ditto	80	6	1	18			
Second Furlong from Home	52	3	3	19			
Home Furlong	112	8	1	0			
Wall Furlong	68	2	1	20			
Furlong heading the Barns	52	3	1	18			
Chalk-pit Furlong	52	3	3	32			
Furlong next Chalk-pit	56	4	1	11			
					102	0	21

CHURCH HILL.

Church Hill	62	47	2	32			
West side of ditto	216	42	0	16			
Lead's Furlong	72	7	0	13			
					96	3	21

* Part of this furlong was lost by the sea.

LITTLE LAINE.							
Upper Furlong	292	24	2	23			
Cliff Furlong	278	13	1	4			
					37	3	27
EAST LAINE.							
Cliff Furlong	444	26	0	20			
Furlong next Newbroke Ground	202	14	1	20			
Second Furlong	116	11	0	16			
Third Furlong	163	15	2	10			
Fourth Furlong	72	5	2	34			
Fifth Furlong	102	7	0	31			
Sixth Furlong	108	8	3	30			
Baker's Bottom Furlong	253	21	0	13			
Coombe Furlong	240	17	2	9			
					127	2	23
WHITE HAWK.							
South side of the White Hawk*		22	1	31			
West side do†		23	0	19			
East side do‡		24	0	25			
North-east side do		14	1	13			
					84	0	11
HILLY LAINE.							
Islingword Furlong	200	26	1	34			
Shepherd's Acre Furlong	112	11	0	18			
Fifth Furlong	298	25	1	14			
Fourth Furlong	193	14	2	2			
Third Furlong	366	29	3	21			
Second Furlong	320	22	3	26			
Gold's Butts		1	0	12			
Home Furlong	247	26	1	12			
Breach Furlong	266	20	1	2			
					177	3	21
NORTH LAINE.							
Home Furlong	247	16	3	25			
Church Furlong	62	6	1	36			
Second Furlong	216	14	1	15			
Third Furlong }	262	17	2	30			
Shepherd's Acre }		0	3	20			
Fourth Furlong	254	17	3	35			
Fifth Furlong	220	20	2	1			
Crooked Furlong	97	8	2	24			
Rottingdean Hedge Furlong	100	8	2	23			
Home Butts	32	3	1	6			
North Butts	52	6	3	0			
The Crook		6	2	35			
					128	3	20

* Set off in February 1765: 22a. 1r. 27p.
† Set off in February 1773: 24a. 3r. 16p.
‡ Set off in February 1773: 24a. 3r. 26p.

	A.	R.	P.	A.	R.	P.
The North side of Round Hill	34	3	16			
South part of ditto	22	3	32			
Scabb's Castle	82	1	37			
Tenantry Sheep Down	400	0	36			
Field in Level	14	1	23			
Black Rock Arable	20	2	0			
Black Rock Down	112	2	16			
The Town of Brighthelmston, including the Steine, North Inclosures, Level, &c	118	2	28			
				806	2	28
Contents of the whole Parish				1562	0	12

Within the Laines were portions of ground termed "yardlands," but where situated has not been fully defined. The chief record of them is respecting the

STOCK OF SHEEP.

68 Yardlands, at 16 sheep per yard	1088
The Reeve ,, ,,	20
The Dooling Leases ,,	16
The Shepherd to keep	none
Widow Barnard ,,	none
	1124

In the "Nonarum Inquisitiones" is the following descriptive valuation of Brighthelmston:—

"This indenture testifies that an acquisition was taken before Henry Husse and fellows, collectors, and assessors of the ix*th* of garbel fleeces and lambs, and of the xv*th* granted to our lord the king, in the county of Sussex, assigned at Lewes, on a Sunday, in the middle of the xl*th* year of the reign of King Edward the Third, from the nonal inquest, and the quindecimal concerning the true value of the ix*th* of garbel, (corn) ix*th* of fleeces, and ix*th* of lambs, by commission of our lord the king, directed to the aforesaid Henry and his fellows, by the oath of John de Erlee, Hugh Russell, John Dac', and Ralph Grabb, parishioners of Brighthelmston who say, that the extent of the church there is taxed at xxv pounds with the vicarage. And they say that the ix*th* part of garbel is worth this year, there, ix pounds, viii shillings, and x pence from the community of the town. Also the ix*th* part of fleeces there is worth xxvi shillings and vi pence, and the ix*th* part of lambs there, is worth vi shillings and viii pence. Also they say, that the ix*th* part of garbel and fleeces of the prior of Lewes there, is worth, vii shillings and viii pence. Also the ix*th* part of garbel and fleeces of the prior of Michelham, is worth xxx shillings and iv pence. And so is the sum of the whole ix*th* of garbel, fleeces, and lambs, this year, xiii pounds. Also they say that the ix*th* part aforesaid cannot answer nor attain to the taxation of the church aforesaid; for that xl acres of land are drowned by the sea for ever, which were worth per annum xl shillings. And also clx acres of land in the common plain, which have been deficient there this year in corn sown, to the value of x pounds. And because the wool cannot be sold as it was wont, the value of xiii shillings and iv pence is deficient. And also the lambs there will be deficient in the pasture this year, by defect of value vi shillings and viii pence. And the vicar has there the first-prints of one dove-house, value ii shillings. And the same has there in offerings, small tithes of geese, sucking pigs, honey, milk, cheese, calves, and eggs, and other small tithes which are worth yearly lxx shillings. Also they say, that there are here no merchants, but tenants of land who live by their own lands, and their great labours only. In testimony of which thing, the aforesaid sworn men have affixed their seals to this indenture."

Chapter VIII.

THE BARTHOLOMEWS.

The chauntry, or free chapel, dedicated to St. Bartholomew, was erected on a piece of land granted by the lord of the manor of Brighthelmston, to the Priory of St. Pancras, at Southover, Lewes, under a quit rent of 3d a-year. It was built to the south-west of the knappe or knab, originally called by the Saxon settlers, *cnæp*, (the summit or crown of a hill) from its elevated position. It is now generally known by the name of Brighton place. Attached to the chauntry was a dwelling for the two or three monks who officiated there. The chauntry was destroyed by the fire which devastated the town, on the landing of the French, under Primauget, and it never after recovered its accustomed use and influence. The almshouses, which were afterwards built on the site, were sold to the parish in 1733, for the sum of £17, and the dwelling of the monks, called the Prior's Lodge, became the residence of the vicar of Brighthelmston, after the Reformation.

"Magna Britannia" mentions, "that there was a church near the middle of the town, and it was burnt down some years ago by the French." This probably refers to the chapel or chauntry of St. Bartholomew. The Prior's Lodge was pulled down by the Rev. Thomas Hudson, in 1790, the year he was collated to the rectory of Blatchington and vicarage of Brighthelmston. From the style of the architecture, and the decayed state of the timbers, there was ample room for supposing the building to have been erected not later than the close of the thirteenth century. In 1665 the Bartholomews is mentioned as a parcel of pasture. The parish workhouse, demolished in 1823, was erected on its site, and the rest of the space continued nearly plain ground till, in 1774, the market place was built, where the present Town Hall stands. The original market-place, that possessed by the town under the charter of Edward II., was on the cliff, where it had continued from the year 1313 till the close of the seventeenth, or the beginning of the last century; when, that part being sapped by the waves, the building was demolished. The vicarage house, which was substituted for the Prior's Lodge, by the Rev. T. Hudson, was vacated by the present vicar, the Rev. Henry Michell Wagner, in 1835, and pulled down in 1837. The old vicarage garden was about a quarter of an acre in extent.

The first stone of the present vicarage was laid on the 24th day of June, 1834, and in the following year the structure was completed, and accepted by the Bishop of the Diocese, on the unanimous recommendation of six commissioners, namely, three laymen and three clergymen, to the effect that the exchange would be, in every respect, beneficial. It stands in a garden of exactly two measured acres; and was built by Messrs. George Cheesman and Son.

In 1584, William Midwinter, a sailor, sold the site of the chauntry to Thomas Friend and others, in trust for the said town, in consideration of the sum of £44, which had been raised by subscription among the inhabitants. It had been granted to Lord Cromwell, on the dissolution of the Priory of Lewes; and on his attainder and execution, to Anne of Cleves. It reverted to the Crown in 1557, after the death of that Princess, and afterwards came into the possession of Roger Blackbourne, a farmer of Yorkshire. In 1577 he aliened it to Milo Taylor, servant to Lord Buckhurst, and John Codwell, both of Southover, Lewes. Taylor soon after released his share to Codwell, who sold the whole to Midwinter.

In 1773, an Act of Parliament was obtained for erecting and holding a daily market, Sundays excepted; and the waste land of the Bartholomews being a central situation, and the common property of the town, it was fixed on for the site of the said market.

The workmen, who were employed in digging for the foundation of this building, happened to cut through a little cemetery, which seems to have belonged to the chauntry of St. Bartholomew, and were so strongly impressed with superstitious awe, by the bones which they uncovered, that they refused to proceed with their work. The vicar, the Rev. Henry Michell, being informed of their scruples, came to the spot, and instead of exerting his personal influence, which was very great over all classes of his parishioners, or vainly combating the prejudices of ignorance with reason, applauded their veneration for the supposed remains of Christians, but assured them that all who had ever been interred there were rank Papists. Their first prejudice being thus laid by a stronger, the men resumed their work, and turned over the rest of the bones with the apathy of grave-diggers.

About fifty years since, in one of the old tumble-down houses which occupied the site whereon now stand the Schools of Mr. Henry Catt, by the "Knab Pump," resided Thomas Herbert, a short, stout, fat, and greasy old fellow, possessing but one eye, who professed to make the best sausages out of Germany. He was a maker of small meat pies and sausages; and with these he exhibited his "Publications for Sale." He was the author of the play, "Too much the Way of the World," and likewise of "A Brief Sketch of Human Life;" which, with his other literary works, lay cheek by jowl with his comestibles. He had been a butcher; and the following specimen of his literary talent, written in a bold hand, in his window, expressed the cause of the change in his occupation; as he stated he was one

> "Who, for want of cash, the shambles spurn'd,
> And is for once a play-wright turn'd."

Chapter IX.

THE WORKHOUSE.

From the deepest research which the compiler of this work has been able to make, he cannot find that any Workhouse existed in

Brighton prior to 1727, in which year the following entries appear in the Town book :—

February 26th, 1727,—That a mortgage be effected on the workhouse, to indemnify Thomas Simmons, in paying the moneys he made of the materialls of Blockhouse, to the constable and churchwardens ; by them to be disbursed in payment of materialls and the workmen employed about building the workhouse.

May 10th,—Order in Vestry for Churchwardens and Overseers,—with all speed to borrow £50, to pay for materials and workmanship about the Workhouse, in the building of it, to be repaid out of the poor rate, or taxes to be raised in the parish, on or before the 10th of May, 1728.

At a public vestry meeting, held at the Old Ship, October 18th, 1727, it is agreed that the Churchwardens and Overseers shall take up with all convenient speed, and borrow one hundred pounds, upon interest at 5 per centum per annum, towards building the new workhouse.

Amongst the minutes of the public vestry, 13th November, 1727, there is the entry of a contract being entered into, between the parish and Thomas Fletcher and Thomas Tuppen, for digging and steining the well to the new workhouse, complete, with fittings, for ten guineas.

The Workhouse at this period was evidently of very limited extent. But in 1733 a portion of the Almshouses in connexion with the chauntry of St. Bartholomew was added to the building. The spot is now occupied by the east end of the Brighton Market. A tenement for the poor previously existed in East street; and in 1690, in consequence of the great increase of the poor-rates, on account of the inroads of the sea, and the injury experienced by the town from the civil and foreign wars of that and the preceding century, by order of the Justices at the quarter Sessions, at Lewes, the following parishes, that had no poor of their own, were called upon to make the following contributions :—

	£.	s.	d.
Patcham, the yearly sum of	17	16	7
Hangleton	4	16	9
East Aldrington	6	1	1½
Blachington	4	2	6
Ovingdean	6	0	10½
	£38	17	10*

* *Anno* 18, *Elizabethæ*, cap. 3. sec. 3.—And be it also enacted, That if the said Justices of Peace do perceive, that the Inhabitants of any Parish are not able to levy among themselves sufficient Sums of Money for the Purposes

Formerly the recipients of parish relief were compelled to wear an insignia of their pauperism; as in a vestry minute appears the following:—

At a monthly meeting of the Churchwardens and Overseers, held 27th August, 1696, an accompt was given that Susan Stone, the widdow of Thomas, refused to ware the Town badge, (viz[t.]) the letters, (B: P:) upon which she was putt out of the weekly pay.

The present Workhouse, on Church Hill, was commenced in 1820, Mr. William Mackie, Architect, Charlotte street, Blackfriars' road, London, furnishing the design, which was selected from forty others by the Directors and Guardians, who had advertised a premium for the best design; as it was then considered it combined a proper degree of elegance with economy, and was replete with more convenience than any other institution for the same purpose in the kingdom. Great alterations and additions have been made to the original building, according to the fancy or caprice of the boards of Guardians for the time being. Mr. John Cheesman was the builder. The ceremony of laying the foundation stone was not of the imposing character which is assumed on commencing similar public buildings in modern times. The stone was merely one that had been dug up while getting out the ground for the foundation of the house, and was of the rudest shape, about two feet in length, eighteen inches in width, and ten inches in depth. It was laid by the Vicar, the Rev. Dr. Carr, afterwards Bishop of Chichester, and subsequently of Worcester.

Brighton, at that time, had a population of 24,000, and there were about 4,000 inhabited houses. Fields surrounded the Workhouse grounds; that to the south, the detached grave-yard of the Old Church, being used for occasional festivities, and for the practice of the Royal Artillery. The first building erected near the House was a soap manufactory, by a Mr. Heard. The premises are now the residence and establishment of Dr. Foreman. On the failure of the soap works, which were to astonish the good people of

aforesaid; that then the said Two Justices shall and may tax, rate, and assess, as aforesaid, any other of other Parishes, or out of any Parish within the Hundred where the said Parish is, to pay such Sum and Sums of Money to the Churchwardens and Overseers of the said poor Parish for the said purposes, as the said Justices shall think fit, according to the Intention of this Law.

Brighton, Mr. Airey converted the building into school premises, and for a few years had a good school there,—the Church hill Grammar School. The Rev. Dr. Butler succeeded him, and then, for a short time, the Rev. Mr. Pugh carried on the establishment.

Mr. Thorncroft was the first person who took up his abode in the new Workhouse, which had a tablet over the main entrance, thus inscribed:

Brighthelmston Poor-House,
Erected A.D., 1821.
Vicar, Rev. R. J. Carr, D.D.
Churchwardens { Edward Blaker. Robert Ackerson. Richard Bodle.

At the old Workhouse, or rather Poor-house as it was called, the average number of inmates was 150, and the only labour consisted in collecting and crushing oyster-shells in a large iron mortar. This work was done by the able-bodied out-door poor, in the winter months, at a fixed price per bushel. The material thus produced was sold for manuring land, and for constructing paths in parks, lawns, &c. The Governor at that time, was Mr. Hayward, he having succeeded Mr. Bailey, and the inmates were farmed to Mr. Rice, at a contract price for their board, of about 4s a-week per head. Previous to Mr. Bailey, Mr. Sicklemore was the Governor, he having succeeded Mr. William Pearce, who was appointed March 25th, 1779. Mr. Samuel Thorncroft, the present Assistant-Overseer, was Mr. Rice's assistant, and helped Mr. Chassereau, the then Assistant-Overseer, in preparing the present Workhouse for the reception of the poor, who were very reluctant to leave the old house, to be transported out of the world, as they termed the removal to the new house on Church hill, which certainly then had as desolate an appearance as the "howling wilderness," the name now given to the Industrial Schools at the Warren Farm, by the opponents of that juvenile establishment. The Assistant - Overseer, previous to Mr. Chassereau, was Mr. White, who succeeded Mr. Jonathan Grenville. At this period the principal officers in connexion with the poor of the parish, were an Assistant-Overseer, at a salary of £200, and a Vestry Clerk, at a salary of £100 a-year. Mr. Thomas Attree, of the present firm, Messrs. Attree, Clarke, and Howlett, solicitors, Ship street, was the Clerk, and used to make out the poor-rates, attend—usually by deputy—the meetings of the Directors and Guardians, record the meetings of the Board, and the Committees, and prepare reports.

The removal from the old to the new house took place on the 12th September, 1822, when 27 persons changed their residence. On the 20th of the same month, nine others followed; and on the 24th, sixty-four more were removed, making a total of ninety-five inmates. Mr. Baldey was the parish surgeon. The new governor—Hayward,—remained only a few days on the removal to the new house; as, without the least intimation to any one, he abruptly took himself off. His successor, Mr. Nuttall, remained only four or five weeks, when he was summarily dismissed by the Guardians, on the 5th of November, 1822. Mr. S. Thorncroft was then appointed Governor, a situation which he continued to fill with great honour to himself and satisfaction to the town, till April, 1834, although he did not leave the house till April, 1835. Mr. John Harper was Mr. Chassereau's successor. Mr. Thorncroft was appointed Assistant-Overseer—a position which he still so ably holds—in October, 1834. Mr. Collington, at the close of 1834, succeeded Mr. Thorncroft as Governor; and he held the office till the middle of the summer of 1836, when Mr. Bartlett entered on the duties of Governor, he having been previously the superintendent of pauper-labour, at a salary of £160 a-year.

At the old house Mrs. Idle was a species of matron; but when the inmates went "up the hill," Mrs. Harriet Dennett held that appointment, and continued it till 1827, when she was succeeded by Mrs. Alice Pickstock. Mrs. Pickstock,—the mother of Mrs. S. Thorncroft,—died in 1843. As a memento of respect, her tomb, erected by subscription in the Cemetery Ground of the Old Church, expresses the appreciation of her valuable services. On her death, Mrs. Bartlett, the wife of the Governor, was appointed Matron. Mr. and Mrs. Bartlett resigned in June, 1848, and were succeeded by Mr. and Mrs. Cuzens. About the middle of the year 1849, Cuzens absented himself from his duties, and they were in consequence both discharged in September. Mr. and Mrs. Hodges were appointed to the vacancies, and they held their respective offices till September of the following year. Mr. and Mrs. C. J. King succeeded them, and in October, 1854, on their resignation, Mr. and Mrs. Passmore entered upon their duties. On the 7th of June, 1859, Mr. Passmore absconded; the dismissal of himself and wife ensued in consequence, and on the 15th of July, Mr. and Mrs. Sattin were appointed to fill the vacancies.

The poor-rate collectors hitherto have been Mr. Edward Butler, Mr. Harry (Captain) Blaber, Mr. W. H. Smithers, and Mr. Frank Butler. The parish assessors have been Mr. Saunders, Mr. Robert Ackerson, Mr. Richard Bodle, Mr. Henry Styles Colbron, Mr. Richard Edwards, and Mr. George Maynard.

The original cost for building the Brighton Workhouse was £10,000, and the land was purchased for £1,400, and paid by a rate expressly raised for that service. In the year 1853, the then Board of Directors determined upon disposing of the present Workhouse and grounds, and the erection of a Workhouse and Industrial Schools, and they purchased ground on the Race Hill, as the site for the former, and the Warren Farm, beyond the Race Hill, for the latter. The Schools are completed, and will be ready for occupation when a sufficient supply of water is obtained from the notorious Warren Farm Well.

There have been occasions when the Guardians, in the plenitude of their duties towards the poor, and also to the ratepayers, have made their Board meetings the opportunity for feasting and guzzling. The most memorable time was in the summer of 1837, when they pampered their appetites with john-dorees, salmon, lobsters, Norfolk squab pie, poultry, and joints in profusion; red and white wines by the dozen, and spirits by the gallon; cigars by the box, and snuff by the pound; with a handsome snuff-box, too; and, the usual services of the House being too mean for them, sets of dish-covers were ordered, and dishes, dinner and pie plates, jugs, sauce tureens, cut decanters and stands, rummers, knives and forks, waiters, and a teaboard. Blacking too, was ordered, and one Guardian, Mr. Paul Hewitt, actually sent his boots to the Workhouse to be cleaned, and when done they were returned to his house again. Another Guardian, Mr. Storrer, also sent his dog to the Workhouse to be kept, as it was inconvenient to have it at home. The Guardians had also a summer house, wherein they smoked their cigars and quaffed their grog. This was at the period when out-door paupers had to slave up the Church hill for relief. The removal of the Board-room to Church street, the Pavilion property, has been a great convenience to the poor, and it has been the means of preventing even a hint that the present Board feast at the parish expense.

Immediately in connexion with the Workhouse, the two following extracts from the parish books, will not be found out of place:—

"*Coppy of the Order for the Removal of Stephen Agnus.*"

"SUSSEX.

"To the Churchwardens and Overseers of the POOR of ye Pish. of Brighthelmstone, in ye sd. County, & to the Churchwardens and Overseers of the POOR of the Pish. of Sittingbourne, in ye County of Kent, & to every of them.

"HEN. PELHAM

"GEO. GOREING

"Forasmuch as Complaint hath been made to us, whose hands & Seales are hereto sett, being two of his Majtes. Justices of the Peace for the sd. County (one of which is of ye QUORUM) by the Churchwardens and Overseers of the poor of the sd. Pish. of Brighthelmstone that Stephen Agnus came Lately into ye said pish. not having nor renting Ten pound p. annum, nor otherwise gained a legal settlement there according to ye severall statutes in that case made and provided, but is likely to become chargeable to the said parish of Brighthelmstone.

"These are, therefore, in his Majts. name, to will and require you, the Churchwardens and Overseers of the Poor of ye sd. pish, of Brighthelmstone or some of you, to convey the said Stephen Agnus from the said pish. of Brighthelmstone To the said Pish of Sittingbourn, in Kent, where, upon the examination of the said Stephen Agnus upon oath, it appears that the said Stephen Agnus was last legally settled as an householder. And you, the Churchwardens and Overseers of the poor of the said pish of Sittingbourne, are hereby required and commanded him to receive and provid for, as an Inhabitant of yr sd pish. hereof, fail not at yr perril. Given under our hands and seals this 27th day of January, in the 13th year of his Majst's reign, Anno Domi. 1701.

"*Certificate acknowledging a Parishioner.*

"Wee, Andrew Godwin, John Tappenden, William Ffullager, and William Deane, Churchwardens and Overseers of the Poore of the Parish of Sittingbourne, in the County of Kent, doo hereby owne and acknowledge Stephen Agnus, of the same Parish, to be an inhabitant, legally settled there. Witness our hands and seales this one and thirtieth day of January, Anno Dni. 1701.

"Attested by us
"W. H. HAUSSETT,
"JO. HAWKES,

"ANDREW GODWIN, *
"JOHN TAPPENDEN, *
"WILL. FFULLAGER, *
"WILLIAM DEANE. *

"*To the Churchwardens & Overseers of ye poore of ye parish of Brighthelmstone, in ye County of Sussex, or to any of them.*"

"Wee, whose hands are hereunder written, Justices of ye Peace of the County of Kent, aforesd., doo allowe of the Certificate above written, dated ye 2nd day of February, Anno Dni. 1701.

"Tho. Osborne,
"Waltr. Hooper."

"Bastardy Bond, *given by a Security, that the putative father shall indemnify the Parish against any expence that may be incurred in the birth of a Child.*

Stamp One Shilling and Sixpence.

"Know all Men by these presents, that I, Buckrell Bridger, of the Parish of Brighthelmstone, in the County of Sussex, mariner, am held and firmly bound unto Stephen Richwood, and Stephen Poune, Churchwardens, and Robert Davis and Edward Stiles, Overseers of the Poor of the Parish of Brighthelmstone, aforesaid, in trust for themselves and others, the parishioners of the said Parish, in Fifty Pounds of good and Lawfull money of Great Britain, to be paid to the said Churchwardens and Overseers, or their certain Attorney, Executors, Administrators, and Assigns, for which payment well and faithfully to be made, I bind my Heirs, Executors, and Administrators, and every of them, firmly by these presents, sealed with my Seal, dated this sixth day of May, in the Ninth year of the reign of our Sovereign Lord, George the Third, by the Grace of God, of Great Britain, France, and Ireland, King, Defender of the Faith, and so forth, and in the year of our Lord One thousand, Seven hundred, and Sixty-nine.

"The Condition of this obligation is such, that, whereas Mary Hill, of the Parish of Brighthelmstone, aforesaid, single-woman, hath, in and by her voluntary examination, taken in writing and upon oath before John Fuller, Esquire, one of His Majesty's Justices of the Peace in and for the said County, declared that she is with child, and that the said child is likely to be born a bastard, and to be chargeable to the said Parish of Brighthelmstone, and that Buckrell Bridger, the younger, of Brighthelmstone, aforesaid, mariner, is the father of the said child. If, therefore, the above bounden Buckrell, the elder, or the above named Buckrell Bridger, the younger, or either of them, then, or either of their Heirs, Executors, or Administrators, do or shall, from time to time, or at all times hereafter, fully and clearly indemnify, and save harmless as well, the above named Churchwardens and Overseers of the Poor of the said Parish of Brighthelmstone, and their successors for the time being, and also all other the Parishioners and Inhabitants of the said Parish which now are, or hereafter shall be for the time being, from and against all kind and all manner of Costs, Taxes, Rates, Assessments, and charges whatsoever, for or by reason of the birth, education, and maintenance of the said child, and of and from all Actions, Suits, Troubles, and other charges and demands whatsoever, touching or concerning the same, then this obligation to be void, or otherwise to be and remain in full force.

"BUCKRELL BRIDGER. *
"The mark of BUCKRELL BRIDGER X the elder. *

"Sealed and delivered, being first stamped in the presence of us, the interlineations being first made.

"GEO. ABINGTON,
"THOS. SCRASE."

But a quarter of a century since it was customary to employ the out-door paupers in scavenging, cleansing, and watering the streets, the poor creatures being harnessed, by means of ropes, to the muck-trucks and barrel-constructed water-carts, after the manner that convicts are put to labour in the Government penal establishments and the navy dockyards. The parish officers eventually got shamed out of the system of thus employing those whose only crime was poverty; and for awhile they substituted the health-destroying and heart-breaking plan of wheeling shingle and sand from the beach to the Workhouse-ground in barrows, till one unhappy creature sunk beneath his burthen and died of "disease of the heart!" The custom then was abandoned. The course now pursued towards the indigent is thoroughly to investigate their several cases, and relieve them according to their necessities and deserts: and where laziness and not misfortune is the cause of their penury, to give them an "Able Bodied Ward" ticket of admission to the Workhouse, which not one indolent person in fifty avails himself or herself of, but rather leaves the Board of Guardians, dissatisfied, and eventually resolves upon an attempt at industry, which results in a benefit to themselves and the ratepayers. The system has succeeded beyond all expectations; and many a man who considered the "house" his birthright, because his father and his grandfather from time immemorial wintered there, has taken to provident and industrious habits, and learned the sweet uses of adversity.

Chapter X.

THE ATTACK ON BRIGHTHELMSTON BY THE FRENCH, IN 1545.

Henry the Eighth having ravaged Artois and Picardy, by the superiority of his forces, and made himself master of Boulogne, the French king to retaliate the wanton desolations, sent Admiral D'Annehault with a considerable fleet to devastate the country on the southern coast of the island. The invasion is thus described by Holinshead:—

"In 37 Hen. 8th, 1545, July the 18th, the admiral of France, Mons. Donebatte, hoisted up sails, and with his whole navy (which consisted of 200 ships and 26 gallies,) came forth into the seas, and arrived on the coast of Sussex, before Bright Hampstead, and set certain of his soldiers on land to burn and spoil the country: but the beacons were fired and the inhabitants thereabouts came down so thick, that the Frenchmen were driven to their ships with loss of diverse of their numbers, so that they did little hurt there. Immediately hereupon they made to the Isle of Wight, when about two thousand of their men landed, and one of their chief captains, named Chevalier Daux, a Provençois, being slain with many others, the residue, with loss and shame, were driven back again to their gallies. And having knowledge by certain fishermen whom they took, that the king was present on the coast, (Portsmouth) and a huge power ready to resist them, they dis-anctioned (disanchored) and drew along the coast of Sussex, of whom few returned to their ships; for divers gentlemen of tho country, as Sir Nicholas Pelham and others, with such power as was raised upon the sudden, took them up by the way and quickly distressed them. When they had searched every where by the coast, and saw men still ready to receive them with battle, they turned stern, and so got them home again without any act achieved worthy to be mentioned. The number of the Frenchmen was great, so that diverse of them who were taken prisoners in the Isle of Wight and in Sussex, did report they were three score thousand."

A curious Picture Map of this attack is engraved in the 24th vol. of the "Archæologia" of 1832, from the original in the Cottonian Library. A copy of this map is in the possession of the compiler of this history. It bears date, "1545, July, 37 Henry VIII," The number of ships attacking the town is twenty-two; and the largest, probably the Admiral's, lying nearest the shore, has four masts; seven have three masts, three two masts, and eleven are galleys with one mast and numerous oars. Eight of the latter are on shore, and the armed men from them have disembarked on the beach, the place where they landed being inscribed,—"here landed the galleys." On the shore also, high and dry, are six large boats of the inhabitants, and several smaller ones. On the beach, likewise, at Hove, are five small boats. On the sea, towards the west side, is inscribed,—"Shippes may ride all somer tem in a myle the town in V fathome water;" and on the east,—"Thesse grete shippes rydeng hard abode shore by shoting into the hille and wallies on the towne, so sore oppresse the towne that the countrey dare not adventure to rescue it." The ships are pierced for guns, and the prows and sterns are raised three or four stages. Numerous pennons and streamers adorn each ship, some bearing a *fleur-de-lys*, and others a cross. On shore the houses under the cliffe are on fire; from the upper town also flames are issuing from almost every house. There are five rows of houses running from north to south; and at the extreme north a row of houses runs from east to west. A square space in the centre is marked,—"A felde in the middle of the town." A road to the east of the town, about the spot now occupied by the Old Steine, and going in the north-east direction is inscribed,—"the valey comyng from Lewes town to Brighthampston." On this road and on the hill adjacent bodies of armed men are marching towards the town. On the cliffe, eastward of this road, is an erection from which is suspended a frame containing some burning substance, and is inscribed,—"the towne fyre cage." This is at about the spot where the offices and auction room of Messrs. Parsons and Son now are. From thence, eastward, is inscribed,—"The East pte of brighthampston riseng onelye on cleves high." North of the town is the church, about which persons, some armed, appear in the attitude of prayer. Beyond the church are two mills, marked,—the "wynde mylles;" and still farther a blazing construction on a pole, marked,—"the bekon of the towne." A road from this spot is continued to the sea, about midway between the church and Hove Church, marked,—"hoove Churche." This road, along which armed men are coming towards the town, is inscribed,—"the valey comyng from ponynge (Poynings) betwixt brighthampston and the vilage, hove." As this road approaches the beach it is inscribed,—"Upon this west pt may lond CM psones (100,000 persons) unletted by any pvision there." At the back of the town is inscribed,—"The towne of brighthampston," and immediately to the east of the town is a body of armed men. Hove,—two rows of houses,—is marked, "hove village," and the road running westward from thence, "the west parte of brithampston lowe all daungerous and wout cleves (without cliffs.)"

The next attempt of the French was on Newhaven, where they landed to a considerable number, and proceeded to pillage the town and environs; but the gentry and yeomen of the coast having been collected on the neighbouring hills to oppose the expected descent, attacked the invaders so vigorously that many were slain in attempting to recover their galleys.

Chapter XI.

FORTIFICATIONS OF THE TOWN.

In consequence of the frequent incursions of the French, and the inhabitants being harrassed by frequent alarm, the town resolved, in 1558, to erect fortifications, to afford them some protection for the future. A Court Baron of the manor of Brighthelmston-Lewes was therefore held on the 29th of September in that year, of which the following entry appears in the Court Rolls:

1 Eliz. At a Court Baron, holden for this manor, 27th September, there was granted to the inhabitants of Brighton town by the lords, one parcel of land, containing in length 30 feet, in breadth 16 feet, to build thereon a store-house to keep armes, &c., now called the Block-house. Also at the Court holden for Atlingworth manor, 3 Jac (1606) January 9th, the homage presented that the

north part of the Block-house aforesaid is built on part of the demesnes of that manor.

The land granted was on the Cliff between Black-lion street and Ship street, and about 215 yards westward of East street. The Block-house was circular, about fifty feet in diameter, and the walls were about eight feet in thickness, and eighteen feet in height. Several arched apartments in its thick walls were depositories for the powder and other ammunition for the defence of the town. In front of it, towards the sea, was a little battery called the Gun Garden, on which were mounted four pieces of large iron ordnance. Adjoining the Block-house, on the east, stood the Town-house, with a dungeon under it for malefactors; and on the summit of this building rose a turret, on which the town clock was fixed At the same time with the Block-house, were erected four gates of freestone, (three of which were arched) leading from the Cliff to that part of the town which lay under it, namely, the East Gate at the bottom of East street; the Portal, which was called the Porter's Gate, and was less than any of the others; it stood next the East Gate; the Middle Gate, opposite the end of Middle street, commonly called the Gate of All Nations; and the West Gate, which stood at the end of West street. From the East Gate, westward, there was, at the same time, a wall built about fifteen feet high, and four hundred feet long, where the Cliff was most easy of ascent: and from the termination of that wall, a parapet three feet high, was continued on the verge of the Cliff to the West Gate, with embrasures for cannon. The Block-house was built at the expense of the mariners of the town; but the gates and walls were erected partly if not wholly by the government.

The south of the town was thus effectually secured. For the security, then, of the other three sides, on any emergency, trenches might be cut at the end of the streets which led into the town, or the entrances might be barred to the enemy by lumber carriages and household furniture, while the inhabitants annoyed them from every quarter. The "Magna Britannia," in addition, says, "The town contains seven streets, and as many lanes, but the most spacious of them is devoured by the Ocean," alluding to South street, under the cliff, which it is supposed formed the sea front of the town.

The town book, under the date 1580, has the following inventory of the "great ordnance, and other munition and furniture in Brighthelmston," viz., four iron pieces delivered out of the tower, on the bond of John Slutter, together with powder and shot delivered with the same, two pieces of great ordnance, and ten "qualivers with their flasks and touch boxes," and a drum belonging to the town.

The town also at that time possessed one windmill, purchased of Queen Elizabeth, and the site of another mill then in ruins; "the town-house, situate to the east side of the block-house," granted by a copy of court roll by the lords of the Manor of Brighthelmston, and the said block-house, "of flint, lime, and sand, of late years erected, and built in warlike manner, by the fishermen, with the profits of their quarter share." *

There is no record as to the date when the fortifications in general were destroyed; but it is generally supposed the gradual inroads of the sea sapped them and caused them to fall. Certainly they were not demolished by any foreign invader, as after 1545 the town was never attacked.

In 1586, when the whole kingdom was alarmed with rumours of the Spanish Armada, a fleet of about fifty sail were discovered off the town, apparently waiting for a favourable opportunity to land. The terrified inhabitants, concluding it was the great Spanish force, fired the beacons and sent off for Lord Buckhurst, who was lord of one of the manors of the town. His Lordship attended with as many armed men as he could muster on so sudden an emergency, and took post on the brow of the cliff between Brighthelmston and Rottingdean, in order to oppose the landing of the supposed enemy at their place. In the course of the ensuing night, his force increased to the number of 1,600 men: and a considerable body of Kentishmen were on their march to join him. Next morning, the ships appeared in the same place; but those on board showed no disposition to land. A few boats, belonging to the town, ventured out at last, a little way, to reconnoitre the fleet, and soon discovered, to their great joy, they were only Dutch merchant-

* See quarter share in "Ancient Customs." page 34.

men laden with Spanish wines, and detained by contrary winds in the Channel.

Towards the end of July, 1588, the town was more justly alarmed at the Spanish Armada; and the inhabitants neglected no means in their power to defend themselves and their country from the threatened desolation by a powerful and inveterate enemy. They had then in the town, belonging to Government, six pieces of great iron ordnance, and ten qualivers, a species of small cannon. With a determination of the most obstinate resistance, the shores of Sussex in general were lined with the people, when this tremendous armament passed in their view, pursued by the light and expert navy of England.

In 1597, in consequence of the continued war with Spain, and Brighton being exposed, by an order of Sessions, dated July 13th, and signed Robert Sackville, Thomas Pelham, Nicholas Parker, Antho. Sherley, and Ran. Nevill, by command of Lord Buckhurst, Lord Lieutenant of the County, there were sent from Lewes to Brighthelmston, one saker and one minion, with their carriages, shot, horse-harness, budges, barrels, ladles, sponges, and all other necessary implements belonging to the same, with six barrels of gunpowder; and such was the educational condition of the people at that period, that Thomas Jeffery, the Constable of Brighthelmston, to whom the artillery and stores were delivered, could not write his name. In 1642, the four pieces of iron ordnance, sent to Brighthelmston in 1597, were returned to Lewes. In the same year, also, a barrel of gunpowder was sent from the town house, Lewes, (where was the powder store,) to Brighthelmston.

In the Court Rolls, according to the Burrell MSS., 1st April, 1645, there are the following records:—

Homage present Willm. Gallan, jun., for not paying to Rd. Cook, lord's reeve, for his lady nets fishing, according to ye ancient custom, 4d, give him time to pay it to the said R.C., at or before St. Jn. Baptist next, on payn of 5s.

25 Aug., 1648. We present Nichs. Payne for building his new house and shop under the cliffs, upon the bank of the cliff, to the hurt and annoyance of the whole towne, if we shd have any occasion to use the ordnance, or that there shd be any invasion by a foreign enemy.

25 Aug., 1654. We present Nics. Payne for encroaching on the lord's waste, and building of his walls 14 feet, or thereabout, more than he is admitted to, to ye cliffe side, before ye place where ye great guns path doth stand, to the

great annoyance and hindrance of ye whole towne and country, and we fine him for it.

In the year 1658, John Pullat, a Quaker, for speaking to the priest and people in the Steeple-house (the church), was put prisoner into the Block-house, which, at that time, was the place of confinement for malefactors.

In the course of the encroachments of the sea during severe storms in 1703 and 1705, the Blockhouse and Gun-garden, wall and gates, were gradually sapped, and at last so completely destroyed, that in the course of thirty years afterwards, scarcely any of their ruins were perceptible. The following is the record of these storms in the Brighton town-book :—

Memorand.—November 27th, 1703, there was a very great and remarkable tempest,* which begun after midnight, and continued in its violence till about 8 in the morning, being Saturday. Many houses in town were damnified, two wind-mills in the east blown over, several of the church leads turned up, and several vessells belonging to the town were Shipwracked, to the great impoverishment of the place.

Another storm, 11th of August, 1705, did equal damage.

The Burrell MSS. record, Jan., 1748-9, that by reason of extraordinary high tides the sea broke in at Brighthelmston, washed away part of the Block-house, and the farm lands called Salts, and did considerable damage to the lands adjacent.

On digging out the shingle for the purpose of laying in the foundation of the wall which forms the south boundary of the King's Road, the ruins of the Block-house were discovered in so compact and firm a state that much difficulty was experienced in excavating them and breaking them up. Less than ninety years since at low water, the well of the old town was visible off the Old Ship Tavern, its steined form standing somewhat high above the sand and shingle.

Lord Macaulay, in his history of England, speaking of the time of Charles II., says:—"Brighton was then described as a place which had once been thriving, which had possessed many small fishing barks, and which had, when at the height of prosperity, contained about two thousand inhabitants; but which was sinking fast into decay. The sea was gradually gaining on the buildings,

* This was the storm which destroyed the Eddyston lighthouse.

which at length almost entirely disappeared. Ninety years ago the ruins of an old fort were to be seen lying among the pebbles and sea-weed on the beach, and ancient men could still point out the traces of foundations on a spot where a street of more than a hundred huts had been swallowed up by the waves. So desolate was the place after this calamity that the vicarage was thought scarcely worth having. A few poor fishermen, however, still continued to dry their nets on those cliffs, on which now a town, twice as large and populous as the Bristol of the Stuarts, presents, mile after mile, its gay and fantastic front to the sea." The Rev. William Gilpin, prebendary of Salisbury, and vicar of Boldre, near Lymington, in "Observations on the Coasts of Hampshire, Sussex, and Kent, made in the Summer of 1774," states:—"The cliff on which Brighthelmston stands, is composed of a mouldering clay; and the sea has gained upon it, at least fifty yards in the memory of man. A fort which stood on the edge of the cliff, gave way in the year 1761, and was shattered into a ruin; but it is now taken entirely down." This, probably, refers to some portion of the old fortifications of the town, which stood to the east of the Block-house.

About the year 1761, a battery, with an arched room under it for ammunition, was erected at the bottom of East (great) Street, not far from the site of the ancient East Gate. A letter dated Brighthelmston, August 12th, 1782, states:—"About seven o'clock yesterday morning, I was awaked by the firing of guns, which made me rise sooner than I should otherwise have done, and upon going to the beach, was informed that a French privateer, of 16 or 18 guns, and about 130 men, had just taken a collier close to the shore. After having turned the collier's men in their own boat on shore,—they only wanting the vessel,—the Frenchmen put on board the collier from the privateer, ten stout fellows, and then sailed away with their prize. This being observed from the ramparts, signal was given to a cutter, which happened luckily to be near, and it directly made sail after the collier, and in about an hour and a half retook her, and sent the Frenchmen on shore." The ramparts alluded to were those of the East Street battery, which was wholly unprotected by any groyne, and was completely undermined by the sea on the 17th of November, 1786, and fell to the ground. There were at the time seventeen barrels of gunpowder in the magazine below; but fortunately none of them took fire amidst the crash of the ruins. Dunvan* states that this battery mounted 12 twenty-four pounders; but on the platform as represented in a map of Brighton, 1779, eight guns only are placed. The eight guns were deposited on the Steine, and remained there for several weeks.

The condition of these guns and the value of the battery will be better gleaned from the following memorandum, made Thursday, September 23rd, 1779:—"Some French privateers are said to be hovering about the offing, and we hear now and then a report of firing. Provoking!—They will not come within reach of the only four guns that may be fired with safety—I mean, when properly loaded with powder and ball—a salute is nothing. The rest are all well known to be honey-combed. The small craft, then, may be cut off with impunity. What a pity that a couple of light six-pounders cannot be spared by the Board of Ordnance, to protect the coast! Those with men or horses, might be dragged along the Clift, and prevent every sort of mischief to be dreaded from such despicable picaroons;—instead whereof, two horse soldiers, in long scarlet cloaks, ride along the coast, making their utility to be understood by no one."

The site of this battery is marked by the Old Battery House, opposite the Rising Sun, to which is attached the following legend of

OLD STRIKE-A-LIGHT:—

"A tremendous gale had ceased, but still the mountainous swellings of the sea burst violently on the shore, when the boat of Swan Jervoise came into the Brighton roadstead, having weathered the storm. The night was pitchy dark; scarcely could the outline of the horizon be perceived, and not a light illumed the blank. The surprise of Jervoise and his crew was therefore great when they beheld a stream of meteor-like splendour burst from every window of the 'Rising Sun' Inn, and as suddenly all was

* Paul Dunvan, the author of "Lee's History of Lewes and Brighthelmstone," published in 1795, was for some time an usher in the Lewes Grammar School.

again involved in utter darkness. This terrific appearance was repeated many times. Swan Jervoise was one of those men who never conjecture, but proceeded at once to ascertain a cause. He therefore, with two of his men, went ashore; but proceeded alone to the 'Rising Sun,' expecting to find the people up. After knocking and bawling loud enough to rouse all the dead in the Bartholomew's Chapel, without wakening the landlord, he was about to force the door, when the light again burst from the windows, and he distinctly heard a ticking as of a person striking a light with a flint and steel, each stroke producing this supernatural blaze of light. In a moment afterwards the door was opened, and a being seven feet high, wrapped in a large black cloak, with a high conical white hat, issued forth. He noticed not the poor drenched fisherman, but he strode on until he disappeared in the darkness. Jervois's hair stood stiff on his head; his limbs trembled with fear; and he shrieked aloud with terror. The landlord heard his cry, and came down with his torch. Seeing his neighbour in such a plight, he bade him come in, roused up a fire, made him take a seat in the capacious chimney, and—having comforted him with good words—placed a rushlight on the table, and then retired to procure a jug of ale. Jervoise, scarcely recovered from his fright, was thus again left alone. As he sat musing by the crackling fire, the dim rush throwing a fitful light around the room, he chanced to turn his head; when, from over the back of the settle, he beheld the death-like features—pallid as a sear cloth—of the tall man in the conical hat. His countenance was most ghastly, and he fixed his grey-glazed eyes full on Jervoise, and pointed to the hearth. This was more than he could bear,—he uttered one loud scream, and fell senseless to the ground. He was thus found by the landlord, who conveyed him to bed; and the next day Jervoise related the particulars to Father Anselm, of St. Bartholomew, and then expired. But the blessed Virgin and Saint Nicholas oft-times bring good out of evil; for on examining the hearth to which 'Old Strike-a-Light' (as the apparition has since been called) pointed, a vast treasure was found, which is still safely deposited with the principal of this order in Normandy; nor has the 'Rising Sun' since been haunted by the unholy spirit of 'Old Strike-a-Light.'

The faithful may therefore know there is no truth in the story that 'Old Strike-a-Light' has lately been seen seated astride a barrel of beer in the cellar chinking a piece of money on a pewter dish. The family vault of Jervoise, the oldest in the churchyard of Brighthelmston, Anno Domini MCXVII, may still be seen on the south side of the church—near Tattersall's."

Towards the latter end of the year 1793, two new batteries were commenced for the defence of the town; one on the West Cliff, which mounted eight 36-pounders, and the other on the East Cliff, which mounted four of the same weight. The guns of these batteries were of French casting, ship guns, taken from the French fleet captured by Lord Howe, in his memorable victory of the 1st of June, 1794. The latter of these batteries was at the bottom of the Marine Parade, opposite the south-end of German Place; but after being in position about ten years,—as the explosions of the guns and the encroachments of the sea had made the walls dangerous,—it was removed. The west battery was opposite Artillery Place. The Sea Fencibles, volunteers, during the war with France used to practice at this battery. They were accustomed, also, to exercise with boarding-pikes, in Belle-vue field, now Regency Square. Colonel Moore's volunteers went through their initiation drill, with faggot-sticks, on the ground behind the battery house, Artillery Place. Colonel Moore resided on the Old Steine, in the mansion which was afterwards occupied by Lady Ann Murray, and then by Mr Harrington, (Squire Harrington, as he was usually spoken of,) now the residence of Captain Thellusson. This noble structure was erected by the Right Honourable W. G. Hamilton, Esq., formerly M.P. for Haslemere. According to a manuscript diary in possession of the compiler of this history: "On the 17th of August, 1805, soon after 12 o'clock, a shot was discharged from this battery by the Sea Fencibles, at a cask moored purposely in the offing, and it fell very close to the object: a second shot was also fired, of 42 pounds weight, merely to ascertain to what a distance the gun would throw it. From the time of the explosion until it struck the water, there was a lapse of 27 seconds; the ball consequently, ere it was received by the liquid element, must have traversed to a distance of three miles. The weight of the cartridge used was 14 pounds." Also, June 13th, 1807: "The Volunteers this morning, for the first time this year, were practised at the Fort, in discharging the forty-two-pounders at a cask, moored, and floating on the water, at about three quarters of a league distant from the shore. Twelve rounds were fired; and though some of the balls immediately struck the object, they generally dropped so close to it, that a moderate sized fishing-boat would scarcely have escaped being injured by either of them. Many elegant spectators were on the Cliff during the exercise." The west battery was removed in 1859. A flagstaff within a railed space, marks its last site; as, twice after its original construction, it was removed with the sanction of Government, to admit of widening the King's Road at that spot, to accommodate the increased traffic. The battery house and the other buildings in connexion with the Battery, were disposed of by auction by Mr. P. R. Wilkinson, on Monday, September 9th, 1861, and by the 28th of that month the space was entirely cleared for the erection of an hotel, Government having disposed of the ground to the Brighton Hotel Company. The remnant of the battery platform, marked by the flagstaff, belongs to the town, the Corporation having purchased it of Government to prevent any other purchaser placing buildings upon it. Brighton thus, wholly depends upon such means of defence as the emergency of the occasion may require to be brought into operation, by means of the railway, the facility of transit offering the full assurance that every *materiel* would be at hand for the ready service of our Volunteers, should an enemy have the temerity to invade our shores and put to the proof every Englishman's motto, "*Pro aris et focis.*"

Chapter XII.

THE INCURSIONS OF THE SEA UPON THE TOWN.

Brighton has not had merely to defend itself against the aggressions of foreign invaders, but the encroachment of the sea at various times has checked its prosperity. Between 1260 and 1340, upwards of 40 acres of land had become submerged,* and the sea made continual inroads upon the lower town. Previous to 1665 twenty-two copyhold tenements under the Cliff, belonging to the manor of Brighthelmston-Lewes, alone were swept away. Amongst them were twelve shops, with four stake places and four capstan-places attached to them, and three cottages and three parcels of land adjoining them.† There still remained under the Cliff, 113 tenements (shops, capstan and stake places, and cottages) which were destroyed by the memorable storms of 1703 and 1705.

The storm of 1703 commenced about midnight on the 27th of November, and continued for eight hours with unabated fury. Many houses were demolished; and others were unroofed: the church leads were torn off; and the two mills belonging to the town, were prostrated by the storm. The town presented the ruinous appearance of a place severely bombarded. Nor was that the only disaster looked for by the dismayed inhabitants, from so dreadful a conflict of the elements. The bulk of their property, and their dearest relatives, were at the same time exposed to its utmost fury on the ocean, and the most dismal apprehensions for their fate were in many of them but too fully realised. Deryck Paine, master of the ketch, "Elizabeth," was lost with all his crew. George Taylor, master of the ketch, "Happy Entrance," was lost with all his crew, except Walter Street, who supported himself on a mast for three days, between the Downs and North Yarmouth, and was taken up at last. Richard Webb, master of the ketch, "Richard and Rose," was lost with all his crew, near St. Helen's. Edward Freind, master of the ketch, "Thomas and

* See foot-note, page 47.

† Godwin's Rental of Brighthelmston Manor, made in 1665, *penes Carolum Gilbert de Lewes Armis.*

Frances," was stranded near Portsmouth. Edward Glover, master of the pink, "Richard and Benjamin," was stranded near Chichester. One man was lost; the master and the rest of the crew saved themselves in the shrouds. George Beach, master of the pink, "Mary," was driven from the Downs to Hamburgh, with the loss of anchors, cables, and sails. Richard Kitchener, master of the "Chomley" pink, was lost, with nine of her crew; five men and a boy were saved by another vessel. Many able seamen, belonging to the town, were also lost in the Queen's (Anne's) ships of war, transports and tenders.

The 11th of August, 1705, was marked by another dreadful storm, which began at one in the morning, attained its greatest fury at three, and raged until eight. It completed the destruction of all the lower buildings which had escaped the fury of all former inundations. Every habitation under the Cliff was utterly demolished, and its very site concealed from the owner's knowledge beneath a mound of beach. The roof of the parish church again also suffered much, the lead being completely stripped away. A record of this event is preserved in the tower of the church, beneath the bell storey; on the wall of which is nailed a tablet of sheet-lead, measuring 4ft. 6in. by 2ft. 6in., that was taken from the roof of the sacred edifice on the restoration of the church in 1853. It is inscribed in raised cast characters, thus:—

RICHARD MASTERS.

RICHARD TVPPEN.

JOHN MASTERS.

CHVRCHWARDENS.

17 05.

Above the names is a cherub at each corner of the tablet; and between the 7 and 0 are represented two nude children amidst scroll-work, which is surmounted with an angel in the act of sounding a trumpet.

Dr. Mantell remarks that at Brighton the inroads of the sea have been very extensive. The whole of the ancient town was situated on the spot which is now covered by the sands, and the present cliffs were then behind the town, like those of Dover; and Mr. Lyell, in his "Principles of Geology," says:—"The sea has merely resumed its position at the base of the cliffs, the site of the old town having been a beach which had for ages been abandoned by the ocean." In the *Taxatio Ecclesiastica Angliæ et Walliæ, auctoritate P. Nicholas* (A.D, 1292), and *Nonarum inquisitiones in coria scaccarii* (A.D. 1340), mention is made that the losses of land sustained by the action of the sea, between the years 1260 and 1340, a period of only eighty years, were in Brighthelmston, 40 acres; in Houve, 150 acres; Aldrington, 40 acres; and in Portslade, 60 acres.

The "Magna Britannia," of 1737, says:—"About 90 years ago, this Town was a very considerable Place for Fishing, and in a flourishing Condition, being then one of the principal Towns of the County, containing near five hundred Families; but since the beginning of the Civil Wars it hath decayed much for want of a Free Fishery, and by very great Losses by Sea, their shipping being often taken from them by the Enemy: Nay, it is the Opinion of the most judicious Inhabitants, that had not Divine Providence in a great Measure protected them by their Town being built low, and standing on a flat ground, the *French* would several times have quite demolished it, as they had attempted to do, but the low Situation of it prevented their doing it any considerable Damage, the Cannon Balls usually flying over tho Town; But the greatest Damage to the Buildings has been done by the breaking in of the Sea, which within these forty years hath laid Waste about 130 Tenements; which Loss, by a modest Computation, amounts to near 40,000*l*. and if some speedy Care be not taken to stop the Encroachments of the Ocean, it is probable the Town will in a few years be utterly depopulated; the Inhabitants being already diminished one-third less than they were, and those that remain are many of them Widows, Orphans, decrepid Persons, and all very poor; insomuch that the Rates for their Relief are at the Rack-Rent of

8d. in the Pound, for there are but few Charities given for their Support, *viz.* one by Mr. Barnard Hilton* of 16*l* *per Annum*, with some other small Benefactions, which make it about 20*l*. a year."

In 1706 there had been considerable wrecks of wines on the Manor of Brighthelmston-Lewes; and the then Lord High Admiral claimed them as his right. But Richard Onslow, Esq., and Colonel Tufton, as proprietors of the manor, kept the wines; and on a full investigation of the business at the assizes for the county, in 1708, their conduct, in that particular, was justified, and their manorial right fully established.

On the 4th of March, 1818, as Mr. Izard was having excavations made for the foundations of two houses on the West Cliff—now the King's Road,—between Ship Street and Middle Street, the workmen discovered the walls of one of the streets under the Cliff, which had been overwhelmed by one of the terrible inundations of the sea. They appeared buried more than fifteen feet with beach.

In 1713, the sea having destroyed everything below the Cliff, encroached with alarming rapidity on the Cliff itself, fragments of which daily crumbled into the sapping tide. It was therefore found absolutely necessary, for the preservation of the rest of the town, to erect groynes before it. These groynes are contrived by means of strong wooden barriers projecting from the Cliff towards the sea, as far as low-water mark, which intercept and confine the beach or sea shingle, that chiefly rolls from west to east in this part of the English Channel. By these contrivances, a large body of beach, rising gradually towards the Cliff, is accumulated on the western side of every barrier, which resists and breaks the impetuosity of the roughest sea. But the reduced state into which a coincidence of unfavourable circumstances had sunk Brighthelmston, about the beginning of the last century, it was impossible for the inhabitants to raise amongst themselves a sum nearly adequate to so expensive an undertaking, A brief was therefore granted them, under which

* Henry Hilton, who was commonly called Baron Hilton, is evidently meant. He died in the year 1648; and in the Town Book is the following memorandum, in reference to the charity:—"Octr. 18th, 1704. Direction how to writ to Baron John Hylton, living at Hylton Castle, by way off Durham, to be left at the post office in Sunderland by Sea."

they collected about £1,700. By means of this public aid, and the internal contributions of the town itself, the Cliff was pretty well secured from the west part, as far as the Old Steine. The groynes eastward of the Steine are comparatively of modern construction, the most important of them being,—in its original state,—that constructed on the suggestion and plan of Mr. Edward Thunder, at Black Rock, about the year 1819, when the sea was rapidly encroaching at that spot and threatening to make inroads upon the whole of the Marine Parade. The barrier was effectual, although on its projection and erection it was called by the shortsighted of the time, "Teddy Thunder's Folly." Thunder, who was one of the Town Commissioners at the time, was an ccentric but shrewd man. He was the inventor of the pedal for shifting the keys of the piano-forte.

Groyne is quite a provincial term of very doubtful origin. It is generally supposed to be a corruption from *royne*. An Act of Parliament was passed in the House of Commons, in 1698, for opening of the ancient *roynes* and water courses in Sedgmore. And it is probable that these *roynes* are the same as *groynes* at Brighton, with this difference, that the latter are artificially constructed for a certain purpose, and the former might have been only a slow acervation of time and nature. The following is an extract from a letter, dated Lewes, September 12th, 1785:—"The violence of the wind on Tuesday last, occasioned the highest tide that has been known on this coast for a great number of years. At Brighthelmston, the fishermen were put to the greatest difficulty in saving their boats; to effect which, many were under the necessity of hauling them up into the town, and others of lashing them to the railing on the bank. Some few, however, that could not be secured, were dashed to pieces; had the storm happened in the night-time, the whole must have shared the same fate.

By the Town Act of Brighton, 1772, a duty of 6d a chaldron was levied on all coal landed on the beach; and by the Act of 1810, a duty of 2s 6d a chaldron—now a ton,—was levied on all coals brought into the town, for the purpose of constructing and supporting the sea-defences of the town. By the construction of these groynes, the sea from time to time was driven back to allow of the building of the sea-wall that protects the whole of the southern road in front of the town, from the bottom of Cannon Place to the extreme east of the parish. The first portion formed was that between West Street and Middle Street, and was opened by George IV. in the year 1821; prior to which time the houses there were only approached at their south front by a temporary wooden platform on poles, for foot-passengers only; and then only during fair weather; as so close to the houses were the rage and flow of the sea during a storm, that the planks which formed the pathway, had to be removed to prevent their being either washed or blown away. At such times a barrier was erected at each end, at Bradley's Library, now Booty's, and the Ship-in-Distress Inn,* now Child's Fancy Repository, bearing the notice, "No thoroughfare." The only way for equestrians and vehicles was the present South Street, where was the following quaint sign over the shop of an eccentric shoemaker:—

Here lives a man that don't refuse
To make and mend your boots and shoes.
His leather's good, his work is just,
His profits small, and cannot trust:
And when grim death doth him call,
Farewell to his old cobbler's stall.

To his blood royal highness P.G.,
And new laid eggs every *day*.†

The last two lines were in red letters, and the initials P.G., were intended for Prince George.

The encroachments of the sea, till the complete groyne system was carried out and the sea-wall completed, extended from Russell

---

* Over the front door of this house was a well painted representation of a Ship in Distress, beneath which was the following couplet:—

"By danger we're encompass'd round;
Pray, lend a hand, our ship's aground."

It may here be added that formerly, throughout the town, the public houses had illustrated signs and poetic effusions. Thus the "Bell," in Russell Street, now the "Nelson," had for its sign, an inverted bell, and the annexed inscription:—

"Good liquor here is to be found;
The Bell for luck's turn'd upside down."

† Day, in the Brighton vernacular, is pronounced dee; hence the rhyme is preserved.

Street to the extreme east end of the parish; and after every storm of any magnitude, the road to the east of the Old Steine,—now known as the Marine Parade,—presented a different aspect, as the inroads of the sea frequently carried away some hundreds of tons of the Cliff; and it was no uncommon thing after a tempest, to find that so much of the roadway had been carried off, from the Cliff becoming undermined by the wash of the waves, as to leave only sufficient space for a single vehicle to pass. On the 15th of December, 1806, during a terrific storm, the roadway between the Royal Crescent and Rock Buildings was completely cut asunder, making the owners of property there uneasy for the safety of their premises. This storm gave occasion to the following trial at the Sussex Assizes, held at Lewes, August 4th, 1807:—

THE KING *v.* GREGORY, PHILCOX, THUNDER, AND THREE OTHERS.

RIOT AT BRIGHTON.

This was an indictment against the defendants, for riotously assembling and pulling down the railing on the road east of Brighton, leading from thence to Rottingdean, and obstructing the Surveyors of the road in the execution of their duty. This case arose out of the falling of the cliff last autumn. The Surveyor of the Road thought it necessary to carry in the railing, and trenched upon the ground of the three first named defendants: they considered he had done more than necessary, and resisted his altering the railing. In consequence of this, on the 11th of February last, they employed men to cut down the polls and rails, which had been erected by the Surveyor of the Road. The next day the Surveyor employed men to re-erect them, and the defendants another party to pull them down. A riot ensued, the one set pulling down as fast as the other erected, until at last the Surveyor's party were the victors.

Mr GURNEY, for the defendants, rested his defence on the ground that the Surveyor was not under the necessity of coming upon their freehold, but that he had acted wantonly and with a view to harass the defendants. He proposed calling evidence to shew that the road at that part of it was perfectly safe.

The Learned Judge held that the Surveyor of the road was clearly right. He was to judge of the necessity if he acted wrong. They ought to have brought an action of trespass, and not to have the law into their own hands.

The jury found them all guilty. The three principals were fined £20 each, and the three workmen £5 each. In the Civil Court an action was tried, arising out of the same transaction, in which the plaintiff had a verdict against the Surveyor. Damages, seven guineas.

CHAPTER XIII.

THE DOWER OF ANN OF CLEVES.

At the Reformation, when the monastery of St. Pancras, at Southover, was destroyed, by order of Henry VIII., on its being surrendered to that monarch, by Prior Robert Crowham, November 16th, 1537, the manor of Southover, Lewes, which included the priory, was granted to Thomas Cromwell, Earl of Essex, who also held one moiety of the manor of Brighthelmston-Lewes :—

4. Hen. VIII. One moiety of this manor, with several other possessions in Sussex, was recovered by petition, by Thomas, Earl of Surrey, they having been devised by the Marquis of Berkeley, to Henry VII., and an act passed in the 7th of that king, whilst the petitioner was absent on the king's business in the north, and ignorant of it till the said parliament was ended. The answer is "*Soit fait come il est desiree.*"

The petition is contained in the Burrell MSS. 5637. Folios 36 and 37.

On the attainder and execution of the Earl of Essex, Sir John Gage, of Firle, was appointed chief steward of Southover and other manors forfeited by that nobleman within the county of Sussex. But on the 20th of Jannary, 1541, they were granted to Ann of Cleves, one of the injured queens of Henry VIII. The Burrell MSS. record :—

32. Hen. VIII. The King granted this manor (Brighthelmston-Lewes) and advowson to Ann of Cleves; with a great many others in Sussex, including the manor of Falmer (originally Fald-mer), which, on her death, again reverted to the crown, and after various successions and alienations, was purchased of Sir John Shelley, of Michelgrove, by Thomas, Lord Pelham, on the 2nd day of May, in the year 1770. It still continues in the possession of the Pelham family, being held by the Earl of Chichester, of Stanmer, the manor adjoining.

Miss Strickland, in her "Lives of the Queens of England," says :—"The marriage was dissolved by mutual consent; and she being content to abide in this realm, and to yield to its laws, and to discharge her conscience of that pretended marriage, the king, of his especial favour, granted to her certain manors and estates in divers counties, lately forfeited by the attainder of the Earl of Essex,—Cromwell, whose spoils formed the principal fund for the maintenance of this princess,—and Sir Nicholas Carew, to be held without rendering an account from the Lady-day foregoing the same grant, which was dated on the 20th of January, 1541."

These grants were made to Ann by Henry VIII., on her assent to the invalidity of her marriage with that monarch, who refused to consort with her. On the 8th of August, 1540, Henry married Catherine Howard. The manor of Falmer was also part of Ann's dower, and in seclusion there she resided some time; though on her divorce she took up her abode at Preston House, in the village of Preston, where still, in one of the rooms, is a large and well executed portrait of her, by some considered the work of Holbein. It was seeing this portrait which induced the king to desire an union with her. She landed at Dover, December, 1538. Henry met her there, and such was his dislike to her, from her beauty not being equal to Holbein's portrait, that he spoke of her as a "Flander's Mare," and used other expressions respecting her of an equally contemptuous character.

Ann died on the 17th of July, 1557, at the Palace of Chelsea, and was buried on the 3rd of August, near the high altar, in Westminster Abbey, near the old portraits of Henry III. and King Sebert.

The manor formerly belonged to the Shirley family, several monumental tablets to the members of which remain within Preston church. Mary, the second sister of Sir Richard Shirley, Bart,, was married to Thomas Western, Esq., of Ravenhall, in Essex, who died April 1st, 1733, leaving an only child, Thomas Western, who married Ann, the daughter of Robert Callis, Esq., and died in May, 1766, leaving Charles Western as his heir. Charles Western, Esq., married Frances Shirley, only daughter and heiress of William Bolland, Esq. His end was of the most melancholy character. Whilst riding with his eldest son, Charles Callis, a child then about four years of age, along the road by Goldstone Bottom, the horse stumbled, and they were precipitated from their carriage, the father being killed on the spot. The life of the child was preserved by his being thrown into a furze bush, by the roadside. This occurrence took place on the 24th July, 1771. The widow, with her two children, Charles and a younger brother, Shirley, about three years old, shortly after left Preston, where none of the family ever after returned, and the estate eventually was purchased by William Stanford, Esq., for £20,000. His grand-daughter, a minor, is his heiress; and so improved is the estate, through the favourable circumstance of the railroad from Brighton to London passing through it, that the portion alone used for the formation of the line realized £30,000.

Charles Callis Western, who was born on the 9th of August, was created Baron Western, on the 28th of January, 1833. He died, unmarried, in 1841, when, his brother being dead, the title became extinct.

Chapter XIV.

THE PARISH CHURCH, ST. NICHOLAS.

This sacred edifice is situated upon a hill north west of the town, about 160 feet above low-water mark. It is a structure of great antiquity, and was originally dedicated to St. Nicholas, Bishop of Mira, in Lycia, who lived about the commencement of the fourth century, and was the reputed patron of fishermen, on account of the following naval miracle recorded of him in the legends of that country: A certain Lycian vessel being in great danger during a storm at sea, the affrighted crew invoked the aid of this pious prelate, and lo! to their amazement and comfort, a venerable personage appeared amongst them, and exclaimed, "Here I am, for ye called me." With his help, the ship was successfully managed until the storm subsided; and then their miraculous assistant vanished. The mariners had no sooner reached the port, than they enquired for Bishop Nicholas, and were directed to the cathedral, where they beheld in him the identical person to whom they owed their safety. His feast is held on the 6th day of December, and used to be celebrated with devout dependence by the mariners of Brighthelmston, before the Reformation. But in the spirit of pious avarice or cunning, the Virgin Mary was, in process of time, made joint tenant with St. Nicholas, in the patronage of this church. "The second dedicator," says Dunvan, "seems to have shrewdly considered that Nicholas could not, either as a saint or a gentleman, object to so fair and exalted a partner; and that in case any of the seafaring inhabitants of the parish were at any time in danger, either their Holy Patron, or more Holy Patroness, would most probably be at leisure to step to their succour."

This church was given by Ralph de Cheney to the Priory of Lewes, in the reign of Stephen. But it appears from the terms of an award or arbitration between Richard de Wich, Bishop of Chichester, and William de Ruslous, Prior of St. Pancras, near Lewes, made in 1252, still extant in the episcopal archives at Chichester, that the priory obtained no full possession of this church before that period. By this award, as soon as the then Rector of Brighthelmston should die, or resign the living, the Prior of St. Pancras was to appoint a Vicar there, who was to have all the offerings of the altar, as far as they belonged to altarage, and the small tithes, viz., those of mills, sea-fisheries, mortuaries, wool, lambs, cheese, cows, calves, hogs, colts, geese, hens, eggs, flax, hemp, and of every thing that grows in gardens, except wheat and barley. He was also to have the third of the tithe of hay, and a convenient mansion assigned him. To encourage a crusade, in consequence of the capture of Acre by the Soldan of Babylon, Edward I. granted to Pope Nicholas IV. the tenths of all the monasteries and churches in England, and in the *Taxatio Ecclesiastica Angliæ et Walliæ auctoritate P. Nicholas*, 1291, occur these entries:—

	£	s.	d.	
"'Eccl'ia de Brighthelmston	20	0	0	P'or Lewens."
"Vicar' ejusdem	5	0	0	

The Vicar of Brighton was at one period saddled with a yearly pension of seven shillings and sixpence to the Vicar of Hove; and in this state the Vicarage continued, the impropriation of the great tithes vesting in the Priory of Lewes, till the suppression of that monastery, in 1538. The impropriation and patronage of this parish were granted by Henry VIII. to Lord Cromwell, his Vicar-General, who in that year, 1538, ordered a public register of baptisms and burials to be kept at Brighthelmston, and in every other parish of the kingdom.

On the death and attainder of Cromwell, the church was conferred by Henry to his repudiated queen, Anne of Cleves, and on the death of that princess, in 1557, it again reverted to the crown. In the reign of Elizabeth, the patronage and impropriation were severed, the former being attached to the see of Chichester; and so it continues to the present day. There is a great tithe on Brighton, of small extent, now belonging to Thomas Attree, Esq., Queen's Park, Brighton, as Lay-Rector, and it formerly belonged to Thomas Read Kemp, Esq., as Lay-Rector.

The church is built of cut flints and grouting of lime and coarse sea-sand, with stone coignes. The old map picture of 1545, represents the church as cruciform, and the tower circular: probably errors of the artist, whose design was doubtless more to illustrate the prominent features of the scene,—the attack upon and burning of the town,—than the architectural details of the buildings. The sacred edifice consists of a body, chancel, and a somewhat low embattled tower, surmounted by a sloping roof, in the centre of which is a cast-iron standard, in which is a flagstaff that may be raised or lowered at pleasure. An arrow vane is on its top. Formerly, within the last half-century, the vane was represented by a gilt fish, doubtless intended as the representation of a dolphin; but in 1796 a visitor, considering that the figure bore more resemblance to a shark than any other fish, penned the following verses upon it:—

Say, why on Brighton's church we see
A golden shark display'd,
But that 'twas aptly meant to be
An emblem of its trade?

Nor could the thing so well be told
In any other way:
The town's a Shark that lives on gold,—
The Company its prey.

A musical peal of eight bells was cast in 1777, by Mr. Rudhall, ironmonger, of the firm Rudhall and Dudlow, North street, Brighton, now Langworthy and Reed, at his foundry, at Bristol. The tenor bell, which is pitched in the key F, weighs 1,500 pounds. The belfry had a peal previous to that date, as in the vestry minutes of of October 25th, 1736, is the order:—

To new cast the great bell belonging to the parish church of Brighthelmston, to agree with Joshua Kipling, bellfounder, to charge on the parish taxes.

In March, 1790, another order was made :—

That the treble bell be repaired by Mr. Palmer.

Two additional bells were hung in 1818, making a peal of ten bells; but when the clock, at St. Peter's church, was put up, the two new bells, which did not accord with the original eight, were removed to the tower of that church, for chiming the quarters.

Doomsday Book, 1086, mentions :—

Ibide' ten' Wills. de Watevile Bristelmestune de Willo. Uluuard tenuit de Rege E. T'c et modo se defd' p. 5 hid' et dim'. T'ra e 4 car. In d'nio e' 1 car', et 13 vill'i, et ii Bord' cu' una car'. Ibi Æccl'a.

TRANSLATION.

In the same place William de Wateville holds Bristelmestune of William. Ulward held it of King Edward. Then and now it defends itself for five hides and a half. The land is 4 carucates. In demesne is 1 carucate and 13 villeins, and 2 bordars, with one plough. There is a church.

The manor was that of Atlingworth,* and there is no doubt the church referred to was the present parish-church of St. Nicholas, which, in its original state, was of Norman construction. It consists of a nave, with side aisles, and a chancel, which is separated from the main body by a richly painted and gilded Tudor screen, over which, at no remote period, was a rood-loft. To the south, also, of the chancel is a small chantry. The five arches which separate on each side the nave from the aisles, and are supported on diagonal pillars, are of the fifteenth century. To accommodate the great increase in the population of the town, from time to time, galleries were constructed wherever it was possible to place them. In 1852, however, in consequence of the dilapidated state of the sacred edifice, the restoration of the church was determined upon. The leader in the desirable movement was the Rev. H. M. Wagner, Vicar, who having invited some of the residents and townspeople to meet at the Town Hall, on the 20th of September, in that year, and having taken the chair, stated the fact, —that many years ago, his Grace the late Duke of Wellington was a pupil of his (the Vicar's) grandfather, the then Vicar of the parish; and that the Duke was wont to worship in the Vicarage pew of their

* "This manor belonged to the Priory of Lewes, and at the dissolution, 29 Hen. VIII., was granted to Sir Thomas Lord Cromwell, as also the rectory, with the advowson of the vicarage."—Burrell MSS.

parish church. He proposed to them the restoration of the church as an appropriate and enduring monument of their gratitude and veneration for his memory. The proposition was unanimously adopted, and a committee was appointed to collect subscriptions, which in less than a month amounted to £5,000, a sum nearly equal to the outlay.

In the chantry, also, a much admired monument or cenotaph was erected to the memory of the Duke of Wellington. This beautiful work of art, sculptured in stone, by Mr. Philip, of Vauxhall, after the design of the late Mr. Carpenter, will henceforth constitute one of the most striking features of the restored church. It is in the decorated period of Edward II. and Edward III., commonly known as the Eleanor Cross. The shape is hexagonal; the height, from the base to summit, 18-ft. 6-in.; the circumferenee, between 15 and 16 feet. The pedestal commences with a richly moulded base, rising from a tesselated pavement On the base of the pedestal rests a plinth, covered with diaper-work, surmounted by another moulding, on the broad chamfer of which is an inscription, in old English characters, in brass, each line being presented by an angle of the monument :—

In Memoriam
Maximi Ducis Wellington,
Hœc domus sacrosancta,
Qua ipse adolescens Deum colebat
Reœdificatur.

[*Translation.*]

IN MEMORY OF
THE GREAT DUKE OF WELLINGTON,
THIS SACRED BUILDING,
IN WHICH IN HIS YOUTH HE WORSHIPPED GOD,
IS RESTORED.

From the pedestal, and above the moulding with this inscription, rise two stories, richly and elaborately decorated, with open tracery-work, and crocketed pinnacles. These are separated by a pierced parapet of chaste design: and a similar one is on the third or upper story, which is a solid stone drum. Each parapet is also ornamented by sunk and carved panels. The crowning ornament consists of a canopied niche, with a pierced spire surmounted by a finial. Enclosed within this niche, is an alabaster figure of St. George, sheathing his sword over the dragon, which lies slain at his feet, symbolical of the career of the great chieftain to whose memory the work is raised. The drum, with all above it, rests on a shaft of dark marble, polished, which springs from the pedestal, and around which winds a scroll bearing the names of four of those achievements which mark different eras in the military career of Wellington, viz. :—

ASSAYE.
TORRES VEDRAS.
VITTORIA.
WATERLOO.

These "crowning deeds" have been well selected. Assaye represents the Duke's Indian campaign; Torres Vedras, his successful defence of Portugal; Vittoria, the victory which delivered Spain; and Waterloo, the battle which saved Europe It is impossible to convey in words an idea of this beautiful monument, which reflects the highest credit on its designer.

Immediately in front of this memorial, is a monumental brass in the pavement, thus inscribed :—

In Memory of R. C. Carpenter, who but a short time survived the completion of his design, the restoration of this Church, MDCCCLV.

The font of the church was much admired for the sculpture which adorned it; but in 1743 its beauty was nearly effaced by the churchwardens, Thomas Stranbido, William Buckell, and G. Warden, who had it cleaned, partially re-cut, and their names carved in the base, a monument of their vitiated taste, confirmed vanity, and profound ignorance. It is of a circular form, and is raised from the floor by one step, It has excited much observation amongst antiquaries, some of whom contend for its early date, whilst others consider it only a copy; but where the original is they are at a loss to say. The sculpture upon it is in four sections. The first represents the Lord's Supper, and consists of seven figures; Our Saviour, crowned with glory, in the centre, is in the act of giving the blessing, and on the table are distributed various drinking vessels, with the bread. The next compartment contains a kneeling figure; the third, which is larger, has a boat on the sea, with the sail unfurled, and two figures, one presenting a small barrel or vessel to a bishop, who has his mitre and crozier, and the other giving bread to a female; both figures in the water. The fourth division consists of three arches, in each of which is a figure, the centre appearing to be the principal. The whole is sculptured in *basso relievo.* Over these compartments is a line of zig-zag and lozenge work, curiously chamfered, and beneath them is a row of exceedingly handsome ornamental work of leaves and flowers.

The following are extracts from a diary :—

Sunday, August 29th, 1778. Have been this morning to the sailor's land mark—to the only church in the town—and collected a number of *novelties.* The Doctor was pleased to inform us, in a religiously political, or politically religious discourse, that when men *tremble* they are generally *afraid*; when they are in danger they should strive to *extricate* themselves; and that *hope* is the expectant of many great and singular *good events.*

Monday, September, 13th.—A new man and wife have just passed me.—The town's-people preserve some customs here that smack of great antiquity, and seem peculiar to the county of Sussex. At a marriage there are strewers, who strew the way from church, not only with flowers, but with sugar-plums and wheat. Why sugar-plums and wheat, I wonder? Many ceremonies have been retained longer than the history of their origin or foundation.

This system of strewing the bride and bridegroom is still pursued, not merely by the friends of the happy pair,—all couples just married are pronounced to be happy,—but by a constant group of women with children in their arms, who scatter their corn, &c., with blessings, in proportion to the harvest of *coin* they reap.

In the beginning of the 16th century, the Rev. Edward Lowe was vicar of the parish. His successor was the Rev. John Bolt, who died on the 2nd of November, 1660. He was succeeded by the Rev. — Falkner, who was incumbent till 1705. The vestry book of the date, "November the 2nd, Anno Domini, 1703," records that :—

That day the Reverend Mr Joseph Grave, Rector off St. Anne's, Lewes, Sent the works off Mr. Charnock, in two Volumes of his for the use off the Vicar of Brighthelmstone and his surveyvors. Each Volume having in gold letters (Brighthelmston) upon both sides off the cover. The benefactor at London would no(t) otherwise be known than by the two letters off his name, H : Y :

The same book has also the following entries :—

March 11th, 1707. John Mockford appointed Clerk at Church ; part of his duty is to wash the church linen, and scour the church plate.

July 8th, 1713. William Cousins appointed Sexton ; Mary Bridger to be equal partner.

March 31st, 1800. That Thomas Waring be appointed beadle and cryer at a salary of Twenty pounds and Cloathes. It is understood that his duty is to make the poor books, the Church Book, the surveyor's book, and the Town book. He is also to attend the North and west galleries of the Church on Sundays. He is to go round the town with the Officers to make the Militia list, and is likewise to officiate as Headborough in the Town; but not elsewhere, and to be sworn for that purpose.

The Rev. William Colbron succeeded to the vicarage in 1705, and held it till his death, on the 20th of July, 1750. The next vicar of Brighthelmston, was the Rev. Henry Michell, who was born at Lewes, in 1714. He finished his studies at the University of Cambridge, and having obtained a fellowship in Clare-Hall college, he, at the age of 25 years, was made rector of Maresfield; and, five years afterwards, the Bishop of Chichester collated him to the Rectory of West Blatchington, and the Vicarage of Brighton. In 1747, he married the only daughter of the Rev. Francis Reade, of Bedford, by whom he had sixteen children. A marble tablet in the church fully delineates his estimable character and profound learning.

The "Magna Britannia" says:—"The church is a vicarage, but meanly endowed. The vicar claims the old episcopal custom of a penny per head, (commonly called smoak money, or a garden penny) as also he requires, as his due, a quarter of a share of all fishing vessels.* The parsonage tythes are about £100 per annum, but are in the hands of an impropríetor, who allows the Vicar no benefit from them, by which means his maintenance is very small: and therefore the neighbouring gentlemen have augmented it by a subscription of £50 per annum, on condition he shall instruct fifty poor boys of the town in reading and writing. The church stands about forty rods from the town, at a little distance from the sea. There was formerly another church, near the middle of the town, which is said to have been burnt by the French."

The Rev. Mr. Michell, died on the 31st of October, 1789, and was succeeded by the Rev. Thomas Hudson, who commenced the chapel of ease, in Prince's place, known as the Chapel Royal.

Mr. Hudson died in 1804, and was succeeded by the Rev. Robert James Carr, afterwards Dr. Carr, of Chichester, and then Bishop of

---

* *Vide.* Quarter-Share, page 34.

Worcester. The present Vicar, the Rev. Henry Michell Wagner, grandson of the Rev. Henry Michell,* was his successor, August 1st, 1824; and during the time he has held the appointment, the number of places of worship attached to the Established Church, which have been erected, will testify his zeal in the support of our Holy Religion.

In 1824, Nathaniel Kemp, Esq., presented the church with a beautiful Communion Service of silver, consisting of a flagon, two cups, and two plates, thus inscribed: "Given by Nath. Kemp, Esq., and Augusta Caroline, his wife, to the Church of St. Nicholas, Brighthelmston. Anno Domini, 1824."

Upon stripping the roof on the restoration of the church, in 1852, three several pieces of inscribed cast lead were preserved, and they are now fixed to the walls of the tower in the chamber below the bell story. One piece has been already described in page 74, the others are as follows:—

THOMAS FRILAND.

THOMAS ROBERTS.

RICHARD ROSSUM.

CHVRCHWARDENS.

1 6 7 5

JOHN VANDYKE

PLVMER.

EDWARD LOWE,

VICAR.

JOHN SCRAS.

HENERY SMITH.

RICHARD HERMAN.

CHVRCHWARDENS.

A O DOM N

16 77.

Between the lines of names and the figures of the date, on the first represented piece of lead, are raised characters, twenty-one in number, intended to denote dolphins, the Arms of Brighton.

Previous to the restoration of the building, the Church, both inside and out, had undergone many changes, to afford space; low,

* Mr. Wagner, the father of the present Vicar, and son-in-law to the Rev. Henry Michell, (Vicar), died at his house in Pall-Mall, London, on Sunday the 17th of February, 1811.

gloomy galleries, scarcely permitting headway for the congregation when standing, whilst the common house-shaped and dormant windows disfigured it in all directions. In a dark gallery at the west, in 1813, was placed an organ,* built by Lincoln. It was opened on the 7th of March, that year, by Mr. Nathaniel Cook. A small organ loft occupies the space over the vestry room, but it does not at present boast of an organ. Formerly there were several tablets on the belfry walls, recording peals which had been rung in the tower. Their places are now occupied by sundry monuments that were formerly fixed in other parts of the edifice; and some few of the ringing records have been removed to the club-room of the Brighton Society of Change Ringers, at the Running Horse Inn, King street,† while the remainder fell into the hands of a marine-store dealer. The Running Horse Inn was formerly known as the Hen and Chicken; and in 1792, and for several years afterwards, was kept by Mr. John Pocock, who at that time was a sawyer by occupation. In 1795, he received the appointment of Clerk at the Chapel Royal, when that place of public worship was first opened; and after retaining the situation for thirteen years, he

* This organ is now stowed away as lumber, in one of the rooms of the Royal Pavilion.

† Although, to many persons, the thus associating of a public-house with the parish church may be considered somewhat out of character, the annexed copy of manuscripts in the possession of the writer of this book, will not only convince them that there is in some measure an affinity, but it will in a degree stagger modern advocates of temperance, not so much that men of the dates recorded indulged in their potations, but that the Vestry Meetings of the time permitted the expenditure out of the Church-rates. Copy:—

"White Hart, Russell Street, Brighton.

1824. The Honourable Churchwardens of Brighton.

To Phinehas Jupp.

	£	s.	d.
March 25th.—61 Pots of Beer	1	10	6
1 Pint do.	0	0	3
June 25th.—74 Pots of Beer	1	17	0
Sept. 29th.—89 Pots of Beer	2	4	6
Decr. 25th.—82 Pots of Beer	2	1	0
	£7	13	3

Jany. 21, 1825.

Received of the Churchwardens, the sum of seven pounds, 13s 3d, as per bill, for Beer for workmen at the Parish Church.

£7 13s 3d. Phinehas Jupp."

Whether the recipients were permitted to indulge in their libations *ad libitum*, is not on record.

was appointed Clerk of the Parish, in which office he continued for thirty-eight years, dying on the 13th of June, 1846, at the ripe old age of four score and one years. The oldest ringers' tablet preserved is thus inscribed :—

May 24th, 1779, was rung in this tower by the Society of Cumberland Youths, a true and complete peal of 11,088 changes, Bob Major, performed in six hours and fifty minutes, in order as follows, viz :

George Cross	Treble,	.... London.
Thomas Jones..........	2nd,	.... Horsham.
Thomas Lintott	3rd,	.... Horsham.
Joseph Willard	4th,	.... Chiddingly.
Edward Simmonds	5th,	.... Islington.
John Wheatly	6th,	.... Epsom.
James Wilson	7th,	.... Cuckfield.
B. Simmonds	Tenor,	.... Leatherhead.

N.B.—The Bobs were called by G. Cross.

The most commemorative is :—

On January 29th, 1820, being the accession of King George IV., was rung in this tower, by the Brighton Society of Change Ringers, a true and complete peal of 5,040 changes of Bob Major, in three hours and six minutes, by persons in order as follows, viz. :—

William Reynolds	Treble.	John Pocock	5th
James Parsons	2nd	James Potter	6th
Richard Bodle	3rd	William Wells	7th
Edward Honeyset	4th	Isaac Tester	Tenor.

Conducted by Isaac Tester.

The present sexton is Mr. John Shelley, who succeeded his father, Mr. William Shelley, on his retirement from the office, at Easter, 1860. The predecessor of Shelley, sen., was Mantell, the successor of Richard Jeffery, in July, 1806.

CHAPTER XV.

DR. VICESIMUS KNOX AND THE SURREY MILITIA.

During the time of the Brighton Camp, in the autumn of 1793, the Surrey Militia were quartered in the town; and the Parish Church being then the only place of worship in Brighton, in connexion with the Established form of Religion, it was not an uncommon occurrence for some of the officers and men of that regiment, to attend at the morning service on the Sunday.

In the beginning of August, Dr. Vicesimus Knox, Master of Tunbridge School, and late Fellow of St. John's College, Oxford, having come to Brighton with his family, in pursuit of health, by sea-bathing, and a salutary change of air and scene, during the anniversary school vacation, hired a house in North Street, at the corner of Bond Street, now the property of Alderman Martin, where on Saturday the 10th, he received, quite unexpectedly, a note from the Vicar, the Rev. Thomas Hudson, to whom he was a perfect stranger, expressing his desire that the Doctor would gratify his congregation, as he politely expressed himself, with a sermon on the morrow. The Doctor shewed some reluctance to assent to the request, but some friends who were present, importuned him, and he wrote a reply expressing a compliance, and on the following morning he ascended to the pulpit, and took his text:—Philippians iv. 7.—"The peace of God, which passeth all understanding, shall keep your hearts and minds through Christ Jesus." "The sermon," says the Doctor*, "was heard by a very large and very respectable congregation, in which were many of the military belonging to the Surrey regiment, quartered in Brighton. The utmost attention was paid to it. The military appeared to be particularly impressed, and highly satisfied. Expressions of approbation were heard, too emphatic for me to repeat. Mr. Hudson, the Vicar, who read prayers, came to my house, on purpose to thank me, in his own name, and that of his congregation. He mentioned the general satisfaction I had given; the many inquiries that had been made after my name by strangers; and expressed a hope, that I would preach once more, as he knew it was the wish of his parishioners. This, however, I declined at that time, and certainly had no intention to preach again at Brighton, though I had every reason to be pleased with my reception."

On the following evening, Monday, August 12th, the birthday of the Prince of Wales, the Doctor was present at the Ball at

* A Narrative of Transactions relative to a Sermon preached in the Parish Church of Brighton, August 18th, 1793, by Vicesimus Knox, D.D. London: Printed for C. Dilly, in the Poultry, 1794.

the Castle Tavern, and partook of the supper which was given in honour of the occasion. Marked civility was shewn him from persons who knew him only from the sermon which had been so favourably received on the Sunday. The Vicar especially, paid him the greatest attention, and continued in his company nearly the whole of the evening, and in the course of it, renewed his request, that as his parishioners very much wished it, he would give him another sermon on the following Sunday. The Doctor's reply was:—"I come here for recreation, after the fatigues of my daily avocations and my own parish church, and I do not wish to be interrupted by exertions of this kind, especially as I find my last sermon has excited so general an attention, and probably raised expectation too high. You mention the praises I have received; but I will not preach for the sake of praise. If you say it will serve you, if you wish to be absent, or if it is any relief to you, I will endeavour to prepare a sermon in the midst of the interruptions of this place, and will preach next Sunday, though I sincerely wish to decline it."

The request was continued, and obtained a compliance.

The subject chosen was, "The prospect of perpetual and universal peace to be established on the principles of Christian philanthropy," his text being, "Glory to God in the highest, on earth peace, good-will towards men." "I was led to the choice of this subject," writes the Doctor, "from observing the extreme bitterness expressed, even in gay and good-humoured companies, against a great part of our fellow creatures; from the almost daily accounts in the newspapers of slaughtered thousands, and the eagerness with which war had been adopted by all the nations concerned, when negociation might have effected every desirable purpose, without expense, and without carnage. * * * * Had I even gone to the camp and discoursed, as a chaplain, on the same topic, it could not have been out of place. But every one who came to the church knew that he must hear peace, charity, good-will, forgiveness of enemies recommended, in hearing the lessons from the gospel. If my sermon was deemed ill-placed in recommending universal peace and universal good will in Brighton Church, what will men, who judge so, say of the gospel read there?

what of the national liturgy, established by law as firmly as the national militia ? * * * * I was heard in silence, and, if I can judge*, with great attention. I was not conscious that any part of the congregation was offended, nor did I surmise it till after the following incident. On going out of the church, a lady, a perfect stranger, accosted me and said, 'I thank you for your sermon. I could have sat hours to have heard such with pleasure. But excuse me—I must tell you, that from what I have observed in the pews, among a certain description of persons, you have offended those, who, I fear, have as little relish for the doctrine of forgiveness as they seem to have of peace. Many, like myself, are highly pleased with every part of your discourse; but there are those who are angry indeed!'"

At the termination of the service, the Doctor and his family unmolested, returned to their residence, where they had a few friends to dine with them; and after dinner he attended the afternoon service, as, understanding that some of the officers were offended at his discourse, he was desirous of meeting them, to learn what had given them offence, that, before misrepresentation could take place, a full and amicable explanation might be given. He did not, however, meet with a single officer; and having heard the Curate, the Rev. J. Mossop, preach, he returned home to tea with his family, and afterwards took a walk on the Steine, still hoping to meet his offended hearers, that he might acknowledge his fault, if he had been in the wrong, and remove their mistake if they thought him so undeservedly; being desirous of a reconciliation. Many officers were there, but he did not recognise any of those who were at the church. From the inhabitants who observed him he received the utmost civility.

On his return home he received a letter from a stranger, who expressed a wish to distribute a number of copies of the sermon in a distant county, concluding his epistle: "A dissemination of such

* In a note, the Doctor says:—"I have since been informed, that in some pews, where a few of the military and their acquaintance were seated, impatience was shewn by such whisperings as this: 'Will the fellow never have done?' A titter was also affected to conceal the choleric affections; and fans played with motions as rapid as the tail of an angry cat. But I was unconscious of these symptoms of stifled rage."

enlightening and convincing knowledge is only wanting to stop the effusion of human blood; for when mankind are well awakened, they will not permit the dignified human butchers, the insolent, unfeeling traffickers in blood, to lead them to destruction.—Sunday, Aug. 18."

The Doctor, in his "Narrative," says:—"I beg leave to mention as I proceed, that from the pulpit, where I must have had a pretty good view of the whole church, I saw very few officers; and of those few I knew not one even by name: I thought there were not twelve. Of common soldiers the number was also inconsiderable; I thought there were scarcely twenty, and these were not of the camp, but of the Surrey militia quartered in the town. There were, indeed, more of the same regiment in the porch or in the church-yard; but too remote from the pulpit to hear a syllable of sedition, if there had been any to hear. I mention the paucity of officers and privates for the following reason; the public has been taught by mistaken prints to believe that I was guilty of preaching peace and good-will before the whole camp, that the aisle was crowded with soldiers, and that all the officers of the camp attended. I appeal to the parishioners present, whether the number of military men, privates and officers included, was greater than I have conjectured. My sermon was not exclusively calculated for a congregation of persons in any particular profession. There was not a word addressed by an apostrophe, as I have heard it asserted, to the officers. I had no reason to suppose that any military men, but those of the Surrey militia quartered at Brighton, would be at the church. I thought, and I believe it was so, that divine service was performed by the chaplains in the camp, and that the soldiers of the camp would not be permitted to straggle to the town or the church, on a Sunday, during divine service. The public has been much deceived in the exaggerated accounts of my preaching to the whole army; but had the whole army been at the church, had it been allowed or been possible, I am certain they would have heard nothing from me, but what was authorized by the gospel, enforced by the law of man as well as of God, tending to promote their happiness in all events, and animating them to the discharge of every duty, on principles of humanity and christianity. I expressly asserted, while I was deploring the calamities of war, that the conductors of war were often men of singular humanity and honour. I expressly commended the beautiful gradation of ranks in society. I enforced good order; I deprecated anarchy as much as despotism.

On the Monday, Dr. Knox visited the Downs, where the army was assembled in review, and in the evening, as usual, he went on the Steine; but though, at both places, as he was afterwards informed, the sermon was a topic of conversation, no insult was offered, nor was any personal application made to him. Tuesday evening was the time when the offence of Sunday was to be avenged. A friend of the Doctor, having to return to London the next day, proposed that they and some of the Doctor's family should go to the Theatre. The Doctor assented; and accordingly Mrs. Knox, Master Knox (aged about 14), and Miss Knox (12), accompanied them, the piece to be represented being the *Agreeable Surprise*. They occupied the right-hand side box, next to the stage box, where the Prince of Wales usually sat: but he was not there that evening. Soon after the curtain drew up, a few officers entered the opposite stage-box. But they had not been there five minutes, before their whole attention seemed fixed on the box where the Doctor and his party were seated. Other officers and several elderly ladies soon appeared in the same box; and they looked at the Doctor in a pointed manner, and then seemed to deliberate. Their attention appeared to be engrossed by the consultation, and they seldom turned to the players on the stage. There were several other officers interspersed in other boxes. Messages were sent to some of them, and they removed into the stage box. A man, whose looks were choleric, and who sat in the same box and on the same seat with Doctor Knox, was sent for, and he left his hat behind him, probably intending to return when he should be excluded. They frequently went in and out, and appeared extremely busy and anxious in concerting the plan of operations. This continued during the whole of the play. The children observed it, and told their father that they suspected some insult. Between the play and the entertainment, the following note, directed to the Doctor, was handed from behind them, to Mrs.

Knox, who gave it to her husband. The son had seen one of the officers writing; and there is no doubt but he was composing this note, which was sent without a name, and couched as follows:—

Your Discourse last Sunday was so offensive, that the gentlemen of this Theatre desire you will quit it immediately."

He read the order, and, giving it to Mrs. Knox, rose, and addressing himself to the opposite boxes, which, however, were now nearly empty, *the military having accompanied their despatch*, requested to know who had sent the impertinent paper without a name. He turned back to a phalanx of military men, who had now come round, and were drawn up behind the Doctor at the door of his box, and in the Lobby. The Doctor stept a little forward, and said:— "Ladies and gentlemen, I have this moment received an extraordinary paper, neither signed nor dated, containing a requisition that I should quit the Theatre immediately, on account of the sermon which I preached last Sunday morning in your parish church. I beg pardon for interrupting you; but under these circumstances, and surrounded, as you see I am, I humbly entreat the permission of the house, to ask aloud who sent me this note, and by what authority I am bound to obey it, in this place of public entertainment, where my family and myself have entitled ourselves to unmolested seats, by paying the price demanded at the door. We have interrupted nobody. Will you authorize the arbitrary expulsion of us all? for my family and friend will certainly follow me. I beg leave, besieged as you see me by a considerable number of men behind me, who are at this moment expressing their anger by opprobrious names, to enter into a short explanation with them, to ask the particulars of my offence in *your presence,* and to declare, that if anything advanced in my sermon gave personal offence, it was unintentional, and that I am concerned at it. If any one of these gentlemen will prove to your satisfaction that he is justly offended, I will immediately beg his pardon. I beg *your* pardon, who are totally unconcerned in this attack, for this singular interruption, which I trust I shall obtain from you, as men and Englishmen; when you have before your eyes a defenceless individual, in a situation so singular, as will, I hope, justify my present address to you."

During the Doctor's address the persons in uniform kept up an incessant clamour, the most outrageous expressions being used, such as:—"A democratical scoundrel that deserves to be hanged,"—"A democrat, a democrat, a d——d democrat,"—"Out with the democrat,—no democrats," the expressions being lavishly interlarded with scoundrel and rascal, and the interjections Bah! Boo! Boh! One of the party exclaimed, "No speech,—that won't do,—he ought to be hanged,—out with him;" while another suggested personal violence before the offender should be allowed to depart. A grim, gaunt figure vociferated, "Irons,—irons, here: he ought to be put in irons directly." All, however, was *vox et preterea nil*, notwithstanding one, very much out of breath with hooting and yelling, crying out "Go directly,—you must go;" whilst from behind resounded the cry "Out with him,—a democrat, a democrat, a democrat,—no democrat, a d——d democrat." Eventually the Doctor and his party were allowed to depart unmolested, though during the time he was separated from his family in the lobby, a tall officer, when Mrs. Knox was turning back to look for her daughter, violently pushed her by the shoulder, and bade her "go along after her husband, and be d——d." One, somewhat ashamed of his companions' behaviour, however, assured her that no violence should be used, and added,—"He should not have come amongst us. Had he stuck to peace we should all have admired him." Another, nodding his terrific plumes, exclaimed, "It is well his wife and children are with him, or else, &c., &c." The son happening to cry "Shame upon you!—near twenty to one," one of the valiant party shook him violently, saying at the same time, "Who are you, you dog? You ought to be hanged as well as your father,—if it is your father: and all such as hold his democratical principles, you dog, you!"

The Doctor avers that though the world had been told that they were a parcel of drunken boys who committed the outrage, the ringleaders were veterans in age, if not in service; and he adds:—"Very few were my hearers in the church, the major part being wholly influenced by the false representations of gossips."

On Wednesday, the 21st of August, Dr. Knox and his family having occupied Mr. Grantham's house, in North Street, a month, the period for which it was engaged, left Brighton; and soon some of the newspapers teemed with magnified accounts of a mutiny having broken out in the Brighton Camp through the Doctor's democratical sermon. The most virulent was the *True Briton.* He also received numerous insulting and threatening letters; and one silly epistle, dated Wick Camp, near Brighton, enclosed a painted bloody hand. The *World,* of August 27th, 1793, declares the treatment which the Doctor and his family received to be most unjustifiable.

The following letters of the Rev. Mr. Mossop, Curate of Brighton, who officiated in the Desk on the 18th of August, and was present during the delivery of the whole of the alleged obnoxious sermon, completely exonerates Dr. Knox from all blame in the transaction:—

Rev. Sir,—From my situation in the church at Brighthelmston the day you favoured us with a sermon, which gave such high offence to a certain description of gentlemen, I have, as may naturally be supposed, had my ears sufficiently stunned with enquiries relative to this sermon, both by many that were present, as well as the absent. From some of the former, I have experienced no small portion of ill-nature, because I could not conscientiously join in the cry with those who can judge the motives of their neighbour better than he can himself, and pronounce it at once seditions, libellous, traitorous, democratic.

The answer I have given to the latter description of inquirers, was in substance, "That I doubted not but that Dr. Knox would submit his sermon, in proper time, to that public at large, which is better able to judge, and generally more candid, than interested individuals, who often misapprehend, but more frequently misrepresent, a subject, to apologise for illiberality and malevolence;" adding, "That that christian charity, which men of our order ought to entertain one towards another, would not allow me to suppose, that Dr. Knox's motive was to hint, in the most distant manner, at the subvertion of our present happy constitution and government, but merely to expatiate on the advantages of universal peace and good-will among mankind, and to reprobate the decision of disputes by the umpirage of the sword."

May I, therefore, take the liberty to ask, whether you have it in intention to publish the sermon, or not? that I may have an opportunity of gratifying my inquirers with a more satisfactory answer. As I am partly a stranger to you, I beg you will excuse this liberty; and remain,

Rev. Sir,

Your obedient humble servant,

J. Mossop.

Brighthelmston, 12th Sept., 1793.

To the Rev. Dr. Knox.

Rev. Sir,—I duly received yours of the 17th inst.; and as I look upon you to be misrepresented to the public, relative to the sermon you preached at

Brighton, and consequently loaded with no small degree of unmerited opprobrium, I shall willingly contribute my mite to exonerate you. You have, therefore, my permission to publish my letter to you of the 12th of September last, in your intended vindication; provided your publication contain no invectives against the present existing government, nor any sentiments which might be improper for one zealously attached to our most excellent constitution to countenance.

I must conclude, by saying, that if every clergyman is to be exposed to insult, for doing what he conceives to be his duty, in exposing the reigning vices of the age, we shall soon find that the feeble rays of religion, which yet remain, to enlighten the christian world, will soon become totally eclipsed.

I am, Rev. Sir,
Your obedient humble servant,
J. Mossop.

Brighthelmston, 19th Nov. 1793.
To the Rev. Dr. Knox.

As a refutation that the appellation "Democrat," could with any degree of truth be attached to Dr. Knox, the following extract from his published remarks cannot fail to suffice :—

I honour the King and the Prince; and I firmly believe that they would scorn to persecute or to oppress, at the instigation of the most opulent peer in the realm, the most defenceless individual, the most abject outcast, the most forlorn beggar in the British empire. I may be abused, reviled, forced out of theatres, but no man shall rob me of my loyalty. The father of his people shall ever find me a dutiful son; and the Prince himself shall not excel me as a peaceable subject, and a friend to law and order. Though he is certainly in all other qualities as much above me, as he is in birth, rank, and the glorious prospect of one day ruling over a great, enlightened, and a free people, he shall not excel me in a zeal for the interests of my country and of the human race.

Many persons endeavoured to induce Dr. Knox to take legal proceedings against his cowardly assailants; but he contented himself by sparing his pocket, publishing a narrative of the transaction, —now a rare work, although it went through three editions,—and lampooning, in a pamphlet called Prolegomena, those "Gentlemen of the Brighton Theatre," who, to be revenged on him, magnanimously insulted and assaulted his wife and his children.

CHAPTER XVI.

THE OLD CHURCHYARDS.

Many persons have a natural predilection for wandering amongst the tombs. Whether in a town or village, their first impulse on arriving at a strange place, is to visit its common burial place, to ruminate amongst the tombs. A vastness, a solemnity, and a hallowedness seem to prevade the spot; and the mind in quietude has an indulgence there, a moralizing never exceeded even within the precincts of a sacred edifice.

The Poet has said,

> The grave can teach
> In silence, louder than divines can preach.

A celebrated moralist thus expresses himself on Epitaphs :—

> When I look upon the tombs of the great, every emotion of envy dies in me; when I read the epitaphs of the beautiful, every inordinate desire goes out; when I meet with the grief of parents upon a tombstone, my heart melts with compassion; when I see the tombs of parents themselves, I see the vanity of grieving for those whom they must quickly follow; when I see kings lying by those that deposed them—when I see rival wits placed side by side, or the holy men that divided the world with their contests and disputes, I reflect with sorrow and astonishment on the little competitions, factions, and debates of mankind; when I read the several dates of the tombs of some that died yesterday, and some six hundred years ago, I consider that Great Day, when we shall all of us be contemporaries, and make our appearance together.

In Brighton old churchyard there is vast material for thought, as great a diversity "In Memoriam" existing as in any burial place in the kingdom; the space being extensive and the monumental inscriptions numerous. Time has obliterated many epitaphs, and destroyed numerous tombstones, few records of the departed being discernible of dates previous to the 18th century. Thirty years since there were several wooden erections to record the memory of the dead; the memorial example of a catachresis, which

> Words abused implies;
> As, over his head a wooden tombstone lies.

According to the minutes of a Vestry Meeting held March 16th, 1791, it was: "Ordered that the Clerk of the Vestry do make enquiry whether the minister of the parish has a right to demand a fee for breaking the ground on the burial of a parishioner." This order was made in consequence of a dispute upon the point, between the inhabitants and the Vicar, the Rev. Thomas Hudson.

The oldest tablet in Brighton churchyard is that at the north of the church, placed—it being a flat stone,—to the memory of Alice, the wife of Richard Masters, who died May, 25th, 1696. It is contiguous to headstones that bear the most quaint epitaphs in the whole ground. Immediately near it is that of Mary Sanders, April, 1753, and bears this injunction to her surviving family:—

My loving children, all agree;
Pray live in Love and Unity.

The tomb next to it is thus inscribed:—

Here lyeth Anne ye wife of Richard Halsted, aged 23, and Elizabeth aged 22 years, both daughters of Henry and Mary Stanbridge, who dyed in May, 1728.

They were two louing sisters,
Who in this dust now ly, that
Uery day Anne was buryd
Elizabeth did dy.

Just at this spot, also, a stone points out the last resting place of the celebrated Sake Deen Mahomed, the introducer of shampooing into England, in 1784. He died on the 24th of February, 1851, at the advanged age of 102 years. By the pathway at the south-east of the chancel are deposited the remains of Martha Gunn, the royal bather of Brighton, who died May 2nd, 1815, at the age of 88 years. Her companion of the bath, Smoaker Miles, is buried near the west boundary wall of the church-yard, immediately opposite Upper North Street. The spot is marked by a tombstone, but the incription has been wholly obliterated by time. To the east of the stone which marks Martha Gunn's grave, is the tomb of Swan Downer, Esq., who endowed the school for girls, known as Swan Downer's School, and immediately to the west is a large headstone thus inscribed:—

PHŒBE HESSEL,
Who was born at Stepney, in the Year, 1713.
She served for many years as a Private Soldier in the
Fifth Regiment of Foot in different parts of Europe,
and in the year 1745 fought under the command of the
Duke of Cumberland, at the battle of Fontenoy,
Where she received a Bayonet Wound in her Arm.

Her long life, which commenced in the Reign of
Queen ANNE, extended to that of King GEORGE IV.,
By whose munificence she received comfort and support
in her latter days. She died at Brighton,
where she had long resided,
December 12th, 1821, aged 108.

The remains of Corporal Staines, a marine who fought under Nelson, at Copenhagen, lie at the foot of old Phœbe's grave.

The following punning epitaph on the headstone, which marks the spot where rest the remains of a Mr. Law, to the south-west of the church, has excited particular notice:—

Stop, Reader! and reflect with awe,
For sin and death have conquered law;
Who, in full hope, resign'd his breath,
That grace had conquered sin and death.

Mr. Law, who was an inhabitant, lost his life by accidentally walking over the cliff, between the New Steine and the Royal Crescent.

To the east of the Chancel door a massive stone points out where are deposited the mortal remains of a great Brighton celebrity, Captain Tettersell. It is thus inscribed:—

P. M. S.

Captain Nicholas Tettersel, through whose prudenee, ualour, and loyalty, Charles II., King of England, after he had escaped the sword of his merciless rebels, and his forces receiued a fatal ouerthrowe at Worcester, September 3rd, 1651, was faithfully preserued, and conueyed to France, departed this life the 26th of July, 1674.

Within this marble monument doth lie
Approved faith, honour, and loyalty;
In this cold clay he has now ta'en up his station;
Who once preserued the Church, the Crowne, and Nation;
When Charles the Greate was nothing but a breath,
This ualiant soule stept tweene him and Death:
Usurpers' threats, nor tyrant rebels' frowne,
Could not affright his duty to the crowne;
Which glorious act of his, for church and state,
Eight princes, in one day did gratulate—
Professing all to him in debt to bee,
As all the world are to his memory.
Since Earth could not reward the worth him given,
He now receives it from the King of Heaven.
In the same chest one iewel more you have,
The partner of his uirtues, bed, and grave.

The special incident referred to in Tettersell's life is recorded in another part of this book. One of the most remarkable tombs was that of the Rev. John Bolt, the vicar of Brighton, who died on the 2nd of November, 1669. It stood at the north-east corner of the Chancel. Not a vestige of the tomb now remains. The main structure of it was brick, and the covering stone was a slab of perriwinkle or Sussex marble: and so great a curiosity was it that it was in no way deemed a sacrilege by the casual passer-by, to knock off a piece with a flint, or even a hammer, for its novelty's sake. Its final demolition took place in 1853, when that and other sacred depositories of the dead—and the remains of the dead too,—were ruthlessly removed to enlarge the church, upon its then restoration. The slab bore the following inscription:—

Here lies interred the body of Mr. John Bolt, Master of Arts of Christ College, in Cambridge, aged seventy-eight years, who was a faithful and laborious preacher of the Gospel for the space of fifty-six years; whom God had blessed with *twenty-nine* children by two wives. He died in full assurance of a glorious resurrection, on the 2nd day of November, 1669, and was buried the 7th, likewise of the same month; in the pious memory of whom, his sorrowful son, *Daniel Bolt*, hath erected this monument.

Stay, passenger, and lett thoughts awhile;
Contemplate Death; Sin curse, which doth beguile
Us of our best enjoyments, and impair
Whatever unto most men pleasant are.
'Tis not thy learning nor thy piety
That can secure thee from Death's tyranny.
Witness this learned, pious man of God,
Who fell a victim to his conquering rod.
Nothing but Virtue can outlive our date
That gives a being beyond mortal fate.

Vivit post funera virtus.

The most quaint epitaph was on a slab in the floor just within the Chancel door. It was nearly obliterated some years since; but shortly after the present Vicar came to the living, he had it fresh cut. It, however, with many other relics, was destroyed during the restoration before mentioned. It was:—

Oh! dear mother, you are gone before,
And I, a wratch, wait at the door:
Sin doth not only keep me thence,
But makes me loath to go from hence.
When Christ hath healed me of my sin,
He'll make me fit and let me in.

Perhaps the most affecting record of the uncertainty of life, is that on the tomb of Robert Augustus Bedford. It is in what is termed the old ground, not far from the poplar tree which marks the spot where once was a well. This well and a wall which went direct north to Church Street, formed the west boundary of a garden that was consecrated as an additional piece of ground for burial, in January, 1818, by the Bishop of Exeter, and about that spot was appropriated for the burial of paupers, and likewise for soldiers; as at that time the Hospital of the Infantry Barracks occupied the site of the present Hanover Chapel burial ground. The inscription—now mostly obliterated,—is as follows:—

This youth, while viewing amidst a large concourse of persons assembled on the Pier Head of this town, on the 17th day of July, 1826, some trials designed to show the practibility of conveying the means of escape to ship-wrecked persons by means of a chain attached to a ball; from which, on one of the experiments, it separated on the discharge of the cannon, and instantaneously deprived him of his life, in the 10th year of his age.

The experiment which was being made was that known as Captain Manby's apparatus for rescuing persons from shipwreck.

On the 20th November, 1819, the funeral of a Sergeant of the 90th foot took place. He was shot on the 17th of the same month, at the barracks, in Church street, by a private of the regiment, who, for the offence, was executed at Horsham.

The well here just alluded to, north of the wall which forms the northern boundary of Queen Square, was, on the restoration of the church, in 1853, filled up with decayed coffins and the mortal remains of those whose bodies were disinterred immediately to the north of the sacred edifice, to afford space and improve the effect of the building. Amongst those whose narrow cell was less violated, was that of Sir Richard Phillips, the natural philosopher, and author of "A Million of Facts." His vault and tomb were reconstructed just within the south entrance to the cemetery ground, in front of Clifton Terrace, whither his remains were removed, and where they now rest. Not far from this tomb lie the remains of Mrs. Pickstock, the headstone to whose grave is thus inscribed:—

In testimony of the
Faithful and zealous
Services of Alice Pickstock,
Matron of the Brighton

Workhouse, and to
perpetuate the recollection of her
many benevolent and pious
offices to the sick and poor of this
Parish,

This stone is erected by the Directors
and Guardians and others, in the year of
Our Lord MDCCCXLIII.

"I bowed down heavily as one that
mourneth for his mother."—Psalm xxxv., 14 v.

To the extreme east of the old ground is the tomb of the real moderniser of Brighton,—whose death took place nine and twenty years ago,—and is thus inscribed:—

MR. AMON WILDS,
Died Sept. 12th 1833, aged 71 years

A remarkable incident accompanies the period at which this gentleman came to settle in Brighton, Through his abilities and taste, the order of the ancient architecture of buildings in Brighton may be dated to have changed from its antiquated simplicity and rusticity; and its improvements have since progressively increased. He was a man of extensive genius, and talent, and in his reputation for uprightness of conduct could only meet its parallel.

Contiguous to this tomb, a stone marks the resting-place of a highly respected inhabitant, for many years the landlord of the Old Ship Hotel:—

LEONARD SHUCKARD,
Died 17th January, 1837, aged 70.

Immediately west is the grave of a Brighton celebrity, whose memory is thus recorded:—

JOHN JORDAN,
Many years a respectable hair-dresser of this town.
Died November 13th, 1810.

Originally the stone was further inscribed:

Say what you will, say what you can,
John Jordan was an honest man.

But there appearing a species of levity about these two lines, unbefitting a place of Christian sepulture, they were removed after the stone had been up but a few days.

To the west of the main entrance from North Street, opposite Wykeham Terrace, is the vault of Mr. Weiss, formerly a surgical instrument maker, Charing-cross, London. His remains are deposited in this vault, his body prior to being screwed down in the coffin, having, by express desire in his will, been pierced at the heart by an instrument which he made expressly for the purpose. His funeral took place with the weapon in him, a special legacy being left to the surgeon, Mr. Benjamin Vallance, who complied with the request, for performing the duty, Mr. Weiss having a dread of being buried alive.

The handsomest monument in the churchyard is that at the north-east entrance, to the memory of Anna Maria Crouch, formerly a performer at Drury Lane Theatre. She died Oct. 2nd, 1805. It was erected by Mr. Kelly.

A large stone cross or crucifix formerly stood immediately in front of the church. The stone steps to it and the lower fragment of the pillar alone remain. A legend in connexion with this cross has been preserved, of which the following is a copy:—

ST. NICHOLAS GALLEY.

"Long had raged the bloody feud between the Lords of Pevensey Castle and the Earls de Warrene, Lords of Lewes; when, early one bright May morning, the warder of Lewes Castle, from the northern turret blew loud his horn. The lady of Earl de Warrene hastened to the turret's height, her infant first-born son kerchiefed on her arm. From thence she viewed the dread conflict which was raging with all the fury of inveterate foes, on Mount Caburn's shelving sides. Lord Pevensey, on his white steed, was seen leading his followers down the hill; Earl de Warrene was urging his men to withstand the charge. In an instant both parties commingled; the strife was desperate, but of short duration. Lord Pevensey, having the vantage ground, drove Earl de Warrene's troops pell-mell down the hill; but the Earl scorned to turn his back upon his foe, and for some time he singly maintained the conflict against a host; until Lord Pevensey came up, flushed with success, and raised his battle-axe to cleave the Earl in twain. It was at this moment that the noble lady of Earl de Warrene, seeing her lord in such imminent hazard, held up her infant son and vowed to Saint Nicholas (the protector of the faithful in dangers) that if her lord's life was spared his son should never wed till he had placed the belt worn by the Holy St. Nicholas, on the Blessed Virgin's tomb, at Byzantium. The saint heard her vow; for the

Earl dexterously avoided the blow, and Lord Pevensey, having lost his balance by the exertion, nearly fell from his horse. In the next moment the Earl's sword appeared through his cuirass behind; Lord Pevensey fell dead; his terrified retainers fled in dismay; and Earl de Warrene returned in triumph to the Castle. Full twenty summers had now passed over, and Manfred, Lord of Lewes, the Earl's eldest son, had not yet fulfilled his mother's vow, to visit the Blessed Virgin's tomb. He was betrothed to Lord Bramber's daughter, the gentle Edona—beauteous as the jessamine's bloom—kind as the Zephyr—good and pure as the saints. Full twenty times had the anniversary of Earl de Warrene's victory been celebrated most gallantly in the Castle's kingly hall. Again the guests had assembled there; the wassail bowl went merrily round; the bards sung in highest strains; Lord Manfred led his betrothed to join in the mazy dance; when—whilst all was merriment and joy,—suddenly a wintry dismal blast passed through the hall. The lights were quickly extinguished, the din and clamour of war seemed to assail the castle walls on every side; and whilst the guests stood in darkness and in stupid wonder, in a moment vivid flashes of lightning shot across the richly tapestried walls, and displayed the fight renewed on Mount Caburn's side. The hill and dale were seen distinctly, as if broad day were shining, and the combatants eagerly engaged. But when Lord Pevensey again lifted his battle-axe to strike Earl de Warrene, all disappeared and total darkness ensued; the clamour ceased against the castle walls; lights were brought, but the guests, terrified, gloomily withdrew. On the morrow, Earl de Warrene hither to Brighthelmston, to St. Bartholomew's Chapel came, and by the counsel of the holy fathers, built a ship, gaily trimmed, and named 'St. Nicholas' Galley,' to bear his son to the blessed Virgin's tomb. It was fixed that when he should return from performing his noble mother's vow, then should he wed the fair Edona. The vessel gallantly dashed from Mecheem* harbour, and bounded over the yielding wave, making his way for brighter—not happier climes. Lord Manfred safely arrived at Byzantium, and performed his sacred duty. It was noon on the 17th of happy

* Ancient name of Newhaven.

May—another year had rolled its wain—when a sail, bearing the well known pennant of St. Nicholas, was descried off Wordinges (Worthing) point by one of the Fathers of this Chantry. Instantly a messenger was sent to carry the welcome tidings to Earl de Warrene, who, with all his retinue, a train of gallant bearing, his noble lady, the Lord of Bramber with the Lady Edona, and the holy Abbot of the priory, with all his brotherhood, had, in a few hours, assembled beneath the Earl's banner, on the hill where now stands St. Nicholas' Church. The day was fair, the wind was favourable, and the 'St. Nicholas' glided swiftly on her way; the holy fathers sang with cheerful voices. The Earl watched, with beaming eyes, for the signal agreed upon. It was made; shouts rent the air; every face shone with joy, every heart beat with gratitude; when, in a moment, the progress of the vessel was checked; she reeled on her side, and sank before their eyes. She had ran full on the hidden rock off Shore-ham* harbour. The Earl and every soul around him stood motionless; not a word broke the silence of that sad scene. To move was useless. One sad, last, long-drawn sigh burst from Edona, and she fell never more to rise. The Earl passed his hands over his eyes; dropped his head on his bosom; no smile ever rested on that face again. One foreign sailor alone of the hapless crew survived to describe (feebly indeed) the ecstacy of Lord Manfred when he beheld his native shores and discerned his father's banner waving on St. Nicholas' hill. Slowly as the cavalcade descended, each cast a look of despair on that sea which had swallowed all their hopes. Earl de Warrene survived a few years only; but before he died he built the church to St. Nicholas on the hill, to be an everlasting remembrance to all who go upon the mighty deep not to neglect their vows. Lady Edona lies under the cross at the entrance to the church, being the spot where she fell and died; but still, on the anniversary of that day, 'St. Nicholas' Galley' glides at midnight past the town of Brighthelmston, and is seen from the cliff by hundreds of the inhabitants, to sink.† The Earl leaving no children, his family became extinct, and the estates passed to the heir, Lord Arundel, to whom they still belong."

* The rock is still there, and is well known to mariners.

† A tradition is still held by the old inhabitants that a galley is seen here in the offing before a storm.

A very quaint epitaph was (it is now obliterated by age) on the late sexton of the period:—

RICHARD JEFFERY.
Died 10th July, 1806, aged 64.

When Barb'ra died, O Lord, prayed I,
Let me die too, and near her lie—
The Lord was good, and heard my pray'r,
And here we lie a faithful pair.

Preceding it, on the same stone, was the following:—

Sacred to the memory of
BARBARA wife of RICHARD JEFFERY;
Who having for upwards of 50 years diligently performed
the office of Sexton in this Parish, died
30th September, 1805, aged 63.

Look, mingled lie, the aged and the young,
The rich and poor,—an undistinguish'd throng;
Death conquers all, and Time's subduing hand
No tomb, no marble statue can withstand;
Mark well thy latter end,—in Bab'ra see,
What, reader, thou, and all mankind must be.
The Grave for thousands though she toilsome made,
Yet here at last her lifeless body's laid,
In joyful hope, as Christian hope will be,
To rise to life and immorality.

On the tombstone of a Captain Cook was formerly:—

Many a hard tempestuous gale he's known,
But on his native shore at last he's thrown;
No rocks or quicksands has he now to fear;
Safe from all storms he rides at anchor here.
Go, and be wise then, 'ere it is too late,
With firm resolve to meet the arm of fate.
A few short years, Alas! how quick they pass;
To this complexion must you come at last.
Death conquers all, and drags them to the grave,
The rich, the poor, the coward and the brave.
Think then, ye youth in time, and dying say,
Come when thou wilt, O Lord! I ready am to-day.

From their exposed position, the inscriptions on many of the tombstones have been erased by the hand of time; nor can one be found of the many recorded in a Diary, kept in 1778 and 1779, of the character alluded to.—"Monday, September 7th, 1778. My landlord is persuading his eldest son, and of course heir apparent, a young prince Crispin, to go to sea. I desire the father to visit the churchyard, and upon various monuments of youth he may observe the following inscription :—

Parents and Friends, weep not for me,
Tho' I was drownded in the sea !—

and then, after due deliberation, if he chose to renew his persuasions he must use his pleasure. The poor man seemed overwhelmed in thought, and much struck. Perhaps the lad may suffer no further solicitation on this account, unless his father should turn out to be a staunch predestinarian."

To the north of the church is a dwarf head-stone, thus inscribed:—

Sacred to the memory of EDMUND BORMAN, who was accidently killed, February 11th, 1796—aged 49 years.

His death was caused thus : — He was superintending the erection of a new flag-staff, for the vane, mentioned in page 84, for Mr. Stephen Poune, the Churchwarden; and having gone aloft, within the tower, to make everything safe in lowering the remains of the old flag-staff, he hastened down, to receive it below, when, just as he emerged from the belfry door, the mass, which was being lowered, having descended much quicker than he expected, came down upon him, crushing him fearfully, so that he died within an hour of the accident. Deceased was bowler to the Prince of Wales and the Duke of York, leader of the ringers and conductor of the choir at the Church, and, being a person of good education, a generally useful man.

On the west portion of the ground, the record of the death of Miss Coupland, who was killed by the fall of a wall, in Church Street, where the Royal Stables now are, whilst walking to the Parish Church, to act as bridesmaid at the wedding of a young friend, cannot fail to be read with interest. The shoes which she wore on the occasion are still preserved by a member of her family named Hibben, who worked for her father, the owner of the premises and smithy, which for so many years formed the obstruction to the Royal Entrance at the bottom of Church Street, The epitaph runs :

Sacred to the memory of MARY COUPLAND, died 9th November, 1800—aged 19.

Underneath this turf, in dust is laid,
A blooming and a virtuous maid ;

In virtue's path she always trod,
And trusted in Almighty God.
For virtue, modesty, and truth,
A perfect patron was for youth;
She lived in love, and feared the Lord,
We hope her soul has met reward;
Lamented was, by great and small,
Was crushed underneath a blown down wall—
Going to church on the Lord's day;
This maid's sweet life was snatched away.
A tender mother left to mourn,
Enough to wound a heart of stone;
God grant his blessing to be given,
For them to meet again in Heaven.
Short was thy life, fair flower, how soon removed,
Sudden thy summons to the realms above.
Vain man, as well on sands may structors raise,
As build on early youth or length of days;
A thousand accidents frail life attend,
And none can tell how soon this life may end.
'Tis not for age that here she lie,
Therefore, in time, prepare to die;
Death does not always warning give,
Therefore be careful how you live.

A headstone that stands about the centre of the ground to the east of the church, and yet bears the name of Lucy Fermor, formerly had on it the following acrostic, now wholly effaced by age:—

L ook here, ye gay and giddy throng,
U nmindful as ye go;
C all'd you may be as soon as I,
Y oung, strong, and healthy too.

F or eighteen years I had not seen
E 'er death did cut me down,
R eturned to dust as now you see;
M ore quick may be your doom.
O h do not then forget, your souls
R equired may be soon.

Perhaps no inscription throughout the whole of the hallowed grounds, affords a theme for deeper meditation than that which here follows, associated as it is with marriages, births, and deaths, through a period of half a century: the plighting of solemn vows, vows how often broken; the promise of suretiship to renounce all evil works, a promise how seldom kept; we may rest in Him, as our hope is this our brother doth, a hope how soon forgotten! It is upon a head-stone, on the left, just within the southern entrance to the Old Ground, and is as follows:—

Here lies all that is mortal of
JOHN POCOCK,
Who was, during 13 years, Clerk of the Chapel Royal, and 38 years Clerk of this Parish.
In the discharge of his duty how simple, upright, and affectionate he was, will alone be known at the last day.
He came to his grave on the 13th of June, 1846, like a shock of corn cometh in his season, aged 81.

The following, which is on a stone by the footway, just south of the tower, has a melancholy history attached to it:—

Sacred to the Memory of John Rowles, who, in discharging his duties as a Peace Officer of this Town, was unfortunately killed by a Wound from a Bayonet, on the 5th Nov., 1817, Aged 40 years.

The circumstances were: On Tuesday, the 4th of November, 1817, a public notice was issued, warning the inhabitants against illuminating their houses, or celebrating the anniversary of the Gunpowder Plot, by means of fireworks. Notwithstanding this prohibition, a number of persons, chiefly boys, assembled on the Old Steine, at twilight, in the evening of Wednesday, the 5th, and let off squibs, serpents, crackers, &c. The civil power, in number 16,—headboroughs and patrol,—at the head of which was Mr. John Williams, the High Constable, immediately interfered, and took into custody the offenders against the edict. This sort of warfare lasted until nine o'clock, when a lighted tar-barrel made its appearance. The authorities espied it, and, after a stout resistance by the populace, it was captured and extinguished. Much irritation was engendered in consequence, and the mob, deprived of their fun, seemed inclined to mischief, and, the principal object of their displeasure being the High Constable, they attacked his house, the Baths, which stood on the site now occupied by the Lion Mansion. Mr. White, also, in Castle Square, who had made himself very prominent in the affair, came in for his share of the spleen of the rioters. Stones were hurled with great violence, and the windows of their houses were soon smashed in. Greatly alarmed, Williams sent a message to Mr. Serjeant Runnington, the resident magistrate, and also to the guard-house at the Infantry barracks,

Church Street, demanding the aid of the military. Several companies of the 21st regiment of Fusileers, who had but that day arrived in Brighton, marched with fixed bayonets to the Steine, the avenues to which they quickly occupied.

The Riot Act was read by Serjeant Runnington, and the utmost dismay prevailed. About this time several squibs being let off near the soldiery, an attempt was made to capture the offenders. Dreadful to relate, however, while charging, one of the military accidentally thrust his bayonet into the body of Mr. Rowles, a headborough. The steel entered just above the hip, and, passing through, appeared three inches on the other side,—the wound proved to be mortal,—and the ill fated man lingered, in the utmost agony, until half-past seven on Thursday evening, when he died, leaving a pregnant wife and three infant children to lament his untimely end. Two of the patrol, Slaughter and Burt, were also so wounded with the stones, cast by the mob, that they were obliged to be carried home, where they remained for some time in a very dangerous state. A woman, also, was wounded in the head with slugs, fired from a pistol. The disturbance lasted until a late hour of the night, and the military did not repair to their barracks until two or three o'clock the next morning.

On the following morning, the persons who had been apprehended for creating the disturbance, were brought before the sitting magistrates, Mr. Serjeant Runnington and Mr. Hopkins, at the Town Hall.

The civil power was blamed for calling in the military. The coroner's inquest on the body of Mr. Rowles, after having sat eight days, returned a verdict of "Wilful Murder" against James Day, the principal, and John Williams, High Constable, and James White, stationer, general collector of rates, as accessories before the act. They surrendered to their bail at the Horsham Assizes, on the 25th March, and were found "Not Guilty," and the judge said, that, so far from any blame being attached to Williams and White, he was fully persuaded that they had acted throughout with the greatest prudence, coolness, and discretion.*

* A criminal information was moved in the Court of King's Bench, against the publisher of the *Brighton Herald*, Mr. William Fleet, for having, pending the

The base of the stone cross, to which is attached the legend of St. Nicholas Galley, is a remnant of the superstition that prevailed prior to the Reformation. In primitive times, the south side of every churchyard contained a column placed on a pedestal, having on its summit a cross; and the nearer to this a corpse was interred, so much the sooner—it was believed—would the soul be relieved from purgatory. Hence the reason why the south side of a churchyard most frequently contains the greatest number of interments, individuals having a solemn dread of being buried in the north, where there was no cross. So far, indeed, did primitive Christians carry their devotion for this figure, that they have been accused of worshipping the cross itself. Such was their blind zeal for the sign of the cross, that they violated all bounds of prudence, and Flecknoe quaintly observes:—"That had they their will, a bird should not fly in the air with its wings *a-cross,* a ship with its *cross-yard* sail upon the sea, nor profane tailor sit *cross-legged* upon his shop-board, or have *cross-bottoms* to wind his thread upon."

With reference to the particular pillar in question, no records, beyond the legend, exist which might contribute to the solution of its origin, but the probability is that it was erected about the seventh century, when the mania for columns and crosses prevailed.

The New Burial Ground, as it is termed, was added in 1824; and the Cemetery Ground was opened in what was known as Butcher Russell's field, in 1841, the first burial in it being that of Mary Wheeler, the wife of a labourer, who was employed in laying out and levelling the ground. She died June 27th, 1841, and an obelisk marks her grave.

At the time when grave-yard robbers, termed Resurrectionists, were the dread of surviving relatives, in 1820-21, these desecrators of the silent tomb paid the Old Churchyard a visit, in the autumn

---

investigation before the Coroner, published certain matters which, it was alleged, tended to create a prejudice against Messrs. Williams and White. Lord Ellenborough observed, that the Court felt itself bound in point of law to grant the rule, but thought it would be advisable for the parties to stay where they were, and not carry the proceedings farther. His lordship expressed a wish that peace and harmony might be restored to a town in which so much division appeared to exist. All parties concerned in the indiscreet affair were severely lampooned in a poem called the "Battle of the Tar Tub," very few copies of which are extant.

of the former year, and conveyed away at least one body, the chief of the sacrilegious wretches being Williams, who, in 1831, was executed at Newgate, with Bishop, for "Burking" an Italian boy. The circumstance of the body being stolen greatly alarmed the inhabitants, and for many years afterwards it was the constant practice to have watchers, under a species of impromptu tent, night after night, for months together, upon the death of a person, to prevent the body from being conveyed away. At one period the system of watching had become such a nuisance that persons were afraid to venture through the burial ground after dusk—the time when the watchers went on duty—as the parties were not satisfied with being there to scare off the expected marauders, but they took with them creature comforts in the form of beer, spirits, and tobacco, and armed themselves with pistols, guns, and swords, so that, when the alcholic spirits began to rise, there was a great lack of discretion, and frequent broils in consequence ensued. The churchwardens, therefore, interfered and prevented their having any other arms than stout sticks. This reckless and indecent profanation of the sacred dormitory lamentably recalls to one's mind the vitiated taste and customs of the early ages, when churchyards were no sooner enclosed than they were appropriated as places of public amusement. According to Aubrey, "in every parish was a church-house, to which belonged spits, crocks, and other utensils, for dressing provisions. Here the housekeepers met, the young people were there, too, and had dancing, bowling, shooting at butts, &c., the ancients gravely sitting by and looking on." Fosbrook further informs us, that "Whitsun ales were brewed by the churchwardens, and sold in the church; and the profits—there being no rates for the relief of the poor—were distributed amongst them." It was, also, customary for barbers to come and shave the parishioners in the churchyard on Sundays and high festivals, before matins. This liberty continued till 1422, when it was restrained by a particular prohibition of Richard Flemyng, Bishop of Lincoln.

For more than ten years the custom of watching prevailed; but legislation at length suggested a means of supplying subjects for dissection, without despoiling the graves; and, since then, in 1854, intra-mural burials being prohibited, the Brighton Churchyards have been respected, and on the 17th of November, 1859, the first tree was planted in the oldest ground, near Wykeham Terrace, by Mr. Churchwarden Marchant, who had suggested the plantation of the grounds. Other of the authorities and the inhabitants in general, followed his example, and very soon the planting of some hundreds of trees and shrubs was effected; but as yet the vegetation of them has progressed but slowly.*

Brighton Vicarage, with West Blatchington, Rectory, is one united benefice, in the sole gift of the Bishop of the Diocese. The present Vicar was appointed by the Crown; his predecessor, the late Dr. Carr, who died Bishop of Worcester, having been made Bishop of Chichester. The Sovereign always takes the appointment to any Ecclesiastical preferment that is vacated by one who is raised to the Episcopate.

Chapter XVII.

MARTYRDOM OF DERYK† CARVER.

Deryk Carver, a brewer, the proprietor of what is now known as the Black-Lion Street Brewery, the oldest building in the town, a Fleming by birth, who had been resident in Brighton about eight or nine years, was the first who suffered martyrdom in Sussex, under the persecution of Mary. About the end of October, 1554, Carver,

---

* The first spot ever set apart as a sacred burial-place,—namely, the field of Ephron, bought by the patriarch Abraham,—was planted round about with trees:—"The field and the cave that was therein, and all the trees that were in the field, and in the borders round about, were made sure unto Abraham for a possession."—*Genesis* xxiii., 17.

† By reference to the signatures of the principal inhabitants to the "Auncient Customs," Page 37, it will be seen that this is the orthography of the name, as written by the son of the martyr. And it is fair to presume that at the time of his signature, 1580, he was a person of no mean importance, and had a vanity that his name should be correctly spelt, as he is the only person who inscribed to the document, that prefixed *Mr.* to his signature. Fox writes it Derrick. The breweries established next after Carver's, were the Ship Street Brewery, by Wichelo, known in modern times as Wigney's Brewery, now no longer in existence; and West Street Brewery, by Mighell, now the extensive establishment of Messrs. Vallance & Catt.

who had adopted the doctrines of the Reformation, and had been in the habit, as opportunity offered, of collecting a few people of his own persuasion in his house, for the purpose of religious worship, was, together with John Launder, of Godstone, apprehended, as they were at prayer, by Edward Gage, of Firle, a gentleman and county Magistrate, and sent up to the Queen's Council. After examination, he and his friend were sent prisoners to Newgate, to await the leisure of Bishop Bonner for his further examination into their heretical practices. The Bishop interrogated them on matters of faith, on the 8th of June following, so that they must have lain in prison for more than seven months, upon a mere suspicion. They made certain confessions, which they duly signed, and then the Bishop, who had no legal right whatever to meddle with their creed, as they were not of his diocese, objected against them certain articles, in the ordinary course of ecclesiastical law, as it existed in those days. Various means were resorted to to induce Carver and Launder to recant, but these they stedfastly resisted. "I will never go from these answers," said the latter, "so long as I live," and so said Carver. Wherefore, on the 10th of June, two days afterwards, they were cited to the Consistory Court of St. Paul's. The "confession" of Carver, as preserved in Fox's Acts and Monuments, was in substance this: "I. That the bread and wine used in the Holy Communion, or as it was then called, the 'Sacrament of the Altar,' is simply bread and wine, and not the material body and blood of Christ. II. That the mass is not a sacrifice; that it does not conduce to salvation; and that it is not profitable to a Christian man, because it is said in Latin, a tongue which he, with the majority of the people, does not understand. III. That although it is requisite to go to a good priest for counsel in matters of religion, yet that priest's absolution is not profitable for a man's salvation. IV. That the faith and religion now set forth in the Church of England is not agreeable to God's Word. That Bishops Hooper, Cardmaker, Rogers, and others of their opinion were good Christian men, and did preach the true doctrine of Christ, and that they did shed their blood in the same doctrine, by the power of God. V. That since the Queen's coronation he hath had the bible and psalter in English read in his house at

Brighthampsted divers times, and likewise, since his coming into Newgate, but the keeper thereof did take them away; and also that about a twelvemonth now past he had the English procession said in his house with other English prayers. And further, that Thomas Iveson, John Launder, and William Veisie, prisoners within Newgate, were taken with this examinate in his house at Brighthampsted, as they were hearing of the Gospel, then read in English." The "confession" of John Launder states, among other things, that he was a husbandman, twenty-five years of age, and an inhabitant of Godstone, and that himself, with Carver, Iveson, Veisie, and other persons, to the number of twelve, had been apprehended by Mr. Gage, in Carver's house, as they were saying the service in English, as set forth in the days of King Edward the Sixth. It appears that Launder, having come down to Brighton to transact business for his father, had heard of Carver's zeal for the Gospel, and had been to his house for religious worship, at the time of Mr. Gage's unfriendly visit. The confession winds up with a statement of his religious views, which, in the main, are identical with Carver's own, as stated. The Bishop's Articles, twelve in number, reiterated the charges already adduced against the prisoners, who, being asked if they still adhered to their opinions, replied affirmatively. Carver added "your doctrine is poison and sorcery. If Christ were here you would put Him to a worse death than He was put to before. You say that you can make a God: ye can make a pudding as well. Your ceremonies in the Church be beggary and poison." The Bishop, seeing their constancy, pronounced judgment upon them both, whereupon they were delivered to the Sheriffs, who were then present, in order that they might be burnt in due course of law. "This Dirricke" records Fox, "was a man, whom the Lorde had blessed as well with temporall ryches, as with his spirituall treasures, which ryches yet were no clogge or let unto his true professing of Christ, the Lord, by His grace, so working in him; of the which, there was such havock, by the gready raveners of that time, that his poore wyfe and children had little or none thereof. During his imprisonment, although he was well stricken in yeares (and, as it were, past the tyme of learning), yet he so spent his tyme, that being, at hys first apprehension, utterly ignoraunt of anye letter of the booke, hee coulde, before his death, read perfectly any printed English. Whose diligence and zeale is worthy no small commendation, and therefore I thought it good not to let passe over in silence, for the good encouragement and example of others. Moreover, at his comming into the town of Lewes to be burned, the people called upon him, beseechying God to strengthen hym in the faith of Jesus Christ. He thanked them, and prayed unto God, that of Hys mercy he would strengthen *them* in the lyke faith. And when hee came to the signe of the Starre, the people drew near unto him, where the Sheriffe sayd that he had found him a faithfull man in al his aunswers. And as he came to the stake, he kneeled downe and made his prayers, and the Sheriffe made hast. Then hys booke was throwen into the barrel, and when he had strypt him selfe (as a joyfull member of God) he went into the (pitch) barrel him selfe. And as soone as ever he came in, he tooke up the booke and threw it among the people, and then the Sheriffe commaunded in the Kyng and Queen's name, on paine of death, to throw in the booke againe. And immediately, that faithfull member spake with a joyfull voyce, saying:—'Deare brethren and sistern, wytness to you all that I am come to seale with my blood Christes Gospell, for because I know that it is true; it is not unknowen unto al you, but that it hath bene truly preached here in Lewes, and in all places in England, and now it is not. And for because that I wyll not denye here God's Gospell, and be obedient to man's lawes, I am condemned to dye. Dere brethren and sistern, as many of you as do beleve upon the Father, the Soune, and the Holye Ghost, unto everlasting lyfe, see you doe the workes appertaining to the same. And as many of you as do beleve upon the Pope of Rome, or any of hys lawes, which he sets forth in these daies, you do beleve to your utter condemnation, and except the great mercy of God, you shall burne in hell perpetually.' Immediately the Sheriffe spake unto him, and sayd: 'if thou doest not beleve on the Pope, thou art *damned* body and soule!' And farther the Sheriffe sayd unto him, 'speake to thy God, that He may deliver thee now, or els to strike me down to the example of this people;' but this faithfull member said, 'the Lord forgive you your sayings.' And then spake hee againe to all the people there present, with a loude voice, saying: 'deare brethren, and all you whom I have offended in wordes or in dede, I aske you for the Lorde's sake to forgeve me, and I hartly forgeve all you, which have offended me in thought, word, or dede.' And he sayd further in his prayer, 'Oh Lorde my God, thou hast written: He that will not forsake wife, children, house, and all that he hath, and take up Thy cross and follow Thee, is not worthy of Thee. But thou Lorde knowest that I have forsaken all to come unto Thee; Lorde have mercy upon me, for unto Thee I commend my spirit, and my soule doth rejoyce in thee.' These were the last wordes of that faithfull member of Christ before the fire was put to him. And afterward that the fire came to him he cried, 'Oh Lord have mercy upon me,' and sprong up in the fire, calling upon the name of Jesus, and so ended."

The order of the Sheriff, that the people should throw Carver's bible into the fire, does not appear to have been complied with, as the book is still preserved, and is in the possession of Mr. Ade, Colonnade, North Street. It is what is termed, a "breeches" bible, from the circumstance that in Genesis iii., 7, the words are: "They"—meaning Adam and Eve—"sewed figge leaves together, and made themselves 'breeches,'" other translations being "aprons." It is in a state of good preservation, but the title page is gone, hence its date cannot be correctly known; but on comparing it with others of apparently the like edition,—an imperial octavo,—it was published in 1550. It received but little injury from the action of the fire upon it; merely a slight discolouration on some of the pages, from the smoke; but the following engrossed memorandum on a blank half-page, between Malachi and the Apocrypha, proves that it is not in the same binding now as it was when Carver had it:

By me, Edward Harffye.
Anno Dom.
1650.

This Bible was Dirrick Carver's; belonging unto his family: of Brighthelmstone: who suffered martiredom ffor Conscience' sake in Queene Mary's Dayes, And bought by Sibbell Clarke, Widdow, of Brighthelmstone; And Given to mee, Edward Harffye of Brighthelmston, Clarke and Writinge Master: And I have now bound him, 1660* 1650. And I doe will him to my Youngest Child.

* This is erased by a mark of the pen being passed through it, in the original.

And Soe the Youngest of my Stock. To hand him ffor ever ffrom one to an other; And now ffirst I give him to Mary Harffye, my daughter, 1664. Wryten by my owne hand. By me Edward : Harffye.

This Carver was Burnt to death, in the Castell of Lewes, Sussex.

On the back of the same half-page, is written, in a good round-hand: "Sarah Clark—1778."

On the inside of the cover, at the commencement, is written, "Wililam Clarke, his book, Septem Ber the 20, 1744." This name also, with the same date, appears on the fly page between the Old and the New Testament. Where, also, previous to the "Holie Gospel according to S. Matthevve," are the annexed entries:—

William Clarke the son of iohn and mary his wife, was Born the 4 of September, near 4 in the morning in the year of our lord 17.11.

the Son of william and Sarah his wife was Born ivne (June) the 13 at a C wor ter past 4 in the after noon on a Sather day, 1747.

William Clark Dyed December the 5, 1747.

In the margin of the 11th chapter of Daniel, is written in good Old English:—

edward Carffre } 1653. his Booke.

January the first.

The blood of the martyr is visible on Chapters 19 and 20 of Judges, and also on Chapters 1 and 3 of Zephania, where the leaves have closed on each other. But the greatest quantity is on the Book of Ruth, which is very much splashed with the vital fluid. Altogether, the Bible is a very precious relic, and its present possessor attaches to it great value, he having refused large sums of money that have been offered him for it.

Stephen Gratwicke, a Brighton man of respectable family, and of liberal education, was put to death in St. George's Fields, Southwark, about the end of May, 1557. At his trial, before the Bishops of Winchester and Rochester, and a priest suborned to personate the Bishop of Chichester, he expostulated with his judges for keeping men a year or two in prison, "permittyng them not so much as a Testament to look upon, for their soules comfort." To this the Bishop of Winchester replied:—"No, syr, we will use you as we will use the child, for if the child will hurt himself with a knife we will keepe the knife from him. So, because you will *damme* your soule with the *Word*, therefore you shall not have it!"

Chapter XVIII.

THE ESCAPE OF CHARLES II.

After the defeat at Worcester, on the 3rd of September, 1651, Charles II., on his arrival at Kidderminster, by the advice of the Earl of Derby, and under the guidance of Francis Yates, brother-in-law of Penderell, retired to "Boscobel," a lone house on the borders of Staffordshire, where lived one Richard Penderell, a farmer, and his four brothers. By the aid of the Penderells, Charles clothed himself in the garb of a peasant, and carried a bill-hook with him into the woods, where daily he pretended to be employed cutting faggots. His only attendant at that time was Colonel Careless, a Roman Catholic. The suspicion of the Parliamentary army was, however, aroused by two strangers staying at such a lone place as Boscobel, and detachments of troops were, in consequence, sent in search of them, and it was then that Charles and Colonel Careless hid themselves in the branches of an oak tree. By the assistance of a Benedictine monk, named Hudleston, Lord Wilmot then joined the King, and by his proposition, they, with Penderell, repaired, at night, to the house of a Mr. Whitegrave, a Catholic gentleman residing some distance from Boscobel. The King, in relating his escape, used to say that the rustling of Richard's calf-skin breeches was the best guide for him during the dark night's walk. Here they were pursued by the parliamentarian army; and Colonel Lane, at whose house Lord Wilmot had been concealed, being made acquainted with the critical position of Charles, offered to conceal him in his house at Bentley. From there he retired to Bristol, at the house of Mr. Norton, a kinsman of Colonel Lane, in the hope of being able to obtain a passage to the continent, as "William," the servant to Miss Jane Lane (sister of Colonel Lane), but no vessel would leave there for a month. Charles, being thus frustrated in his object, placed himself under the guardianship of Colonel Windham, of Dorsetshire, in whose charge he continued nine days, and then went to Heale, within three miles of Salisbury, where he remained until the necessary arrangements had been made by Lord Wilmot, for his passage from Brighthelmston to France.

Lord Wilmot, after receiving counsel from Dr. Hinchman, afterwards Bishop of Salisbury, tried at Lawrence Hyde's Esq., living at Hinton Dambray, in Hampshire, near the sea, what could be done for a passage. Being unsuccessful there, he repaired to Colonel George Gounter, at Rackton, four miles from Chichester, who promised him every assistance in his power. On Wednesday, the 8th of October, the Colonel rode to Elmsworth (Emsworth), a fishing station two miles from Rackton; but as the boats were all away, the Colonel could do no good there. Colonel Gounter then, accompanied by Lord Wilmot, rode to Langstone, a place by the sea, and attempted in vain to arrange for a passage. Colonel Gounter and Lord Wilmot then received the co-operation of Captain Thomas Gounter, who went to Chichester, but was unsuccessful in his object. The Colonel upon this, conceived the next and best expedient, namely, of treating with a French merchant, a Mr. Francis Mancell, at Ovingdean Grange, whither he hastened, pretending to pay him a visit, and to become well acquainted with him. He was there courteously received, and entertained; and, after a while, he broke the business to Mancell, saying, "I do not only come to visit you; but to request one favour of you. I have two special friends who have been engaged in a duel, and there is mischief done, and I am obliged to get them off if I can. Can you fraught (freight) a bark?" Mr. Mancell said he doubted not he could at Brighthelmston. The Colonel pressed him to go immediately, promising, if the business was effected he would give him £50 for his pains; but it being Stock fair-day there, and his partner out of the way, he could not possibly until the next day. On the 10th October, the merchant went to Brighthelmston to enquire, but the seaman upon whom he could with the greatest certainty have depended, was gone to Chichester, he having bargained for a cargo there; fortunately, however, it touched at Shoreham, about four miles from Brighthelmston. Mr. Mancell, therefore, sent immediately to Shoreham, for the man, and on Saturday the 11th October, an agreement was made that he (the seaman), should have £60 paid him, before he took the parties into the boat. And it was arranged that he was to be in readiness at an hour's warning. In the meantime, Mancell was to stay there, under pretence of freighting his bark, so as to see all things in readiness against the arrival of the Colonel and his two friends. The Colonel then returned to the house of Mr. Hyde, afterwards Chief Justice of the King's Bench, with whom Lord Wilmot was staying, and broke the joyful intelligence to him, that all was in readiness; and it was arranged that Colonel Phillips should go for the King on the following day. This was effected, and the King, on horseback, escorted by Colonel Phillips, rode from Heale to Winchester, where they were met by Lord Wilmot, Colonel Gounter, and Captain Gounter, who accompanied them to Brawde Halfe-penny, a little above Hambledon, where Charles expressed a wish that lodgings should be procured in the neighbourhood, and he was consequently conducted to the house of Colonel Phillips's sister, at the rear of Hambledon; where, after partaking of a hearty supper, Charles retired to rest, being much fatigued by his long ride of 40 miles that day. At the break of day the following morning, the party took their leave of Hambledon, and on coming to Arundel, rode close by the castle, where they were met full butt by Captain Morley, the Governor, but whom they happily escaped, and then passed on by Howton to Bramber. The remaining portion of the journey is found thus fully detailed in a very curious and *recherche* article which, about forty years since came into the possession of the British Museum, and is entitled "The last Act, in the miraculous storie of his Mties. escape; being a true and perfect revelation of his conveyance, through many dangers, to a safe harbour; out of the reach of his tyranical enemies; by Colonel Gunter; of Racton in Sussex; who had the happiness to be instrumental in the business, (as it was taken from his mouth by a person of worth a little before his death.)"—"Being come to Bramber, we found the streets full of soldiers, on both sides the houses; whoe unluckily and unknowne to me were come thither the night before, to guard; but luckily (or rather by a speciall Providence) were just then come from their guard at Bramber bridge, unto the towne* for refreshment. We came upon them unawares, and were seen, before we suspected anything. My Lord Wilmot was ready to turne back, when I stept in and said: 'If we do, wee are undone.' 'He saith well,' saith the King. I went before, hee followed, and soe

* Probably Steyning is here meant.

passed through, without any hinderance. It was then betweene three and fower of the clock in the afternoone. We went on; but had not gone farre, but a new terror pursued us; the same soldiers riding after us as fast as they could. Whereupon the King gave me a hem! I slacked my pase, till they were come upp to me and by that tyme, the soldiers were come, whoe rudely passed by us (beeing in a narrow lane) soe that we could hardly keepe our saddles for them; but passed by without any further hurt; being some 30 or 40 in number. When we were come to Beeding, a little village where I had provided a treatment for the King (one Mr. Bagshall's house) I was earnest that his Matie. should stay there a whyle, till he had viewed the coast: But my Lord Wilmot would by noe meanes, for feare of those soldiers, but carried the King out of the road, I knew not whither, soe we parted; they were they thought safest, I to Brightemston; being agreed they should send to me, when fixed any where, and ready. Being come to the said Brightemston, I found all clear there, and the Inne (the George) free from all strangers att that tyme. Having taken the best roome in the house and bespoken my supper; as I was entertaining myselfe with a glass of wine; the King, not finding accommodation elsewhere to his mind was come to the Inne; then upp comes mine hoast (one Smith by name). 'More guests,' saith he; he brought them into another room, I taking noe notice. It was not long, but drawing towards the King's roome, I heard the King's voice, saying aloud to Lord Wilmot, 'Here, Mr. Barlow, I drinck to you.' 'I know that name' said I to my hoast, there by me; 'I pray enquire, and whether he were not a Major in the King's Army.' Which done, he was found to beo tho man, whome I expected; and presently invited, as was likely, to the fellowship of a glass of wine. From that I proceeded and made a motion to join companie, and because my chamber was largest that they might make use of it. Which was accepted, and soe we became one companie againe. At supper the King was cheereful, not showing the least signe of fear or apprehension of danger; neyther then nor att any tyme during the whole course of this busines. Which is no small wonder, considering that the very thought of his ennemies soe great, and soe many; soe diligent, and soe much interested in his ruine; was enough, as long as he was within their reach, and as it were, in the very middest of them, to have daunted the stoutest courage in the world. As if God had opened his eyes, as he did Elisha's servant, at his master's request, and he had seene a heavenly hoast round about him to guard him : which to us was visible, who therefore, though much encouraged by his undauntedness, and the assurance of soe good and glorious a cause ; yet were not without secret terrors within ourselves, and thought every minute a day, a month, till they should see his sacred person out of their reach. Supper ended, the King stood his back against the fyer, leaning over a chaire. Up comes mine host (upon some jealousie, I guess not any certain knowledge;) but up comes him who called himself Gaius, runs to the King, catcheth his hand and kissing it, said: 'It shall not be said but I have kissed the best man's hand in England.' He had waited at table at supper, where the boateman also sate with us and were then present. Whether he had feare, or heard any thing that could give him any occasion of suspicion, I knowe not. In very deede, the King had a hard taske, soe to carry himself in all things, that he might be in nothing like himselfe : Majesty being so naturall upon him, that even when hee said nothing, did nothing, his very lookes (if a man observed) were enough to betray him. It was admirable to see the King (as though he had not been concerned in these words, which might have soumded in the ears of another man as the sentence of death) turned about in silence, without any alteration of countenance or taking notice of what had been said. About a quarter of an hour after, the King went to his chamber, where I followed him and craved his pardon with earnest protestaation that I was innocent, soe altogether ignorant of the cause how this had hapened. 'Peace, peace, Colonel,' said the King, 'the fellow knowes mee, and I him. He was one (whether or not, I know not; soe the King thought att the tyme) that belonged to the back stairs of my father; I hope he is an honest fellow.' After this I began to treat with the boatman (Tettersfield by name) asking him in what readiness he was. He answered, he could not of that night, because for more security he had brought his vessel into a breake and the tyde had forsaken it: so that it was on ground. It is observable that all the whyle this business had been in agitation to this very time, the wind had been contrarie. The king then opening the wenddowe, tooke notice that the wind was turned, and told the master of the shipp. Whereupon, because of the wind, and a cleere night, I offered £10 more to the man to gett off that night. But that could not be. However, we agreed that he should take in his company that night. But it was a great business that we had in hand; and God would have us to knowe soe, both by the difficulties that offered themselves, and by his helpe he afforded to remove them. When we thought we had agreed, the boatman starts back and saith, 'noe, except I would ensure the barke.' Argue it we did with him, how unresoanable it was, beeing soe well paid, &c., but to no purpose, soe that I yielded att last, and £200 was his valuation, which was agreed upon. But then, as though he had been resolved to frustrate all by unreasonable demands, he required my bond. At which, moved with much indignation, I began to be as resolut as he; saying, among other things, 'there were more boates to bee had, besydes his; if he would not another should,' and made as though I would go to another. In this contest the king happily interposed. 'He saith right,' saith his Matie., 'a gentleman's word, especially before witnesses, is as good as his bond.' At last the man's stomach came downe, and carrie them he would, whatever became of it; and before he would be taken he would run his boate under the water. Soe it was agreed that about tooe in the morning they should be aboard. The boateman in the meanetyme went to provide for necessaries, and I persuaded the king to take some rest. He did, in his cloaths, and my Lord Wilmot with him, till towards tooe in the morning. Then I called them up, showing them how the tyme went by my watch. Horses being ledd by the back way towards the beache, we came to the boat, and found all readie. Soe I took my leave, craving his Maties. pardon if anthing had happened through error, not want of will or loyalty. How willingly I would have waited further, but for my family (being many) which would want mee, and I hoped his Matie. would not, not doubting but in a very little tyme he should be where he would. My only request to his Mtie. was that he would conceal his instruments, wherein their preservation was so much concerned. His Matie. promised noebody should know. I abided there keeping the horses in readiness in case anything unexpected had happened. At 8 o'clock I saw them on sayle, and it was the afternoon before they were out of sight. The wind (O Providence) held very good till the next morning, to ten of the clock brought them to a place of Normandie called Fackham, some three miles from Havre de Grace, 15 Oct. Wenseday. They were no sooner landed but the wind turned, and a violent storme did arise, in soe much that the boateman was forced to cut his cable, lost his anchor to save his boate, for which he required of me £8, and had it. The boate was back againe at Chichester, by Friday, to take his fraught. I was not gone out of the town of Brighthelmston twoe houres, but soldiers came thither to search for a tall man 6 foot and 4 inches high."

By the foregoing it will be seen that Charles never visited, much less slept at Ovingdean Grange, as has been stated by some historical writers, playwrights, and writers of romance.*

The vessel in which Charles escaped, was the "Surprise," the property of Captain Nicholas Tettersell, whose virtues are engraved upon his tomb in the Old Church-yard,—*vide* Chapter XVI. The vessel was a brig which had been detained a few years previously, in the Downs, by a royal squadron, on her way from Newcastle, with a cargo of coals, but was released by a personal order of Charles, then Prince of Wales, whose features were consequently known to Tettersell, notwithstanding the king's attempt to disguise himself. The brig at the time of the engagement with Tettersell, was half laden with coals, and the sailors were in a great measure disengaged from duty. In order, therefore, to collect them without exciting suspicion, he announced that she had broken from her moorings. By this means, having got his crew on board, he signified to them his engagement in a secret expedition, in which their service should not go unrewarded. Matters being thus prudently adjusted, Tettersell went ashore by himself, in order to get a bottle of spirits, and to inform his wife that he should be

* Colonel Phillips went for Charles on Sunday, 12th October; they started on the 13th, and remained at Hambledon the night of the 13th. On the night of the 14th they slept at the George Inn (King's Head) Brighton, from whence they departed at 2 a.m. on the 15th, arriving at Fechamp at 10 p.m. of that day.

absent for a few days. Curiosity urging the good woman to dive into the mystery of so sudden and unreasonable a departure, he was at last constrained by her importunity to reveal to her the nature of the service he had undertaken; and she, with a fortitude and fidelity which reflect a lustre on her memory, earnestly exhorted him to an honourable performance of his engagement with the illustrious fugitive. It is recorded by Baker, in his Chronicles, that in the course of the day, as the king, who still retained his disguise, that of a Puritan, was sitting on the deck, one of the sailors stood close to windward of him smoking his pipe, and on being rebuked by the captain for making so free, retired, muttering, "truly a cat may look at a king," but without being aware how personally apposite the adage was.

After the Restoration, Tettersell, in 1671, in consideration of his loyal services, was appointed by James, Duke of York, (then Lord High Admiral of England,) Captain of the "Royal Escape," as a fifth-rate; and the year ensuing, the king granted the reversion of that sinecure to his son.

The following is the patent for the reversion of the appointment:—

CHARLES R.

Whereas our dear brother, James, Duke of York, Lord High Admiral of England, hath by his orders, dated the 4th of September last past, directed you to cause Captain Nicholas Tetershall to be borne in pay, together with one servant, as captain of our vessel called the Royal Escape; and that he should be allowed pay as captain of a fifth-rate ship, and he and his servant paid with the yard at Deptford; and whereas the said Nicholas Tetershall hath humbly besought us to continue the said allowance unto his son, Nicholas Tetershall, after his decease, in consideration of his faithful and fortunate service performed unto us, we have thought fit to condescend unto that his request, and it is accordingly our will and pleasure that after the decease of the said Nicholas Tetershall, the father, he, the said Nicholas Tetershall, the son, be borne in pay, together with one servant, as captain of our said vessel, the Royal Escape, and that he be allowed pay as captain of a fifth-rate ship, and he and his servant paid with the yard at Deptford, in the same manner as his father now is. Given at our Court at Whitehall, the 29th day of August, 1672, in the four-and-twentieth year of our reign.

By His Majesty's command,
HENRY COVENTRY.

To the Principal Officers and Commissioners
of our Navy now and the time being.

By the following minute in the record book of the House of

Commons, Wednesday, 19th of December, 1660, it will be seen that His Majesty was not unmindful of the services in effecting his escape, that were rendered by Mr. Lane and his family :—

Resolved.—"That as a mark of respect to Mrs. Lane, and in testimony of her services, in being instrumental to the preservation and security of the person of his royal Majesty, there be conferred on the said Mrs. Lane the sum of £1,000, to buy her a jewel, and that the same be, and hereby stands charged on the arrears of the grand excise, and paid to her assigns, in course, after the other sums are satisfied which are charged on the grand excise, by former orders of this Parliament. And the commissioners of excise, for the time being, are hereby impowered and required to satisfy and pay the same accordingly. And this order, together with the acquitance of the said Mrs. Lane, or her assigns, testifying the receipt thereof, shall be to the commissioners of excise a sufficient warrant and discharge."

And letters patent, bearing date, 12th day of July, Anno 1677, were granted by the king, to John Lane of Bentley, in the County of Stafford, that henceforth he and his lawful descendants shall bear in augmentation of their fraternal arms, *three lyons passant guardant, or in a Canton Gu.*

The "Royal Escape" was Tettersell's coal-brig ornamented and enlarged; and shortly after the Restoration, she was moored in the Thames, opposite Whitehall, to receive the veneration of the fickle multitude. "But, some time after," as Dunvan says, "when the increasing guilt of Charles proved to them a bitter restorative from political insanity, she dropped down to Deptford, where she remained in a progressive state of decay, till, in the year 1791, her mouldering remains were broken up for fuel in one of the dock-yards there."

The descendants of Tettersell long enjoyed an annual pension of £100. Sir John Bridger, the grandfather of Sir Henry Shiffner, of Combe Place, was the last of the family who received the pension. A ring which was given to Tettersell by Charles, is in the possession of the Shiffner family.

The name of the Inn, in West street, was, after the return of Charles from exile, changed from the "George" to the "King's Head," and as a memorial of the royal visit, the portrait of his Majesty became the sign of the house. It remained some years fixed on the outside of the premises; but about forty years since, when it was going rapidly to decay, it was taken down by the then landlord, Mr. Eales, and, having received a coat of varnish, was placed in an oak frame and hung up indoors. That, however, like every other memento of the flight of Charles, has some years been a thing of the past, the bedstead with its appurtenances whereon the royal personage slept, the chair whereon he sat, the cooking apparatus of the occasion, and every article connected with the event having long since been purchased at long prices to those persons who set store upon historical relics. On Royal Oak Day, the anniversary of the 29th of May, 1660, commonly called Restoration Day, it is customary for a large bough of oak to adorn the front of the "King's Head."

The only relic in Brighton, in any way connected with the "Merrie Monarch," is Nell Gwynne's looking-glass. This glass is amongst the curiosities in the Brighton Museum, at the Royal Pavilion, and is the property of Sir Charles Dick, of Port Hall, Dyke Road, Brighton. It bears the likeness of Nell Gwynne and King Charles, which are modelled in wax; and also the supporters or crest which Nell assumed, namely, the lion and leopard. The whole is curiously worked in various coloured glass beads, and the figures with the dresses are made to project in very high relief; indeed, they are merely attached to the ground-work. In the upper compartment is Charles in his state dress, and in the bottom one that of Nell Gwynne in her court dress—the pattern of which is very tasteful. On the right is Charles in his hunting dress, and on the left is Nell in her negligée dress. The beads have retained their colours, which are very appropriate to the subject, and must have been a work of considerable time and patience; but whether done by Nell or not, there is no record. Mrs. Jameson says:—"Charles, in spite of every attempt to detach him from her, loved her to the last, and his last thought was for her—'Let not poor Nelly starve!' Burnet, who records this dying speech, is piously scandalized that the King should have thought of such a 'creature' in such a moment; but some will consider it with more mercy, as one among the few traits which redeem the sensual and worthless Charles from utter contempt."

CHAPTER XIX.

PERSECUTIONS FOR CONSCIENCE' SAKE.

During the persecutions for conscience' sake, several inhabitants of Brighton underwent sundry pains and penalties. In 1658, John Pullot,* for speaking to the Priest and people in the Steeple-house, was put prisoner into the Block-house;—Churches or houses having a steeple and a bell, were termed Steeple-houses. The next day Pullot was sent to the County gaol till the Sessions, when he was sentenced to Bridewell for six months' hard labour, and to be whipped. In 1659, Nicholas Beard, for going into the Steeple-house, was much abused, and haulèd out by the hair of his head.

The "Abstract" referred to recites:—"1658.—A meeting being held at the house of William Gold, in Brighthelmston; the professors of that town, coming from their worship, first broke the windows, which work one zealous woman was observed to do very devoutly with her bible; then they flung in much filth on those that were there met, and at length thrusting in upon them, hauled out Joseph Fuce and some others, throwing him very dangerously on the ground, and hauling him and others out of the town, threatened that if he came thither again they would throw him into the sea. After this manner did the people there frequently abuse those who were assembled together; of which abuses Margery Caustock had a large share. Her daughter also, of the same name, going from a meeting was cruelly stoned and wounded in the face, to the endangering her eye; and her blood was spilt to that degree that some of her wicked persecutors boasted that they had killed one Quaker, as they had almost done another, namely, Richard Pratt, by stoning him."

Pratt had previously, in 1656, delivered in a paper to the Bench of Justices, at the Lewes Sessions, representing the cruel usage and stoning of his friends at Brighthelmston, and desiring them to exert their authority for protecting the innocent from such

* An abstract of the Sufferings of the People called Quakers, for the Testimony of a Good Conscience. London: The Bible, George Yard, Lombard Street, 1733.

abuses; when he was by them committed to the House of Correction, and ordered to be whipped there, and kept to hard labour. As the officers were dragging him away to Bridewell, one William Hobbine, seeing him in danger from the pushing of the people, laid hold of him to keep him from falling. This being interpreted an attempt to rescue the prisoner, Hobbine was fined three pounds, and sent to prison for not paying it.

Thus the persecutions of the Quakers continued in all parts of the kingdom, till General Monk having had complaint made to him of the rude disturbances of Meetings by his soldiers, while at Westminster, he, with complete success, issued the following order:

St. James's, March 9, 1659-60.

I do require all officers and soldiers, to forbear to disturb the peaceable meetings of the Quakers, they doing nothing prejudicial to the Parliament of England.

GEORGE MONK.

In consequence of Monk having declared for the Commonwealth, Charles II., who for some years had resided on the continent, after his escape from Brighton, by his advice repaired to Breda. But it being resolved in England to recall him to the throne, he made, on the 14th day of April, 1660, his celebrated Declaration of Breda, whereby he granted a free and general pardon to all offenders against himself and his royal father, and "liberty of conscience, that no man shall be disquieted or called in question for differences of opinion, in matter of religion." His Restoration was the result on the 18th of May following, and on the 29th of the same month, his birthday, he made his public entry into London.

The Act of Uniformity, which was passed in 1662, and was called the St. Bartholomew Act, because it was to take effect on the 24th of August, the feast of that apostle, produced a kind of ecclesiastical revolution, and shewed the invincible determination of the enthusiasts. The date of the Bi-centenary of this Act, is the 24th of August of the present year, 1862. The Act was short, but very stringent, as the annexed extract "XIV. Caroli II., 1662.—

Be it enacted by the King's most excellent Majesty, by the advice and with the consent of the Lords spiritual and temporal, and of the Commons in this present Parliament, that every Parson, Vicar, or other Minister, who now hath any Ecclesiastical Benefice or Preferment within the Realm of England, shall, in the Church, Chapel, or place of public worship, upon some Lord's Day, before the Feast of St. Bartholomew, which shall be in the year of our Lord God, 1662, publicly and solemnly read the morning and evening prayers, according to the said Book of Common Prayer, at the times appointed, and after such reading thereof, shall openly and publicly, before the congregation, declare his unfeigned assent and consent to the use of all things in the said book in these words and no others—I, A. B., declare my unfeigned assent and consent to all and everything contained and prescribed in and by the Book of Common Prayer. And that every such person who shall (without some lawful impediment) neglect or refuse to do the same, shall be deprived of all his spiritual promotion; and the Patron shall present or collate, as if he were dead.

In one day, and by a concerted resolution, 2,000 presbyterian ministers resigned their livings, because they would not conform to the articles of the Act. They were even, some time after, prohibited from coming within five miles of those places where they had exercised their ministry, except on journeys, under pain of six months' imprisonment, and paying a penalty of five pounds. These rigorous proceedings were by no means agreeable to the king, who was solicited by his brother James, to grant a general toleration. Charles, in consequence, proclaimed an indulgence to those whose consciences would not permit them to conform to the established worship; and as Parliament was then prorogued, he gave his royal word, that at the approaching session, he would endeavour to procure a confirmation of that indulgence. On the 18th of February, 1663, therefore, on the assembling of Parliament, Charles endeavoured to fulfil his promise; but the Parliament strongly suspected that he had another and much deeper design in view, his avowed intention being to gratify the Dissenters, but his secret resolution being to support the Catholics, so they determined to defeat him. He in consequence, from a remonstrance which they drew up, issued a proclamation against all Popish Priests and Jesuits.

In 1664, the Parliament, not content with the penalties contained in the Act of Uniformity, passed the notorious Conventicle Act, whereby it was enacted that if any one should repair to Conventicles,—the name they gave to the meeting-houses of all Dissenters,—he should be fined £5 for the first offence, or suffer three months' imprisonment; for the second offence £10, or six months' imprisonment; but for the third offence, after being convicted by a jury of his peers or fellows, he was to be transported to some foreign plantation, or pay the penalty of £100.

In 1665, upon the assembling of the Parliament at Oxford, a Bill was brought before that august body, that no dissenting teacher, who refused to take the oath of non-resistance, should, except upon the road, come within five miles of any corporation, or of any place where he had discharged the offices of a minister, after the Act of Oblivion, as it was called, under the penalty of £50. The Commons rejected the Bill, which imposed the oath of non-resistance on the whole nation.* The Conventicle Act was passed in 1670. By it every member of a Conventicle, or assembly of Non-Conformists, consisting of more than five persons, exclusive of the family where it was held, was liable to a fine.

One of the most virulent officials in persecuting the Non-Conformists, was Captain Tettersell, who effected the escape of the King. On Sunday, the 29th of May, 1670, while exercising his authority as High Constable of Brighton, he, with the zeal of a bigot, and the malign industry of a ministerial spy, discovered in the town a house in which a few Dissenters had privately met: and the door having been barred against so unfriendly an intruder, he surrounded the premises with his creatures, until a warrant for breaking the door open arrived from Sir Thomas Nutt, of Lewes. When the warrant arrived, the door was opened upon the demand of the Constable; but no minister could be found; nor were the company engaged in any religious ceremony. It was, however, asserted by some of the Constable's assistants, that they had heard from within a voice in the elevated tone of prayer or instruction, and for this imputed offence, the whole party was summoned before the said Sir Thomas Nutt, and other Justices at Lewes. But there being no proof to justify conviction under the Conventicle Act, the bench insidiously counselled the objects of their persecution to confess the whole, and promised they would permit them to set their own fines. Finding them averse to self-accusation, where they were conscious of no crime, these upright dispensers of justice, even on the vague conjecture of the spies, fined to the full penalty of the Statute, not

* The Corporation and Test Act which prohibited a Non-Conformist taking any Civil or Military office, was repealed May 8th, 1828.

only such as were found in the house, but also a man who had been seen coming out some time before the said spies approached it. William Beard, the master of the house, having been fined £20, Captain Tettersell broke open his malthouse, and took thereout sixty-five bushel sacks of malt, which he sold to one of his partisans for twelve shillings a quarter.* Sir Thomas Nutt was a most malign retailer of penal law, and he prevailed on three other justices to co-operate with him in order to sanction the rancour of persecution. Other Constables besides Tettersell, also, were the too willing harpies of oppression under the mask of law.

Fastened in the back cover of Deryk Carver's bible (the particulars of which are in Chapter XVII.) is a permission signed by Lord Arlington, for holding a Conventicle. The mark where the royal seal had been affixed, yet remains. The following is a correct copy of the license :—

(The Regal Seal.) CHARLES R.

CHARLES, by the Grace of God, King of England, Scotland, France, and Ireland, Defender of the Faith, &c. To all Mayors, Bayliffs, Constables, and other Our Officers and Ministers, Civil and Military, whom it may concern, Greeting. In pursuance of Our Declaration of the 15th of March, 1671-2. We have allowed, and we do hereby allow of a Room or Rooms in the house of Elizabeth Hopdon, widd. of Gouldhurst in Kent, to be a place for the Use of such as do not conform to the Church of England, who are of the Perswasion commonly called presbyterian to meet and assemble in, in order to their publick Worship and Devotion. And all and Singular Our Officers and Ministers, Ecclesiastical, Civil, and Military, whom it may concern, are to take due notice hereof: And they and every of them, are hereby strictly charged and required to hinder any tumult or disturbance, and to protect them in their Said Meetings and Assemblies. Given at Our Court at Whitehall, the 9th day of December, in the 24th year of Our Reign, 1672.

By His Majesties Command,
ARLINGTON.

Wi dd. Hopdons house.

The Toleration Act, 1 Wm. and Mary, 1. c. 18, which exempted Dissenters from the penalties of certain laws, was confirmed by statue 10 Anne, c. 2.

---

* Crosby's History of the English Baptists.

Chapter XX.

THE BIRDS AND THEIR HAUNTS IN THE NEIGHBOURHOOD OF BRIGHTON.

The Sussex coast is a favourite locality for the greater portion of our British Birds, more particularly the migratory species. The high headlands to the eastward seem to be a great attraction to them by day, and, as a great many take nocturnal flight, the glare of light at night sent high into the vault of the heavens from the gas lamps in the town of Brighton, attracts a great number to this neighbourhood, and many rare specimens have been obtained. The migration of birds is a subject of considerable interest in their natural history to the Ornithologist. It was formerly supposed that many birds, which now are known for a certainty to migrate, retired to some secure retreat, and remained dormant through the winter. So general was this impression that in some districts of England seven of the migratory birds obtained the names of the seven sleepers. The Cuckoo was one of these; and the Swallows were supposed to lie up in a torpid state during the winter. Most birds migrate, and those which cross the seas are called "Birds of Passage." A great number of our birds remove as the cold weather sets in, from the inland districts towards the sea shores, which afford them a better supply of food.

In the Spring of the year—March and April—we have the greatest arrival of our summer visitors, and it is astonishing with what order and punctuality they arrive and depart. They are the unerring messengers of Spring; and, true to Nature's laws, arrive generally within a few days of the time pointed out by the scientific observations of the Ornithologist.

The poets, from Chaucer downwards, have largely introduced birds into their works. Chaucer, in his "Assembly of Fowles," says—

> On every bough the birdis herd I syng,
> With voice of Angell in their harmonie.

Milton, in praising the nightingale, says—

> As the wakeful bird
> Sings darkling, and in shadiest covert hid,
> Tunes her nocturnal note.

Shakspear writes—

> The poor wren,
> The most diminutive of birds, will fight;—
> Her young ones in her nest—against the owl.

Byron, in his "Bride of Abydos," says—

> There sings a bird unseen, but not remote,
> Invisible his airy wings,—
> But soft as harp, that Houri strings
> His long entrancing note.

Lord Erskine, in beautiful words, says—

> They whisper truths in reason's ear,
> If human pride would stoop to hear.

All our poets, from the greatest to the least, from the first to the last, acknowledge by their writings how much they owe to the productions of Nature, both animate and inanimate.

The Golden Eagle—*Falco chrysaetos*—is mentioned by Yarrell, in his "History of British Birds," as having been shot near Bexhill, but none of our late writers on Ornithology have been able to authenticate the fact. We have not been honoured with a visit from his imperial majesty the king of birds. Several specimens of the White-tailed Eagle—*Falco albicilla,*—have been shot in the immediate neighbourhood, and the parties have always fancied they have been lucky enough to obtain the true Golden Eagle. A gentleman from Brighton, being at Shoreham some years ago, just after the landlord of the Dolphin Inn had shot what he considered was the Golden Eagle, somewhat surprised the imagined lucky shot by assuring him that it showed too much of its legs, and that it was only an immature specimen of the Sea Eagle; and so it turned out. Several others are likewise recorded as having been shot in this neighbourhood.

The Osprey, or Fishing Hawk—*Falco haliætus,*—has of late years been a rare visitant in this vicinity, though several are authenticated as having been shot here formerly. They are occasional visitors along our shores, but seldom go far inland for their prey, as they are true fishermen, living entirely upon the fruits of their labour; and they are very formidable, and powerfully winged birds, darting down from a great height, like an arrow from a bow, upon their prey with unerring certainty. In North

America they are welcomed in the Spring by the fishermen, as the happy omen of the approach of herring, shad, &c., which periodically arrive there on the coast, in prodigious shoals.

Eastward of Brighton, about fourteen miles, is Beachy Head, the home, from time immemorial, of a pair of Peregrine Falcons—*Falco peregrinus*; another pair is generally to be found in the high cliffs near Seaford. This noble bird was the pride of our ancestors in their sporting diversions, and was considered very valuable when possessed of the particular qualities most in request. Yarrell, in his "History of British Birds," mentions that in the reign of James I. Sir Thomas Monson is said to have given one thousand pounds for a cast (a couple) of these hawks. The high perpendicular cliffs at Beachy Head have always been a favourite breeding place for the Peregrines, and where their young are generally every year taken by a man whose companions let him over the cliff by means of a derrick. The derrick is simply a pole with a sheave-wheel at one end of it, for the rope to pass over, and is run about two feet over the edge of the cliff, and at the other end it has a hole, through which an iron bar is passed and driven firmly into the ground to keep it steady. By this contrivance the man is lowered to the required spot, and hauled up again in safety, and though the process has been going on for many years, no instance is recorded of any accident having occurred. By this means also a great many of the eggs of the Willock—*Uria troili*—and Razor bill—*Alca torda*,—are taken; these birds breed here in great numbers every year. The derrick is a familiar machine to the smuggler, as it enables him to get his tubs very expeditiously from the bottom to the top of the cliff, which is done by several men on the beach taking hold of the end of the rope, and running straight out with it, and then fastening on the tubs in clusters. Sometimes they are brought up in this way four or five hundred feet. These cliffs are likewise the resort and breeding places of a great many Jackdaws—*Corvus monedula*.

Sixty years ago the Red Legged Crow, or Cornish Chough—*Pyrrhocorax graculus*—was common here, though now the species is nearly or quite extinct all along our southern shores. A man, now between sixty and seventy years of age, who has been in the constant habit of going nearly all his life, to Beachy Head to catch prawns for a livelihood, says that he remembers the Red-billed Daw perfectly well, and that the last he saw there, was fifty-three or fifty-four years ago, and that he recollects to this day the precise spot where he saw them. There were seven in company, and he describes their flight to be a succession of jerks, or in the manner of a Dishwasher, which is very peculiar. It was ninety years ago that Gilbert White, of Selborne, recorded the fact of their abounding at Beachy Head and all along the cliffs of the Sussex Coast.

A little to the westward of the highest part of the cliffs, upon a projecting portion, called Beltout, stands Beachy Head lighthouse, a very handsome and solid structure, built entirely of granite. It is supposed that it will last till the solid chalk cliff washes away from under it. It stands about thirty yards from the edge of the perpendicular cliff, which is here about one hundred and forty yards high, with the sea at highwater washing its base. It has a revolving light of three sides, with ten argand lamps in each with highly polished reflectors, kept in motion by machinery wound up like a clock, two or three times in a night. It is managed by two light-keepers, whose duty is to keep the lamps burning and revolving from sunset to sunrise, all the year round. It has no doubt been the means of saving numerous vessels from being lost upon that once very dangerous part of the Sussex coast.

At the foot of the cliff, nearly under the Lighthouse, is a cave called "Darby's Hole," said to have been cut out more than a hundred years ago, by a clergyman of that name living at East Dean, a little village about a mile-and-a-half off, for the philanthropic purpose of saving the lives of shipwrecked sailors; and it is handed down as a fact that he had the pleasure at one time of saving nearly a dozen poor men from a watery grave. Formerly, hardly a winter passed without three or four wrecks occurring, which proved a great assistance to the poor villagers of East Dean. A laughable story is told of a wreck happening a great many years ago, on a Sunday morning whilst most of the villagers were in church, when a man wishing to inform some of his friends there of the circumstance, quietly slipped in for that purpose, and it was soon whispered from one to another that there was "a wreck," and they so kept going out one after the other that the church got considerably thinned. The clergyman seeing that he was likely to be left nearly alone, and suspecting the cause, he in a loud audible voice said, "If there is a wreck, say so, and let's all start fair."—The story goes that the news of the wreck was rather a hoax than otherwise, as the fact of "a four-mast vessel laden with wool and tallow ashore," proved to be nothing other than the carcase of a South-down sheep washed up by the tide.

The lighthouse has a very pleasing effect when viewed by night from the sea, and on a fine summer's evening, parties frequently make excursions from Eastbourne and other places to visit it. Being situate on the South Downs the walk to it is most delightful, the turf being so very fine, that it may be compared to a Turkey carpet, and in July and August the air is highly fragrant with wild aromatic herbs, thyme, &c. At the same time of the year great quantities of those delicious birds, Wheatears—*Sylvia œnanthe,*—arrive, and are scattered over the extensive Downs in vast numbers, but not in flocks, as they are almost invariably seen singly. It is a great perquisite to the shepherds to catch them, which they do by cutting out lines of traps in the turf in the form of a T, and inverting the turf over a couple of horse-hair nooses. Pennant states, that in his time the numbers snared about Eastbourne amounted annually to about one thousand eight hundred and forty dozen. They are called the English Ortolan, from their being so fat and plump and of such a delicious flavour. They are a great delicacy potted. They are, however, gradually lessening in numbers, year after year, so that it hardly pays the shepherds now, for their time and trouble to get their traps ready.

Along the whole range of the South Downs the Wheatear has its haunts, especially about the vicinity of the Devil's Dyke, which is a place of general rendezvous for sportsmen and pleasure-seekers. It was formerly known as the Poor Man's Wall, and even now, in its deep trenches, exhibits the form and extent of a Roman encampment.

About five-and-forty years ago, in consequence of the large extent of company that frequented the spot in summer-time, to view the vast expanse of country which the site commands, Mr. Sharp, a confectioner, then carrying on his business in North Street, on the spot now occupied by the premises of Mr. Abrahams, outfitter, conceived the idea of establishing a place for refreshment near the summit of the hill, and for that purpose hired a piece of ground north of the high vallum which runs westward from the top of the Dyke to the brow of the hill. Thither he conveyed a wooden house that had been used as a bacon shop by a man named Smith. It formerly stood upon wooden wheels opposite the shop of Mr. Hyam Lewis, silversmith, in Ship Street Lane, now the upper end of Ship Street; but it at present forms a dwelling place, under the hill, by the turnpike road to Fulking, at the base of the Devil's Punch Bowl, close by the village of Poynings.

The person who first superintended the Dyke establishment was Mr. Russell, who was succeeded by Mr. Thomas Sturt. His successor was Mr. Thomas King, familiarly then and now known as "Tommy King," whose refreshing beverages and exhilirating fiddling gave him a far and near notoriety. The premises were only occupied and opened during the Summer season, from May to October; and although stabling and other accommodation were constructed, in a few years the public requirements induced the erection of the present building, the Dyke House, by Mr. Hardwick, and it has successively passed from King to Mr. Edwards, of Horsham, the tenant who obtained the spirit license; Mr. Ade, of Huntingdon; Mr. William Cooper, of Brighton; Mr. Peter Barkshire, now of Patcham; to its present occupier, Mr. William Thacker, who has been landlord of the house, and tenant of the farm attached twenty-seven years, during which period he has received the royal patronage of William IV. and Her present Majesty and the late Prince Consort. The house has also been the resort of many illustrious foreign visitors, amongst whom may be named Prince Metternich and Count Nesselrode.

The most notorious character who took up his abode here, was Azimullah Khan, the great promoter of the Mutiny in India. He was a resident in Brighton during the Spring and Summer of 1846; but towards the latter end of the Autumn of that year, by the alleged advice of his physician, he, for three weeks, had apartments at the Dyke House; and during that time he was constantly receiving and sending off Indian overland messengers with enormous despatches, without doubt having reference to that shocking revolt which will for ever remain an odious blot upon the history of our East Indian dominions. Azimullah was the Prime Minister of the arch fiend, Nana Sahib; and though it might be saying too much in declaring that the plan of the insurrection was decided upon at the Dyke House, there is little doubt that the first copy of the proclamation was prepared there. Lieutenant Delafosse, one of the few survivors of the Cawnpore massacre, on his return to England visited the Dyke, and there assured Mr Thacker that he saw Azimullah on the river bank at Cawnpore, in the company of Nana Sahib, waving his sword when the guns were discharging their murderous balls into the boats which contained the defenceless victims.

The steep sides of the Dyke have been the scenes of numerous accidents, from persons having the temerity to run down them. Some daring feats of riding and driving have also been exhibited here. The most memorable and daring act was that of Tom Poole, who, for the wager of a champagne dinner for twelve, drove a tandem down the most abrupt part. It was most cleverly accomplished, without the least accident; but that he might not be disappointed in participating in the wagered repast,—in the event of the loss of life or limb in the performance of the exploit,—he insisted upon having the dinner before he undertook his task. Many other dare-devil tricks have been attempted here; and perhaps the most remarkable is that related in what is familiarly known as the

LEGEND OF THE DEVIL'S DYKE.

"Once upon a time, at the period of yore, in the days of mistletoe and harvest-homing, when our country merited the title of 'merrie England,' there was to be found on the edge of the South Downs, opposite the pleasant little village of Poynings, in Sussex, a humble hostel, or village Inn, yclept 'The Jolly Shepherd,' kept by one Dame Margery, who, in her younger days, had followed the camp, but had long since retired upon her reputation as a trooper's widow. The accommodations of the 'Jolly Shepherd' would be held in slight repute in modern days, but in the time of which we are speaking they were reckoned all-sufficient, although consisting chiefly of a warm seat by a cheerful fire, fresh eggs and bacon, and good honest home-brewed ale; and accordingly some half-dozen rustic customers were seated round the widow's hearth, to escape the cutting blast of the Downs without, and commemorate the eve of Holy Saint John, within. Suddenly the song and the tale of the party were interrupted by a most mysterious knocking at the door, and a shrill, querulous voice demanding instant admittance. The active old hostess hastened to obey, but made a kind of a jump, step, and hop backward, on beholding the unusual appearance of the new arrival, exclaiming, 'Lord preserve us! what is it?' 'A gentleman from below,' replied a little, decrepid, wizened old man,

> Whose coat was red, whose breeches were blue,
> With a little hole where a tail came through.

He glided into the room and crept along by the wall, with the most infernal ceremony and politeness, to the inner recess of the chimney corner, without having once shown his back to his hostess or any of the good company there assembled, and quickly finding himself comfortably seated, the queer little old gentleman produced a blackened 'Dudeen' and a velvet tobacco pouch, but somehow or other the clouds of smoke he emitted were, so pervaded with the smell of brimstone and bitumen, that the rest of the guests did nothing but sneeze and knock their heads together in a regular hob-and-nob fashion. To stop this nuisance, the worthy hostess placed before her mysterious guest a frizzing hot dish of eggs and bacon, but upon tasting the same, he expressed his dissatisfaction, declaring it was as cold as charity, and demanding 'more pepper.' He, upon receiving it, emptied the contents of the pepper-box over the dish, and having thus formed a regular *pate au diable,* he swallowed it down with considerable apparent relish. With the ale it was pretty much the same; the hostess first mulled it, but her refractory guest declared it was as cold as ice; then she boiled it with a vast quantity of ginger, but with little better success, and it could only be brought to suit his fiery palate by being stirred up, when boiling, with a red hot poker. These strange proceedings of the mysterious visitor mightily astonished the rest of the guests, their faces becoming much elongated; and after staring at each other in stupified bewilderment, they stealthily took to their homes, exclaiming, 'Did you ever see the Devil?' The whole of the company had departed long ere the cause of their uneasiness left his chimney corner and glided to his sleeping apartment, which he managed to do in the same mysterious manner as he had entered the house, never once removing his back from the wall. About three o'clock in the morning, our worthy hostess of 'The Jolly Shepherd' was awakened from her balmy slumbers, by a strange thumping, bumping kind of noise just under her window, seeming to resemble the hubbub made by a shoal of whales or other such lumbering monsters, who had quitted the ocean deep, and taken to wallowing and gambolling along the Downs by way of pastime. The trooper's widow possessed a bold heart, and, added thereto, she had a woman's curiosity, which induced her to creep out of bed, and cautiously to take a peep at what was going on. She was amazed? She did not behold half a dozen Leviathans having a game at leap-frog, nor the like number of griffins playing at snap-dragon. No, no, nothing of that sort; but the queer little old gentleman aforesaid, mounted on a pair of lofty stilts, with a huge spade in his hand, was digging away at the edge of the ancient Roman encampment, like the very 'old-un,' shovelling out the chalk and flint stones by waggon loads, and his tail whisking about like a serpent in fits. The bold hostess did not hail him to stop his digging. Not she, good honest soul, as she was desirous of seeing a little clearer what he was about, before giving any alarm; so she quickly struck a light, and lest the candle should alarm her ancient guest, she caught up something to put before it, and this something fortunately happened to be a sieve. Suddenly the old gentleman ceased working, looked up at the window, and when he saw the candle behind the seive, surmounted by the old woman's night cap, he exclaimed 'Oh! Beelzebub, the rising sun,' and folding his stilts across to form a spindle, he ducked his head forward and rolling himself into a ball like a hedgehog, he went bounding along the Downs with fearful rapidity. The Right Rev. Rector of Poynings had been to a jolly christening, had made a wet night of it, and was endeavouring to navigate his road homewards, when he saw a sort of galvanized harlequin whirling and tumbling along straight towards him. The Rev. Rector stopped short; when, just on passing, a sharp pointed sting was protruded from the rolling mass; and having slightly touched his Reverence's great toe, the whole ball exhaled, evaporated and vanished—*exit in fumo*. The parish duties of Poynings were performed by the Curate for the next three months; the doctor said his Reverence was laid up with the gout, but the Rector himself maintained it was the Devil. The question has ever since been, what could induce this queer old gentleman to set to work and dig away in such an outlandish fashion? Some old gossips say that his evil intention was to let in the salt sea, and flood all this most beautiful valley of pleasant Sussex. Be that as it may, one fact is worth noting, that the hostelry of 'The Jolly Shepherd,' from that period ceased its existence, and never, in the village of Poynings, since that night, when his Satanic Majesty was foiled, has a license been held by any person *again* to 'sell spirits.'"

The largest attendance of visitors to the Dyke, is during the months of August and September, when, frequently, as many as a hundred carriages a-day arrive with parties, either to view the magnificent expanse of scenery which the spot commands, or on pic-nic excursions, as the establishment has accommodation for many sets of visitors at the same time. The predilection which the English have for displaying their wit in snatches of their poetic genius, has, on the walls of the rooms, the looking-glasses, and the panes of glass in the windows, extensive scope, and signatures innumerable crowd every available spot.

> O! foul attempt to give a deathless lot
> To names ignoble, born to be forgot,
> In vain recorded.

The house being erected in so exposed and elevated a situation, one of the highest of the South-Down range, damage by gales and storms is very frequent. From the loneliness of its position, too, burglars have made various attempts to obtain spoil, but the reception they have always met with has rendered their expeditions a trouble rather than a profit. The spot was especially chosen by the late Duke of St. Albans for his hawking excursions, as it afforded an extensive range of sight to the numerous company of nobility and gentry, who attended upon such occasions to witness that old English pastime. The Brighton Harriers, at least once a week during the season, throw off here, and other packs make it their place of meeting.

But to return to the more immediate subject of this Chapter, the feathered tribe, from which there has been a slight digression, for the record of facts that form an important link in the chain of local history :

The Buzzard—*Falco buteo,*—is another of our indigenous birds, which has nearly disappeared from this district, and what was many years ago called the Common Buzzard is now very rare. They were formerly frequently met with among the furze near the edge of the cliffs, where they were constantly at war with the Jackdaws.

The Black Redstart—*Sylvia tithys,*—is considered rare in this country; but Brighton has been fortunate in affording several examples of this handsome and graceful bird, which is a winter visitor.

The Common Redstart—*Sylvia phœnicurus,*—unlike his *confrere,* is a summer visitor, generally arriving about the second week in April. Their migration seems to be gregarious, as they are to be met with in flocks of ten or a dozen, close by the sea shore, a little to the westward of Brighton, where they have apparently just arrived. In a day or two, they distribute themselves over the country, and are hardly ever seen again, but singly, or at most in pairs. This bird has several dark red feathers on the rump, and the country people call it the Fire Tail.

The Grasshopper Warbler—*Sylvia locustella,* is a very shy bird, and consequently is very rarely seen. It is a great ventriloquist, and its note is exactly like the grasshopper, (hence its name), only very much louder, and so very peculiar, that a person may be within a yard or two of the bird, and yet be unable to define the exact spot. It is not a scarce bird, and several nests of it have been found at the Holm-bush, and almost any fine evening in June it may be heard there. Its haunts are at the edges of large woods, in low scrubby bushes.

The Sedge Warbler—*Sylvia phragmitis,*—may be found in the

Summer months in the marshes that run up from Shoreham to Beeding. It is one of our night singing birds.

The Reed Wren or Reed Warbler—*Sylvia arundinacea,*—is found in precisely the same locality as the last, and where, during the Summer months, several of their extraordinary nests have been found. They generally prefer the ditches where the reeds grow the thickest. In making their nest, which is very deep, they bring three or four stout reeds together with their materials, near the water, and it is so beautifully and scientifically constructed, that in case of floods, the nest will rise up the stems. Any lover of Natural History, if he is not aware of the fact, or seen their nests, would be delighted with the beautiful provision which Nature here carries out.

The Nightingale—*Sylvia luscinia,*—is the most musical, most melancholy of birds, the poet's bird,—*par excellence.* On Poynings Common, through May, they may be heard in the greatest perfection, where they tune their melodious nocturnal love song through the livelong night. They generally arrive about the second week in April.

The Dartford Warbler—*Sylvia provincialis,*—is said by most writers on British birds, to be extremely rare, but on the Downs, two or three miles to the north-east of Newhaven, they have been seen among the furze. They have a propensity for keeping near the ground in the high furze, and a great dislike to exhibit themselves. They are local, and tolerably abundant in their *habitat.*

There are five species of Wagtail that are visitors in the neighbourhood of Brighton. The White Wagtail—*Motacilla alba,*—so nearly resembles the common Pied Wagtail—*Motacilla yarrellii,*—that to a common observer there appears scarcely any difference. The Gray Wagtail—*Motacilla boarula,*—and the Grayheaded Wagtail — *Motacilla flava,* — are rare birds to this country; but both have been shot in this locality. The Yellow or Rays Wagtail—*Motacilla campestris,*—is common in the Spring of the year, and may be found by the edges of running streams. To the eastward of Brighton the whole family of the Wagtails are called Dishwashers.

Sky Larks—*Alauda arvensis,*—in October, come in large flights from the east. It is a favourite amusement with the Cockney sportsmen of Brighton, on a nice sunshiny morning, to go just outside the town, with what is called a lark glass, which is simply a piece of wood about a foot long, planed like the ridge of a house, having small pieces of looking glass let in the sides, and a wooden pin fitted in a socket or stump which is firmly driven in the ground, and is set spinning backwards and forwards by a string. By this means the poor birds are decoyed down; and they seem fascinated by the glitter of the glass, as they keep hovering within a few feet of it, and are not easily driven away; consequently they present easy marks for the shooter. A dozen or more will hover over the glass at one time, and a tolerable marksman will sometimes kill three or four dozen of a morning. The sport is generally over by half-past nine or ten o'clock. In the winter,—generally at the first fall of snow,—immense flights of larks come coasting along, driven apparently from the cold northern climes, towards the more genial west. The numbers that pass over Brighton are incredible, they sometimes extend to millions a-day, as from early light to dusk there is a continued stream, at least a quarter of a mile wide, passing along. On the road to Rottingdean is where the greatest flights may be observed. They are apparently continental visitors, coming across the German Ocean in a north-east direction. The flight seldom lasts more than two or three days.

The Ortolan Bunting—*Emberiza hortulana,*—has twice been obtained in and near Brighton; but it is a very rare bird in this country.

The Hoopoe—*Upupa epops,*—the most beautiful of all our British birds, is a frequent visitor in the Spring of the year to this part of the country. In May, 1845, Mr Swaysland, Naturalist, Queen's Road, had to preserve and mount six Hoopoes, which were killed within a few miles of Brighton.

The Great Norfolk Plover, or Stone Curlew — *Œdicnemus crepitans,*—is becoming very scarce now, though formerly these birds were tolerably abundant. Their haunts were generally to be found among the large open stony fallows of our downs. They are like all the family of Charadriidæ, very shy birds.

The Golden Plover—*Charadrius pluvialis,*—the Ringed Dotterell

—*Charadrius morinellus,*—the Grey Plover—*Vanellus melanogaster,*—the Turnstone—*Strepsilas interpres,*—the Sanderling—*Calidris arenaria,*—the Oystercatcher—*Hæmatopus ostralegus,*—are all, every year, to be met with in the little bays and inlets, on the beach between Brighton and Shoreham Harbour; as are also the Curlew—*Numenius arquata,*—the Whimbrel—*Numenius phæopus,*—the Redhawk—*Totanus calidris,*—the Sandpiper—*Totanus hypoleucos,*—the Greenhawk—*Totanus glottis,*—the Blackheaded Godwit—*Limosa melanura.* The Ruff—*Machetes pugnax,*—is also found in the above locality, as well as several other species of the Waders. The Curlew Sandpiper—*Tringa subarquata,*—and the Little Stint—*Tringa minuta,*—have both been killed in the same place, though their visits are rare and far between.

The Gray Phalarope—*Phalaropus platyrhynchus,*—has occasionally been met with, generally in flocks of from ten to fifteen, and upwards. They are nearly or quite the smallest web-footed birds that are known; their homes are in the cold northern climes, and they are so unacquainted with man and his terrible engines of destruction, that they are apparently tame. Two gentlemen once fell in with a flock, in Shoreham Harbour, and killed seventeen, being nearly or quite all there were. They described them as miniature ducks swimming swiftly about on the still water, and did not attempt to escape; consequently they were all shot down.

In very severe winters, immense flocks of Wild Fowl fly near the shore, from east to west, and a great many specimens of the Goose and Duck tribe are obtained, some of them very rare to this county. The Egyptian Goose—*Anser ægyptiacus,*—was shot a few miles from Brighton, two years ago. So rare is this beautiful bird considered, that there is still a doubt amongst Ornithologists that the examples which have been met with, have only strayed from gentlemen's parks, &c. They have generally been seen and shot in the severest winters, and are apparently a sort of "frozen-out gardeners."

During the winter of 1860, owing to its severity, several specimens of the Hooper—*Cygnus musicus,*—and Bewick's Swan—*Cygnus minor,*—were shot in this neighbourhood. A great many Swans were likewise observed flying a little distance out at sea.

The Great Northern Diver—*Colymbus glacialis*—is occasionally met with, as also the Black and Red Throated Diver—*Colymbus arcticus*,—and *Colymbus septentrionalis.*

There are several species of Terns to be met with in this locality. The Gullbilled Tern—*Sterna angelica*,—and the Lesser Tern—*Sterna minuta*,—are both rare, particularly the former, and have been shot near Shoreham. A few examples of the rare Little Gull—*Larus minutus*,—have been shot near Brighton; likewise the Ivory Gull—*Larus eburneus*,—both very rare. Most of the common Gulls are abundant, being near their breeding places.

Several specimens of The Forktailed Petrel—*Thalassidroma Leachii*,—and of the Storm Petrel or Mother Carey's Chicken—*Thalassidroma pelagica*,—have been obtained generally in the severest gales, about the time of the Vernal and Autumnal equinoxes, when they have frequently been found blown ashore, by stress of weather; and instances have occurred here, when they have been picked up in areas of houses near the sea, generally in a most exhausted state.

The House Sparrow,—*Fringilla domestica*,—is a well-known young gentleman, that may be seen almost any day, at every man's door, whether poor or rich, in town or in country. He is the most familiar and domesticated wild bird in England. In town he puts on his black, dirty, scavenger's dress, which completely disguises him,—his appearance being so different from his *confreres* in the country. His destructiveness among the newly sown seeds in the garden, and in the ripe standing wheat, is proverbial;—but then, in the consumption of grubs and caterpillars, he is eminently serviceable, which greatly compensates for the harm he may do in the garden or in the field.

The Rook—*Corvus frugilegus*,—during the latter part of the Winter, the whole of the Spring, and the former part of the Summer, takes up his abode in the elm trees of the Pavilion Grounds, which form a breeding colony in immediate connexion with the Rookery at Stanmer Park. About Christmas the Rooks arrive to reconnoitre, and in February they commence building their nests, much to the entertainment of persons whose business or pleasure takes them by way of the New Road. For some few years previous to the re-building of Union Street Chapel, in 1825, a pair of Rooks annually took up their abode in a large elm tree which stood in the small burial-ground of that place of worship. The Jackdaw—*Corvus monedula,*—and the Starling—*Sturnus vulgaris,*—in various parts of the town are annual visitors, year after year occupying the same blank chimneys or neglected gables.

All Naturalists attached to the scientific expeditions for the exploration of the Arctic regions, speak of the myriads of water fowl met with, in those immense reservoirs of snow and ice, the accumulation of ages, where, in the midst of plenty, they rear their young, unmolested by man. There, amongst lagoons, and bays, and swamps, and lakes, and where an impenetrable barrier is firmly fixed to the prying eye of man, they find an asylum to propagate their different orders, and genus, and species, surrounded by a profusion of food; and, at the end of the long Summer day of weeks of unsetting sun, with instinctive knowledge they gather together their separate families, in innumerable flocks, and proceed southward, to replenish the warmer regions of the globe, and to furnish man with some of the luxuries of life.

Brighton and its surrounding locality, including Lewes, have obtained considerable repute amongst entomologists for producing a great many rare insects, owing, no doubt, to there being several persevering and good collectors in the district.

There are only sixty-four indigenous Butterflies in England,—certainly very few when compared with the number of species found in Europe. Of those sixty-four, Brighton and its neighbourhood contribute forty-eight, and of Moths,—of which there are upwards of two thousand found in England,—nearly the same proportion. It is a curious fact in Natural History, that some families, which years ago were rare in England, have now become common; and, others which were frequently met with, are very rare; some species have disappeared altogether, while new ones,—owing to the great addition and perseverance of collectors,—are every year discovered and added to the lists.

The Holmbush,—about eight miles from Brighton, and the commencement of the Weald of Sussex,—has hitherto been the great emporium for moths, and a good many butterflies, particularly the *fritillaries*, whose resort is in and near the large woods there.

A few years ago, the Wood White,—*Leucophasia sinapis*,—in June could be found there in abundance. Now the species is rarely seen; but, being a denizen of the interior of the woods, and the woods all about there being strictly *tabooed*, the collector has not the opportunity to get them he formerly had.

The Green-veined White,—*Pieris napi*,—the pretty little Orange Tip,—*Anthocharis cardamines*,—and the Brimstone Butterfly,—*Gonepteryx rhamni*,—are common in that locality; but for the Clouded Yellows,—genus, *Colias*,—Brighton must be closer approached in the clover fields, about August. They are of a rich golden colour, banded with black; and there is a variety called *Helice*, which are considered a prize to any entomologist. *The* great prize, the Queen of Spain,—*Argynnis lathonia*,—*has* been taken in a garden at Kemp Town; but like "Angels' visits," they are very "few and far between." The gorgeous Large Copper,—*Polyommatus hippothoe*,—whose wings, edged with black, shine like burnished gold, and cast into shade any colour which the device of man can create,—was once plentiful in two counties of England, Cambridgeshire and Huntingdonshire; but it is now considered by our best entomologists extinct in this country.

The Purple Emperor,—*Apatura iris*,—may be seen in all his glory on a hot Summer's day, the first week in August, in the above locality, soaring round the high oaks, in all imaginable grandeur. He is rightly termed Emperor, as no other butterfly dares to invade his imperial aerial realms. His magnificent purple wings defy the highest skill of the artist to imitate. These simple, beautiful butterflies whisper in reason's ear, truths, which, alas! humble the pride of man. There is the Painted Lady,—*Vanessa Cardui*,—but she will not do for the present fashionable generation, as she does not wear crinoline, and her food is of the most vulgar description,—the common thistle, from which she derives her specific name.

The family of the Argus Butterflies,—the Hair Streaks,—genus *Thecla*,—are of five distinct species, three of which are obtained near Brighton. Their haunts are likewise amongst the large oak trees, where they play and gambol in the hot sunshine, the live-long day. The last family of the butterflies are the Skippers,—in science, *Hesperidæ*,—or, to use the generic name for this family—*Hesperia*. The first is the Grizzle—*Syrichthus elveolus*, whose specific name means chequered, the spots on the wings of the Imago, being somewhat like a chessboard, the fore wings being black, interspersed with about fifteen or sixteen squarish white spots. The next is the Dingy Skipper—*Hesperia paniscus*,—and then the Large Skipper—*Hesperia Sylvanus*,—from "Sylvan,"—being found in the woods. The Pearl Skipper—*Hesperia Comma*,—takes its name from a mark on the fore wings, and is found in low swampy situations, and in almost every locality for Butterflies. Then, there are the Small Skipper—*Hesperia Linia*,—and the Lulworth Skipper — *Hesperia Acteon*. The latter derives its English name from the only place where it has been found, viz., near Lulworth Cove, on the Dorsetshire Coast; and it receives its Latin name, Acteon, from his being a great hunter.

This ends the list of the British Butterflies in the vicinity of Brighton, with the exception of that which was taken by one of the most honest and persevering collectors, in August, 1860, near Kemp Town. No one doubts of its being taken there, as several entomologists of the highest respectability, saw it on the spot *alive*, immediately after it was taken; but a very small clique of savans will not allow it to be put on the list as a new British Butterfly, because they have a theoretic fancy that it might be blown over from the coast of France, a distance of nearly a hundred miles, across the English Channel. The idea, however, is absurd. A little delicate butterfly, with all the appearance of having just emerged from the chrysalis, to be blown that distance without apparently ruffling a feather, is out of all character. If it had been a new bird that had been obtained on our shores, the ornithologists would have been only too happy to have had the opportunity of adding it to their list, as a new British species.

Mr. Edward Newman, of Bishopsgate Street, the great naturalist, and prince of writers, and publisher of works on Natural History, has stood sponsor to this new British Butterfly, and named it—The Brighton Argus—*Lycaena Bœtica*.

Bewick has expressed the wish that mankind could be prevailed upon to read a few lessons from the great book of Nature, to see the wonders which the Universe presents, and to reflect on the wisdom, the power, and the goodness of the Great Creator that planned and formed the whole.

How necessary is it, then, that we should direct our attention to the sowing of the seeds of knowledge in the minds of youth. The great work of forming the man cannot be begun too early; and agreeably with this sentiment, how many writers are there who spend their lives in contributing in various ways to turn the streams of instruction through their proper channel into this most improvable soil,—taking children by the hand, and directing their steps like guardian angels, in the outset of life, to prevent their floundering on in ignorance to the end. In these undertakings the instructors of youth are often assisted by the fertile genius of the artists, who supply their works with such embellishments as serve to relieve the lengthened sameness of the way. Among the many approved branches of instruction, the study of Natural History holds a distinguished rank. To enlarge upon the advantages which are desirable from a knowledge of the Creation, is surely not necessary. To become initiated into this knowledge is to become enamoured of its charms; to attain the object in view requires but little previous study or labour; the road which leads to it soon becomes strewed with flowers, and ceases to fatigue; a flow is given to the imagination which banishes early prejudices and expands the ideas, and an endless fund of the most rational entertainment is spread out, that captivates the attention and exalts the mind. For the attainment of this science in any of its various departments, the foundation may be laid, insensibly, in youth, whereon a goodly superstructure of useful knowledge can easily be raised at a more advanced period. In whatever way, indeed, the varied objects of this beautiful world are viewed, they are readily understood by the contemplative mind, for they are found alike to be the visible works of God. The great book of Nature is amply spread out before mankind, and could they but see how clearly the hand of Providence is in every page, they would consider the faculty of reason as the distinguishing gift to the human race, and use it as the guide of their lives. They would find their reward in a cheerful resignation of mind, in peace and happiness, under the conscious persuasion that "a good naturalist cannot be a bad man."

Chapter XXI.

THE WILD FLOWERS AND MOSSES ABOUT BRIGHTON.

To an unobservant eye the vicinity of Brighton possesses no wild vegetable productions worthy of notice, and, apart from the cultivated fields, all else appears a barren waste, save and except the short sweet verdure whereon our favourite South-Down flocks luxuriate. Upon peering, however, into the hedgerows, and the waysides and the furrows, a volume is opened to the student of Botany, and there is that whereon he may sumptuously feast. Fifty years since, the observation that "Brighton was a place without trees," was a truism; but since then, irrespective of the success in planting the Squares, Enclosures, Steines, and the ornamental gardens of private residences in the town, where formerly, only hardy tamarisk grew, belts and copses of thriving trees have reared their towering heads, and the elm, fir, sycamore, horse-chesnut, larch, beech, hazel, birch, hawthorn, and the holly and other evergreens, having, by culture, become acclimatised, thrive so well as to induce the belief that they are indigenous to the South East Coast.

Immediately along our sea-shore, to the westward, upon leaving the grass-plot at Adelaide Crescent, a low trailing plant is met with, and is more or less abundant at some distance beyond the reach of the tide, as far as the lock of the Shoreham Harbour Canal, at Fishersgate. It is known as the Orach—*Atriplea postulcoides,*—and has succulent silvery leaves, upon a woody stem. The Yellow Horned Poppy—*Glacium luteum,*—is equally abundant in the same localities, and a few years since was very thriving on the sites of Adelaide Terrace, Mills's Terrace, and the houses adjacent. Its leaves are sea-green, and its flowers are of a pale yellow, resulting in long seed pods. It has a tap root, which, on being broken, exudes an acrid juice. A species of Samphire, or Jointed Glasswort, grows in profusion about the pools in the vicinity of Copperasgap. It is gathered and pickled; but it is altogether of a different character to the Samphire which is gathered on the cliffs of the Isle of Wight, and at Dover. Thrift Grass, about the wide expanse of the beach in the vicinity of the Canal Basin, flourishes in extensive patches, and its lilac flowers are a pleasing relief to the eye during the bright rays of the meridian sun in Summer. The most prolific plant in this neighbourhood is the Stonecrop, known by the several names, Ginger, Wall-pepper, and Gold-chain. It is leafless, and grows as it were, in links, from which issue golden flowers of dazzling brightness. The vitality of this little plant is incredible, and, like the several species of the *Cacti*, it absorbs and retains a vast amount of moisture. It may be propagated from very small portions of the plant. A dwarf kind of the Bitter Sweet Nightshade—*Solanum dulcamara,*—abounds in the same locality. It differs from the Deadly Nightshade, the former having purple flowers and yellow stamens; whereas the latter bears a large cup-shaped flower. The berries of both are poisonous. A rough hairy plant, the Viper's Bugloss—*Echium vulgare,*—also grows here. It bears large and handsome purple or blue flowers. A very common plant along the banks of the Canal, and likewise on the banks of the shelving cliffs, between Hove and Kingston, is the Sea Starwort, or Michælmas Daisy—*Aster tripolium.* It is of the same kind as that which formerly was so common in flower gardens. Another plant which grows abundantly about here, is the Common Mallow—*Malva sylvestris,*—and bears purple flowers, succeeded by seeds, well-known amongst children as "cheeses." Formerly, the whole range of the dwarf cliff from Russell Street to Hove, abounded with the Common Mallow, the leaves of which possess valuable properties when boiled and applied as a poultice to whitlows, There also, as many an ass well knew, the Milk Thistle—*Carduus marianus,*—which was formerly held sacred to the Virgin Mary, was very prolific. Specimens of it may be found now upon the banks south of the turnpike road beyond Hove. Some years since, some rare roots of this superbly prickly plant protected the bank which forms the northern side of the cricket ground belonging to Hove House School. It may be known by the white streaks on its leaves. The unfinished embankment between the Chain Pier and Kemp Town is a fine nursery for this thistle, emblematical of the amazing quantity of the same species which occupied the rugged slopes that formed some portions of the East Cliff, now the Marine Parade, before the erection of the sea wall.

The other plants along the sea-side are the Wild Beetroot—*Beta maritima,*—bearing greenish white flowers on a straggling stem, with a large root; the Sea-side Campion, or Catchfly, a white trailing flower with a globular calyx and dark stamens; the Starry-headed Clover—*Trifolium stellatum,*—the Tree Mallow—*Lavater arborea,* and three species of Plaintain—the Common Plaintain, with acorn shaped seeds grouped up a rat-tailed stem, the kind given to birds; the Ribwort Plantain, bearing similar seeds, borne in a cluster at the end of a similar stem; and the Buck's-horn Plantain, so called from the irregular shape of the leaves, resembling a stag's horn, with the seeds like the other kinds.

In the fields in general, about Brighton, is the Scentless Mayweed—*Matricaria inodorata,*—with a large radiating flower like a daisy, having a yellow centre and white outside. The simple, yet pretty Daisy abounds about the general field herbage:

> Daisies, the flowers of lowly birth,
> Embroiderers of the carpet earth,
> That stud the velvet sod.

The most prolific source of the wild flowers near Brighton is the plantation on the Dyke Road, upon the estate of Lady Ogle. There

> The Violet in her greenwood bower,
> Where birchen boughs with hazels mingle,
> May boast herself the fairest flower,
> In glen, or copse, or forest dingle.

Both the Sweet Violet—*Viola odorata,*—and the Dog Violet—*Viola canina,*—grow there, the latter in profusion. The Wild Heartsease—*Viola tricolor,*—is not to be found there; but it abounds in the hedge-rows about Preston, where also the Sweet Violet may be found. In this plantation are the several kinds of Nightshade; the Bitter-sweet, as before described; the Black Nightshade—*Solanum nigrum,*—a rare species in this district; and the Deadly Nightshade—*Atropa belladonna,*—which may be known by its large dark tobacco-leaf shaped leaves, cup-shaped purple flowers, and cherry-like fruit, the produce of a root,

> That takes the reason prisoner.

Considering the easy access to this plantation, and other copses where this death-plant flourishes, and reflecting upon the natural proneness of children to pilfer and consume all within their reach, when they are upon their marauding expeditions, it is really surprising that there are not numerous instances of poisoning by misadventure. It can be but the special Providence, which it is presumed watches over children, that prevents the tasting of the forbidden fruit.

The Black Bryony—*Tamus communis,*—thrives here to perfection. Its flowers are of a greenish yellow, but its berries, like the Nightshade, are poisonous. The Geranium — *Geraniaceæ,* — signifying Crane's Bill, — from the seed vessel and pistil resembling a crane's head and bill,—may be found here of three distinct species. Each, being in its wild state, is very diminutive; but they all are as perfect in their form and colours as the most highly cultivated of the genus. In the hedges by the London Road, just beyond Preston, the Lewes Road, beyond the Cavalry Barracks, and Preston Drove, the Dove's-foot Geranium, — *Geranium molle,*—vegetates. Its flowers are pink or purple, and its leaves, which grow in clusters, are flat, and velvety to the touch.

An English species of the Arum Lily is very common in this and other plantations, and in the damp and shady hedge-rows to the north of Brighton. Its leaves are of a dark green, spotted with purple, and it has, instead of a flower, a sort of leaf, containing a green spadix, which is also purple. The stem of this leaf has a ring of glands, beneath which are anthers and ovaries, which, as the plant matures, are succeeded by scarlet berries, that are commonly known as Lords and Ladies. The plant yields an acrid juice, which is very poisonous; and about eighteen years since, a servant girl at the Synagogue, in Devonshire place, unwittingly poisoned herself, in consequence of eating some Lords and Ladies. The juice, mixed with vinegar, was formerly taken as an antidote against the plague, and even against other poisons.

The two species of Stitchwort, the Lesser—*Stellaria graminea,* —and the Greater—*Stellaria holostea,* or satin flower,—grow on the bank by the Dyke Road copse. Both kinds are beautiful star-like wild flowers. And, a little further on, the Wild Marjoram—*Origanum vulgare,*—is very plentiful amongst the furze that dots the green sward. Buttercups and cowslips grow plentifully in the Hove fields, and in the meadows which abut the railway at Preston.

The three several species of Nettle are met with in various localities. The largest is the Roman Nettle—*Urtica pilulifera*,—from the pill-like shape of the flowers,—formidable in its appearance, and pungent to the touch. The next is the Common Nettle, with which most persons are conversant; and the other species is the Burning Nettle—*Urtica ureus*,—which grows about a foot high, and whose leaves are a very dark green. All these species have a venomous sting of a hair-like character, which possesses at its root a poisonous bulb that discharges itself when the sting is pressed gently. When, however, the stings are grasped firmly. the fine points become bent or broken, and are thus rendered harmless. They point upwards, so that if the hand be passed up the plant briskly the sting is ineffectual. The Dead Nettle—*Lamium album*,—has no sting. Its flowers are white, whereas the blossoms of the stinging Nettles are green.

The hedge-rows of the Hove and Preston Droves are composed principally of Brambles, Dog-wood, the Wild Rose, a species of willow, called Palm; Black Horehound, Traveller's Joy, Alder, Ash, and Ivy. By the pathway on the upper road to Shoreham, and on the London, Ditchling, Lewes, and Dyke roads, just upon the outskirts of Brighton, the Burdock—*Arctium lappa*,—commonly called the Dock, thrives amidst burdens of dust. The flower is purple, and is thrown out from a ball, after the manner of the bloom of the Corn Flower. A thistle-like cone succeeds, and forms a means for amusement to schoolboys, who gather them and stick them on persons' clothes.

The Wall Pellitory—*Parietaria officinalis*,—which has reddish stalks and flowers, and hairy leaves, yields a cooling extract. It is found in different localities, but does not require much nutriment for its dwarf growth. The Shepherd's Purse, so called from its heart-shaped seed pods, resembling old-fashioned money purses, is found growing about most hedged-in fields. On many of the hillocks upon the meadow land Knot Grass is very prevalent. It may be found also amongst the vegetation between the carriage road and pathway just beyond Preston.

On the Ditchling Road, and the Roman Encampment on Hollingbury Hill, Wild Mignionette, Heath, Thyme, Gentian, Whitlow-grass, Carline and Plume Thistle, and Hawkweed grow in profusion; and in the fields immediately south of the pond there, Dandelion, Adam's Needles, Centaury, Convolvulus, Yellow Snapdragon, Yarrow, Cockle, Perriwinkle, Poppy, Milkwort, Dropwort, Cropwort, Fleabane, Yellowwort, Henbane, and Groundsell form a pleasing diversity; while, in the copses contiguous, the Rock Rose and the Sun Rose give their Summer refreshing odours.

In speaking of the Mosses in the vicinity of Brighton, the area will be restricted to the range of the Downs in which the Town is placed, and the coast line of the same distance. Therefore, assuming the limit to be bounded on the east by the Cliffs as far as Newhaven, and the Downs that slope to the west side of the river Ouse, and gradually heighten until passing Lewes, Offham and its chalk-pits are reached. Following, then, the base of the hills by the Devil's Dyke, and the Fulking Downs to Beeding, and thence continuing the marginal line to Shoreham, a tract of country will be embraced, that will be bounded on the south by the sea-shore. Thus, the sandstone plants, and those found in arenaceous soil will be represented by the species from the banks on the beach, near Aldrington Basin, and a few from the tertiary sandstone at Newhaven Cliffs—chalk, clay, and argillaceous soils determining the remaining species.

The list is as follows :—

Archidium phascoides.
Acaulon muticum.
triquetrum.
Flörkeanum.
Phascum rectum.
curvicollum.
cuspidatum.
bryoides.
var γ
Pleuridium subulatum.
alternifolium.
Astomum crispum.
Gymnostomum microstomum.
tortile.
Gymnostomum var β subcylindricum.
Weissia controversa.
mucronata.
Seligeria calcarea.
calcicola.
Dicranella varia.
Dicranum scoparium.
palustre.
Ceratodon purpureus.
Pottia cavifolia.
var δ gracilis.
minutula.
truncata.
Heimii.

Anacalypta Starkeana.
var β brachyodus.
caespitosa.
lanceolata.
Didymodon rubellus.
luridus.
Trichostomum subulatum.
mutabile.
flavo-virens.
tophaceum.
flexicaule.
Tortula aloides.
unguiculata.
var β apiculata.
fallax.
vinealis.
insulana.
squarrosa.
revaluta.
Hornschuchiana.
convoluta.
muralis.
subulata.
laevipila.
ruralis.
rupestris.
papillosa.
Encalypta streptocarpa.
Schistidium apocarpum.
Grimmia pulvinata.
Racomitrium canescens.
Orthotrichum saxatile.
tenellum.
affine.
rupestre.
Lyellii.
diaphanum.
leiocarpum.
pulchellum.
Ludwigii.
Ulota crispa.
phyllantha.
Zygodon viridissimus.
Atrichum undulatum.
Polytrichum commune.
piliferum.
Webera carnea.
albicans.
Bryum pseudo-triquetrum.
cernuum.
inclinatum.
intermedium.
bimum.
torquescens.
capillare.
var β flaccidum.
Donianum.
Billarderii.
caespiticium.
sanguineum.
atropurpureum.
argenteum.
roseum.
Mnium affine.
rostratum.
hornum.
undulatum.
Funaria hygrometrica.
Physcomitrium pyriforme.
fasciculare.
Fissidens bryoides.
adiantoides.
taxifolius.
Leucodon sciuroides.
Cryphaea heteromalla.
Leptodon Smithii.
Neckera pumila.
crispa.
complanata.
Anomodon viticulosus.
Cylindrothecium Montagnei.
Homalothecium sericeum.
Thuidium tamariscinum.
Plagiothecium denticulatum.
sylvaticum.
Rhyncostegium tenellum.

Rhyncostegium depressum.
confertum.
megapolitanum.
Thamnium alopecurum.
Eurynchium circinnatum.
striatulum.
striatum.
praelongum.
Swartzii.
hians.
pumilum.
crassinervium.
piliferum.
Isothecium myurum.
Brachythecium velutinum.
rutabulum.
campestre.
glareosum.
Brachythecium albicans.
Scleropodium illecebrum.
Camptothecium lutescens.
Amblystegium serpens.
riparium.
Hypnum polymorphum.
chrysophyllum.
cupressiforme.
resupinatum.
molluscum.
filicinum.
cuspidatum.
purum.
Hylocomium splendens.
brevirostrum.
squarrosum.
loreum.
triquetrum.

Tortula Hornschuchiana, *Orthotrichum rupestre*, and *Orthotrichum Ludwigii*, *Bryum torquescens*, *Eurynchium circinnatum*, and *Eurynchium striatulum* have been found by Mr. Mitten only, about Woolsonbury Hill.

The plants growing on chalk, are: *Seligeria calcarea*, on inclined faces of chalk pits, and occasionally on detached chalk. *Seligeria calcicola*, in simliar situations on Woolsonbury. This is nearly allied to *Seligeria pusilla*, and has the capsule always ovate. *Anacalypta caespitoso* in some seasons is in plenty on Woolsonbury. Only two localities are known in Sussex, and it is not found elsewhere in Britain. *Bryum intermedium* is frequent in chalk pits, and remarkable for having the fruit on the same tuft in all stages of maturity. *Encalypta streptocarpa*, Woolsonbury, under beech trees. *Neckera crispa*, on Woolsonbury and Newtimber; in fruit on the first hill. *Cylindrothecium Montagnei*, Saddlescombe. *Rhyncostegium depressum*, Newtimber woods. *Hypnum polymorphum*, Patcham enbankment. *Hypnum chrysophyllum*, common everywhere. *Eurynchium circinnatum*, Clayton.

The clay summits of the hills, as at Woolsonbury, give *Phascum alternifolium* and *Weissia mucronata*, and *Physcomitrium fasciculare* on Pyecombe downs. *Racomitrium canescens* is frequent in similar localities, and fruited on Woolsonbury in December, 1858. *Tortula subulata* and *Eurynchium hians* are also frequent, the latter differing from *Eurynchium Swartzii*, its near ally, in its wider, not acuminate, leaves.

The stiff soils of the hills furnish *Phascum rectum*, *Phascum curvicollum*, *Astomum crispum*, *Gymnostomum microstomum*, *Pottia minutula*, *Anacalypta lanceolata*, *Didymodon luridus*, *Tortula convoluta*, also *Phascum bryoides* in disused roads.

A rivulet at Gin Gap, near Newhaven, with its miniature ravine, gives *Webera albicans*, in fruit, *Trichostomum topnaceum*, and *Hypnum riparium*.

On the cliffs, east of Brighton, are found *Acaulon triquetrum*, the only British locality for this; also, *Gymnostomum tortile*, the *var β subcylindricum* of which occurs on a hill near Greenway Station, *Phascum curvicollum*, *Pottia cavifolia*, *Trichostomum mutabile*, and *Trichostomum crispulum*. *Anacalypta Starkeana*, *β brachyodus*, are all frequent, and *Webera carnea*, at Black Rock.

The sides of Woolsonbury have numerous species, as follows; —*Phascum bryoides var γ*, *Archidium phascoides*, *Fissidens adiantoides*, *Dicranum palustre*, *Hypnum molluscum*, *Brachythecium glareosum*, *Bryum bimum*, *Bryum pseudo-triquetrum*, *Bryum roseum*, and *Bryum Billarderii*; this last plant is exceedingly rare. It is the only known British locality, and it is not known to have been gathered elsewhere north of the Colosseum at Rome.

Brachythecium campestre is common in fields among grass, differing from *Brachythecium rutubulum* by its its gradually tapering, not suddenly acuminate leaves. *Bryum capillare β flaccidum* is found in a field in Newtimber valley. On walls *Tortula vinealis*, *Tortula revoluta*, *Tortula rupestris*, *Grimmia pulvinata*, *Orthotrichum saxatile*, *Orthotrichum diaphanum*, and *Rhyncostegium tenellum*, are luxuriant; but *Bryum sanguineum* is rare.

In Poynings springs *Mnium affine* and *Hypnum filicinum* are frequent. In the stubble fields at Aldrington are found *Acaulon Florkeanum* and *Acaulon muticum*, and in the near hedge-banks, *Anacalypta Starkeana*, *Tortula insulana*, *Bryum Donianum*, *Scleropodium illecebrum*. Once, in November, 1858, the very rare fruit of *Eurynchium piliferum* was gathered.

Around Aldrington Basin are seen *Tortula ruralis*, *Tortula squarrosa*, *Trichostomum flavo-virens*, *Pottia Heimii*, *Pottia cavifolia δ gracilis*, *Physcomitrium pyriforme*, *Bryum cernuum*, *Bryum caespiticium*, *Bryum inclinatum*, *Bryum atropurpureum*, and *Rhyncostegium megapolitanum*; also fertile *Brachythecium albicans* and *Camptothecium lutescens*.

In woods are *Bryum torquescens*, *Orthotrichum Lyellii*, *Orthotrichum Ludwigii*, *Orthotrichum rupestre*, *Mnium hornum*, *Mnium rostratum*, *Mnium undulatum*, *Anomodon viticulosus*, *Neckera pumila*, *Neckera complanata*, *Isothecium myurum*, *Leucodon sciuroides*, *Cryphaea heteromalla*, *Leptodon Smithii*, (fruiting at Poynings), *Plagiothecium denticulatum*, *Plagiothecium sylvaticum*, *Eurynchium Swartzii*, and all the species of *Hylocomium*: the last mentioned abundantly, with capsules, at Clayton. On detached ash trees at the feet of the hills, *Orthotrichum tenellum*, *Orthotrichum pulchellum*, and *Tortula papillosa* are not unfrequent. On beech stems about Woolsonbury, *Zygodon viridissimus* fruits freely, and a most diminutive state of *Schistidium apocarpum* is seen.

The Mosses already indicated are not the only species found on these soils; for, on the Arundel Downs, precisely similar in formation to those of our range, *Encalyta vulgaris*, *Antitrichia curtipendula*, *Thrudium abietinum* and some others may be met with.

In proof of the extreme beauty of the form of these objects and the marvellous design of our Great Creator, a more positive instance of the perfection of vegetable organization could not be adduced than *Acoulon Florkeanum*. Taking a single plant, radicles are found, corresponding to roots in flowering plants, at the bottom of the stem. Next rise the overlapping leaves, disposed, for instance, as are those of the lettuce. When these leaves are dissected off, the stem is exposed to view, consisting of a pedicle with a capsule at the top, terminating in an oblique apiculus or small point, and covered by a membrane, called a calyptra, or hood. And clustering around the base of the pedicle are the sexual flowers. The whole plant does not exceed the sixteenth of an inch in height and width, the size of a small pin's head.

Thus, after enumerating most, if not all the Wild Flowers and

Mosses which attach themselves to the natural history of Brighton, we may say,

> Beautiful children of the glen and dell,—
> The dingle deep—the moorland stretching wide,
> And of the mossy fountain's sedgy side,
> Ye, o'er my heart have thrown a lovesome spell.
> And though the worldling, scorning way deride—
> I love ye well.

Chapter XXII.

BRIGHTON CAMP AND THE TRAGEDIES OF GOLDSTONE BOTTOM.

The hills and the vales about Brighton, have more than a natural history in connexion with the animal and vegetable kingdoms, to give them a feature in the nation's chronicles. Not the least important events have been the Camps, lyrically handed to posterity by one of the most martial and spirit-stirring pieces extant, the "Brighton Camp, or, the Girl I left behind me," music that seems inherent to drums and fifes.

Although "Brighton Camp" is the familiar term used, it must be understood that there have been several Camps held here. The first was in 1793, and was formed on Tuesday, August 13th. The troops composing it the previous morning at three o'clock, struck their tents on Ashdown Forest, from which they marched at five, and reached Chailey Common at half-past eleven. There they pitched their tents for the night. On the Tuesday morning at four o'clock, they were again on the march, and at noon they arrived on the hills over Brighton. The baggage, part of the heavy artillery, and the corps of artificers, marched by way of Lewes; but the army in general, consisting of about 7,000 men, took their route over the South Downs. By two o'clock the Camp had formed in the presence of the Prince of Wales, who met them as they came over the hill. The left of the encampment was close to the town, in Belle-Vue Field,—now Regency square,—and stretched in a direct line along the coast. The encampment, which increased to 10,000 troops, was composed of regulars and militia, and was continued, on account of some apprehensions of an invasion by the New Republic of France, till the 28th of October.

As a matter of course, during the time of the encampment, there was a Sham Fight. Its plan was, an enemy attacking Brighton and the Camp. The enemy consisted of eight regiments of infantry, with their battalion guns, under General Sir William Howe; while four battalions of infantry, the light horse, and the mounted artillery, defended the country. Brighton was denominated Dunkirk, and was of course taken by the British. But one prisoner was captured, an officer of the East Middlesex, by his own Major, after a stout resistance, for the offence of sitting on a drum, during the inactivity that generally prevails for hours in the field. The officer was put under arrest, but the next day he was liberated.

The Camp of 1794, was formed early in the summer, about a mile and a half to the west of the town. It consisted at first, of 7,000 men; but when the harvest was got in, it was increased to nearly 15,000, as the militia regiments were not called out till the crops were cleared, the men then composing the militia corps being principally agricultural labourers. On the breaking up of this Camp many of the regiments remained in Barracks at Brighton. The Barracks then were in West Street, at the corner of Little Russel Street, afterwards the Custom House; in North Street, on property now known as the Unicorn Yard,—Windsor Street; and in Church Street, the present Infantry Barracks.

Nothing of any particular importance took place during this Camp. But that of the following year will ever be memorable in the history of Brighton, inasmuch as it is connected with the trial and execution of two men and the flogging of several others for mutiny. Not that the mutiny took place here, but Brighton was the military head quarters of the troops, hence the Court Martial was held in the town.

East Blatchington, near Newhaven, was the theatre of the disaffection, arising from the shortness and bad quality of the bread and flour supplied to the troops; in consequence of which, some men of the Oxford Militia broke into the mill in the vicinity of the barracks, and also, in a rebellious mood, emptied the contents of a vessel laden with corn, into the river, at Newhaven. The Court Martial was held at the Castle Tavern, which occupied the site whereon now stand the buildings which form the north-east corner of Castle Square. The trial occupied eight days; and ended in Edward Cooke,—termed Captain Cooke, from his taking the lead in the mutiny,—and Henry Parish being found guilty and sentenced to be shot. Six others were also convicted, but their sentence was only that they should be flogged. Much sympathy was shown by the inhabitants to the poor fellows, who were each day marched under a strong escort, from the guard house of the Battery, Artillery Place, to the Castle and back. Many of the residents in Russell Street, every night and morning took them provisions, which they were able to pass to them through the bars of their airing ground; and on the morning of the execution of the sentence upon them the wretched men were unable, from their emotion, to express their thanks for the kindness the people showed them.

From the hour of four in the morning of the day appointed for them to suffer, the whole lines of encampment were ordered to hold themselves in readiness; at five, however, in the evening, the officers were given to understand that the execution was countermanded for that day. The cause of this short respite was attributed to the absence of the Prince of Wales's 10th Regiment of Light Dragoons, afterwards the 10th Hussars, which did not march into Brighton till nine o'clock on the following morning, and of course could not pitch their tents till late in the evening. When this regiment was seen on the march to their station, all hopes of an expected reprieve seemed entirely to vanish. The most respectable people, however, of Brighton took this opportunity of one day's delay, to repeat their petition in favour of the two men; but all proved ineffectual, for early on the 13th June, 1795, the Oxford Militia—the regiment to which the mutineers belonged,—began their march from the Barracks at Blatchington to Brighton, to be made awful spectators of their unhappy comrades' punishment, and to be their executioners. At four o'clock the whole were ordered to accompany them from the ground to Goldstone Bottom, at which place they arrived about five. The six men—for there were thirteen mutineers,—that were sentenced to be flogged, proceeded afterwards in a covered waggon, guarded by a strong escort, which was composed of select men, picked from every regiment of the line. The two condemned to be shot followed in the rear in an open cart, attended by the Rev. Mr. Dring, and guarded by a second escort, under the command of Captain Leigh, of the 10th Regiment of Light Dragoons, and one of the Captains belonging to the Lancashire Fencibles. When they arrived, however, at the winding road which leads to Goldstone Bottom,—or Vale,—which is surrounded by an eminence, both the escorts were commanded to halt. The six men sentenced to be flogged were then taken from the covered waggon, and, having been marched through the entire line, which was under arms to receive them, they were brought back to a whipping-post, that was fixed in the centre of the different regiments. The drummers selected to flog them were men belonging to their own corps. To three of them were given three hundred lashes each. This was the number they then received, as, from their long durance, and consequent weakness, the surgeon pronounced that they could suffer no more. The fourth was then stripped, and, after being tied to the flogging-post, was reprieved, as were also his two other comrades.

This part of the distressing ceremony being gone through, the two unfortunate men condemned to be shot were taken from the cart and marched, as the others had been, up the line, with this difference only, of being conducted also through part of the outer line, which was composed of the Prince's Regiment, and the Lancashire and Cinque Port Fencibles. They were then marched to the front of the Oxfordshire Militia, where the coffins stood to receive their bodies, the Artillery being planted on the right, with lighted matches, in the rear of the Oxfordshire, to prevent any mutiny, if attempted, and the whole height commanded by two thousand cavalry.

Cooke and Parish being conducted to the fatal spot, exchanged a few words with the clergyman, and then kneeled, with the greatest composure and firmness, on their coffins; the first time, however, they kneeled, it was done the wrong way, but being placed in a proper situation they received their death from a delinquent platoon of twelve of their own regiment, at the distance only of six paces. One of them was not quite dead when he fell, and was therefore shot through the head with a pistol. This, however, was not the last awful ceremony the line had to experience; for, to conclude the dreadful tragedy, every regiment on the ground was ordered to file off past the bodies before they were suffered to be enclosed in their coffins. The whole scene was impressibly awful beyond any spectacle of the kind ever exhibited.

No disturbance whatever resulted from the melancholy affair; everything was conducted with the greatest solemnity and order: the awe and silence that reigned on the occasion infused a terror, mingled with an equal degree of pity, that was distressing beyond conception. The Oxfordshire Militia naturally experienced more afflicting sensations than any other regiment on the ground.

Cooke and Parish were both young men, and behaved with uncommon firmness and resignation; they marched through the lines with a steady step, and regarded their coffins with an undaunted eye.

On the morning of his execution Cooke wrote to his brother a letter, the original of which is in the possession of the author of this book. It is written in a free and bold style, very different to what might be expected from a man under sentence and at the point of an ignominious death. The following is a correct copy, *verbatim et literatim*, of the original:—

Brighton, 13th of June, 1795.

Dear Brother,—This comes with my kind Love to you, and I hope you be well. I am brought very low and weak by long confinement and been in great trouble. Dear Brother,—I am sentenced Death, and must Die on Saturday, the 13th of June; and I hope God Almighty will forgive me my Sins. I never was no body's foe but my own, and that was in Drinking and breaking the Sabbath, and that is a great Sin. I have prayed night and Day to the Almighty God to forgive me and take me to Heaven, and I hope my prayers be not in vain. I am going to die for what the Redgment done; I am not afraid to meet Death, for I have done no harm to no person, and that is a great comfort to me: there is a just God in heaven that knows I am going to suffer innocently. Dear Brother,—I should be very glad to see you before I Depart this Life. I hope God Almighty will be a Guardian over you and all my relations, and I hope we shall meet in heaven, where we shall be ever happy without End. So no more from the hand of your ever loving and Dying Brother,

Edward Cooke.

A print extant of the execution of these misguided men, is in the possession of Mr. Benjamin Kent, the landlord of the Good Intent Inn, Russell Street. It is thus inscribed :—

"The Awful Scene or Ceremony of the Two Soldiers belonging to the Oxfordshire Militia, which were shot on June 13th, 1795, in a Vale, while in Camp at Brighton, by a party of the Oxfordshire Militia which were very Active in the late riots, the men appeared very composed and resigned, the party which shot them were much affected, Infantry, and Artillery, were drawn up in lines on the occasion."

The engraving, which is about 18 inches by 15 inches, represents the men kneeling on their coffins, the figure signifying Cooke being in the attitude of prayer, with clasped hands and a firm countenance; while Parish, though with his hands clasped denoting his devotion, is dejected in his general position and has downcast looks. Three lines of four men each are at "present," the front rank kneeling, while at each side of the men to be executed is a man at "ready." The Rev. Mr. Dring, who is in his clerical robes, is departing from the scene towards the rising ground to the right, at the foot of which is an infantry regiment at "attention," with the 10th Regiment of Light Dragoons at their rear. On the crown of the hill are the civilians, male and female; in front of whom, to the right, are soldiers formed in a circle, within which, at a triangle, is a man undergoing the punishment of the lash, an officer, evidently the surgeon, superintending the proceedings. Immediately in the rear are the tents of the encampment.

Thirteen regiments were present at the execution, which for nearly fifty years was pointed out by the form of the coffins, the positions of the men firing, and other incidents of the scene, being cut out in the turf by the shepherd, whose innocent flocks browsed where so tragic an affair occurred. The plough has since obliterated all traces of the tragedy from the spot.

A singular instance of the effect of nervous excitement is connected with the execution. The Rev. Mr. Dring, the Chaplain of the regiment, who attended the culprits in their last moments, being a nervous man, and having a great horror of the duty which he had to perform, made a special request that after he had administered to them the last religious consolation, he should have sufficient time to get beyond the sound of the report of the fatal muskets before the order to fire was given. Promise of compliance with his request was made; but either from his tardy progress in leaving the spot, or a miscalculation of time, the word of command was given, and the firing took place while he yet was within hearing. The effect upon him was that he fell to the ground, and never after recovered the shock upon his nerves.

The bodies of the two mutineers were interred in Hove churchyard, contiguous to the centre of the old north boundary wall, where their remains continued undisturbed till the restoration of the Church, in 1834, when a saw-pit was dug at the actual spot, and a few of their bones were exhumed. The burying party was under Sergeant-Major Masters, who afterwards was a publican at Witney. The receipt for the burial fees on the interment of the bodies is still retained by his family. A few years since, Mr. Samuel Thorncroft, the Assistant-Overseer of Brighton, being at Witney, by chance called at Masters's house, when, the subject of the execution of the two men being introduced, the receipt referred to was shown him, and Masters stated that so infamously constructed were the coffins in which the corpses were put that, notwithstanding they were buried in their regimental attire, their blood oozed through the coffins and ran down the backs of their comrades who conveyed them to their grave.

The vicinity of Goldstone Bottom is memorable not only for these military executions, but, also, for the hanging and gibbeting of two men, James Rook and Edward Howell, on the 26th of April, 1793, just north of the Old Shoreham road, beyond Hove Drove. Their crime was robbing the mail, at that time conveyed between Brighton and Shoreham by a lad, named John Stephenson, on horseback. The robbery took place on the night of the 30th of October, 1792. What they took was of little value; and they used no violence. In a barn adjacent they broke open the letters and shared their trifling contents.

Their apprehension was effected by an old woman, named Phœbe Hassell, who happened, as was her frequent custom, to be taking some refreshment at the Red Lion public house, at Old Shoreham, kept at that time by a man named Penton, when Rook came in and ordered some beer. In the course of conversation with the persons present, the subject of the mail robbery came up, and from some observations made by Rook, Phœbe, in her own mind, was convinced that he was one of the party in the affair. She in consequence, went out and gave information of what had transpired to the parish constable, Bartholomew Roberts, who was well acquainted with Rook, then living with his mother in a small cottage close by, on the spot now occupied by Adur Lodge. On being taken into custody, Rook, whose age was about 24, a simple, inoffensive fellow, who had been the dupe of his companion in the crime, admitted the offence, and afforded such intelligence as led to the apprehension of Howell, at Old Shoreham mill, where, at the time, he was reading a pamplet to the miller. Howell was 40 years old, and by trade a tailor.

Some of the stolen property was found upon them; and their identification by the mail-boy being complete, they were committed from the Fountain Inn, for trial at the Spring Assizes, at Horsham, when, being found guilty, they were sentenced to be executed at the spot where the robbery had been effected. They were conveyed to Horsham on horseback, and for their safe custody, not only were they handcuffed, and pinioned with strong cords, but each had his legs roped together under the horse's belly, and, besides the constable that accompanied them, there was a military escort of four cavalry.

An immense concourse of spectators witnessed the execution of these unfortunate men, whose bodies, according to the barbarous custom of the times, were afterwards encased in an iron skeleton dress and gibbetted. The disgusting sight of their decaying bodies remained some time a terror to the timid, but a mark of recreation to the reckless and thoughtless, who were accustomed to throw at them and practise many revolting tricks.

Many relics of the event remain in the possession of inhabitants of Shoreham and Hove; Mr. Alderman Martin, in Brighton, has, at the present time, a tobacco stopper which was made from the bone of a finger of Rook.

When, however, the elements had caused the clothes and the flesh to decay, the aged mother of Rook, night after night, in all weathers,—and the more tempestuous the weather the more frequent the visits,—made a sacred pilgrimage to the lonely spot; and it was noticed that on her return she always brought something away in her apron. Upon being watched, it was discovered that the bones of the hanging men were the objects of her search, and as the wind and rain scattered them on the ground she collected the relics, and conveyed them to her home, and when the gibbets were stripped of their horrid burthen, in the dead silence of the night she interred them, deposited in a chest, in the hallowed ground of Old Shoreham Churchyard.

Besides being found guilty of robbing the mail, the Grand Jury, at the same Assizes, returned a "True Bill" against James Rook, for horse stealing; but he was not put upon his trial for that offence, in consequence of being left for death upon the other charge. The "Brief" for the prosecution in the horse stealing case, now "held" by the author of this book, runs thus:—

BRIEF for the Prosecutor. THE KING agst. JAMES ROOK } On the Prosecution of JOHN BOYCE, For Horse Stealing.

INDICTMENT—STATES—That the Prisoner James Rook on the 31st of October 1792 at the Parish of New Shoreham in the County of Sussex feloniously did steal take drive and carry away a Brown Gelding the property of John Boyce the elder of New Shoreham aforesaid.

Case

In the Afternoon of the 30th of October 1792 about 3 o'Clock John Taylor the Servant of the Prosecutor turned his Master's Brown Horse and another Horse into a field a short distance above the Street at Shoreham and fastened the Gate

And the next Morning about 5 o'Clock he went to the Field in order to get the Horses up to Work when he found the Brown Horse missing.—On the Morning of the 1st of Novr. between 10 and 11 o'Clock the Prisoner was seen by Henry Strivens on the Prosecutor's Horse in company with one Edward Howell who came to water their horses at a Pond near a Barn at Perching belonging to Mr John Marchant about 3 or 4 Miles from Shoreham Strivens says he had seen the Horse before and knew him but did not know at the time who he belonged to—On the Evening of the said 1st of Novr. John Stephenson the Boy who Carries the Mail from Steyning to Brighthelmston was stopped and robbed of the mail in Goldstone Bottom near Brighthelmston by the prisoner and Howell at which time the Prisoner was on Prosecutor's Horse which the Boy knew, having several times seen the Prosecutor's Man with the Horse and having seen the same horse in the Prosecutor's Field at New Shoreham both before and since the robbery.

Proofs.

Proof	Witness
To prove that this witness (who is servant to the Prosecutor) about 3 o'Clock in the Afternoon of the 31st of Octr. 1792 had the Prosecutor's Brown Horse with another up to the Field—That the next Morning about 5 o'Clock he went to get the Horses up to work when he found the Brown Horse missing ....Call..............	JOHN TAYLOR.
To prove that between 10 and 11 o'Clock in the Morning of the 1st of Novr. 1792 as he was Threshing at a Barn at Perching about half a mile from the Hill and about 3 or 4 from Shoreham he saw two men the Prisoner and Howell come to a Pond to water their Horses within about forty yards of the Barn. That the Prisoner was upon a large Brown Gelding with a Sprig Tail and a large Miller's Pad upon it. That the next day he saw the Prisoner and Howell in custody on the Hill near Shoreham for robbing the mail and also saw the Horse on which the Prisoner Rode which he was informed belonged to the Prosecutor and was the one he had lost and which was the same the Prisoner was on when he and Howell came to Water their horses and to Prove that he has since seen the Horse at Prosecutor's at Shoreham ..Call	HENRY STRIVENS.
To prove that he was stopped and robbed of the Mail on the Evening of the first of Novr. 1792 by the Prisoner and another Man whom this Witness believes to be Howell at a place called Goldstone Bottom near Brighthelmston. That the Prisoner was on the Prosecutor's Horse which he knew by having several times before seen the Prosecutor's Man with the Horse and having seen the horse several times in the Prosecutor's Field at New Shoreham both before and since the Robbery. Call the Postboy.....	JOHN STEPHENSON.

The Brief, from the trial not having been proceeded with, is not endorsed to any Counsel, but is marked "Brooker, Brighton," the original of the firm, Messrs. Brooker and Penfold, now Messrs. Penfold and Son, solicitors.

Phœbe Hassell, the person who was chiefly instrumental in bringing Rook and Howell to justice, was a very celebrated character. She was born at Stepney, London, in March, 1713, of respectable parents, named Smith. Of her early life little is known; but the first incident of her remarkable career, as related by herself to the compiler of this work, was her falling in love with Samuel Golding, a private in the regiment known as Kirke's Lambs. Phœbe Smith then was but fifteen years of age, being, as she used to remark, a fine lass for her years. Golding's regiment being ordered to the West Indies in 1728, such was Phœbe's attachment for him, that, donning the garb of a man, she enlisted into the 5th regiment of Foot, commanded by General Pearce, then under orders, also for the West Indies, and embarked after him. There she served for five years without discovering herself to any one. She was likewise at Monserrat, and would have been in the action there, but her regiment did not reach the island till after the battle was over. Soon after her return to England her regiment was ordered to join the forces under the Duke of Cumberland, on the continent, and she was present at the battle of Fontenoy, May 1st, 1745, when she received a bayonet wound in her arm. Golding's and her regiment were afterwards at Gibraltar, where he got wounded, and was then invalided home to Plymouth. Phœbe then informed the Lady of General Pearce of her sex and story, obtained her discharge, and was immediately sent to England. She went to the military hospital at Plymouth, with letters of recommendation from her late Colonel, and there nursed Golding; and when he came out of the hospital they were married, and lived happily together for more than 20 years. Golding had a pension from Chelsea.

After but a short widowhood, she married William Hassell, of whom little is known beyond what is recorded in the parish book of Brighton; extracts from which will show that in 1792 they were in poverty, as at a meeting of the Churchwardens and Overseers, held at the Castle Tavern, on the 5th of December that year, it was: —"Ordered that Phœbe, the wife of William Hassell, be paid three guineas to get their bed and netts, which they had pledged to pay Dr. Henderson for medicine."

Hassell died about this period, and Phœbe then, by the assistance of a few of the inhabitants, purchased a donkey, and travelled with fish and other commodities to the villages westward; and it was on one of these journeys that she obtained the capture of Rook and Howell for robbing the mail.

The following minute appears in the Vestry book :—

1797.—20th May, at a meeting of the Churchwardens and Overseers held at the Hen and Chickens, (now the Running Horse, King Street)—Ordered, that Phœbe Hassell's rent be paid from the present time, and that her weekly allowance be discontinued.

In the early part of the present century the infirmities of age began to tell upon her, and, being no longer able to get about the country, she was taken into Brighton Workhouse ; from which, however, at her own request, she was discharged in August, 1806, as a minute of the vestry held on the 14th of that month states :— "That Phœbe Hassell be allowed a pair of stockings and one change on leaving the poor-house."

After this period she obtained a subsistence by selling fruit, bulls-eyes, pin-cushions, &c., at the bottom of the Marine Parade, near Old Steine Street, where, in sunny weather, she used to sit in a chair with her basket of wares beside her, and obtained a good amount of custom. Her costume would, at the present day, form a great attraction. She wore a brown serge dress, a white apron,—always clean,—a black cloth cloak with a hood, surmounted by a red spotted with white handkerchief. Her head-dress was a black antique shaped bonnet over a mob cap. Her shoes were for service and not look, without any regard to "rights and lefts;" and her hands and arms were usually encased in a pair of long woollen mittens. Her walking-stick, now in the possession of Mr. Edward Blaker, of Portslade, was a serviceable piece of oak.

Hone, in The Year Book, date, Sept. 22, 1821, says, "I saw this woman to-day in her bed, to which she is confined from having lost the use of her limbs. She has even now, old and withered as she is, a fine character of countenance, and I should judge, from her present appearance, must have had a fine though perhaps masculine style of head when young. I have seen many a woman, at the age of sixty or seventy look older than she does under the load of 106 years of human life. Her cheeks are round, and seem firm, though ploughed with many a small wrinkle. Her eyes, though the sight is gone, are large and well formed. As soon as it was announced that somebody had come to see her, she broke the silence of her solitary thoughts and spoke. She began in a complaining tone, as if the remains of a strong and restless spirit were impatient of the prison of a decaying and weak body. 'Other people die and I cannot,' she said. Upon exciting the recollection of her former days, her energy seemed roused, and she spoke with emphasis. Her voice was strong for an old person, and I could easily believe her when, upon being asked if her sex was not in danger of being discovered by her voice, she replied that she always had a strong and manly voice. She appeared to take a pride in having kept her secret, declaring that she told it to no man, woman, or child, during the time she was in the army; 'for you know, Sir, a drunken man and a child always tell the truth. But I told my secret to the ground. I dug a hole that would hold a gallon, and whispered it there.' While I was with her the flies annoyed her extremely: she drove them away with a fan, and said they seemed to smell her out as one that was going to the grave. She showed me a wound she had received in her elbow by a bayonet. She lamented the error of her former ways, but excused it by saying, 'when you are at Rome, you must do as Rome does.' When she could not distinctly hear what was said, she raised herself in the bed and thrust her head forward with impatient energy. She said, when the King, George IV,—saw her, he called her 'a jolly old fellow.' Though blind, she could discern a glimmering light, and I was told would frequently state the time of day by the effect of light."

Phœbe had nine children, but none of them attained any age except the eldest son, who was a sailor, but she had neither seen nor heard of him for many years prior to her decease.

On the 12th of August, 1814, at the festival which took place at the Royal Cricket Ground, to commemorate the peace on Napoleon Buonaparte retiring to Elba, Phœbe, as the "Oldest Inhabitant," sat on the left of the Vicar, the Rev. Robert Carr, and was an interesting object, then 99 years of age, and many presents in silver and one pound notes found their way to her from the opulent and enquiring part of the crowd. On the celebration of the Coronation of George IV., Phœbe, at the age of 107, and totally blind, took part in the ceremonies, and was present on the Level in a carriage with the Rev. R. Carr, (Vicar), and cheerfully joined in the National Anthem. This incident brought her into great notoriety;

and several ladies being struck with her appearance, and pleased with the respectable character she bore, raised a subscription, each subscriber being presented with Phœbe's likeness, beneath which was inscribed, "An Industrious Woman living at Brighton, with very slender means of Support, which she can only earn by selling the contents of her basket, for whose assistance this Etching is sold."

For some few years previous to her decease, which took place on the 12th of December, 1821, she was allowed half-a-guinea a-week by the King. It is related that His Majesty offered her a guinea a-week, but she refused it, saying that half that sum was enough to maintain her.

Phœbe, in support of a good old Sussex custom, regularly, on St. Thomas's Day, 21st of December, went out "Gooding," visiting well-to-do parishioners, to gossip upon the past, over hot elderberry wine and plum cake, and to receive doles, either in money or materials, to furnish home comforts for the celebration of the festivities of Christmas. One of her places of call was the residence of Mr. Robert Ackerson, where the author of this book has many a time and oft heard the old female warrior tell of her deeds of arms. She made a prediction that the wife of Mr. Ackerson would live to a good old age; and so it came to pass, as, on Friday, the 2nd of February, 1855, she expired, being then in her 97th year.* On the St. Thomas's Day previous to her decease,

* We have to record this week the death of, we believe, the oldest inhabitant of Brighton, Mrs. Ackerson, who had reached her 97th year. She was the widow of the late Mr. Robert Ackerson, who filled the offices of High Constable, Overseer, Churchwarden, and Parish Assessor of Brighton. When Royalty smiled on this little fishing village, the not least important of the Brighton fair was the wife of Bob Ackerson, whose merits were prominently blazoned by one who loved the comforts of the world,—no less a personage than Johnny Townshend, the celebrated Bow-street runner, who lived, during the residence of the Prince in Brighton, with the old Brightonian, at the corner of Duke Street, West Street, where Royalty itself was wont to take a luncheon. Cribbage was ever a favourite game with her, and till within a few months of her death her knowledge and play were as acute as ever. She read much: the Bible, the Book of Common Prayer, and the Sermons of the Rev. J. S. M. Anderson being her universal favourites. It is worthy of record that she was a twin, the other infant, a boy, surviving but a few hours. She was childless; yet many an orphan will long revere her memory. Nearly up to the close of her long life Mrs. Ackerson was in possession

not one of her pensioners, as she termed them, paid her a visit, they having all died off, gone as she said, after Old Phœbe, and she felt assured that she then should soon follow.

Mr. Hyam Lewis, father of Mr. Benjamin Lewis, silversmith and jeweller, Ship Street, erected the tombstone in the Old Churchyard, which marks the spot where the remains of Phœbe are deposited.

Chapter, XXIII.

THE STEINE AND ITS TRIBUTARIES.

No part of Brighton has undergone so many changes during the last century as the Steine, which was at first the drying-ground for fishermen's nets and the "laying-up" place for such boats as were not in use at particular fishing seasons of the year. The term Steine is of Flemish origin, and is derived from *Ein, Stein*, or *Steen*, a rock, as at the time when the town received its Flemish colony, the southern extremity of the valley in which Brighton lay was edged and protected from the sea by a ledge of chalk rocks, and from these the name Steine, or rocky, was given to the field or meadow, which was called the Steine Field. The word is generally, but erroneously written Steine, in

of her faculties; her hearing was not greatly impaired; her eye-sight was what would be considered, for persons many years her junior, good; and her recollection was astonishing. She delighted to hold converse with persons who taxed her memory, and would relate the reminiscences of her youthful days with much glee. She loved to talk of her old associations in the early years of George IV.; and would do so with all the freshness of a person in the prime of life. She was a remarkably fine woman, and her carriage was almost as erect just before she died as it had ever been. Perhaps so noble and firm a pattern of old age has scarcely been witnessed. During the last few years of her life she had resided with her nephew, Mr. J. A. Erredge, on the London Road, to whose family she was much attached. We understand that she retained her recollection and composure to the last, and died most tranquilly.—*Brighton Herald*, Feb. 10th, 1855.

Her baptism is thus recorded in the parish register of Pyecombe, Sussex, the village in which she was born:—December 26, 1758: Baptised Richard and Jane, children of Robert Marchant and Sarah his Wife."

conformity with the old corrupt spelling of the Normans and Normanized English in this country. "The final *e*," says Paul Dunvan, "which our ancestors borrowed from the French language, was apposite to the genius and usage of the Saxon and Teutonic: and in the modern English language, the use of it is admissible in words of Saxon origin, only to denote the elongation of the preceding vowel, or the liquidity of the letter *g*. The obvious power, therefore, of the dipthong *ei* makes the attendance of this Norman lackey after the Teutonic noun, Stein, or Steen, totally unnecessary." The addition of the final *e* is a modern innovation, as on the Court Rolls of a Court Baron, held for the Manor of Brighthelmston-Lewes, is the following entry:—"March (27 Elizabeth) it is ordered, that no hog go unringed on the Stein, where nets lie, under a penalty of eight-pence *toties quoties*."

In 1779, according to a map of that date, the only building on the east side of the Steine, was Thomas's Library; just to the north-west of which, on the grass, was a slight erection much after the style of the judge's stand at races. This structure was the orchestra, in which the town band, of three performers, discoursed their music under their leader, Mr. Anthony Crook, whose instrument was the trombone. The side of the hill whereon St. James's Street, Edward Street, and the numerous streets which swell the town to the east and north-east now stand, was, "a delightful and rich tract of down, arable and pasture:" and in an old print of Brighthelmston, in 1765, reapers are represented employed in cutting and teams of oxen in carrying the crops on the ground now occupied by the Marine Parade, Grand Parade, &c. Thomas's Library was the building now modernized and in the occupation of the Electric Telegraph Company. The Steine at that period was of much larger dimensions than at present. In Godwin's rental mention is made of "the common pound of Brighthelston manor, together with a cottage and garden adjoining the said pound, situate on the Steine on the west side of East Street;" and in the same rental a bowling-green on the Steine is occasionally mentioned.

In tempestuous weather and during the winter, the boats of the fishermen were hauled up for safety on the Steine. A Diarist, dating his memorandum, Wednesday, September 8th, 1778, says,

"An old well is half open among the boats; a little child has just now waddled off the Steyne towards it. I ran to prevent mischief, and succeeded.—Have remonstrated against this dangerous neglect in vain. There are one dry and two wet wells open thereabouts. When a child of fortune or two shall have been lost therein, the wells may be boarded over.—The Commissioners by the Act have sufficient powers, and collect money enough to answer its purposes; yet the Cliff-side is all along covered with rubbish, offensive to the sight and smell. Indeed, there is no occasion to search much for nuisances, obstructions, and inconveniences, in this place.—*Mem.* —Since the above complaint, some loose boards have been laid across one of the wet wells."

In the time of Elizabeth, and even at a more recent date, the inhabitants were wholly supplied with water from the public wells, which were town property, under the control of the Lords of the different Manors. Thus, at a Court Baron held for the Manor of Brighthelmston-Lewes, in October (20 Elizabeth) a bye-law was made that nothing should be laid within four feet of any well within the said Manor. On the Court Rolls, also, of the same Manor, appears the following:—"April (19 Jac.) it is ordered at the Court-Leet, that a building which Richard Scrase, gentleman, has erected over the common well in the upper end of North Street, shall not convey to the said Scrase, or his heirs, any right in the said well, more than as an inhabitant." This well remained in use till within the last few years, and was known as the Unicorn Yard well, and was situate in the present space immediately in front of Blaber's eating-house, at the south end of Windsor Street. Another well was in West Street, in the water channel before the premises now occupied by Mr. Feldwick, cabinet maker. The curb of it was raised, on a brick-work platform, around which was the main water-course of the street. About eighty years ago, in consequence of the well becoming an impediment to the increased traffic in the street, and being but little used, it was domed over, and for some years a square stone at the edge of the pavement marked its site. The other town wells still in use by means of pumps, are on the Knab; in East Street, by the Sussex Arms, formerly the Spread Eagle; in Market Street, opposite Payne's Hotel; and in Pool

Valley, adjoining the Duke of Wellington Inn. The well situate just without the poultry portion of the Market, and likewise the one in Little East Street, from being put out of use by the service of the Water Company, have been closed over, as has also the great northern well which but a few years since supplied a large tank that was erected on the area between St. Peter's Church Enclosure and the Level, for the street watering service. The remaining town wells and their pumping gear, now out of use, are situate, one at the Grafton Street Police Station, and the other under the roadway at the entrance to the Pier Esplanade, at the bottom of the Steine. The pump of the last mentioned well, about forty years since, was worked by a donkey, which traversed, "on the getting up stairs" principle, the interior of a wheel that was fitted to the groyne. On a brisk March day, however, when the wind was blowing up more of the dust of that month than is proverbially required to be equal in worth with a king's ransom, while the machinery was working under the influence of the usual propelling power, Old Father Neptune, as if envious of the poor animal's dominion over the aqueous element, mounted a foaming billow and rushed into the wheel after the donkey. Neddy's good genius, who was in constant attendance upon him,—just to sharpen his appetite for work when he felt disposed for a rest,—luckily superseded the design of the mythological sovereign of the deep, by whipping-out his quadruped friend, before the turbulent king could lash around him. This increased the rage of Neptune, who, on retiring to his deep abode, bodily tore away the wheel and its fixings.

Previous to the supply from the town pumps, the water for the streets was obtained from the sea. The water carts then were of the most primitive description, and consisted of barrels on wheels, similar to those now in use for the conveyance of water upon farms. But they had in addition, fixed at the backs of them, an oblong perforated box each, for the distribution of the water, which was supplied from the barrels by pulling out plugs of wood that projected into the boxes. The barrels were filled by backing them some distance into the sea, when the water was lifted into funnels fitted to the bung holes, by a species of scoop at the end of a pole, the operator of this intelligent process the while, standing on the shafts of the carts, or Bacchus like, and bare-legged, bestriding the barrels.

The Steine then was entirely open, and was a country walk for visitors. That is to say, in the Spring, Summer, and Autumn; as in Winter time, from its then lying very hollow, the southern part was generally flooded, and in severe weather the sheet of ice which was there formed was a general rendezvous for sliding and skating. When fashion made the Steine a place of public resort, attention was paid by the town authorities, to make it in some degree, attractive. The ground was made level, and verdure was encouraged to ornament it. On it the old Duke of Cumberland, of Fontenoy, delighted to turn out the stag and hunt the bounding deer, as the place was entirely open to the full extent of the Downs; and the inhabitants were gratified with repeated spectacles of the kind, sometimes as often as twice or thrice in a season.

Sports of a less aristocratic character sometimes took place here, as the following extract from the *Morning Herald* will verify:—

1805, September 11th.—A pony race on the Level, this morning afforded much diversion to a very numerous assemblage of spectators. After this, donkey races took place: seven started for the first heat, and what is very singular, two, on this starting, ran a *dead heat*; a circumstance, probably, with quadrupeds of this sluggish tribe, never recorded in the annals of sporting. The donkies having performed their task, the company removed to the Steyne, to the South, where *jumping in sacks*, and a jingling match kept hilarity alive for about two hours longer.

There were Jenkinses of the Press even at this period, who watched with keen eye the doings of royalty, and of the nobility, as will be seen by the following extracts:—

Morning Herald, August 9, 1805.—This morning, the Prince of Wales and the Duke of Sussex honoured the Steyne Promenade with their presence, and for a short time before dinner, rode on horseback. Mr. Mellish drove Lord Barrymore's curricle two or three times round the Steyne, this morning. The quartern loaf here, now sells for one shilling and six pence.

August 19th.—The Duke of Sussex rode out in an open barouche and amused himself in smoking a pipe.

The following are also extracts from a private diary kept in 1805:—

August 4th.—The Cliff Parade, from the South end of the Steine to the unfinished Crescent, displayed much genteel company this afternoon. The Cyprian Corps have much increased in number within the last two or three days. We have now *little French Milliners* in every part of the town.

August 27th.—Townshend and Sayers, two Bow Street officers, arrived here this morning, in quest of an individual who has been guilty of a burglary in the metropolis. They had been here but a short time when the object they were in search of, in a laced livery, was descried by them in the act of crossing the Steine. They took him into custody, and having ornamented his wrists with a pair of iron ruffles, they bore him off in triumph to London.

September 19th.—About half-past one o'clock the Prince of Wales returned from a walk to the west of the Steine, to the Pavilion. His Royal Highness, who was habited in a black coat and waistcoat, and nankeen pantaloons, appeared rather lame from the recent hurt he had received in his ankle. He walked with a stick, of sufficient dimensions occasionally to bear his weight.

September 26th.—The Duke of Clarence was to-day, for a short time, on the Steine. Some of His Highness's sons are at this time here, and were under the military instructions of a sergeant of the South Gloucester Militia this morning on the Pavilion lawn.

The Steine was first partially enclosed with common hurdles; then it was partly paved and railed in. At last the present massive iron railings were erected. But not as they at present stand. They surrounded a much larger area, and the lamp-posts were the main standards, the rails being fastened in them. At that period the paving around the Steine, under the then Town Surveyor, Mr. Thomas Harman, was considered a master-piece of the art of paving in brick. Previous to this improvement, there was no carriage road completely round the Steine, vehicles of every description, from Castle Square to Prince's Street, having to pass down the west of the Steine and Pool Valley, along at the back of the York Hotel, up the east of the Steine, and by way of the back of (now) the Telegraph Office, down St. James's Street, and then along by the eastern side of the north Steine, as posts erected across from the Castle Tavern to the Steine railings admitted only of foot-traffic, and the coaches for London and Lewes went from Castle Square by way of North Street, New Road, Church Street, &c. The road across from Castle Square to St. James's Street was effected on Easter Monday, March 31st, 1834, and appeared to be a work of magic, as the long-desired improvement had met with opposition from parties who feared the alteration would affect their interest in property from which the traffic would be diverted. The resolution was passed by the Commissioners, and on the day above-mentioned, the "trick" was done, although the opposition hastened to town to procure an injunction from the Lord Chancellor; as it so happened, that it was the Easter vacation, so his Lordship could not be approached till all the alterations had been performed. On the reinstating of the iron railings, the lamp-posts were placed at the edge of the pavement, as hitherto, half of the light from the lamps had been cast on the space within the railings, where it was not required. The posts still show the holes through which the iron railings passed when they were in their original position.

The chief modern features on the Old Steine are the statue of George IV., the Fountain, and the Russian guns. The first was put up on the 11th of October, 1828. The idea of its erection originated with a party of tradesmen, who were accustomed to assemble nightly at the King's Arms, George Street; but a subscription which remained open for more than eight years and a half did not provide the sum, £3,000, agreed to be paid Chantry for his artistic skill. The Fountain, known as the Victoria Fountain, was also erected by subscription, procured through the indefatigable exertions of Mr. Cordy Burrows, to whom also the credit is due for the planting of the Steines with flowers and trees. The Fountain was inaugurated on the 25th of May, 1846. The design of the structure was furnished by Mr. Henry Wilds, the model of the dolphins by Mr. William Pepper, and the ironwork was cast at the Eagle Foundry. The rock-work upon which the dolphins rest is formed of huge sand-stones, called in Wiltshire and Berkshire, "Grey Weathers," and breccia, or pudding-stone, which for lengthened periods had lain in Goldstone Bottom, on the Dyke Road, and fields adjacent, by many persons considered to be the remains of Druidical temples or altars. But such a notion must be fallacious, as, at a very recent date, similar accumulations of sand-stone have been dug up about the western part of Brighton, where the soil exhibits many irregularities which geologists are unable to account for. An instance of this occurred in digging out the ground for the foundation of the tower of All Saints' Church, Buckingham Place, the soil to a considerable depth at one particular spot, being so loose and treacherous that great ingenuity and care had to be observed—attended with great expense,—by Messrs. Cheesman and Son, the builders, to make the foundation secure.

A stone also, of the character termed Druidical *cromlech,* was dug out while preparing for the foundation of the present Brighton Workhouse, and was used for the corner stone of the building. In excavating the ground likewise, in 1823, for laying in the gas-pipes across the Steine, from Castle Square to the corner of the Marine Parade, huge unshapen blocks of a like character were turned up. The last memento on the Steine, the Russian guns, are relics of the siege of Sebastopol.

The old maps shew a piece of water on the Steine, between the Castle Tavern and the Pavilion, formed by the spring which rose at Patcham and used to flow by the Pool—Pool Valley. In the year 1793, the Prince of Wales and the Duke of Marlborough, whose house stood at the north end of the Marine Pavilion, made an arched sewer along the Steine, to carry away this water into the sea, and, in consideration of the expense and improvement, the Lords of the Manor, with consent of the homage, gave his Royal Highness and the Duke permission to rail in or enclose a certain portion of the Steine, adjoining their houses respectively, but never to build on or encumber it with any thing that might obstruct the prospect, or in any other way be a nuisance to the Steine. A barn which stood at this spot, the property of Mr. Howell, as shewn in the view of the Steine, 1765, was moved, at the request of the Prince of Wales, to the top of Church Street, into the field whereon also, stood the Infantry Barracks Hospital, a wooden building that occupied the site of the Hanover Chapel Burial Ground. There were two main entrances to the sewer. One was about the centre of the road,—along which the water channel ran,—opposite the Pavilion Parade; and the other was in the roadway immediately to the east of the entrance to Castle Square from the Steine. Each was protected by a wooden railing in a triangular form. The sewer discharged itself by means of a square wooden trunk at the back of Williams's Baths, now the south front of the Lion Mansion.

In 1785-6, the first houses on the South Parade, the east side of the Steine south of St. James's Street, began to be erected, and in a few years the whole of them, as well as the extensive range of buildings which forms the North Parade, were completed.

Mrs. Fitzherbert's mansion, now the residence of W. Furner,

Esq., the Judge of the County Court of this district, adjoining the present mansion of Captain Thellusson, was built in 1804. On the site now occupied by the square block of buildings that form the north-east corner of Castle Square, about forty years since, stood the Castle Tavern, which had been one of the chief rendezvous of royalty, the nobility, and the gentry. It was originally a very small house, but being considered the best in the town for a tavern, it was purchased by Mr. Shergold, who opened it under the sign of the Castle, in 1755. Such was its success, in consequence of the increase of visitors to the town, that, in 1776, Messrs. Tilt and Best joined him in partnership, and the premises were greatly extended. In 1790, the other parties having given up the business, Mr. Tilt carried on the undertaking, and he was succeeded by his widow. In 1814, Messrs. Gilburd and Harryett became the proprietors. It attained the acme of its celebrity when in the hands of Mr. Tilt, who attached to the establishment an elegant suite of Assembly and Concert Rooms, built with great taste and judgment by Mr. Crunden, of Park Street. London, in 1776. The Ball Room was rectangular, 80 feet by 40 feet, with recesses at each end and side, 16 feet by 4 feet, decorated with columns corresponding with the pilasters which were continued round the room, dividing the sides and ends into a variety of compartments, ornamented with paintings from the Admirander and the Vatican, representing a portion of the story of Cupid and Psyche, and the Aldrobrandini marriage; with air-nymphs and divers other figures, in the ancient grotesque style. The ceiling was curved, and formed an arch of one fifth of the height of the room, which was 35 feet. Over the entablature, at each end of the room, was a large painting; the one a representation of Aurora, and the other a figure of Nox. In 1814, a beautifully toned organ by Flight and Robson was erected at the north end of the room.

In the season, from August to March, Assemblies were held every Monday. These were under the management of Masters of the Ceremonies, the first of whom were, in 1805, Mr. Yart at the Old Ship, and Mr. William Wade at the Castle. They were succeeded by Mr. J. S. Forth, in 1808. He acted in the same capacity at the Old Ship and the Castle Assemblies. Lieut.-Col.

Eld succeeded Mr. Forth, and at his decease, December 22nd, 1855, the office fell into disuse; in fact, for some years previous to the decease of the Colonel his services were rarely required, the progress of the age having rendered such an office null and void. The duties of the Masters of the Ceremonies consisted in watching minutely the arrival of the nobility and gentry. For this purpose he attended the Libraries and Hotels regularly once or more a-day to copy the lists of the latest visitors, at whose addresses he then called and left his card, a hint that they should enter their names in his book, which lay at the principal places of fashionable resort, and with each entry deposit a guinea with the custodian of the M.C.'s book, who received a per centage for his trouble and attention. The payment of the fee ensured a mutual recognition upon all occasions of meeting between the giver and the receiver during that visit of the donor at Brighton, and, on the occasions of balls and assemblies, he was expected to make all the necessary arrangements, and for dances provide all unprovided ladies and gentlemen with partners. Masters of the Ceremonies orginated at a period when balls and routs terminated at ten o'clock in the evening, when "We won't go home till morning," had not come into vogue, but the sedan chair of "my lady" was in punctual attendance, and the fair burden was wafted home to admit of repose before midnight, and to give the sterner sex an opportunity for a carouse or a spree.

The following is an extract from a private diary:—"July 30th, 1805. This evening, at nine o'clock, the first assembly of the season, the Grand Rose Ball, was held at the Castle Inn, under the patronage of the Prince of Wales. The Ball Room is large, lofty, and noble, and commands a full view of the Steyne; looks, also, into the Pavilion Gardens, the beautiful shrubberies of which are worthy of the Royal resident. The ceiling forms an arch, and is painted to represent the rising sun. Every part of the room is ornamented with various masterly paintings of classical antiquity. It was lighted up in a superior style, suited to the dignity of the guests, with three cut-glass chandeliers, 100 lights, and forty lustres and side-lights. The Prince entered the room at half-past nine, and at ten o'clock the Ball opened."

During the erection of the Royal Stables, in Church Street, in 1809, a carpenter, who lived in Jew Street, named John Butcher, uncle to Mr. Butcher, of the present firm, Messrs. Cheesman and Butcher, chinamen, North Street, accidentally fell and injured himself. Upon his recovery, not being able to resume the heavy work of his trade, he constructed a machine of a similar make to the sedan chair, and placed it upon four wheels. It was drawn by hand, in the same manner as Bath chairs, while an assistant, when the person being conveyed was heavy, pushed behind. Its introduction was quite a favourite feature amongst the nobility, and a second fly, in consequence, was soon constructed. These two vehicles were extensively patronized by the Prince of Wales and his noble companions; and from being employed by them on special occasions of a midnight "lark," they received the name of "Fly-by-nights," and soon entirely superseded sedan-chairs, except for invalids on their conveyance to and from the Baths. Butcher, from the great success which attended his project, being desirous that his flys should have a more elegant appearance than his ability in the ornamental could effect, sent one of them, for the purpose of being repainted and varnished, to Mr. Blaker, coach-maker, Regent Street, and he, having an eye to business, purloined the design, and improved upon it by making two or three to be drawn by horses. The most remarkable vehicle of this description, for the conveyance of one passenger only, was that made for Mr. George Battcock, surgeon, who died on the 3rd of February last. It was called Dr. Battcock's "Pill Box."

When George IV. expressed a desire of converting the Castle Assembly Room into a Chapel to be attached to the Royal Pavilion, the fee simple of it was transferred to his Majesty, and as a tavern attached to a place of divine worship would be a great incongruity, the transfer of the license of the Castle was made to premises in Steine Place, the Royal York Hotel, so designated in reference to the Royal Duke, Frederick, whose permission for the name was applied for and obtained from his Royal Highness. The house was opened by Mr. Sheppard.

The Royal Albion Hotel, which has so conspicuous a position to the south of the Steine, occupies the spot whereon formerly stood

Russell House, once the residence of Dr. Russell, and afterwards of the Duke of Cumberland. In 1805, it was the residence of Miss Johnson. It stood abruptly to the sea, the waves in stormy weather laving the brick boundary wall to the south. Immediately under its east wall was Haines's Repository for toys, where, too, was also an apartment in which were exhibited the wonders of the Camera Obscura. The Junction Road now occupies the site; it was a favourite lounge with visitors. The latter years of Russell House were of a remarkable character, some portion of it being devoted by its owner, Mr. John Colbatch, to copper-plate printing; while in the largest apartment the wonders of Khia Khan Khruse, the chief of the Indian Jugglers, were exhibited, in the Autumn of 1822. The building eventually had a most neglected appearance, and was pulled down. The purchase of the space then was contemplated by the town, in order to keep open the southern extremity of the Steine to the sea. Mr. Colbatch required £6,000 for it, a sum which the Town Commissioners assented to give; but after numerous delays the bargain was off, and soon the present noble building rose to shut out the southern aspect from the Steine.

In 1792, during the Revolution which deluged France in its own blood, there was a great influx of refugees from Dieppe to Brighton, to escape the savage and unrelenting fury of their persecutors. On the 29th of August, that year, the Marchioness of Beaule landed at the bottom of the Steine, having paid two hundred guineas at Dieppe, for her passage across, and even then she was under the necessity of appearing in the dress of a sailor, and as such she assisted the crew during the whole voyage, not only to disguise herself, but in order to bring with her, undiscovered, a favourite female, whom she conveyed on board in a trunk, in which holes were bored to give her air. His Royal Highness the Prince of Wales, with Mrs. Fitzherbert and Miss Isabella Pigot, received them on landing, and the Prince escorted them to the Earl of Clermont's, where tea was provided for His Royal Highness and twenty of his friends. On the 20th of September, two packets landed several persons of distinction, amongst whom were the Archbishop of Aix, and Count Bridges, one of the household of the hapless Louis XVI. Many priests were amongst the refugees, for the relief of whom subscriptions to a considerable amount were made, for the purpose of relieving their immediate necessities, and to enable them to pursue their journey to London. On Wednesday, October 20th, thirty-seven nuns, in the habit of their order, were landed near Shoreham from the Prince of Wales packet, commanded by Captain Burton. Their destination was Brussels, where a convent was being prepared for them. It had been intended that they should disembark at Brighton, but the roughness of the sea prevented it. Captain Burton's daughter was married to Mr. William Wigney, a north countryman, who had then recently settled in Brighton, in North Street, where he kept a linen-draper's shop. The house,—which he purchased of Lord Leslie, afterwards Lord Rother, who married Henrietta Ann, daughter of the first Earl of Chichester,—he paid for in French money, which he had received in exchange for English coin from the refugees brought over by his father-in-law. It is related of him that he was not over scrupulous in the way of business, of passing half-franc pieces for sixpences to the unwary. He was afterwards the head of the firm of Messrs. Wigney, Rickman, and Co., bankers, Steine Lane.

No part of Brighton has had a more varied character than the Steine. From being the general depository of the materials of the aborigines, for fishing, it became the place of rendezvous for the nobility and gentry, the beaux and belles delighting to promenade there, expend their small talk, and listen to the strains of the military bands which daily played upon some portion of it. Even upon Sunday afternoons, so recently as twenty-three years since, the sounds of music attracted immense crowds of the inhabitants and visitors there. Frequent innovations, however, upon its space having taken place, and the southern walks along the whole front of the town, having, by their extension and commodiousness, become the fashionable resort, the Steine has quieted down to a thoroughfare that connects the east with the west portion of the town, and there is a contentment that it shall remain an important lung of the borough.

During the agitation for the Reform Bill, when self-esteemed politicians tried their 'prentice voice upon stump oratory, the Steine was the famous arena for their eloquence. Where now, on gala days, the triple rampant dolphins, which support on their entwined tails the basins of the fountain, belave themselves, a waggon has formed the vehicle for the conveyance of political sentiments under the guise of Toryism, Whigism, Chartism, or any other ism that the whim, rage, or fashion of the day has chanced to assume.

The most memorable event on the Steine was the dinner given there on the 3rd of September, 1830, to the children of the various charity schools in the town, to commemorate the first visit of William IV. and Queen Adelaide to Brighton. Their Majesties arrived on the previous Monday, great preparations having been made for their reception, triumphal arches and other erections forming emblems of rejoicing throughout the space from the extreme north of the town, on the London Road, to the entrance of the Pavilion Grounds. Probably, now, when there is so great a facility for the transmission of large masses of people by means of the railway, the numbers of persons who came into the town on the occasion, would be considered of little moment; but then the quantity was estimated as vast, vehicles of every description arriving in the town, heavily laden with human beings, not only from all parts of the county, but even the distance of two hundred miles was not considered too great to travel in order to witness the imposing sight. For more than a week prior to the appointed day, numbers of persons had arrived in the town to ensure being present; and lodgings of every description were seized with avidity, at—to use a commercial term—long prices. The stage coaches from London,—many of which were specially placed on the road to meet the demands,—were crowded to excess at extra fares; and the vans and spring waggons—as they were termed—nightly bore heavy freights of provisions to meet the anticipated rapid consumption.

Their Majesties arrived shortly after five o'clock, and were met by the High Constable, the Clergy, and a Committee of the principal inhabitants, the children of the various schools forming a line along the route through which the royal carriages passed. The waving of handkerchiefs by the ladies from the balconies, the shouts and huzzas of the people, the roaring of cannon, the ringing of bells, the music of various bands, the tramp of horses, the rattling of carriages, the floating of hundreds of flags and banners, formed altogether a spectacle that had never been previously, nor has it been since, equalled in Brighton. The crowning feature of the day was a structure in the form of a triumphal arch, which was of vast proportions, fifty feet in height, the opening of the arch having a span of twenty-five feet, and the whole was clothed with evergreens and flowers. The top was covered with a profusion of flags and streamers, from the Hyperion frigate, then stationed at Newhaven, in the midst of which flaunted the Standard of England. A body of sailors, belonging to the Coast Blockade service, dressed in blue jackets and white trousers, were arranged pyramidically on the top, and gave a crowning character to the spectacle, as they gave three hearty cheers for the "Sailor King." They were seventy in number, supplied by Captain Mingaye, of the Hyperion. The structure was crowded with gaily dressed ladies, and the galleries of the archway were filled with the girls of Swan Downer's Charity School, and those of the National School, who at that time wore green dresses and white mob caps. In the evening the town was one blaze of light from a general illumination.

The preparations for dining the children were completed by noon on Friday. Three rows of tables, with benches on each side, were ranged round the whole area of the southern division of the Steine, which at that time was one grass plot, to which the spectators were admitted by tickets. The centre of the lawn was left entirely open, no persons being allowed upon that portion except the committee of management and the bands of the Horse and Foot Guards. At the southern extremity of this open space was a capacious marquee, erected for the accommodation of their Majesties. The interior was laid out very tastefully, and refreshments were prepared. At its entrance waved the two large town flags, supported by two of the Committee in blue sashes. Across the pavement between the two divisions of the Steine a space was boarded off, as also, across the northern division, and thence to the private entrance of the Pavilion at the north end of the Steine. At this period posts and rails skirted the outer edge of the pavement around the whole of the Steine.

The spectators began to assemble on the pavement about one o'clock, at which time the whole circumference outside the fence was belted with carriages, some of which had taken up their position at an early hour in the morning. The parade of the children to the grounds was a most pleasing sight, their general cleanliness and their appearance of health and happiness, imparting a most gratifying charm to the scene. By two o'clock the whole of the children were seated, and the ampitheatre of the Steine, gradually rising from the children at the tables to the spectators that girted them, and then on to the carriages covered with persons, and beyond that the thousands which crowded the windows, balconies, and the very roofs of the houses that bound the Steine, afforded a spectacle far more imposing than the most vivid imagination can conceive.

Precisely at two o'clock, their Majesties, accompanied by the Princess Augusta, the Landgravine of Hesse Homburgh, the Duke of Cambridge, Prince George of Cambridge, Sir Augustus and Lady D'Este, and others, came across from the Pavilion Grounds to the boarded-off avenue, where they were met by the High Constable, who had received His Majesty's commands to escort the royal party to the festive scene, where they received the respects of the Magistrates, Clergy, and Gentry. Having surveyed the scene for some time, their Majesties and suite passed along the line close to the children, frequently returning the salutations of the people with the utmost affability and condescension. Having returned to the entrance, their Majesty's bowed to the vast assemblage and withdrew, attended by their royal relatives. At that moment the regimental bands struck up the National Anthem, and shouts simultaneously burst from every lip. Even the children, whose eyes only, as yet, had been feasted, rose and mingled their shrill voices with the harmony of throats.

It was calculated that more than 60,000 persons were present to view the feeding of the youthful multitude, who, immediately on the Grace having been said by the Rev. H. M. Wagner—Vicar,—were supplied with an unlimited quantity of roast and boiled beef and plum pudding by the numerous carvers who had volunteered their services, lady waitresses with the utmost alacrity attending most assiduously upon the youthful guests. It was an occasion that formed an epoch in the life of every person present. On the occasion of the first visit of Queen Victoria to Brighton, October 4th, 1837, a similar banquet was given to the children upon the Steine.

The most celebrated public buildings of the Steine were the libraries, which were the principal resort of the visitors. The first library here was instituted by Mr. Woodgate, at the southern extremity, on the premises at present occupied by Mr. Shaw, confectioner, and others, contiguous to the York Hotel, where also was the Post Office. Mr. Woodgate was succeeded by Miss Widget, who resigned it to Mr. Bowen; after whom came Mr. Crawford, and, lastly, Mr. F. G. Fisher.

The other library was that of Mr. Thomas, after whom was Mr. Dudlow, who was succeeded by Mr. James Gregory, whose successor, Mr. Donaldson, resigned the establishment to Mr. Thomas Lucombe. Mr. Donaldson pulled down the original low building in 1806, and erected the present structure, which has however, since the carriage road has been formed in front of it, been much modernized to suit the various businesses to which the premises have been devoted.

"A Diarist," writing August 23rd, 1779, says, "There is a sort of rivalry between the two Librarians on the Steyne, as to their subscription books; which shall most justly deserve the title of the book of Numbers.—There is a constant struggle between them, which shall be most courteous; and the effects are those usually consequent upon an opposition. Sir Christopher Caustic, this morning was turning over the leaves, at Bowen's, which contains the names of the subscribers. Mr. Bowen bowed *a la Novarre* or *Gallini*, and with offered pen and ink, craved the honour of—an additional name: this being his first season, and having been purposely misinformed by some would be witty wag; 'Sir,' said Mr. Bowen, displaying, all the time, two irregular rows of remarkably white teeth, 'yours will stand immediately after that of the Honourable Charles James Fox, Esq., and before that of Mrs. Franco, the rich Jew's lady. Esquire W——d's was to have been on the medium line, but, poor gentleman, he is unfortunately *detained* near London, on *emergent* business.' To what a degree was the dealer in stationery let down, when he was afterwards regularly rectified; when by explanatory notes, and critical commentations, he came to be fully informed that the individual Mr. Fox in question was not the celebrated senator of that name, but an Irish *Jontleman*, who condescends in winter to keep a chop house at the corner of the play-house passage, in Bow Street, Covent Garden; and every autumnal season, has frequent opportunities of storming and swearing at the ladies who may have the good fortune to belong to the Brighthelmstone company of Comedians, he being sole manager thereof. And such management!—*Scarrons Rancour*, who filled all the characters in a play by himself, was a fool to him. That Mrs. Franco was, to be sure, the temporary wife of young Mr. Franco, last season, but seems at leisure this to be the temporary wife of even Mr. Bowen, if he pleases; and that poor Billy, who was the *Beau*, is confined, *custodia marcellis, Banco Regis*, on suspicion of debt, where he blacks shoes, cleans knives, and turns spits, for the privilege of dipping sops in the dripping-pans of poor prisoners."

"Mr. Thomas, the other librarian, must be noticed in turn. He hath been years enough practising small talk with the ladies and gentlemen upon the Steyne, and hath arrived at a surprising degree of precision in pronouncing French-English. He is now reading the newspaper to some of his subscribers, with an audible voice, and repeatedly calls a detached body of troops a *corpse*; a *tour* he improves into a *tower*; and delivers his words in a *promiscas* manner. It is near seven in the evening, and the widow Fussic has just waddled into his shop, with a parasol in her right, and a spying-glass in her left hand. Thomas offers her a *General Advertiser*. 'Lord bless me!' says she, 'Mr. Thomas, how damp this paper is tho' it it has come so far, and must have been printed so long since! What reason can you give for it?'—Mr. Thomas observes, considers and explains, in a most explicit manner, the cause and the effect, to the inquisitive lady, naturally speaking, as a body may say; proving to a demonstration, according to Candide, that there can be no effect without a cause; and that of course, damp papers, closely compressed, will continue damp a considerable time. In the interim, Miss Fanny Fussic stares and whispers to her brother Bobby, while he is subscribing to a raffle, that Mr. Thomas must be a most prodigious man, monstrously intelligent, and withal, that he is amazingly communicative: 'He knows but every-thing,' says she, 'and tells but every-thing he knows.'"

Another Library was also established on the Steine, on the premises which had been known as Raggett's Subscription House, at the opposite corner of St. James's Street. "In this house," writes Mr. H. R. Attree, in his Topography of Brighton, "the dice are often rattled to some tune, and bank-notes transferred from one hand to another, with as little ceremony as bills of the play, or quack doctor's draughts to their patients." This library was established by Mr. Donaldson, jun., who disposed of it to Mr. Osborne, from whom it passed to Mr. Nathaniel Turner.

Originally, beneath the balconies in front of the two first-mentioned libraries, were seats, with and without reclining backs, upon which, in genial weather, subscribers were accustomed to lounge and peruse the newspaper or the last new novel of the day. Cigars then were unknown, and short pipes had not come into vogue, so that these retreats were not disfigured with the notice "No smoking allowed," as the "weed" was not indulged in, except behind a long "churchwarden" at the tavern, where gossips nightly met to chat over the scandals of the day. Besides these retreats beneath the balconies, there were open high-backed seats, called Settles, much after the structure of rustic chairs in parks and pleasure grounds, upon various parts of the promenade around the Steine. At the bottom of the Steine, also, facing the sea, was the Alcove, a summer-house kind of building, capable of seating something like half-a-dozen persons. Bew,* in his diary, date, Thursday, August 26th, 1779, says, "This morning I edged away towards the Alcove, at the east end of the bottom of the Steyne, wherein were seated *two* Elders, and perhaps, a *chaste Susanna;* at any rate, she was not naked. On my approach they departed hastily, and I joined the deserted lady—in discourse, by observing that the town was thin, and that I heard trade in general was very bad. 'Very bad, indeed, Sir,' said she; 'I suppose you are a

* Mr. Bew, who afterwards lived in East Street, was dentist to George IV., and, in conjunction with Mr. Frederick Vining, lessee of the Theatre Royal Brighton.

fellow sufferer. You belong to the players, Sir, don't you?' 'My dear,' replied I, 'why should you think so?' 'Because you are seldom without a book in your hand.' 'Do few read besides players, then?'—'Yes, Sir, I beg pardon; I had another reason; but you'll excuse me.' 'Indeed I will not my dear.'—'Why then, Sir, as you advanced towards us, one of those *elderly* gentlemen—by their discourse I believe they are parsons,—said to the other, 'Come, Sir, let us be gone, or we shall be taken off; *Mr. Diarist* is coming this way.' 'Now, Sir, if that is your name, tho' I have never seen it yet in the play bills, was it wonderful that I should imagine you to be one of the gentlemen players.'—I assured her, nevertheless, that I was not entitled to that honour; and here you may imagine our conference ended."

Another retreat for a lounge or promenade was the Colonnade under the balcony of the library on the Marine Parade, established in 1798, by Messrs. Donaldson and Wilkes, and afterwards carried on by Mr. Pollard, and then by Messrs. Tuppen and Walker. This library, and the original two on the Steine, were not merely the resort of visitors for the purpose of literary pursuits, as their name legitimately implies, but after eight o'clock in the evening, during the Summer season, that portion of the business in connexion with books ceased, and holland blinds being drawn down to cover over the whole of the books and book-shelves, a saloon was formed that nightly attracted hundreds of *tonish* idlers to the vocal and instrumental music that was discoursed, and to join in the raffles, similar to those that were going on at Raggett's subscription room.

Bew, in his Diary, date, Saturday, September 4th, 1799, writes,—"Every article of convenience, every trinket of luxury, is transferred by this uncertain, quick mode of conveyance. Not a shop without its rattle-trap,—rattle, rattle, rattle, morning and evening. Here may be seen,—walk in and see,—an abridgment of the wisdom of this world;—the pomps and vanities are at large, varying like yonder evanescent clouds. Observe the fond parent initiating her forward offspring in the use of the dice-box, and herself setting the example; yet may she wonder, at some future day, and think her throw in life's raffle extremely severe, that a propensity to that and similar habits should continue and increase."

Fisher, in August, 1805, established a new Auction Mart in St. James's Street, that was open morning and night. The following extracts from a private diary will in some degree explain the rage which was on at those periods for this and similar virulent pastimes :—

August 2nd, 1792.—But little company stirred out to-day, on account of the intense heat of the weather. Sporting men of fashion, dashers, and blacklegs certainly assembled on the Steine, to make their bets for to-morrow's Lewes Races, where much excellent sport is expected. The other part of the day was spent mostly in Raggett's Subscription House, at Billiards, Dice, &c. *On dit.*—Lady Lade is returning from Brighton in much dudgeon,—because, forsooth, Lady Jersey, she says, made *wulgar* mouths at her yesterday on the race-ground!

July 23rd, 1805.—A very select and elegant assemblage of nobility last night paraded the Steine until a late hour. Donaldson's library, also, was very fashionably filled; and Wilks's Pic-nic Auction exhibited a blaze of rank and beauty.

August 23rd.—Wilks's bargains were in fashionable request last night, and the knock-down blows of Fisher were directed with his usual ability and effect. Fisher's New Auction Lounge was again well filled with rank and beauty this morning. A monster of the finny tribe has been exhibited in a marquee, pitched purposely for the occasion, on the Steine to-day. It is called a Star *Fish*, and is so worthy the attention of the curious that it has divided the attention of the public with *Fisher*.

August 27th.—Wilks's Auction Lounge, last night, was immensely crowded until a late hour: nor has the magnetical hammer of Fisher, at his new room, been less attractive this morning.

September 21st, 1807.—Donaldson's and Pollard's libraries have had crowded assemblages, and the game of Loo has had more than its usual number of votaries. This evening Mr Cartwright will perform at Fisher's Lounge, on the musical glasses, under the patronage of Mrs Orby Hunter.

October 8th.—Pam still possesses his original attraction, and the Belles are nightly *looed* in his presence.—Rather a *bad* pun that, eh?

May 9th, 1810.—Donaldson's and Walker's spacious and airy Steine and Marine Lounges have not been so interestingly decorated with rank and beauty as they have to-day appeared for many preceding months, though the amusements of one card loo, &c., are not yet there introduced. The diversion of raffling has not been permitted at either for some years past, nor will it again be allowed, so long as the Little-go Bill remains unrepealed; we may therefore conclude that the rattle of the dice will hever be heard at either again.

Trinket Auctions were established when an Act of Parliament, called Mr. Vansittart's Little-go Bill, was passed, that did away with raffling at all places of public resort, as the profits to the librarians at the watering places generally, arose from these diversions, rather than from the high literary character of the books upon their shelves, or the erudite position of the persons whose names were in their subscription books because fashion ruled it so. The novelty of Trinket Auctions soon wore off, and then another pastime, under the name of Loo, was introduced. The game was very diverting in its progress, and afforded an occasion for many agreeable sallies of wit, according to the talent of the conductor of it and the disposition to replications of those about him. The Loo Sweepstakes, as they were termed, were limited to eight subscribers, and the individual stake, one shilling. The full number being obtained, a certain quantity of cards, amongst which was a Knave of Clubs, or Pam, were shuffied, cut, and separately dealt and turned: the numbers were called in rotation during the process, and that against which Pam appeared was pronounced the winner.

In September, 1810, an attempt was made to constitute the game of Loo an illegal act. For that purpose informations were lodged against Messrs. Donaldson and Walker, the proprietors of the Steine and Marine Libraries, and the case was heard at Lewes, before a full Bench of Magistrates. Mr. Courthorpe was counsel for the prosecution, and Mr. Adolphus appeared for the defendants. The only case that was argued was that of an information against Mr. Walker, founded on the 12th of Geo. II., c. 28, and which was dwelt on with much force,—such indeed as a confidence of success only could inspire —by Mr. Courthorpe. To prove that defendant had offended within the meaning of the Act, and consequently was liable to the penalty therein expressed, i.e., two hundred pounds, Mrs. White, the wife of one of the informers, was called and examined. This witness hesitated considerably in her evidence, particularly when interrogated by Mr. Adolphus, as to her motive in becoming a subscriber to the Loo amusement at Walker's and whether or not she had so acted with the sole aim and purpose of lodging an information against Mr. Walker, which she at last admitted. The substance of her evidence was "That she attended at Walker's library on the 30th of August; that she stood next to Mr. Walker on that occasion; that she heard him say, 'Ladies and gentlemen, three shillings are only wanting to complete the sweepstake for this elegant Lady's Morocco work-box;' that she gave him a shilling for a chance, when he asked her in what name she would have it, and she said Mrs. Goodlove; that a lady at length shuffled and cut the cards; that Mr. Walker dealt them; that the first dealt was called Mr. Bangup; that she won Pam, and got the prize; that Mr. Walker told her she had won it, and that she was to receive seven shillings in goods, or subscribe an extra sixpence, and have two chances for another box of much superior value; that she took the prize she had won, and lost two shillings in other ventures, &c." When questioned by the Earl of Chichester, one of the magistrates, as to the real value of the prize that had been nominated at 7s, her husband whispered to her what to say; which being overheard by the Noble Earl, Mr. White was compelled instantly to quit the room, and to wait without, that he might be at hand in case he should be wanted. Mr. Adolphus (the witness being dismissed) addressed the Bench in a most able speech, concluding by producing an Act of Parliament passed in 1806, by which he clearly evinced that the present informations could not be sustained, as the said Act dispossessed magistrates of all jurisdiction and control in matters of that sort then before them. Mr. Courthorpe laboured hard, notwithstanding, to gain his point; but as his oratory had not the power to supersede an Act of Parliament, his labour was in vain. As authorities in support of the Act he produced, Mr. Adolphus was upheld by the opinion of the Attorney-General, and a decision in the Court of King's Bench. The Magistrates, from what had been brought forward by Mr. Adolphus, saw their incompetency in so strong a light, that they dismissed the business, even without hearing the reply which Mr. Adolphus was about to make to his learned friend. There were three other informations, all of which of course were withdrawn. The librarians returned home in high spirits, and the Loo parties, subsequently, and exulting in the success of the day, were more numerous than usual.

Pam, the good genius of Loo, continued to hold sway at the libraries till 1817, when the magistrates took an antipathy towards him, owing to the unbounded patronage which he received from the ladies in general. They considered him an unwelcome resident; so, by their mandate, supported by an obsolete Act of Henry VIII., he was excommunicated from all the libraries, as, at this time he had taken up his abode at Mr. T. H. Wright's Library, then just established at the south-west corner of Pavilion Street. Gradually, however, he resumed his position at the establishments of Lucombe and Tuppen; but notwithstanding the presiding influence of those two patterers and wits, assisted by Mr. Stacy, the present librarian at the Royal Albion Rooms, and Mr. Wheeler, the box book-keeper at the Brighton Theatre, the destruction of the fashionable promenade, by curtailing the Steine of its fair proportions, so distorted the throng and habit of fashion, that Pam fell into desuetude and the libraries, unsupported by him, became failures.

Five and twenty years since, Brighton abounded with libraries, Wright's, in the Colonnade, North Street, removed from the Pavilion Parade, and Eber's, in Castle Square, a branch of the London establishment, being amongst the principal of those that then existed. Furnishing food for the mind, however, was a less profitable speculation than supplying materials for the understandings, as Mr. Tozer on the former premises, and Messrs. Dutton and Thorowgood on the latter, by the sale of boots and shoes, have matured businesses that may vie with any of the same trade in the kingdom. It is somewhat remarkable, too, that a portion of the premises in Prince's Place, occupied by Mr. Lulham, boot and shoemaker, and the house in the occupation of Messrs. Sharman and Co., North Street, as a boot and shoe mart, were the library of Mr. Taylor. These facts certainly confirm the adage,—at any rate when besieged by the multitude with a civil view, — that "there is nothing like leather."

From time to time libraries of more or less pretensions have been started, either by private parties or by societies of membership; but most of them have become things of the past, which in their short lived career possessed nothing to warrant a recital of their history.

The oldest established now in existence is Mr. Folthorp's North Street Library, originally Choat's, and then Loader's. It is admirably situated, and has a supply of books, periodicals, and newspapers equalled by no other circulating library in the county. The only proprietary literary establishments, with the exception of those attached to the several places of public worship and their schools, are the Brighton Royal Literary and Scientific Institution, Albion Rooms, to which a Chess Club is attached; the Railway Library and Scientific Institution, for the use of persons employed on the railway; and the Young Men's Christian Association, in Middle Street. Some of the booksellers have a lending library connected with their businesses. The principal of these are Dollman's, Western Road, and Burrett's, Waterloo Street, Hove; Styles's, North Street, Sugg's St. James's Street, and Grant's Library and Reading Room, Castle Square. The literary character of which the Steine formerly boasted is now entirely gone, and it is content to be considered the emporium of the followers of Galen and Æsculapius, who as much there abound as the students of Coke and Blackstone throng Ship Street, and give that locality of quips, quirks, and the law's delays the appellation of Chancery Lane.

Chapter XXIX.

THE THEATRES.

Besides the Assembly Rooms at the Castle Tavern and the Old Ship Hotel, and the Libraries, the Theatre has been, and still is, a place of fashionable resort in Brighton. The remnant of the first Theatre ever erected in the town has recently been restored to public notice in consequence of the premises undergoing alterations in the process of converting them into ale and porter stores, by Messrs. Charlton and Co. They are situated in North Street, and are approached by a doorway between the shops of Messrs. Cunditt, jewellers, and Mr. Pritchard, confectioner. To the old inhabitants they are better known as Wallis's wine and spirit vaults; and at a recent date they were occupied by Mr. Cordy, the son-in-law and successor of Mr. Wallis. In 1789 they were used as the printing office of Messrs. William and Arthur Lee, who in a few years removed their establishment to Lewes, and then Mr. Wallis took possession of them.

In this building David Garrick displayed his inimitable histrionic talent. The main structure and its original front have long since passed away; but the stage yet remains entire, with its several traps and appointments. An excellent portrait of Garrick, till lately graced the wall, but the modern destroyer of many a work of art, whitewash, has entirely obliterated every feature of it.

Annexed is a copy of the "Bill of the Play," in the possession of Mr. Cunditt, referring to this Theatre:—

Theatre, North-Street, Brighthelmston,
On WEDNESDAY, October 5, 1785, will be presented,
A COMEDY, called THE

SUSPICIOUS HUSBAND.

Ranger, ... by Mr. GRAHAM, Jun.
Frankly, ... by Mr. WEWITZER.
Bellamy, ... by Mr. WILLIAMS.
Jack Meggott, ... by Mr. FROST.
Tester, ... by Mr. FOLLETT, Jun.
Buckle, ... by Mr. PHILLIPS.
Simon, ... by Mr. DANIELL.
And Mr. *Strickland*, ... by Mr. LESTRANGE.
Mrs. *Strickland*, ... by Mrs. WALCOT.
Jacintha, ... by Mrs. BOLTON.
Lucetta, ... by Mrs. EDGAR.
Millener, ... by Miss STEVENSON.
And *Clarinda*, ... by Mrs. ELLIOTT.
(From the Theatre Royal, Dublin, Being her First Appearance on this Stage.)

Dancing, between the Acts, by *Master* and *Miss* Michel.

To which will be added a FARCE, called,

WHO'S THE DUPE?

Old Doiley, ... by Mr. FOLLET.
Sandford, ... by Mr. FROST.
Granger, ... by Mr. WILLIAMS.
And *Gradus*, ... by Mr. GRAHAM, Jun.
Miss *Doiley*, ... by Mrs. BOLTON.
Charlotte, ... by Miss EDGAR.

TICKETS and PLACES for the BOXES to be taken of Mr. *Baily*, at the *Theatre*.

Doors to be opened at SIX, *and to begin exactly at* SEVEN.

The Tragedy of RICHARD III, and the New Pantomime of ROBINSON CRUSOE, or, HARLEQUIN FRIDAY, (as performed for *Eighty Nights*, at the Theatre Royal, Drury Lane) is obliged to be postponed till *Friday* Evening, on account of the machinery not being quite ready.

The following are extracts from the Diary of Mr. Bew:—

1778.—Tuesday, September 1. — *The Settle.* — STEINE. —Mr. Griffith, of

Drury Lane playhouse, with much civility, conducts me to the Theatre, in North Street, in which *company* he is *concerned*, am fearful the manager is most *concerned*, at—the badness of the season, for there seems a *plentiful lack* of company. But, not to play too much upon words, it is a pretty building, something larger than that at Richmond, and seems well adapted to its intended uses.

Friday, 4.—*At the Theatre.*—In the evening went to Griffith's benefit, the *West Indian*, by desire of Lady Mills; much, but pleasingly disappointed, because the company performed a great deal better than from information I had been taught to expect; the ladies also were, what all stage-ladies not always are, —extremely decent.

Previous to 1774 there was no other temple dedicated to Thalia and Melpomene, than a barn. The first theatre was built by the late Mr. Samuel Paine, and let in 1774, to Mr. Roger Johnstone, formerly the property-man at Covent Garden Theatre, who, having continued it for three years only, it was then leased to the late Mr. Fox, of Covent Garden Theatre also, in 1777, for the term of fifteen years, at the annual rent of sixty guineas.

It was understood, however, between the lessor and the lessee, that the former, in addition, was to have the *net receipts* of the house on one night, to be called his benefit night, clear of all expenses, in every succeeding year; and that *his family* should be free of the theatre, or possess the right of witnessing the performances there, at all times, without being liable to any charge as the consequence of their visits.

The latter stipulation was correctly introduced into the covenants of the lease, but not so the former, *net profits* being there stipulated instead of *net receipts*; the issue of which was, that Mr. Paine was called on to defray the expenses of his first benefit night, contrary to what had previously been understood, and orally agreed upon, between him and Mr. Fox.

This circumstance had nearly given rise to an unpleasant litigation between the parties; in which Mr. Paine, in all probability, would have been the sufferer, for the want of a document to establish the propriety of his claim; but such a mortification and injury he preserved himself from, by having recourse to the following expedient:—

The right of gratuitous admission to the theatre, to himself and family, as above specified, was undisputed; and as no place in the house was stipulated as the only part they should be permitted to enter in their visits, he determined to avail himself of his privilege to the full extent of its bearing. He, therefore, collected his family together, and with them entered the theatre for a succession of nights, resolutely occupying the best seats in the boxes, to the exclusion of other and more profitable applicants.

The manager, thus opposed, and law and equity pronounced by the public as both in favour of Mr. Paine, consented to ratify his first agreement, and the system of warfare adopted to harass and punish him, ceased. Before the expiration of the fifteen years' lease the house was found inadequate to the accommodation of the increased population of the town, and a new one was erected in Duke Street. The license for the theatre was yearly obtained from the magistrates at the Quarter Sessions at Lewes; and Mr. Fox, on finishing the house in Duke Street, applied for the removal of the the license to that place. His application was granted, no opposition being offered to the measure by Mr. Paine.

The latter, however, discovered the error of his non-resistance before the next application for the license became requisite, when his opposition to it was a matter of course; but which proved ineffectual from the delay, and the license was granted to the same house, on which, without opposition, it had been bestowed the year before. The family of Paine were, therefore, pecuniary sufferers of several hundred pounds per annum by this event, and for which the only compensation ever received fell short of one hundred and twenty pounds, or guineas.

On the death of Mr. Fox, the Duke Street Theatre was purchased by H. Cobb, Esq., of Clement's Inn, who built the present house in the New Road, 1807, and removed the license thereto, having first satisfied the ground-landlord in respect to the measure.

The building had a plain front of wood, drawn out to imitate blocks of stone, unpierced with windows, and was approached by a semi-circular carriage and foot-way from the street, as it was set back from the main road to nearly the present frontage of Mr. Patching's house, on the site of which the Theatre then stood. The projecting entrance to the Boxes, in the centre of the front, was by a Grecian portico supported by four Tuscan pillars, from which branched brackets supporting two round shaped oil lamps. The buildings abutting east and west had also similar lamps. The Pit and Gallery entrances were on the east side, approached by an external passage, that had a door, over which was painted "Pit and Gal." The stage door was a little to the west of the principal entrance, where the word "Boxes" was conspicuously painted. Five posts divided the footway on each side of the portico. A print of the Theatre was published in London, April 1st, 1804, by T. Woodfall, Villiers' Street, Strand, and several figures therein exhibit the peculiar fashion of the day in dress. The license to this Theatre Royal was granted by a special Act of Parliament, which passed in the year 1788.

An anecdote connected with this Theatre, and noted in "Brighton Past and Present," by Mrs. Merrifield, is worthy of quotation:—"It was during the time that Fox was manager that the celebrated Mrs. Jordan trod these boards as an actress. A friend of mine, who sometimes visited the green room, one day found her in great distress, threatened by a Sheriff's Officer, on account of the debt of an extravagant brother. Mrs. Jordan solicited my friend to become surety for her. 'When I went into the room,' said my friend, 'I thought her one of the plainest little women I had ever seen, but I had not been in her company half-an-hour before I thought her charming.' It is almost unnecessary to say that he complied with her request, and relieved this fascinating actress from her embarassment; nor had he cause to repent of his goodnature, for Mrs. Jordan paid the debt as soon as she was able, and thus released him from his engagement."

Annexed is a copy of a bill of the performance at this theatre:

For the Benefit of

Mr. PALMER, JUN.,

The last night but Two of performing this Season.

Theatre, Brighton,

On Wednesday, October 15th, 1794, will be presented, the popular play of

THE JEW.

Sheva (for that night only,) .. by Mr. Bannister, jun.
From the Theatre Royal, Drury Lane.
Sir Stephen Bertram .. . by Mr. Dormer.
Charles Ratcliffe .. .. by Mr. Palmer, jun.

Jabel .. .. by Mr. SIMPSON.
Frederick .. .. .. by Mr. PALMER.
From the Theatre Royal, Drury Lane,—positively the last time of his performing here this Season.
Eliza .. .. by Mrs. SIMPSON.
(End of the Play.)
A COMIC MEDLEY, by Mr. EDWIN.
After which, the Farce of

THE VILLAGE LAWYER.

Sheepface (for that night only,) by Mr. PARSONS.
From the Theatre Royal, Drury Lane.
Snarl .. .. by Mr. SIMPSON.
Scout .. .. by Mr. BANNISTER, jun.

The whole to conclude with the favourite Entertainment of

THE LYAR.

Young Wilding .. .. .. by Mr. PALMER.
Papillion .. .. by Mr. PALMER, jun.
Miss Grantham .. .. .. by Mrs. PALMER, jun.
Being her first appearance.

⁎ The Nobility, Gentry, and Public are respectfully informed that, on account of the great call for places, part of the PIT will (for that night) be laid into the Boxes.

Tickets to be had, and places for the Boxes taken, of Mr. PALMER, jun., No. 11, Russell Street, and at the Theatre, from Ten till Three o'clock.

The returns for the house on the occasion were: —

	£.	s.	d.
Six Box Tickets	1	4	0
Fifteen Pit ditto	1	10	0
Two Gallery ditto		2	0
Taken at doors	7	8	0
Total	£10	4	0

The "Brighton New Guide," 1800, published by Fisher, Old Steine, says: "The scenes are painted by Mr. Carver, of Covent-Garden Theatre, and they do honour to the abilities of that ingenious artist; and if the abilities of the actors are not sufficiently powerful to excite the enthusiasm of applause, they are not so contemptible as to create disgust. Candour must acknowledge, that the theatrical business at Brighthelmston is conducted with great regularity, and that if perfection is not reached, mediocrity is surpassed."

In 1672, a tax on plays was proposed; but the court party objected to it. They said the players were the King's servants, and administered to his pleasures. Sir John Coventry pleasantly asked, "Whether the King's pleasures lay among the male or the female actors?" Charles, who, besides his other mistresses, entertained two actresses, Mrs. Davis and Nell Gwynne, was hurt by this sarcasm, and took an unworthy revenge. Some of his guards attacked Coventry, and slit his nose. The Commons expressed their indignation, by passing what is called the Coventry Act, by which maiming and deforming were made capital crimes, and those persons who had assaulted Coventry were rendered incapable of receiving the King's pardon.

In July, 1805, when the Prince of Wales bestowed his patronage upon the Duke Street Theatre, and first attached to it the gracious adjective, "Royal," great improvements were effected in the house, those in his Royal Highness's box particularly so: blue panels, with sparkling gold stars, on a dark ground, and ornamented with festoons of roses, superbly distinguished it; a crimson curtain of velvet depending from the ceiling also heightened the effect, and gave an indescribable appearance of grandeur to the whole. The box was also carpeted throughout, and handsome painted chairs with cushions in lieu of fixed seats, made part of its furniture.

On the 13th of August, 1805, a piece was produced in honour of the birthday of the Prince of Wales, and was called *The Twelfth of August*. The plot of the piece was: "Sofa Hazleby," the daughter of an opulent farmer, a resident of Brighton, who has numerous suitors, has promised to become the bride of him who can give the best solution to a question which she will submit to their consideration on the Green, on the Twelfth of August; and the reason she assigns for choosing that day for a decision so momentous to her, is because it gave birth to England's Heir,—a Prince whose suavity of manners, benevolence of heart, and mental endowments have rendered him the pride of his country and the admiration of Europe. "That auspicious morn," she continues, "could but appear to me as most grateful and best adapted to my purpose, in which every honest countenance I might gaze at should be brightened with exulting smiles."—The preceding part of the drama being over, in which her eccentric suitors afforded much mirth to the audience, the final scene presents a supposed view of the South Downs, and the entrance of Brighton, the latter brilliantly illuminated, the initials P. W., the feathers, and a blazing star, being appropriately conspicuous.

In 1799, Mr. Alexander Archer was manager of the Duke Street Theatre. Upon stripping the paper from the walls of 34, Bond Street, on the 20th of May, in the present year, to effect some alterations, a relic in the character of a "play bill," was brought to light. It is thus worded: "Engagement of Mr. Quick. Doors open at half-past six. Begin precisely at 7 o'clock. Mr. Quick's fifth night. Theatre Brighthelmston. On Tuesday, July 13th, 1802, will be performed the admired comedy of *She Stoops to Conquer;* the part of 'Tony Lumpkin,' by Mr. Quick. After which will be added *St. Patrick's-Day, or the Scheming Lieutenant.* Lee, Printer, Brighton." The house had just been vacated by the descendants of Johnson, who for many years was the bill-sticker of the town. The first stone of the present Theatre was laid on the 24th of September, 1806, by Mr. Brunton, senr.; and the building was opened on Saturday, the 6th of June, 1807, with the tragedy of *Hamlet,* when Mr. and Mrs. Charles Kemble represented the Prince and Ophelia.

The *Brighton Ambulator*—a publication almost extinct,—thus speaks of the present theatre as it was when opened by the first lessee, Mr. Trotter:—

THE THEATRE.

This place of public amusement is situated in the New Road, leading into North Street. It is a very handsome structure, having a colonnade, which runs along its whole front, supported by neat stone pillars. The entrance into the Boxes is in the centre; and that to the Pit is on the right, and the Gallery on the left of the building.

The interior has two tier of boxes. The Prince Regent's box is on the left of the stage, divided from the other boxes by an iron lattice work, gilded, which gives it a pleasing and private appearance. The pit and gallery are well constructed for the audience, particularly the latter, which has a prominent view of the stage.

The house is illuminated by nine cut-glass chandeliers, and a range of patent lamps at the foot of the stage. The stage is exceedingly convenient, and has a length proportioned to the structure. The whole is fitted up with a tasteful elegance, and we must acknowledge, that it reflects honour on the discriminate judgment of Mr. Trotter, the manager.

This account of the theatre describes it as it was more than half a century since; as of late years it has been, externally and internally, greatly modernized; although the chief lighting attraction in its transition from oil and wax to gas, a noble and well supplied chandelier, which was lowered and raised at pleasure over the centre of the pit, has long since been removed, the light from it detracting from the scenic effect, and the great heat which it disseminated militating against the comfort of the audience, especially the "gods."

The present owner of the property is George Cobb, Esq., an Alderman of the Borough of Brighton, who, a few years since, purchased of the executors of the late Sir Thomas Clarges the moiety which that baronet held.

Sir Thomas, in his latter days, was what is modernly termed, a little "cracky" in the cranium. Just about the period of the murder of the Italian boy, by Bishop and Williams, when pitch plasters were in vogue, and were as much terrors in the public mind as garottings now are, Sir Thomas had a pony which he imagined was unwell, and beyond the aid of veterinary skill. He therefore, with the manual service of his groom, undertook to cure it himself, and thus proceeded:—He procured a sheet of canvass, which he spread with a composition of pitch, tar, and tallow, and in this cere-cloth he encased the body of the animal, and twice daily, in the midst of Summer, took it, with merely a horse-cloth over it, on the Race-hill and submitted it to severe exercise, the groom walking it briskly, and himself riding beside it on horseback for two hours at a stretch. His intention was to pursue this course till all the virtue in the composition would become absorbed by the afflicted system of the animal, when its cure would be effected and the canvass would of its own accord drop off. The severity, however, of the process, was too much for the poor creature; for having borne the punishment somewhat more than a week, one morning, when Sir Thomas and his man went to the stable in Rock Mews, where a box had been specially fitted up, the straight-jacketed small edition of a horse was a stiffened corpse.

Immediately previous to her retirement from the stage, Mrs. Siddons filled an engagement here for three nights, namely, Tuesday, August 8th, 1809, as "Mrs. Beverley" in *The Gamester*,*

* A copy of the bill of the performance on this occasion is in the possession of Alderman Martin.

Tuesday, 15th, as "Lady Macbeth," and on Thursday, 18th, as "Isabella," in the tragedy of that name. The receipts of the house for the 15th, amounted to £172 16s, a sum by far exceeding that which the Theatre could boast of having held on any night previous. On August 29th, she also appeared as "Margaret of Anjou," in the tragedy of *Earl of Warwick*, for the benefit of Mr. Murray, on which occasion the receipts amounted to £150 5s; and on September 12th, as "Lady Macbeth," for the benefit of Mr. Cresswell. On the last occasion Mr. Charles Kemble, for the first time on any stage, made his appearance as "Macbeth." Every actor of celebrity has trodden the boards of the Brighton Theatre, which has been the nursery for supplying many first-rate performers to the patent houses of the Metropolis. At a Masquerade which took place here, October 8th, 1812, a great disturbance arose in consequence of Theodore Hook and his friends appearing unmasked.

The several lessees have been Mr. Trotter, Mr. Grove, Mr. Brunton, sen.,—father of the late Dowager Countess of Craven, who at the time of her marriage was acting on the stage of this Theatre, in her father's company,—Messrs. Jonas and Penley, Mr. (Romeo) Coates, Mr. John Brunton, jun., Mr. (Jerry) Russell,—when the house was open only on Mondays, Wednesdays, and Fridays,—Messrs Bew and Vining, Mr. Charles Hill, Messrs. Walton and Holmes,—a commonwealth,—Messrs. Saville and Harroway, Mr. Hooper, Mr. Poole, Captain Belcour, Mr. H. Farren, and the present respected lessee, Mr. H. Nye Chart. Formerly, the season extended from July to October; now the house usually continues open from the latter end of July until the beginning of March.

Upon the completion of the present Theatre in the New Road, a permanent building for a Circus was erected on the Grand Parade, between Carlton Street and the weigh-bridge, which, for obtaining the weight of the loads in the waggons and carts that traversed the turnpike road to Lewes, stood at the spot that forms the bottom of Sussex Street. It was completed by Messrs. Kendall and Co., and opened in August, 1808. The building had a frontage of neat design, in width one hundred feet, which was also its depth, that extended into Circus Street. A wing to the north of the Circus was appropriated for a billiard lounge, confectionary, &c.; and the corresponding wing to the south for a coffee-house and hotel. The representation of a prancing horse surmounted the centre of the structure.

The only incident worthy of record which took place in this building during the few years that it was devoted to equestrian exhibitions, was an accident which befel the daughter of the lessee, Mr. Saunders, on the evening of Monday, August 28th, 1809, on the occasion of a bespeak of the Duke of Marlborough, when, while riding round the ring, which was thirty-six feet in diameter, Miss Saunders lost her equilibrium and fell. She was borne away insensible, amidst the intense anxiety of a most fashionable audience. The announcement, however, of the Acting Manager, Mr. Clark, that she had received but a slight injury, gave a salutary relief to all present. At her benefit, which took place on the previous Thursday, under the patronage of Lord and Lady Somerset, the house was crowded in every part.

In 1812 the Circus closed from want of support, and for a few years the premises were occupied as a Bazaar, a speculation which was quite a failure, although every inducement in the way of loos, lotteries, and lucky-bags, was introduced, with occasional displays of fireworks and the ascents of fire-balloons from the parade ground opposite, now the extreme north Enclosure. At that period, and for some years afterwards, the land northward from the Pavilion boundary wall to the Level was enclosed with posts and rails in areas like the present, and formed a public promenade, and the parade ground of the military. How it became enclosed with iron railings and planted with trees and flowers, to the exclusion of the inhabitants, has never been satisfactorily explained. Occasionally attempts have been made to investigate the business; but inasmuch as money is required for such a purpose, and the majority of the ratepayers are contented with the excellent manner the Enclosures are conducted, they allow the Trustees who have possessed themselves of the right, to continue in undisturbed possession.

From time to time since the demolition of the Grand Parade Circus, various troupes of equestrians have visited Brighton. Saunders's was the first, his exhibition, which took place on the present site of St. George's Place, being termed a Mountebank performance, and consisting, besides feats of horsemanship, of such tricks as are witnessed in shows at fairs and races. On Thursday evening, June 21st, 1821, from six to eight thousand persons assembled to witness the equestrian exploits, &c., of this company. In the midst of the amusements one of the scaffoldings, on which were nearly a hundred persons,—men, women, and children,—gave way, and the whole fell to the ground, a depth of about four or five feet. Many persons received severe bruises, and Mr. Siller, of His Majesty's private band, had his leg broken in two places. The chief prop of the scaffolding was some slight paling, the yielding of which to the great pressure above occasioned the accident, which, under the circumstances, might have produced far more serious results, as many persons were immediately under it at the moment. Cook and Bridges — familiarly known to the juveniles of the time as "Cock and Breeches," —afterwards came and took up their position on the Level; and then followed Ryan, Cooke, Batty, Tournaire, &c., in more or less permanent buildings; followed by the flying visits of troupes in mammoth tents. The last erection for the exhibition of horsemanship, and that still in existence, is the affair in Sussex Street, the hitherto success of which is evidence that the intelligent portion of the community have not failed to appreciate the talent which has been produced.

Chapter XXV.

BRIGHTON FROM ITS SIMPLICITY TO ITS PRESENT RENOWN.

The primitive state of Brighthelmston, both as respects the condition and habits of the inhabitants and the position and style of the habitations, must to a considerable extent be left to conjecture, as there is no doubt the great changes which have taken place in and about the town to give it the importance which it at present possesses as England's "Queen of Watering Places," have all been effected within the last 150 years.

An engraving in "The Antiquities of England and Wales," published in 1775*, showing the ruins of the Blockhouse at that period, gives a representation of the houses on the Cliff at the spot whereon now stand the Old Ship Hotel and the premises adjacent. The south end of Black-lion Street is very conspicuous, the corner houses consisting only of dwellings one story in height, of a cottage or hovel-like appearance, very singular in architectural design when compared with the present noble block of buildings of Messrs. Hedges and Butler, the wine merchants, on the east side.

The author of a "Tour through Great Britain," date, 1724, says:—"Bright Helmston, commonly called Bredhemston, is a poor fishing town, old built, and on the very edge of the sea. The fishermen have large barks, in which they go away to Yarmouth, on the coast of Norfolk, to the fishing fair there, and hire themselves for the season to catch herrings for the merchants; and they tell us that these make a very good business of it. The sea is very unkind to this town, and has, by its continued encroachments, so gained upon it that in a little time more they might reasonably expect it would eat up the whole town, above one hundred houses having been devoured by the water in a few years past; and they are now obliged to get a brief granted them to beg money all over England, to raise banks against the water; the expense of which, the brief expressly says, will be eight thousand pounds; which, if one were to look on the town, would seem to be more than all the houses in it are worth."

The Rev. William Clarke, Rector of Buxted, and grandfather of the celebrated traveller, thus writes to his friend:—

Brighthelmston, July 22, 1736.

Dear Bowyer,

We are now sunning ourselves upon the beach at Brighthelmston, and observing what a tempting figure this Island made formerly in the eyes of those gentlemen who were pleased to civilize and subdue it. Such a tract of sea; such regions of corn; and such an extent of fine carpet, that gives your eye the command of it all. But then the mischief is, that we have little conversation

* By Francis Grose, Esq., F. A. S. London: Printed for S. Hooper, No. 25, Ludgate Hill, 1775.—(Imp. 4to.)

besides the *clamor nauticus*, which is here a sort of treble to the plashing of the waves against the cliffs. My morning business is bathing in the sea, and then buying fish; the evening is riding out for air, viewing the remains of old Saxon camps, and counting the ships in the road, and the boats that are trawling. Sometimes we give the imagination leave to expatiate a little;—fancy that yon are coming down, and that we intend next week to dine one day in Dieppe, in Normandy; the price is already fixed, and the wine and lodgings there tolerably good. But though we build these castles in the air, I assure you that we live here *almost underground*. I fancy the architects here usually take the altitude of the inhabitants, and lose not an inch between the head and the ceiling, and then dropping a step or two below the surface, the second story is finished something under 12 feet, I suppose this was a necessary precaution against storms, that a man should not be blown out of his bed into New England, Barbary, or God knows where. But as the lodgings are *low* they are cheap; we have *two parlours, two bed chambers, pantry, &c.*, for 5s per week; and if you will really come down you need not fear a bed of the proper dimensions. And then the coast is safe; the cannons are all covered with rust and grass; the ships moored, and no enemy apprehended. Come and see.

Nec tela temeres
Gallica, nec Pictum tremeres nec littore toto
Prospiceres dubiis ventura Saxona ventis.

My wife does not forget her good wishes and compliments upon this occasion. How you would surprise all your friends in Fleet Street, to tell them you were just come from France, with a vivacity that everybody would believe to be just imported from thence!

In this year, 1736, the poor rates were eight pence in the pound on the rack rent, "which was then," says Dunvan, "an intolerable burthen." About this time visitors of distinction began annually, in Summer, as soon as the deep roads of Sussex became passable with any degree of convenience, to frequent the town; but lodging-houses had not then been put in requisition, the only accommodation being a few indifferent inns; and the principal diversions were hunting, occasional horse-racing, and water excursions.

About the year 1750 the medical use of sea-water in scrofulous and other glandular complaints, under the unwearied and successful attention of Dr. Richard Russell, who removed hither from his seat at Malling, near Lewes, established his fame and also that of the town all over the kingdom. He, may in truth, be considered the founder of Brighton's greatness; and it is much to be regretted that the inhabitants while appreciating the laudable services and good qualities of modern Royal and Noble patrons, and perpetuating individual virtues by works of art in marble and on canvass, have hitherto omitted to mark their gratitude to the memory of the learned Doctor, there being amongst the treasures of the town no memento whatever of him. His portrait, it is true, graces the Telemachus room of the Old Ship Hotel, but it might as well be stowed away in the ex-clock tower of the Pavilion, so rarely have the public an opportunity of seeing it. This hint perhaps may induce the possessor of the portrait to make a present of it to the Corporation, who have recently received several additions by gift to their choice collection of paintings.

The erection of lodging-houses soon became a profitable speculation in Brighton, and that late obscure fishing village began to increase in population and celebrity. The wonderful success of the industry and discernment of Dr. Russell appeared by several cases of cures which he cited in his work, "A Dissertation on the use of Sea-water;" and the most eminent members of the faculty in England bore willing testimony to the great acuteness and utility of his professional investigations. The benefits which the diseased have ever since received from sea-water are, therefore, in a great measure, to be imputed to the medical labours and sagacity of this good man, in grateful commemoration of whom the proprietors of a new street,—the first that was erected, composed principally of lodging-houses for the accommodation of invalid visitors,—named it after him, Russell Street, many of the original houses of which that still remain, though now occupied by a different class of persons than those for whom they were designed, show the improvement that had then taken place in house property. The Rev. Dr. Mannington, of Jevington, in the following epigram, simply, yet elegantly estimates the philanthropical abilities of Dr. Russell :—

> Clara per omne ævum Russelli fama manebit,
> Dum retinet vires unda marina suas.

Thus translated : —

> Admiring ages Russell's fame shall know,
> Till ocean's healing waters cease to flow.

Dr. Russell's son, William—afterwards Mr. Sergeant Kempe, on assuming the name of his maternal grandfather,—however, who appeared to have been one of the wits of the town at that period, by the following lines, knew the limit of his father's skill :—

> Brighthelmston was confess'd by all
> T' abound with females fair;

But more so since fam'd Russell has
Prefer'd the waters there.

Then fly that dang'rous town, ye swains,
For fear ye shall endure
A pain from some bright sparkling eye,
Which Russell's skill can't cure.

Dr. Russell died in 1759, aged 72 years, and was interred in the family vault at South Malling, on the 25th of December. He was the son of Mr. Nathaniel Russell, a surgeon and apothecary of Lewes, and clandestinely married the only daughter of Mr. William Kempe, of South Malling. After his marriage he studied at the University of Leyden, and received instruction under the learned Boerhaave. His death took place in London Dr. A. Relhan was his worthy successor, inasmuch as he fully developed the causes of the salubrity of Brighton, the invaluable efficacy of sea-bathing, and the medical virtues of the chalybeate spring, at the Wick, now the property of Sir Francis Goldsmid. In his "Treatise on the Salubrity of the Town and Neighbourhood," the Doctor writes:—

The town, (June, 1761,) at present consists of six principal streets, many lanes, and some spaces surrounded with houses, called by the inhabitants squares,* The great plenty of flint stones on the shore and in the neighbouring cornfields, enabled them to build the walls of their houses with that material, when in their most impoverished state. At present they ornament the windows and doors with the admirable brick which they burn for their own use. The town improves daily, as the inhabitants, encouraged by the late great resort of company, seem disposed to expend the whole of what they acquire, in erecting new buildings, or improving the old ones. Here are two public rooms, the one convenient, the other not only so, but elegant, (the Old Ship), not excelled perhaps by any in England, that of York excepted.

The *endemial* or popular disorders of temperate people being the product of air and diet, the best proof of the healthfulness of the air of any place is deduced from the customary longevity of the inhabitants, and the rate of the Bills of Mortality. By the poor's rate of this parish, there are 400 families in Brighton, each of these may be supposed to contain five souls (the common calculation in England is six in a family), and consequently the number of inhabitants, exclusive of those supported in the work-house, who, at a medium, amounted to 35, may be estimated at 2,000.

In seven years, beginning with 1753, and 1752, the baptisms were 388, and the burials 227; so that the baptisms were annually to the deaths, nearly as five to three.

But as the dissenters are nearly a tenth of the whole, I may be allowed to add to the number of baptisms 35 for the seven years, which is five annually,

* Castle Square and Little Castle Square.

and nearly a-tenth, and makes the whole of the baptisms 423 to 227 burials. By this the baptisms are annually to the deaths as 60 to 32, which is nearly two births to one death. In London there is annually a death in every 32 persons, which is nearly two to one in favour of Brighton.

With regard to the sea water at this place, it appears by experiments that in Summer (weather tolerably dry) there are in every pint of it at least five drachms and fifteen grains of defecated salt; about five of bittern, or a decomposed earth, attracting humidity from the air; and six grains of white calcarious earth. This proportion of clean contents, being nearly a twenty-third of the the whole, is as great, or perhaps greater, than is to be found in the sea water of any other port in England, and must be owing to its peculiar distance from the rivers, it being further from such, I apprehend, than any other sea port in England.

Dr. Coe, writing in 1766, says:—" Brighton is a small ill-built town, situated on the sea-coast, at present greatly resorted to in the Summer season by persons labouring under various diseases, for the benefit of sea bathing, and drinking sea water; and by the gay and polite on account of the company which frequent it at this season. Until within a few years it was no better than a mere fishing town, inhabited by fishermen and sailors; but through the recommendation of Dr. Russell, and his writings in favour of sea water, it has become one of the principal places in the kingdom. It contains six principal streets, five of which are parallel with each other, and are terminated by the sea, namely, East Street, Black-lion Street, Ship Street, Middle Street, and West Street; and North Street runs along the other ends of the five, from the Assembly Rooms, kept by Mr. Shergold, almost to the Church."

The Rev. William Gilpin*, in his " Observations on the Coasts of Hampshire, Sussex, and Kent," made in the summer of 1774, observes:—" Soon after, we reached Brighthelmstone, a disagreeable place. There is scarcely an object either in it or near it of nature or of art, that strikes the eye with any degree of beauty," and then in a somewhat contradictory manner, adds:—" One of the most picturesque sights we met with at Brighthelmstone, was the sailing of a fleet of mackarel-boats to take their evening station for fishing, which they commonly continue through the night. The sun was just setting when all appeared to be alive. Every boat began to

* Vicar of Boldre near Lymington. The book published by his trustees for the benefit of his school at Boldre, and printed by T. Cadell and W. Davies, Strand, London, 1804. Imp, 8 vo. 136 pp.

weigh anchor and unmoor. It was amusing to see them under so many different forms. Some in a still calm with flagging sails, were obliged to assist their motion with oars; others were just getting into the breeze, which rippled the water around them, and began gently to swell their sails; while the fleet, the water, and the whole horizon, glowed with one rich harmonious tint from the setting sun."

Mrs. P. Hill, in her " Apology*,"—now a very rare work,—in 1787, five years after the Prince of Wales first honoured the town with his presence, complains of the "doors opening direct into the sittings rooms," and of the inconvenience of not being able to be 'out' to any visitor."

Bew writes, Sunday, August 30th, 1778:—"This town is built on spots, in patches, and for want of regularity does not appear to advantage: every man, as to building, seems to have done what appeared right in his own eyes. Here is no magistracy: if there is an affray, the parties must go as far as Lewes, which is much the prettier town, to have it settled. Upon recollection, this town may be quieter for having no trading justices resident on the spot. Am since informed, a gentleman in the commission of the peace attends here occasionally from Lewes.—There can be no antiquities; for Brighthelmston was only a small obscure village, occupied by fishermen, till silken Folly and bloated Disease, under the auspices of a Dr. Russell, deemed it necessary to crowd the shore, and fill the inhabitants with contempt for their visitors." In his "Diary," also, Tuesday, September 7th, 1779, he writes:—"Am viewing my worthy friend, Mr. Bull's house, or rather box, upon the Clift, between Ship Street and Black-lion Street.—He beckons me in, and shews it throughout. It is one pretty room to the height of three stories, with a semicircular window comprising most of the front,

* Mrs Hill's "Apology," for having been induced, by particular desire, and the most specious allurements that could tempt female weakness, to appear in the character of Scrub, Beau Strategem, for one night only, at Brighthelmston, last year, 1786, when the Theatre was applied for by the Honourable George Hanger, and engaged for that purpose; with an address to Mrs. Fitzherbert. Also, some of Mrs. Hill's letters to His Royal Highness the Prince of Wales, Mrs. Fitzherbert, and others. The denouement with events and remarks that may not be deemed uninteresting to this nation at large. By Mrs. Hill.

and on each floor overlooking the sea all ways, which makes the situation most delightful. The ground whereon it stands is copy-hold—indeed the ground in and about Brighton is mostly so—measuring nearly eighteen feet square. The fine is both certain and small. About fifty years ago, this piece of land was sold for four pounds; thirty years since, a purchaser gave eleven; and about this time two years, the Alderman bought it for one hundred pounds to build upon." The premises here referred to are 35, King's road, those in the occupation of Mr. Ridley, boot and shoe maker. In the same Diary, date Monday, September 7th, 1778, he remarks: "Mr Alderman Bull, of London, is building a house on the Clift; a semi-circular window is in each story. Am told he meets with many obstacles in the execution of his design.—Surely it is to the interest of these people (meaning the inhabitants) to have such men become resident among them; but he is denied a convenient entrance to his building. A cellar window to the adjoining house projects before his street door."

That Brighton at the present day possesses fine architectural features cannot be denied. The magnificent Squares and Crescents which flank its sea-frontage, and even form part of the frontage, possess strong claims on our admiration, especially when we glance at the general state and style of architecture of our time, and reflect upon the rapid rise and development of the town—looking to what it was and considering what it is.

During the close of the last, and the beginning of this century, architecture had reached its lowest ebb in England. Our true indigenous Gothic had almost passed into a tradition: the Classic models, from their extreme ill-adaptation to our climate, had undergone such deterioration, that the application of the term even to the best of later works was an absurdity. The influence of Sir Christopher Wren had been of the most baneful character; not that he was himself deficient in genius, but that his style, which hardly attains to grandeur even in the Metropolitan Cathedral, was of a character which inevitably degenerated in feeble hands. Thus it happened that we were left almost without a national style, or, at least with one utterly devoid of intrinsic merit of any kind. The churches and other public buildings were erected upon no principles; and in accordance only with the taste, or want of taste, in the architect, who no longer represented an Art, but devoted himself to a Profession.

Of course, when all the higher and more important offices of architecture were thus indifferently served, it was not to be expected that street-architecture would fare very happily. Our streets, in fact, gradually lost all their picturesqueness and variety of the olden times, and gained neither dignity nor beauty. Complacent builders shrugged their shoulders in pity at ancestors who had covered houses with roofs like over-sized wigs; or had recourse to hanging stories one projecting over the other until the light of heaven only stole into the streets through a narrow aperture above the road. But though these things were quaint and barbarous, there was a something about them which had in it the sense of beauty,—something which makes one even now prefer the High Street of Eastgrinstead to the latest built, the most elegant and supernaturally genteel of our modern terraces.

This, however, has only just begun to be felt, and when Brighton rose like a dream upon the remains of a fishing village, none of these things were thought of. People had certainly discernment enough to see that the rude village style would not do. A visitor of Dr. Russell's time describes Brighton houses as consisting of one or more stories, and with the door-ways so low that you must stoop to enter, and then probably stumble down a step or two into the sitting room. A person has only to go into the Twittens, the narrow lanes between Middle Street and Black Lion Street, to witness even now such illustrations. The Railway booking office, in Castle Square, is a specimen of the architecture of Brighton after this period; and under George IV. it was beginning its marvellous development.

This sort of thing it soon became necessary to alter, and year after year saw the gradual improvement in the streets of the town. But though this resulted in fine streets, and in lofty and commodious houses, the element of beauty was always wanting, simply because there was nothing like a principle in the minds of builders. They had some vague notions of the Palladian oracles, of a bastard Italian, a debased Renaissance, applicable to dwelling-houses; but the results of the application were and have been, up to the present time, deplorable.

Brighton is not alone in this matter,—indeed, it rises superior to very many of its compeers; but when its position and infinite diversity of sight are reflected upon, there cannot fail to be regrets upon the Brighton it might have been. Supposing, for example that an earlier recognition of the claims of Gothic and an English style had taken place. Suppose that the public buildings, instead of being of the packing case order in beauty—hollow cubes with a sham frontage of stuccoed pilasters—had presented the variety in structure and beauty in detail which is found in a minor degree in St. Peter's Church. Suppose further that the streets, instead of having, as at present, flat, level surfaces, without a line of beauty in themselves, without a curve or an angle to reflect the sunshine or hold the shadow, which is so exquisite, had retained even the quaintness of early times, what a town Brighton would have been! No continental town could, from its very situation and the formation of the ground upon which it stands, have exceeded it in picturesque loveliness. And short of this, even had the purer Italian models been followed, had builders attempted such erections as those of Palmeira Square, or those of the Pavilion Buildings,—and they are the best specimens of that class of street architecture which we possess,—the result would have been a grandeur and a beauty which would have left the visitor no ground for a moment's doubt that Brighton is indeed the "Queen of Watering Places."

The improvement in the style of the buildings was the natural result of the great accession of visitors for the benefit of the sea-bathing. Bew remarks, Sunday, September 13th, 1778:—"Took the liberty of surveying all the bathing-machines. Fine ladies going,—fine ladies coming away. Observe them at the instant of bathing,—how humiliating! They appear more deplorable than so many corpses in shrouds, and put me in mind of the old dialogue between Death and the Lady. Methinks the guide is saying, in the character of Death,—

> Fair lady, lay your costly robes aside,
> Nor longer think to glory in your pride."

An idea may be formed of the rage for bathing at this period from an entry of the same diarist, Thursday, September 9th, 1779:—"Each man runs to a machine-ladder as it is dragging out of the sea, and scuffles who shall first set foot thereon: some send their footmen and contend by proxy; others go in in boots, or on horseback to meet the machines:—so that a tolerably modest man, on a busy morning, has generally an hour and a half, perhaps two hours, for contemplation on the sands, to the detriment of his shoes, as well as the diminution of his patience." And on Saturday, the 11th of the same month, he writes:—"Have matched the bathers and bathees this trip however, having corrected them all handsomely—without quarrelling—have given them the slip; but take the particulars:—About 6 a.m., I drew along the sands, the machine of which I had become seized by prescriptive right, by legal possession, having deposited part of my wearing apparel therein, tho' I had requested the assistance of the *marine centaur*, the man on horseback, in vain. As the tide was flowing, I soon plunged into the sea, stretched a long way out into the offing, and continued rolling and laughing among my brother porpoises, to think what a loss the company on shore would sustain for want of one machine out of seven, it being a very fine busy morning. The bathers holloa'd and bawled in vain; for I could not, indeed would not hear them. After swimming backwards and forwards along the shore, about four miles in the whole, the tide setting strong to the eastward all the time, I returned about nine; and Smoaker, growling like a bear with a sore head, swore bitterly."

William (Smoaker) Miles was a great celebrity, being the principal bathing man. One day, when the Prince of Wales was bathing, he ventured out further than Old Smoaker considered prudent. In vain Smoaker called "Mr. Prince, Mr. Prince, come back," his holloas only causing His Royal Highness to dash out further. As the only means to exact obedience, in rushed the old man, swam up to the Prince, and, seizing him by the ear, lugged him, *nolens volens*, to the shore. When his young aquatic student remonstrated upon receiving such treatment, Old Smoaker rolled out a round oath or two, adding, "I ar'n't agoen' to let the king hang me for letten' the Prince of Wales drown hisself; not I, to please nobody, I can tell'e." The incident pleased the Prince, who ever afterwands patronised him. To testify, also, His Royal Highness's respect for the straightforward, honest, but blunt fellow, he established the Smoaker Stakes, which were run for at the Brighton Races, Friday, July 25th, 1806, with the following result:

The Smoaker Stakes of 20gs. each, one mile; 8 yr. olds to carry 7st. 4 yr. olds 8st. 3lb. 5 yr. olds 8st. 9lb. 6 yr. olds 9st. 11lb., and aged 9st. 1lb.

His Royal Highness the Prince of Wales's b.h. Albion, 6 yrs. old .. 1
Mr. Fermer's b. c. Hippomenes, 4 yrs. old 2
Lord Egremont's b. m. Slipper, 5 yrs. old.. 3
Mr Howorth's ch. c. Patagonian, by Pegasus, 3 yrs. old 4

At starting the odds were 8 to 2 in favour of the field. Albion was the favourite; 2 to 1 against Hippomenes, and Slipper; and 3 to 1 against Patagonian. A good heat between the two horses first in. Won by about a neck.

Old Smoaker was a bit of a wit in his way. On one occasion, while he was standing near the Ship in Distress Inn, now the Sea House Hotel, two dandies of the day addressed him, stating that they had come down to Brighton for the benefit of their health, and had been recommended to drink asses' milk, could he inform them how it was to be obtained. Miles, more plain than polite, replied that he did not then exactly know, but he should advise them, for the sake of saving themselves trouble, to suck each other.

William Miles was succeeded, as Royal Bather, by his brother John, who, when too old to follow his occupation, was pensioned off by Royalty, as long as he lived. A song of the time, then very popular, ran thus:—

There's plenty of dippers and jokers,
And salt-water rigs for your fun;
The king of them all is "Old Smoaker,"
The queen of 'em, "Old Martha Gunn."

The ladies walk out in the morn,
To taste of the salt-water breeze;
They ask if the water is warm,
Says Martha, "Yes, Ma'am, if you please."

Then away to the machines they run,
'Tis surprising how soon they get stript;
I oft wish myself Martha Gunn,
Just to see the young ladies get dipt.'

Martha Gunn had a world-wide fame, and was the cotemporary of Mrs. Cobby, the original bather. Old Smoaker's daughter was known as Martha's handmaiden, she being the chief dipper with the "Lady of the Bath."

The following extracts from the *Morning Herald* will give an idea of the importance of Martha and her occupation :—

July 15th, 1805.—The venerable Priestess of the Bath, Martha Gunn, was busily employed this morning.

August 4th, 1806.—The bathing machines were in active use this morning, and Neptune's *pickling tub* exhibited many beauties in brine.

August 16th.—Many of our lovely belles took *ducks* for their breakfast this morning, purchased of their cateress, Martha Gunn, who boasts that from the fair profits she gains by the sale of her *ducks*, she is often enabled to purchase a goose for dinner.

August 28th.—The Beach this morning was thronged with ladies, all anxious to make interest for a dip. The machines, of course, were in very great request, though none could be run into the ocean in consequence of the heavy swell, but remained stationary at the water's edge, from which Martha Gunn and her robust female assistants took their fair charges, closely enveloped in their partly coloured dresses, and gently held them to the breakers, which not quite so gently passed over them. The greatest novelty, however, that this part of the coast exhibited this morning, was in a gentleman's undressing himself on the Beach, for the purpose of a ducking, in front of the town, attended by his lady, who *sans diffidence*, supplied him with napkins, and even assisted him in wiping the humid effects of his exercise from his brawny limbs, as he returned from the water to dress.

In the following season the practice of bathing from the beach became so general that on Thursday, August 19th, a Vestry Meeting was held at the Old Ship, for the purpose of adopting measures to prevent the indecent practice of indiscriminate bathing in front of the town. Earl Bathurst and Mr. Wilberforce were present, and subscribed five guineas each to defray any expenses of prosecutions that might be deemed requisite to rid the town of the evil. The resolutions passed, that proceedings should be taken against offenders, for awhile had the desired effect; but in 1808 the nuisance was revived, resulting in a prosecution at the Horsham Assizes, on Monday, March 21st, 1809. The case was :—

THE KING *v.* JOHN CRUNDEN.—The defendant was indicted for indecently exposing himself on the beach at Brighton, on the 26th of Jnne, and 2nd of July last.

Mr. Gurney having opened the indictment, Mr. Serjeant Shepperd stated the circumstances of the case. He observed, that it had long been the practice of various persons to undress and bathe so near to the houses, and within view of the inhabitants of the town of Brighton, that at length many respectable persons had associated themselves into a Committee, to prevent such an indecent nuisance. They had accordingly met and pointed out the limits within which persons not using machines might bathe in the sea, and in general most persons acquiesced in their resolution. In order, however, that no person might complain of any hardship, they resolved that all persons who were invalids, and to whom it might be inconvenient to walk to the distance prescribed, should have tickets given them on application to the Committee, which would entitle them at any time to the use of a bathing machine gratis. And still further, to preserve public decency they had built a hut on the beach, wherein any person might undress himself under cover. Notwithstanding these different accommodations, the defendant, who was a tailor, at Brighton, refused to conform to these reasonable regulations, but obstinately persisted in the indecent practice of bathing within a few yards of the houses. He had been frequently remonstrated with, but his uniform answer was, the *sea was free*, and he would bathe when and where he pleased. Nor was he merely content in doing this in his own person, but he had induced many others to follow his example, and he constantly came at the head of his companions, by whom he was denominated the Captain, and in defiance of all decency and remonstrance, daily exposed himself naked on the Beach. The Learned Serjeant here called witnesses to prove the facts he had stated.

Mr. Marryatt addressed the jury for the defence, in which he stated it had been the custom at all times for persons to bathe where the defendant now bathed, and they ought not to be disturbed because Mr. Ellis, the witness, had thought proper to run up houses within view.

The Chief Baron thought this a serious question, and stated his opinion that it was an offence against decency and morality. If a town grew up, the inhabitants must not be annoyed with indecent spectacles; and therefore it became the duty of the bather to retire to remoter situations.—The Jury found the defendant *Guilty*.

For awhile this example had a very salutary effect; but, more or less, until the present season, the nuisance has continued. Now the New Bye Laws prohibit bathing from the beach in front of the town, except before the hour of six in the morning or after nine in the evening; and all persons bathing from the machines are compelled to wear gowns, drawers, or some such suitable covering. Less than thirty years since the bathing from the Ladies' Bathing Machines, between West Street and Middle Street, was not of the most pleasant character, as it was customary for coal brigs in fine weather, to discharge their cargoes at that spot, and frequently, so was the surface of the water covered with fine coal dust, that many a child who dreaded bathing, was compelled to be dipped an extra time or two by the bathing women, to rinse off the black particles.

Some years have elapsed since the universal practice prevailed of discharging cargoes of coal, stone, timber, &c., in front of the town, greater facilities than formerly existed being offered now, at Shoreham, for unloading at the wharfs, without the risk of the vessels—as was very frequently the case,—being stranded. Great quantities of coal is also transmitted to Brighton by rail from Deptford Creek, so that that useful household commodity is much reduced in price to what it formerly was. In the week prior to Christmas, 1812, such was the scarcity of coal in the town, from adverse winds prevailing and preventing the arrival of shipping from the north, that persons in even comfortable circumstances, whose cellars were exhausted, purchased only to the extent of a bushel at a time, and so indifferent were the coal merchants to part with their coal even at £5 a chaldron—about equal to the present ton,—that at the coal-yard of Messrs. Edmund Savage and Bonham, which was situate opposite Ship Street Lane, in North Street, immediately above the shop of Messrs. Palmer and Green, ironmongers, the purchaser of half-a-bushel of coal was compelled likewise to buy at the same time sixpenny worth of uncleft wood.

The following will show the cost of coal per chaldron at that period to the coal merchants in the town:—

Newcastle on Tyne, the Sixteenth day of November in the year of our Lord One Thousand Eight Hundred and Thirteen.

It is this day mutually agreed between Mr. William Spence, owner of the good ship or vessel, called the "Eliza," Wm. Hunter, master, of the burthen of 96 tons, or thereabouts, now on her passage to Sunderland; and Messrs. Savage and Bonham, of Brighton, merchants, freighters of the said ship, for one voyage, at and from Sunderland to Brighton Beach. That the said ship being tight, staunch, and strong, and every way fitted for the voyage, the said master, with said ship, shall, with the first opportunity, after arriving at Sunderland, take on board a full and competent cargo of Nesham Main Coals. And being so loaden, the said master, with said ship, shall therewith proceed to Brighton Beach, or so near thereunto as he may safely get, and deliver the same to the order of the said freighters, on being paid freight, at the rate of Thirty-eight Shillings per chaldron, Winchester measure; the freighters paying King's duty, Town dues at Brighton, Ramsgate and Dover Harbour dues, and the owner lights, metage, delivery, and pilotage, during said voyage. (Restraints of princes and rulers, the dangers of the seas, of whatever nature, fire, and enemies, always excepted.) Freight to be paid on delivery by what cash wanted for ship's use, and for the remainder a good Bill on London, at two months' date. Two days allowed said freighters (if the ship is not sooner despatched), for unloading the said ship at Brighton. Demurrage, Three Guineas per day, for every day's detention, over and above the days allowed as aforesaid. Witness our hands the day and year above written.

Witness, MATT. FAIRLESS. WILLIAM SPENCE.

The incidental expenses attendant upon freighting a vessel brought the actual cost to £3 16s. 3d. per chaldron, as thus:—

	£.	s.	d.
Freight per chaldron..........................	1	18	0
Nesham Main Coals at		17	0
King's Duty per chaldron		10	0
Town Duty do		3	0
Spoutage at Newcastle do			6
Cartage from Beach do		4	0
Metage and Trimming do		1	0
Ramsgate and Dover Lights do		2	6
Beer to men do			3
	£3	16	3

Added to this, Mr. Savage, upon this occasion, to obtain the cargo with the least possible delay, made a journey to Newcastle, the expenses of which amounted to £20.

In 1805, persons interested in shipping, the coal merchants especially, entertained the idea of a basin or harbour for the safety and accommodation of vessels trading hither. The project did not meet with approval amongst the inhabitants generally, as they were desirous of retaining the town as a place of fashionable resort, rather than make it a trading port; and in April, the following year, His Royal Highness the Prince of Wales having caused it to be signified through Mr. Thomas Saunders, High Constable, that he had not bestowed his sanction or patronage in favour of the project, and that he did not intend to possess any such intention, the idea was abandoned. Some of those, however, interested in the scheme, bore their disappointment with but an ill grace, and for some years after the payment of the coal duties was the source of much disaffection. The principal of those who combatted against the payment was Mr. William Izard, whose reasons of objection were embodied in a handbill which he issued, as follows :—

To the Vistors and Inhabitants of the Town of Brighthelmston, and to all such other persons as it may concern.

Whereas sundry reports and misrepresentations have been propagated, and widely circulated concerning myself, in consequence of my having lately refused to pay the Coal Duty of three shillings per chaldron on all coals landed *(from my own vessels)* at this place, for the use and consumption of the inhabitants, as heretofore levied by the Commissioners acting under the Town Act, for the express purpose of "Building and repairing Groyns, Sea Walls, and other works, for the protection of the town of Brighthelmston against the encroachment of the sea, pursuant to the powers and by virtue of and by the authority of an Act of

Parliament made and passed in the 50th year of his present Majesty," for the before-named purposes;

In vindication of my own conduct, and in strict justice to myself and family, and that the public may not form an opinion which may in any wise operate to my prejudice, I do hereby beg leave to state my several objections for so refusing to pay the said Coal Duties, so unwarrantably demanded, viz:—

First.—Because it clearly appears to me, from the best account that I have been able to obtain from Mr. T. Attree, the Commissioners' Clerk and Treasurer, that since the passing of the aforesaid Act of Parliament and the levying of the said Coal Duties, that the Commissioners have actually been in the receipt of near Eight Thousand Pounds from that source only!

And that it also appears that the said Commissioners have not expended *Three Thousand Pounds* of such monies so received, for the protection of the town, agreeable to the express provisions and in strict conformity to such enactments as are set forth in the said Act of Parliament; so that it seems that there is now a balance of between four and five thousand pounds in favour of that particular and specific account, and which balance of Surplus Duties now remains unapplied towards those sacred purposes for which it was raised, by and under the authority of the aforesaid Act of Parliament.

And notwithstanding the immense balance in favour of the Groyns just before stated, and irreconcilable and incongruous as it may appear, these very same Commissioners are now actually paying the interest on the sum of £1140 money borrowed on the credit of the said Coal Duties, and that, in direct opposition to the very terms of the aforesaid Act of Parliament, which strictly restrains Commissioners from applying any money arising from that branch of their finance to any other use or purpose whatever, whilst there shall be any money due or be owing upon the credit of that account.

And yet under all these circumstances the Commissioners are still endeavouring to increase their balance of Coal Duties, although it is not wanted for the purpose for which it is levied; and were the Commissioners to convert such balance to any other use, it would in them constitute a great abuse of power, and a high breach of their trust!

As I do not chuse to participate in either of these crimes, I am unwilling to increase the guilt of such a portion of the Commissioners as may chuse to indulge in such gross misconduct, by continuing to do that to my own wrong, which would ultimately increase theirs.

It is upon these grounds and upon them only, that I have been induced to refuse the payment of Groyn Dues; and I must also beg it to be unequivocally understood, that when the before-named balance of between Four and Five Thousand Pounds shall have been legally and fairly expended and properly accounted for, and if circumstances should hereafter make it necessary, I shall most willingly and cheerfully submit to the payment of the Coal Duty as heretofore.

Brighton, August 24th, 1814. Wm. Izard.

Since the publication of the above address, Mr. Wm. Gates, principal Coast Officer of the Customs at this place, and the Commissioners' Collector of Groyn Dues, assisted by Mr. T. Attree, their Clerk and Treasurer, accompanied by the Brighton Magistrates, and also by Mr. Robert Ackerson, the present High Constable, and a great possy of "Headboroughs" and other persons have thought proper to make a seizure in my Coal Yard of Eight Chaldron of Coals, to satisfy themselves for the payment of such Dues as they pretend to claim as due from myself: to effect which, the violent measure of breaking open my Coal Yard gate, by forcing the lock, was resorted to, on Thursday last; but as the merits of this transaction are put into a fair train of legal investigation, I have to request that the candid public will be pleased to suspend judgment till the issue shall be so determined.

WM. IZARD,
Ship Owner and Coal Merchant.

Brighton, August 29, 1814.

The power of the authorities prevailed, and the Dues continued to be exacted.

The female attendants of the machines are, as respects dress especially, of the primitive order of their race, except that they do not in the afternoon appear in their best prim attire, as of yore they were wont to do, to "tout" in Castle Square, on the arrival of the coaches. Their last grand show day in their aquatic costume was on the occasion of their visit to the Exhibition, in Hyde Park, 1851, when, to defray their expenses, subscriptions were raised amongst the inhabitants. At the Exhibition they were the observed of all observers; and had but the original idea been carried out of their travelling from the London Bridge Terminus to the building, in their machines, the arrangements of the day would have been complete, and the unsightliness and primitive construction of the vehicles would have excited the sympathy of some inventor and induced him to bring out something that would have had a creditable appearance.

Almost coeval with sea-bathing in establishing the reputation of Brighton, were the baths, first established by Dr. Awsiter, on the spot now occupied by Brill's Ladies' Swimming Bath, and for so many years known as Wood's Original Hot and Cold Sea-water Baths. The first stone of these baths, which were after a plan of Mr. Golden, architect, was laid in the year 1759. Mr. George Lynn erected the present building.

Dr. Awsiter, in a pamphlet, called "Thoughts on Brighthelmston," published in 1768, says, "The utility of these baths is obvious: they may be used either for hot or cold bathing. There are some individuals to whom cold bathing would be serviceable, could they be able to bear the fatigue of being dipt in the sea, and (what is more material), to be exposed to the cold air. If the weather happens to be stormy, and the sea so rough, as not to admit of bathing in it, recourse may be had to the baths: by this means bathing would become more universal, be unattended with terror, and no cure protracted. Moreover, invalids would have the advantage of this bathing remedy all the year round; whereas, on account of the variableness of our climate, it is denied them at present, except in the Summer months, and then only in calm weather."

The Artillery Baths, the next established, obtained their original fame from the proprietor, Mr. Smith, having discovered a method of curing the gout, by means of an air pump, from whence many persons of rank and consequence received great benefit. They are known now as Hobden's Artillery Baths.

Williams's Hot and Cold Baths, which occupied the site of the present Lion Mansion, at one period received extensive patronage, and the *Morning Herald* of August 17, 1807, says, "Williams's Baths are in very fashionable request. Numberless *elegantes* were in hot water there this morning." On Mr. Williams's decease they were carried on by Mr. Bannister, who was succeeded by his son-in-law, Mr. William Knight. The halcyon days, however, of these baths had fled, and the premises, after remaining in a very dilapidated state for some time, were cleared off for the erection of the present noble mansion.

The personage who acquired the greatest fame for his baths, and obtained the highest and most extensive patronage, was Sake Deen Mahomed, who, although not born in Brighton, yet, this highly favoured town was the theatre where his name became patent for the alleviation of suffering mankind, and hence he is entitled to special notice.

He was a native of India, and was born at Patna, the capital of Bahar, about 290 miles N.W. of Calcutta, in the year 1749. Having been educated for the surgical profession, he entered the East India Company's service in that capacity, which he afterwards relinquished, and for fifteen years acted exclusively in a military character. In the year 1780 he was appointed by Major, afterwards General Popham, to a company, but in 1784, he left the service and came to England, where he continued to reside the remainder of his valuable life. In his early days having devoted much time and attention to Oriental bathing, both medicinally and as a luxury, on his arrival in England, he was induced to think seriously of introducing the Indian Vapour Bath, and the art of Shampooing, and sedulously employed himself in preliminary experiments, to prove the correctness of the hypothesis he had formed, that what was a luxurious restorative in India, might prove in England a wonderful remedy for many diseases.

Justified by proof, he repaired to Brighton, where he promulgated his discovery, but at first with little success, as the public were ill-prepared to receive a system which should supercede Warm Sea-water Bathing. Fortunately, however, he effected several gratuitous cures,—cures which quickly gained circulation amongst those who had prejudged and condemned his bath; and adduced the most positive and convincing proof of tho great superiority of Shampooing over every other description of treatment, in particular cases. All prejudices were quickly removed, and his wide-spread fame soon gained him the appointment of Shampooing Surgeon to their Majesties George IV. and William IV. Presents, conveying the expressions of the deepest feelings of gratitude and thankfulness, crowded upon him. The Muses poured forth their eulogiums; the several organs of the press—national and local—their panegyrics.

He exemplified the curative and invigorating influence of his Art in his person and his longevity. He died the 24th of February, 1851, at the advanced age of 102 years, and was buried in the church-yard of St. Nicholas, Brighton, where an unassuming tomb records his age and death. He was father of Mr. Frederick Mahomed, of the Gymnasium, Palace Place.

Mahomed's Bath establishment opposite the Star and Garter Hotel, King's Road, is now the property of Mr. Charles Brill, who is likewise the proprietor of the Ladies' Swimming Bath, before mentioned, and the extensive baths and the Gentlemen's Swimming Bath, originally Lamprell's, at the bottom of East Street. Buggins's Baths in Western Street, are a great acquisition to the western part of the town; where also, in the Western Road, Hove, is the Turkish Bath of Dr. Toulmin, who is well supported in his popular treatment. Other baths have from time to time, been started, mostly, however, with a very ephemeral existence.

Great as was the success of Mahomed's process, he was in no inconsiderable degree indebted for the many cures he effected to the perseverance of Mr. Henry Harrap, to whose memory the author of this book has a grateful respect, for enabling him to retain and ably use a leg, the amputation of which had been recommended by the faculty. Little is known of his early career, more than that he was born at Helston, in Cornwall, October 21st, 1794. He left home at an early age, and during the short peace previous to the Battle of Waterloo, he was a private in the 51st Foot, the Duke of York's Own. In 1817, he was with his regiment stationed at the Infantry Barracks, Brighton, being then an officer's servant. His brother Richard was also in the same regiment, as Sergeant-Bugler, and, during his location here, he married, at Preston, a young woman, the widow of Corporal Fudge, late of the Gloucester Militia. But shortly after his marriage he deserted. His wife however, provided two substitutes, and paid £40 for his discharge; she also bought Henry off, and the two brothers, till the year 1828, followed the trade of boot and shoe making, in Ivory Place. The maiden name of his wife was Short, a native of the village of Hangleton, and she was married to Fudge before she was 14 years of age, in consequence of her mother, who was a widow, being about to be married to another corporal in the same regiment, the man refusing to wed her with an incumbrance. Richard died in 1828, and in the following year Henry was married to his brother's widow, at St. George's in the Borough, London. By neither brother had she any family; but by her first husband she had four daughters. She died in July, 1843. In 1838, Mr. Harrap discontinued the business of shoemaking, and converted the shop-front of his premises on the Grand Parade, at the corner of Sussex Street, to one of a more private character, devoting the whole of his attention to professional rubbing.

At the zenith of the career of Sake Deen Mahomed, Mr. Harrap obtained the custom of that professor, and for a long time continued to make and repair shoes for the family. This circumstance caused him frequently to visit Mr. Mahomed's establishment, where he principally obtained that information which enabled him to commence the practice of rubbing, omitting the shampooing process, his inventive genius enabling him to substitute as many contrivances as the numerous cases of affliction entrusted to his skill and care required. Many of his inventions, which had been of benefit to sufferers, formed a species of Museum in a room at Mahomed's establishment. From Mrs. Williams, too, a neighbour, in Ivory Place, who was celebrated for her healing unguents, Mr. Harrap gained much of his surgical knowledge.

Mr. Harrap was totally uneducated, and, at the commencement of his professional career, entirely unacquainted with medical science and nomenclature; yet, progressively, by natural instinct as it were, and studied practice, he acquired a knowledge of anatomy which astonished those who were conversant with that science; and gentlemen of high position in the medical profession—including the late Sir Matthew Tierney, Sir Astley Cooper, Sir Benjamin Brodie, &c.,—acknowledged his worth by awarding him that credit which they considered due to an energetic and gifted man. His perseverance enabled him to amass a large fortune; and after having been a great sufferer for more than two years, from a cancer of the bowels, he was removed by death from the scene of a most useful life, on Saturday, the 12th of October of last year, leaving a wife, the widow of the late Sidney Walsingham Bennett, Esq., solicitor, to lament her irreparable bereavement, and a large circle of grateful patients and sincere friends the remembrance of an honourable and honoured man.

For some time previous to his decease he had been unable to attend actively to his professional duties; yet, he was present daily, at his house of business on the Grand parade, watching, and instructing his step-son, now his successor, Mr. Sidney Bennett, who qualified as a surgeon on the 29th of May, 1861, and there is little doubt his perseverance in the course pursued by the deceased will add a lustre to his father-in-law's name, and confirm a credit due to the memory of a man who was never ambitious of praise, but perseveringly sought a remedy to alleviate the sufferings of the afflicted. Deceased was buried at the Parochial Cemetery, Lewes Road.

Nature has been peculiarly bountiful in her goodness towards Brighton; as, independent of the salubrity of the position of the town and the superlative excellence of its sea-water, the Chalybeate spring at the Wick is possessed of great curative properties, the opinion of Drs. Russell and Relhan, being confirmed by Dr. Henderson, who thus writes :—

This water, when first taken from the spring in a glass, in appearance greatly resembles a solution of emetic tartar in common water. The taste is not unpleasant, something like that upon a knife after it has been used in cutting lemons. It does not seem to contain the smallest portion of sulphur; it neither changes vegetable blues, red, nor does it effervesce with alkaline salts, calcareous earths, magnesia, nor fossil alkali; neither does it change vegetable blues, green, nor does it effervesce with acids; yet it curdles soap, and renders a solution of it in various spirits milky.

It seems to contain a considerable portion of calcareous earth, mixed with vitriolic acid in the form of its selenites, and also a considerable portion of iron, as will appear from the following experiment: Sixty-four ounces of this water by measure being evaporated to dryness, there was a residuum of a brownish colour, full of spiculæ, weighing eight grains, four ounces of which, with an equal quantity of charcoal, was made into a paste with oil, and calcined. On trying the calcined matter with the magnet, two pieces nearly in the metallic form adhered to it; and when put upon paper, at the distance of half an inch, moved in every direction with the magnet. These two pieces weighed one-eighth of a grain.

The gross residuum neither effervesces with alkali nor acids, and is sufficiently soluble in water.

This water becomes instantly transparent, like distilled water, on the addition of any of the mineral acids, especially the vitriolic.

A solution of galls in common water, added to an equal portion of this water, becomes black like ink, in a few minutes.

The Chalybeate has been found serviceable in several cases of general debility, crapulas, indigestion, atony of the stomach, and fluor albus; and in all those diseases where chalybeate and tonic remedies are required, it promises, under due regulation, to be useful.

Dr. Henderson was a physician of eminence in the town; and a minute of Vestry, at the Unicorn Inn, February 10th, 1794, shews the esteem in which he was held by the inhabitants. It runs thus:—"Dr. Henderson presented with a pint silver cup, for his care and attention to the parish."

A character of the time, who also practised the healing art, is not so favourably mentioned in the Vestry Book, February 4th, 1805, the entry of him being:—"Resolved that Michæl Cobby be allowed eight shillings per week, on his quitting the Poor-house; and his drugs and effects delivered up to him." It must not, from this, however, be supposed medicine and surgery were so at a discount that parish relief was requisite to maintain

The wise physician skilled our wounds to heal.

Dr. Cobby, as he was familiarly known, had talent, but he was more a disciple of Bacchus, than of Galen, and the natural reply to him, as he tendered his services in his tattered clothes, which his poverty bespake, and as a foul specimen of the unwashed, would be "Physician, heal—cleanse—thyself." Not that Brighton at that period had waned in the least from the character it had obtained for healthfulness, as a memorandum, made August, 1806, states:— "Such is the healthy condition of the town, that the doctors and apothecaries complain dolefully of their declining businesses, and undertakers are literally starved out, the latter declaring, 'All trades must live,' but the residents are determined not to serve them." In 1580, there was but one medical man in Brighton, Dr. Mathews, who lived in Middle street. His terms for attending in confinements were: At Portslade and Rottingdean, 5s; at Blatchington, 3s 6d; and anywhere in the town of Brighthelmston, 2s 6d.

In the early part of 1786, a sad scourge, the small pox, pervaded the town, and on the 25th of January, that year, when the population amounted to 3620, the following return of its virulence was made:—

	Those who had the small pox.	*Nos. who had not.*
West Street	351	322
Middle Street and Lanes	231	272
North St. and ditto	234	295
Ship and Blk-Lyon do	318	336
Knab, Cliff, Brighton pl. and Little East St.	260	291
East St. and Nth Row, Steyne and Pool Lane	308	291
Poor in the House	31	50
Number supposed After taking numbers	0	30
	1733	1887

A general inoculation in consequence, was ordered at a Vestry Meeting; and the 1887 who escaped the disease were inoculated by Messrs. Lowdell, Gilbert, Pankhurst, and Tilston, the charges being: The poor, servants, and day-labourers, at 2s. 6d. each; and other persons at 7s. 6d. each. The return of the deaths is not made in the Vestry minute book.

One of the crowning features of Brighton, as a health-providing town, is the German Spa, Queen's Park, an establishment for manufacturing the Artificial Mineral Waters, which, by the faculty, are pronounced to be so perfect an imitation of the original springs in Germany, that the most celebrated chemists can detect no difference between them. They are the production of Dr. Struve, of Dresden, who some years ago turned his attention to the analysis and imitation of the original, and patients who have drank both can discover no difference in their flavour or effect. The artificial waters supplied are:—

WARM WATERS	CARLSBAD	The Sprudel	1651°	Fahrenheit.
		Neubrunnen	138°	,,
		Mulhbrunnen	138°	,,
		Theressebrunnen	122°	,,
	EMMS	The Kränchen	117°	,,
		Kesselbrunnen	84°	,,
COLD WATERS	MARIENBAD	Kreutzbrunnen		
	AUSCHOWITZ	Ferdinandsbrunnen		
	EGER	Frazenbrunnen		
	PYRMONT			
	SPA			
	SEIDSCHUTZ			
	PULLNA			

Mr. G. S. Carey, in a "Poetical Tagg, or Brighthelmstone Guide," * July 28th, 1777, gives the following on the rise and progress of the town even at that date:—

This town, or village of renown,
Like London Bridge, half broken down,
Few years ago was worse than Wapping,
Not fit for human soul to stop in;
But now, like to a worn-out shoe,
By patching well, the place will do.
You'd wonder much, I'm sure, to see,
How it's becramm'd with quality;
Here Lords and Ladies oft carouse
Together in a tiny house;
Like Joan and Darby in their cot,
With stool and table, spit and pot;
And what his valet would despise,

* A Rural Ramble to Brighthelmstone, &c. Printed for R. Thoma,s Brighthelmstone.

His lordship praises to the skies;
But such the *ton* is, such the case,
You'll see the first of rank or place,
With star and riband, all profuse,
Duck at his door-way like a goose:
The humble beam was plac'd so low,
Perhaps to teach some clown to bow.
The air is pure as pure can be,
And such an aspect of the sea!
As you, perhaps, ne'er saw before,
From off the side of any shore:
On one hand Ceres spreads her plain,
And on the other, o'er the main,
Many a bark majestic laves
Upon the salt and buoyant waves;
The hills all mantl'd o'er with green,
A friendly shelter to the Steyne,
Whene'er the rugged Boreas blows,
Bemingled with unwelcome snows:
Such is the place and situation,
Such is the reigning seat of fashion.

Brighthelmstone,
July 28th, 1777.

Four years previous to the date of this "Tag," namely, in 1773, an Act of Parliament was passed, giving power to sixty-four Commissioners, elected by the inhabitants, to light and cleanse the streets, lanes, and other places within the town of Brighton, and for the general regulation and improvement of the town. In 1809, meetings of the inhabitants took place at the Old Ship, for and in opposition to obtaining a new Act of Parliament; and on the 21st of February, 1810, a very large majority of the Vestry, at a meeting held at the Old Ship, resolved that the Bill as framed by the Town Committee, which had been appointed by the inhabitants, should be forthwith presented to Parliament, to be passed into a law. The Act passed that year, augmenting the number of Commissioners to one hundred, and raising the duty on coal from sixpence to three shillings per chaldron. On the 22nd of June, 1825, (6 Geo. IV.) this Act was repealed and another passed, extending the number of Commissioners to one hundred and twelve, and giving them increased powers, in consequence of the extensive enlargement and requirements of the town.

Under the provisions of this Act some of the greatest improvements in the town were effected. The most prominent of these was the Sea Wall, which forms the southern front of Brighton from Cannon Place to the west end of Kemp Town. As early as 1799 the requirement of a wall at the foot of the East Cliff, now the Marine Parade, to prevent the encroachments of the sea, occupied the attention of the possessors of property in that vicinity, as amongst the Conditions of Sale of the land for the purpose of erecting the Royal Crescent,—sold by auction by Mr. Christie, at the Old Ship Inn, Monday, September 16th, 1799,—was the following:—

If it shall be judged necessary to build a Sea-Wall under the Cliff, for Use or Ornament, the Purchasers and Plot Holders of each Ground Plot to contribute their Proportion for Building the same.

The building of the Crescent commenced forthwith; but, in consequence of one of the most prominent of the speculators absconding, the whole of the houses were not completed until the end of December, 1807, at which period the area in front of the Crescent measured four acres. No wall was then considered necessary at the foot of the Cliff, but a dwarf wall was built on the south side of the carriage road, in lieu of posts and rails, which guarded in a most irregular manner the other portion of the road-way from the Steine to Black-Rock. On widening the road as now existing in consequence of the construction of the present massive sea-wall, not only was the dwarf wall removed but the crown of the rise of the road, which there ranged with the present paving of the Crescent, was taken off, and the incline made on the turfed area, which was considerably contracted by setting back the iron railings in a line with the front of the other property immediately east and west.

A statue of the Prince of Wales, by Rossi, seven feet high, on an ornamented pedestal, eleven feet high, was, in 1802, placed in front of the Royal Crescent. His Royal Highness was represented as dressed in his regimental uniform, with his arm extended towards the sea. The statue, which was made of plaster, cost upwards of £300. In November, 1807, some person broke off the fingers of the extended left hand. Eventually the other arm with a portion of his mantle was knocked away, and in that condition the mutilated figure was allowed to remain several years, till becoming more and more unsightly from parties continually adding to its disfigurement, it was removed.

Two incidents of a most melancholy character, in connexion with the Royal Crescent, claim a record. The first was the death of a workman, named Leggatt. He was engaged in forming the words "Royal Crescent" on the tablet which surmounts the centre house, and had finished the S, when, on stepping back to observe its agreement with the other letters, he over-balanced himself, and, falling upon the iron railings below, he was unfortunately killed. The other event was the death of a soldier, named Charles Millegan, of the Second Battalion of the Coldstream Guards, which occurred on Christmas night, 1835, he having accidentally fallen down the Cliff from the Crescent wall. A stone to his memory, erected by the privates of his battalion, in the north burial ground of St. Nicholas Church, has the following inscription as a tribute of respect by his comrades:—

Oft may the tear his green sod steep,
And sacred be the Soldier's sleep
Till time shall cease to run.
And ne'er beside his lonely grave
May Briton's pass and fail to crave
A blessing on the fallen brave,
For such was MILLEGAN.

The first section of the town Sea-Wall, that between Ship street and Mahomed's—now Brill's Baths,—was constructed in 1825. Then followed the execution of the difficult enterprise, the union of the east and west sea-drives and promenade, by the formation of the Junction Road round Brill's Swimming Bath, and thence across the outlet of the Pool Valley, and southing the Albion Hotel. To effect this great undertaking, the sea had to be repelled, hence recourse was had to the erection of a series of large groynes, and the facing of the wall, which is of concrete—a due admixture of grey lime and shingle,—with piles and planking; and this proceeding resulted in the sea being forced against the cliffs beyond the Chain Pier, storm after storm making such inroads that in some places the Marine Parade was not of sufficient width for a vehicle to pass. The proprietors of houses along the Marine Parade, in consequence, became alarmed for their property. The Commissioners therefore, took immediate steps to prevent the incursions of the ocean, and numerous groynes, which were erected between the Chain Pier and the Black-Rock groyne, having in some measure answered the purpose of keeping back the raging water, a plan was attempted to be carried out of forming a battering or leaning wall of flint as a facing to the cliff, which was widened and filled in as the wall progressed. The scheme, however, proved a fallacy; as the amazing mass of unsettled earth with which it was backed up, having become saturated with heavy rains, forced out the foot of the wall, the whole of which slid out into the sea, or on the beach.

A concrete wall of amazing substance, was then substituted with the greatest success, at a cost of £100,000, under contracts, by Mr. William Lambert, an extensive builder of the town. In many parts, the wall—which is in some places sixty feet high,—is twenty-three feet thick at its base, and batters—inclines—on an average, four inches to the foot on the face. More recently, other portions of the sea-front of the town have been extended in width, by the same process, to admit of the increased road traffic, so that Brighton may now boast of an uninterrupted sea-drive and promenade of more than three miles' extent.

The other public structures erected by the Commissioners are the Market and the Town Hall. The former is a lofty and commodious building, standing principally on the site of the Old Workhouse and Town Hall. It is T shaped, with the transverse head towards the east, opposite the Town Hall, a building which occupies the space whereon, till the erection of the new structure, the Market formerly stood. The corner stone of the Town Hall was laid in April, 1830, by Thomas Read Kemp, Esq., the contractor for the building being Mr. Doubleday, whose tender was £12,491 1s. 7d. The cost, however, of the building, from the various hewings, hackings, and cuttings, which it has undergone, has exceeded, at a moderate calculation, £60,000. It is after the plan of Mr. Thomas Cooper, but it is minus a most important wing. This defect arose from the Commissioners omitting to purchase land for the south portion, the owner of the property refusing to sell after the building had pretty far advanced. The consequence is that the approaches to the upper rooms of the southern portion are wanting, and hence much inconvenience is experienced.

The Town Hall is used for town meetings, public assemblies, the Council meetings, and the general purposes of the Borough. In it are offices for the Town Clerk—C. Sharood, Esq.,—and his staff, for the Collectors of the Municipal and Parish Rates, and for the Borough Surveyor—Mr. Philip Lockwood,—and his staff. The Magistrates' Court, which occupies the southern basement, is likewise used for the Borough Quarter Sessions, the Recorder being John Locke, Esq., Q.C., and M.P. for Southwark. The police-force originally established on the 15th of April, 1830, under Chief-Officer Pilbeam,—the Police Station then being in Steine Lane,—has at present Mr. George White for the Chief-Constable, he having succeeded Mr. Chase on the 21st of December, 1853, his predecessor,—who succeeded Mr. Pilbeam,—Mr Henry Solomon, having been murdered by John Lawrence, on the 13th of March, 1844. The Superintendents are Mr. Owen Crowhurst and Mr. Isaiah Barnden; and the Inspector of Flys, &c., is Mr. James Terry. The force consists of 80 men,—inspectors, sergeants, and privates,—who occupy the south-west portion of the basement, immediately contiguous to the Magistrates' Court, the dungeons for the uncommitted and, perhaps, innocent, being in the most remote portion of the underground vaults at the north-east of the building.

Prior to the establishment of the Police-force the care of the town was entrusted to a few Watchmen of the antique school, by night, and a Beadle in cocked-hat and general suit of his order, by day, assisted by the Town Crier of similar mien and garb. The Watchmen had succeeded the Patrol, a species of self-guardianship which the inhabitants imposed upon themselves in rotation, under the supervision of the High Constable and his Headboroughs. During the Winter months it was also customary for a bell-man to perambulate nightly most of the old streets of the town, and hourly proclaim the time and weather. The stocks in the Market place, and the parish pound at the back of the Old Church were then in vogue.

A portion of the principal room on the basement, to form the County Court, is temporarily taken off by means of a partition, in two sections which swing back on hinges to the side walls. The Court is held every alternate Friday, William Furner, Esq., being the Judge. The only residents of the building are Friend Paine—the Hall-Keeper,—and his wife. Paine, at one time, was in himself the fire brigade of Brighton. Eight men, whose peculiarity of costume for the office consisted in wearing white hats, had previously been engaged to work the engines in the event of any fires; but none occurring, the white-hatted force was dispensed with, and eventually such an arrangement was made by the Town Council with the Brighton, Hove, and Preston Constant Service Water Company, that the fire-hose being fitted to plugs and standards in connexion with the water-mains, the service of the fire-engines was dispensed with, the position of the reservoir of the Company, on the Race Hill, giving a pressure sufficiently strong to force the water over the highest edifices in the town. In 1825, a Sussex County and General Fire and Life Assurance Company was projected, with Mr. Barnard Gregory as Managing Director. The office of this Company was on the premises in North Street now well known as Folthorp's Royal Library, where, in front of the house, a fire-engine, fire-escape, and other appropriate apparatus, were prominently displayed. Firemen, bedight in the antique fittings of their order in London, with silver-plated badge on their arms, bearing the Brighton Arms,—two dolphins,—surmounted with SVX, and encircled with "BRIGHTHELMSTON IN SIGILVM," and "SUSSEX COUNTY AND GENERAL FIRE AND LIFE ASSURANCE COMPANY," perpetually showed themselves about the premises which had been previously used as the Mess House of the officers of regiments from time to time stationed at the Infantry Barracks, Church Street. The career of the Company was very brief, and the exploits of the firemen were confined to one fire only, namely, that at Major Russell's mansion, Portland Place, September 12th, 1825, known in Brighton,—where the great rage for building had then just set in,—as the year of the panic. Kemp Town at that period, and for some few years afterwards, was a town of carcasses, many of the houses being not only floorless and windowless, but roofless.

In this district, but in the parish of Rottingdean,—to avoid the Brighton coal dues,—the Brighton Old Gas Light and Coke Company erected their works in 1818-19, much to the dissatisfaction of the inhabitants, who petitioned Parliament on the 6th of May, 1818, against the introduction of gas into the town. Some considerable time elapsed before it was much used for in-door lighting, persons, in general, having a fear of explosions. For illuminating it was first used on the 12th of August, 1819, when, to oblige the Company, Mr. Stone, shoemaker to His Royal Highness the Prince Regent, gave them permission to fit up, at their own expense, over his shop in East Street, at the corner of Steine Lane, a design—the Prince of Wales' Feathers,—in gas, the effect of which excited the wonder and admiration of the whole town, and completely reconciled the inhabitants to the use of gas.

As early as 1806 the Incorporation of the town was mooted, and on the 2nd of July, that year, a meeting of the inhabitants, at which the Vicar, the Rev. R. Carr, presided, took place at the Old Ship, respecting a communication which had been made from the Prince of Wales to Sir Henry Rycroft, on the subject. The meeting was numerously and respectably attended, and the subject was ably and dispassionately discussed. After a debate of several hours, the Incorporation by Charter was unanimously negatived, and an address of thanks was voted to His Royal Highness for his condescension, and the kind interest which he took in the welfare of the inhabitants of the town. During the meeting it was announced that the Prince had no particular desire that the Incorporation by Charter should be adopted, unless the inhabitants should conceive that such a measure would promote their interests; and that any other mode which they might better approve of, for the impartial administration of justice in the place, should be honoured with his Royal sanction.

The subject of Incorporation then remained dormant till about the year 1852, when, the inhabitants thinking that Brighton was of sufficient importance to be placed on an equality with other towns of like population and influence, agitated for a Charter. The opposition of the old governing body was very great, and the "tug of war" continued, each party contending and hoping most zealously. At length the contenders for the Incorporation prevailed, and the Charter under the Municipal Act, and bearing date, April 1st, 1854, was granted. In 1860, in order to remedy many known defects, the Local Government Act of 1858, was adopted, after a severe contest. The Corporation consists of the Mayor, the Recorder, 12 Aldermen, and 36 Councillors, six for each Ward, the Wards being the Park Ward, Pavilion Ward, Pier Ward, St. Peter's Ward, St. Nicholas' Ward, and West Ward. The Magistracy consists of the Mayor, the last ex-Mayor, the Recorder, the Stipendiary Magistrate,—at present A. Bigge, Esq.,—and other Magistrates whose appointments are sanctioned by the Secretary of State for the Home Department. The present Magistrates are, His Worship the Mayor, J. Allfree, Esq., J. C. Burrows, Esq., W. Catt, Esq., J. Fawcett, Esq., W. Furner, Esq., W. M. Hollis, Esq., M. D. Scott, Esq., B. Stent, Esq., W. F. Smithe, Esq., T. Warner, Esq., and W. Alger, Esq., who also acts in that capacity by virtue of being the last ex-Mayor. Ewen Evershed, Esq., is the Clerk of the Peace.

The Mayors hitherto, have been :—

1854.—Lieut.-Col. Fawcett.
1855.—W. Hallett, Esq.
1856.—I. G. Bass, Esq.
1857.—J. C. Burrows, Esq.
1858.—J. C. Burrows, Esq.
1859.—W. Alger, Esq.
1860.—W. Alger, Esq.
1861.—H. Smithers, Esq.

The great increase of the population during the course of the last hundred years, is the surest criterion whereby to judge of the rapid progress of the town :—

In 1761 the population of Brighton was	2,000
1786	3,600
1794	5,669
1801*	7,339
1811	12,012
1821	24,429
1831	40,634
1841	46,661
1851	65,573
1861	77,090

Brighton had, comparatively speaking, stood aloof from politics till the passing of the Reform Bill, in 1832, the inhabitants, not being free-holders, having had no voice in framing the House of Commons. Under the fostering wing of George IV. Brighton could not be otherwise than Tory ; but the Royal Patron of the town being dead and his successor William IV. possessing different political views to his deceased brother, and others besides the aborigines

* The year when the first Census was taken.

having taken up their abode in Brighton, diversities of political opinions arose, and hence, on the first election of Members for the Borough there was opposition.

The following have been the polling results of the elections to the present date :—

December 11th and 12th, 1832.

Isaac Newton Wigney, Esq.	873
George Faithfull, Esq.	722
Captain G. R. Pechell, R.N.	613
William Crawford, Esq.	391
Sir Adolphus James Dalrymple, Bart.	32

January 8th and 9th, 1835 :—

Captain Pechell	961
I. N. Wigney, Esq.	523
Sir A. Dalrymple	483
G. Faithfull, Esq	467

July, 25th, 1837 :—

Captain Pechell	1083
Sir A. Dalrymple	819
I. N. Wigney, Esq.	801
G. Faithfull, Esq.	183

July 1st, 1841 :—

Captain Pechell	1443
I. N. Wigney, Esq.	1235
Sir A. Dalrymple	872
Mr C. Brooker	19

May 6th, 1842, on the Bankruptcy of Mr. Wigney :—

Lord Alfred Hervey	1277
Summers Harford, Esq.	640
Mr. C. Brooker	16

July 30th, 1847 :—

Captain Pechell	1571
Lord A. Hervey	1230
W. Coningham, Esq	886

July 8th, 1852 :—

Sir G. Pechell	1924
Lord A. Hervey	1431
J. S. Trelawney	1173
J. Ffooks	119

Upon Lord A. Hervey's appointment as a Lord of the Treasury, under the Derby Administration, his re-election took place on the 4th of January, 1853, without opposition.

March 20th, 1857:—

Sir G. Pechell	2278
W. Coningham, Esq.	1900
Lord A. Hervey	1080

April 30th, 1859:—

Sir G. Pechell	2322
W. Coningham, Esq.	2106
Sir A. MacNab	1327

July 16th, 1860, in consequence of the death of Sir George Pechell:—

J. White, Esq.	1588
H. Mōor, Esq.	1242
F. D. Goldsmid, Esq.	571

Chapter XXVI.

THE MARINE PAVILION AND ITS OCCUPANTS.

The ascendency of Brighton over every other marine resort in the kingdom may be regarded as having been established by the attachment to the town of His Royal Highness the Prince of Wales, George IV., who in 1782—when he was about twenty years of age,—honoured it for the first time with his presence on the occasion of his visit to his uncle, the Duke of Cumberland, who then occupied Grove House. The auspicious event was celebrated by the inhabitants with a general illumination, every pane of glass in the town displaying a candle stuck in a lump of clay, the primitive style of candlestick for illuminations before coloured glass well oil-lamps, called Coronation Lamps, came into vogue, previous to the adoption of gas.

The following year the Prince repeated the visit, occupying the house adjoining Grove House, belonging to Thomas Kemp, Esq., of whom it was subsequently purchased by his Royal Highness. This house formed the nucleus of the Marine Pavilion, the erection of which commenced in 1784, and the building was completed in 1787. At this period a barn stood out abruptly in East Street, at the corner of North Street, but as it incommoded the public drive it was taken down, and a handsome house,—the original of the present north east corner of North Street,—was erected at the rear of its site, by Mr. Hall, surgeon. The other dwellings, northward to Carlisle House, were then built. The east or sea front of the Pavilion, which extended about 200 feet, consisted of a circular building in the centre supported by stone Doric pillars, and crowned with a dome, and on each side there was a range of bow-fronted apartments one story high above the basement, with balconies and verandahs. The entrance front was towards East Street. It consisted of a plain main building to which, in 1802, were added two projecting wings, that formed a square fore-court, in the centre of which was a handsome sun-dial, supported by the figure of a negro that was much admired for its beauty of design and accuracy of sculpture.

Immediately north of the Pavilion was Marlborough House, the property and residence of the Duke and Duchess of Marlborough. It was a massive square building of brick, two stories high, and a part of the east front formed a noble bow having three windows on each floor. There were six windows also on each floor in this front besides those in the bow. A range of nine windows on each floor faced the north. The northern boundary wall of Marlborough House was in a direct line with the present southern wall of the Pavilion Stables, and the cluster of elms on the gentle mound just north of the present Pavilion marks the site of the Duke's residence, which was a temple of benevolence and charity, the poor and needy daily participating in his bounty. The following extracts from the *Morning Herald* will show that his Grace's good deeds to the poor extended over a series of years :—

Brighton, August 10th, 1796.—The Duke and Duchess of Marlborough, with their household, leave here on the 17th inst. Six weeks is generally the time for their Graces' residence here, but this summer they have overstopped their stay. The Duke of Marlborough's liberality affords a good and generous lesson to the other nobility who occasionally reside here; for the victuals and milk (the latter a scarce article in this town), that is left amongst the household, is distributed every morning, in parcels, to the poor of the place; a good day's provision for several fishermen's wife and children.

August 18th, 1806.—The Duke and Duchess of Marlborough and Lady A. Spencer seemed greatly to enjoy, from the windows of Marlborough House, the parade of the South Gloucester Militia on the Level.—A crowd of the indigent inhabitants of this place, from the kitchen of Marlborough House, returned with smiling faces, and aprons, &c., well filled with provisions, to their families, at an early hour this morning.

The entrance of Marlborough House was to the west, where the road formed the public way from East Street to Marlborough Row, which consisted of nine houses, whereof North House—that now contiguous to the northern entrance of the Pavilion Grounds—was No. 9. It was a boulder-fronted house, having adjoining it to the north, Coupland's blacksmith's shop, with three horse-shoes on a board adorning its front. These premises projected from the front line of the south side of Church Street; and, connected with them, were the dwelling-houses of Mr. Coupland and Mr. Beattie, and Beattie's donkey stables, the whole group of buildings, for many years after the Pavilion and Grounds became royal property, disgracing the approach to the Sovereign's residence and destroying the uniformity of the street. Eventually, the town purchased the property, and it was then wholly cleared away. The other houses of Marlborough Row were cant-bow fronted and were approached by four steps each. They were principally lodging-houses; but in 1800, No. 2,—opposite Marlborough House,—was in the occupation of Mr. John Wymark, baker, and in September, that year, on the occasion of a fire breaking out upon his premises, on a Saturday night, the Prince of Wales received the unfortunate family, and exerted himself in protecting their goods, which were taken for safety into the Pavilion.

The grounds attached to the Royal Pavilion and Marlborough House were, originally, of very limited proportions, those to the east front consisting only of a narrow lawn west of a direct line northward from the east front of the houses that form the north-east corner of Castle Square, on the Steine. But in consideration of the Prince and the Duke constructing in 1793, the sewer to carry off the stream which flooded the Steine in winter, the Lords of the Manor,—Brighthelmston-Lewes—with consent of the homage, gave them permission to enclose a certain portion of the Steine,—the Marlborough Steine, as it was termed,—adjoining their houses respectively; but never to build or encumber it with anything that might obstruct the prospect, or be any way a nuisance to the Steine. The ground then taken in was parted from the Steine by park palings, and posts and rails were put along the outer side to form a foot-way for the public.

In 1800, His Royal Highness purchased the principal portion of the Pavilion property to the south, of Mr. Weltjie, but no important improvements were undertaken until the following year, when, His Royal Highness having purchased the Elm Grove Gardens, the permission of the inhabitants was given him to enclose the old London Road, which ran direct northward from the top of East Street, on his making the New Road at his own expense. By this alteration, the Grove, and the shrubberies and pleasure-grounds of the Duke of Marlborough, which he likewise purchased, became united with the Pavilion Grounds.

The Promenade Grove or Public Gardens, which were under the particular patronage of the Prince of Wales, occupied the space of the present Pavilion Grounds, directly south of the Royal Stables, as also the site of the stables, and were approached by way of Prince's Place, an arched gateway occupying the space whereon stand the premises now occupied as the First Sussex Volunteer Rifle Orderly Room. Prince's Place was intended chiefly for the accommodation of the London tradesmen who came to Brighton with their wares for the season. An enclosed shrubbery of small dimensions occupied the centre of the open space, and the carriage drive was about it.

The gardens were surrounded with large overspreading elms, hence the name of the Grove, and in the hottest day of Summer a luxuriantly refreshing shade was afforded the fashionable promenaders who supported by subscription the establishment, which was open every day during the season. On Wednesdays a public breakfast was provided, when a band of music attended, and played at proper intervals select pieces of music. The breakfasts, when the weather was fine, were well attended, and boasted of all the elegance and the fashion in Brighton. Parties also, at other times went there to breakfast, drink tea, take refreshments—which were provided in abundance,—read the papers, &c. It possessed a well-appointed saloon, fitted up in an elegant style: adjoining which was an octagon-shaped orchestra. On particular nights the Gardens were brilliantly illuminated, and displays of fireworks were given; at which times the admissions were half-a-crown, and the entertainments were conducted with the greatest order and decorum. Upon stripping the walls of the house formerly inhabited by Mr. Johnson, recently purchased by Mr. Bradley, in Bond Street, a bill, having reference to these Gardens, and printed as follows, was brought to light:—

Under the patronage of His Royal Highness
THE PRINCE OF WALES.
PROMENADE GROVE.
The Nobility, Gentry, and Public are respectfully informed that there will be
ON THURSDAY EVENING, AUGUST 8TH, 1802,
A GRAND CONCERT,
of
VOCAL AND INSTRUMENTAL MUSIC.
After which a
MAGNIFICENT DISPLAY OF FIRE-WORKS.
Designs and Fire-works by
MR. MORTRAM.
By Permission of Colonel Jones, the Band of the 18th Dragoons will perform on the Lawn.
Admission at Half-past Seven; Concert at Eight, and Fire-works at Nine O'clock.
Managers,—
MESSRS. VERNEY AND JOHNSON.

The Promenade Grove, as a place of public entertainment, closed with a Grand Gala, which terminated with the spectacle of the eruption of Mount Vesuvius, on the 19th of September, 1802.

In 1805, the Royal Stables were commenced, after the plan and under the direction of Mr. Porden. They may be reckoned as the first great architectural work in Brighton. The centre of the building which supports the dome is circular, and contains a spacious reservoir of water for the stables which surround it. In this circular area the doors of various stables, comprising sixty-two stalls, open. Somewhat elevated, a gallery leads, by way of two staircases, to the several apartments of the servants required about the stables. The circumference of this spacious building is 250 feet, and the dome which surmounts it is nearly of the magnitude of that of St. Paul's Cathedral, London. On the west side is the magnificent Riding School, 200 feet long and 50 broad; and eastward of the dome was a spacious Tennis Court. The Parochial Offices occupy much of this latter space, which had previously, by order of William IV., been added to the stables, a blank screen front to the east giving the buildings an appearance of uniformity. There are two grand entrances to the stables, the one from Church Street, through a lofty archway which enters into a spacious square court, containing the coach-houses, carriage-horse stables, and general offices. A similar archway leads to the circular dome, opposite to which is a corresponding entrance from the Pavilion lawn. On the east and west sides of the circle are similar archways leading to the Riding School and the Tennis Ground.

The neglected state of these premises is a disgrace as well to the nation as to the town; for while Englishmen pride themselves on the vaunted greatness of their country, such is the reduced condition of her military resources that she is compelled to beg houseroom of the civil authorities for the accommodation of her soldiers, in a town where two ranges of barracks are inadequate to the requirements of a single regiment. The Town Council are bound in justice to the ratepayers to appropriate the premises to purposes for which little or no provision is made. The Courts of Justice in Brighton are libels on the name; the police accommodation is meagre in the extreme, persons only suspected of a crime being placed in underground dungeons similar to which criminals convicted of the darkest crimes would not by any British Government be permitted to be consigned; and while other towns with less pretensions to greatness than Brighton have their Public Baths and Wash-houses, these premises, which may be easily converted on a small outlay to meet all the requirements alluded to, are permitted to be illegally let and grossly misapplied, to the detriment of the property and the inconvenience of the inhabitants.

The most memorable event, in connexion with the Royal Stables, was the celebration of the Jubilee of the Fiftieth Year of the Reign of George III., by Mr. Philip Mighell feasting 2,000 of the poorest inhabitants of the town, by permission of the Prince of Wales, in the Royal Riding Room, on Wednesday, October the 25th 1809. The following is a copy of the letter to Mr. Mighell, conveying the sanction of His Royal Highness :—

Pavilion, Brighton, Oct. 20th, 1809.

Sir,—I am commanded by the Prince of Wales, to acquaint you that His

Royal Highness will have great satisfaction in affording the accommodation of his Riding House upon the happy occasion to which your letter refers, and which His Royal Highness sees in a most laudable view.

Sir, your Obedt Servt.,

BENJ. BLOOMFIELD*.

P. Mighell, Esq.

The eventful day was ushered in by the ringing of bells, the British Flag majestically waving on the venerable tower of St. Nicholas' Church, to which place of Divine Worship the Freemasons of the Royal Clarence Lodge, and their visiting brethren from the neighbouring Lodges, proceeded in procession, about eleven o'clock, the Band of the South Gloucester Militia taking the lead, and announcing their approach by their harmony. An appropriate sermon was preached by the Rev. Mr. Tilt; at the conclusion of which—there being then no organ in the church,—the Musicians of the Prince of Wales's Band performed the Coronation Anthem. At one o'clock a royal salute was fired from the Battery, and it was repeated by a gun-brig, then lying off the town. About half-past one o'clock the doors of the Royal Riding House, in Church Street, were thrown open for the admission of the benevolent Mr. Mighell's party, in number about two thousand three hundred, exclusive of a hundred stewards, who assisted upon the occasion. The greatest order and decorum prevailed throughout the feast; everybody was happy, and not an unpleasant incident occurred to mar the harmony of the proceedings. Mr. Phillips, of the New Inn Hotel, who was afterwards known as Jubilee Phillips, had the management of the dinner, the potatoes for which were a gift, and were dug from Mr. Mighell's garden,—whereon now stands Queen Squar e,— by his nephew, Mr. Richard Mighell, at present of Albany Villas, Cliftonville. In the farm-yard of Mr. Scrase, about three hundred yards from the Riding House, fifteen hundred poor

* Master of the Household to His Royal Highness. His appointment to that office arose from the singular circumstance of the Prince enquiring of Colonel Slade if he knew of any gentleman who played the violoncello? The Colonel replied, that he knew only of Captain Bloomfield of the Artillery. "Bring him here to dinner," said His Highness, "and tell him to bring his violoncello, and we'll play something." The Captain attended, and pleased the Prince, who desired him to call upon him the next day. He attended at the Pavilion accordingly and soon gained such favour as to obtain the confidence of the Prince. He was first made Sir Benjamin, and afterwards Lord Bloomfield.

persons were also dined, at the expense of a party of gentlemen, who opened a subscription for the same benevolent purpose, and similar order and harmony prevailed. On retiring,—which they did about five o'clock,—the grateful recipients gave expression to their loyalty, and invoked blessings on Mr. Mighell and their other liberal friends. The Freemasons dined in their Lodge Room, at the Old Ship—then kept by Mr. John Hicks,—where, also, in the evening, was a Ball and Supper.

In 1803, the Prince purchased property in Castle Square, adjoining the old stables, and year by year, till 1806, constant additions and improvements were made to His Royal Highness's property. Castle Square, just at its junction with North Street, was, in July 1811, the scene of the last punishment by the pillory in Brighton. The culprit was a man named Fuller, a native of Lewes; at the petty Sessions of which town—Brighton then having no bench of magistrates,—he was convicted of passing at Brighton a two-penny for a two-pound note. The structure of the pillory was upon a platform raised about ten feet from the ground. It consisted of a frame connected with an upright pillar, around which it revolved, and was made with holes and folding boards, through which the head and hands of the criminal were put, and from twelve to one o'clock he continued to take the circuit of an area of about eighteen feet diameter, under the superintendence of Mr. Harry Colbron, the High Constable, who, with his Headboroughs, escorted their prisoner to the place of punishment from the King and Queen Inn, to which house he had been brought from Lewes by the authorities of the House of Correction. A great concourse of the inhabitants assembled to witness the punishment, which was conducted by Catling, the beadle. The stage and pillory were constructed by Messrs. Colbron and Saunders.

In 1814, the Prince purchased Marlborough House; and the same year the houses and shops on the north side of Castle Square, and the whole of the old stables and coach-houses between the south side of the Pavilion, and terminating in a line with the bottom of North Street, were pulled down, and a noble range of domestic offices was erected on the site. Immediately north of the stables were the residence and grounds of Mr. Louis Weltjie, Clerk of the Prince's Kitchen. A portion of his brick-fronted house still remains, just within the southern entrance of the Pavilion Grounds. Weltjie and his wife were Germans, who had saved money while in the service of several of the nobility, and they invested it in the purchase of the property which they afterwards disposed of to the Prince, who reposed such confidence in Weltjie, that in December, 1788, upon His Royal Highness being—as was his perpetual condition,—in pecuniary embarrassment, and it had been determined by himself and his royal brothers, the Duke of York and the Duke of Clarence,—who were also in difficulties,—to speculate upon the prince's accession to power in consequence of the afflicting malady of their royal father, George III., Weltjie was selected as one of a party to effect a negociation in England, Ireland, and Scotland, of some post-obit bonds. Weltjie, however, fearing the consequences, withdrew from the project by introducing two persons of property and extensive money connexions, one of whom on the 16th of that month, perfected a bargain secured by the three royal brothers, for £30,000, payable when a *certain event* should take place. The bonds went into "The Market," and the witless purchasers who had obtained them at a premium, being afraid to acknowledge that they held any such obligations,—inasmuch as by anticipating the death of the sovereign they subjected the parties to all the penalties of petty treason,—their redemption was never claimed. Annexed is a copy of the bond referred to:—

KNOW ALL men by these presents that We, George Prince of Wales, Frederick Duke of York, and William Henry Duke of Clarence, all living in the City of Westminster, in the County of Middlesex, are jointly and severally, justly and truly indebted to John Cator, of Beckenham, in the County of Kent, Esquire, and his executors, administrators, and assigns, in the penal sum of Sixty Thousand Pounds of good and lawful money of Great Britain, well and truly paid to us at or before the sealing of these presents. Sealed with our seals this 16th day of December, in the 29th year of the reign of our Sovereign Lord George III., by the Grace of God, King, Defender of the Faith, Anno Domini 1788.

The condition of the above obligation is such, that if the above bounden George Prince of Wales, Frederick Duke of York, and William Henry Duke of Clarence, or any or either of them, or any other of their heirs, executors, or administrators, shall well and truly pay or cause to be paid unto the above-named John Cator, his executors, administrators, and assigns, the full sum of Thirty Thousand Pounds of lawful money of Great Britain, within the space or time of six calendar months next after any one or either of us, the said George Prince of

Wales, Frederick Duke of York, and William Henry Duke of Clarence, shall come to and ascend the throne of England, together with lawful interest on the same, to be computed from the day that such event shall happen, up and home to the time of paying-off this obligation, then and in such case, the same shall be null and void; otherwise to be and remain in full force and virtue.

George Prince of Wales, *
Frederick, *
William Henry, *

Witnesses,
Andrew Robenson,
Charles Bicknell.

In May, 1813, at a Court Baron of the Manor,—Brighthelmston-Lewes, — leave was given to the Prince Regent* to extend the fence which surrounded the Marlborough domains to the Royal Mews, and in 1815 His Royal Highness erected the lower section of the east and north boulder-fronted wall, placing on it the dwarf palisading that now crowns it, as raised to its present height; and in 1817 Marlborough Row became the Prince's property, and its site was added to the Royal Domain, which was then made to occupy an area of about seven acres.

Prior to 1817, the royal visitors to the Prince of Wales had been his Royal Consort, the Princess of Wales, in August, 1795, his daughter, the Princess Charlotte, July 27th, 1807, his brothers, the Dukes of Sussex, York, Clarence, Kent, Cumberland, and Cambridge, and their Royal Mother, Queen Charlotte, who paid her only visit to Brighton, accompanied by the Princesses Elizabeth and Mary, on the 24th of October, 1814, and they continued their stay till the 29th of that month, during which period Her Majesty graciously ordered the distribution of £50 to the poor, and became, with a liberal donation, the Patroness of the Dollar Society for the relief of the indigent. The Princesses were also donors to the Society. The foreign potentates who had been visitors were the Emperor of Russia and the King of Prussia. Various princes of the crowned heads of Europe had also paid their respects to the Prince, whose companions were the elite, if not the most dissolute of the nobility of the day. So notorious, in fact, were the doings at the Pavilion, that Lord Chancellor Thurlow, himself not the purest in conduct nor the most refined in man-

* Appointed to the Regency, February 5th, 1811.

ners, refrained from calling upon the Prince. One day, while walking on the Steine, his Lordship was met by His Royal Highness, in company with Lord Barrymore, Sir John Lade,* and other like companions. "Thurlow," said the Prince, "how is it that you have not called on me? You must name a day when you will dine with me." Lord Thurlow, casting a look round upon the Prince's friends, said, "I cannot do so until your Royal Highness keeps better company." Lord Thurlow died of the gout at Brighton, on the 12th of September, 1806, his dying words being, "I'm shot if I don't believe I'm dying."

Amongst the most notorious of the Prince's companions were the brothers Barrymore, the eldest,—who had been ordained to the church,—being known amongst them, for his irreligious propensities, as Hellgate; the second, for his immorality, Newgate; and the third, for his lameness, Cripplegate. The latter was the survivor of the infamous trio, his infirmities not permitting him to indulge in the vices which prematurely terminated the career of his brothers. They had a sister, who surpassed them in evil qualifications, and she bore, for her coarse volubility, the nickname of Billingsgate. Another of the *clique* was Colonel Hanger, familiarly known as George Hanger, the Knight of the Black Diamond, the wit and satirist of the party. His Life,† written by himself, abounds with sarcasms and truisms, but though designed to "point a moral," it does not "adorn a tale," that teems with sensualities. Upon one occasion Sheridan and Hanger were dining in the room of the old building where the Prince usually dined,

* Lade was in receipt of an annual pension of £400, as driving tutor to His Royal Highness. His wife, Lady Lade, who was born in Luckner's Lane, St. Giles's, London, was one of the most abandoned women of the Court. She was for some time the mistress of the notorious malefactor John Rann, known as "Sixteen Stringed Jack," who expiated his crime upon the scaffold, at Tyburn. The Duke of York then took her under his protection, and he transferred her by marriage, to Sir John Lade. Such was the style of language of this infamous woman, that when the Prince of Wales wanted an object of comparison in the vulgar practice of swearing, he was universally accustomed to say, "He swears like Letitia Lade." Some of the descendants of Sir John are still living, and reside at Ovingdean.

† The Life, Adventures, and Opinions of Col. George Hanger, written by himself. Two volumes, 8vo. London: Printed for J. Debrett, Piccadilly, 1801.

termed by them, in consequence of its contracted dimensions and generally excessively heated condition, the Royal Oven. In the course of the meal Sheridan said, "How do you feel yourself, Hanger?" "Hot, hot;—hot as h—l," replied Hanger. "It is quite right," was Sheridan's severe rejoinder, "we should be prepared in this world for that which we know will be our lot in another." Reckless roistering and inconsiderate practical joking were the delight of the Pavilion party, the hours of the night being principally the time when they immoderately enjoyed themselves. Upon one occasion, on a dark evening, they procured a coffin, and having put into it something resembling a corpse, dressed in a shroud, they stood it on end, without a lid, in front of the door of a tradesman's house, at which they knocked, and then hid away. On the servant "answering the door," as it is termed, the light of the candle in her hand displayed the spectre-like figure, which so frightened the poor girl that she shrieked and fainted. The inmates of the house, taking the alarm, ran to the door, and were equally terror-stricken. Cries of help quickly brought to their assistance many neighbours; but the concoctors of the joke had taken the precaution to fix to the handles of the coffin a strong rope, by means of which they, with little trouble, drew away the cause of the alarm; and there being thus nothing left to be frightened at, the inmates of the house became, for some time, laughing stocks for their credulity.

The numerous tricks practised upon the townsfolk did not in the least offend them, as in the event of any damage being done, that could be recompensed in a pecuniary way, the greatest liberality was always shown; in fact, the inhabitants had found that Royalty was the staple article upon which they existed, and they so assimilated their ideas with their position, that their chief fears were that they might by some inadvertence or mischance give the Prince offence, hence His Royal Highness was their chief study. The feeling, however, was graciously reciprocated by the Royal visitor, as exhibited upon the occasion of the anniversary of the birthday of His Royal Highness, August 12th, 1806—and it was generally so on like events—when a deputation of the inhabitants presented to the Prince the following address, to which every householder of note had previously subscribed his name :—

To his Royal Highness the Prince of Wales,

We, the Ministers, High Constable, Churchwardens, Overseers, and principal Inhabitants of the Town of Brighthelmston, with the most grateful recollection of the many gracious instances of your Royal Highness's patronage conferred upon us, to which alone are to be attributed that prosperity and those advantages unfelt by, and unknown to, any other Provincial Town, most humbly approach your Royal Highness, to express the dutiful and thankful sentiments which this recollection inspires, and more particularly calls forth on the anniversary of this day. While we entreat your Royal Highness to accept these our humble acknowledgments and congratulations, we devoutly implore the Supreme Disposer of all events long to preserve a life so invaluable to us, to whom your immediate protection is so liberally dispensed, and so dear and important in its general consequences to the nation at large.

His Royal Highness replied :—

Gentlemen,

Accept my best thanks for this Address. Be assured that I feel a lively interest in the prosperity of this place, and shall ever promote its welfare as far as lies in my power.

GEORGE, *Prince.*

It has hitherto, in general, passed current, that the predilection of the Prince of Wales for Brighton arose from the combination of the extent of the marine view which the town commanded, the salubrity of the place, and the great superiority of its sea-bathing; in confirmation of which last attraction prints are extant representing, of life size, Martha Gunn, the bather, bearing in her arms a naked "four-year old" baby, purporting to represent the youthful form of His Royal Highness, about to undergo the process of dipping; whereas it is well known that he had attained the age of a score of years before he first visited Brighton. The portrait of Martha no doubt is correct, but the infant in her arms is but an adjunct to distinguish her from the fishwomen, whose costume at that period was similar to the female bather. The Royal Bathing Machine, which for some years was so conspicuous on the beach at the bottom of the Steine, was that used by the Prince when he bathed under the guidance of Smoaker Miles, at the bottom of Russell street. It finished its days at the Steine, whither it was removed for the transit of His Royal Highness along the sand, at low-water, to the boat that conveyed him to and from the Royal yacht, which, during the temporary abode of the Prince in Brighton, was usually stationed, with a convoy of two ships of war, off Brighton, at the moorings, which were laid down and marked by buoys about six miles from the shore. The Royal machine was retained at the Steine, amongst the ladies' bathing machines, as it was much in request by the gentler sex, who were always anxious to occupy the machine from whence the Prince had taken a "header," or travelled to his yacht.

Much, in the way of anecdote, has been transmitted to us orally, respecting Martha Gunn, especially in reference to the Prince and the Pavilion; but, besides being a bather little of her life is known. In a rare work, "A Donkey Tour to Brighton*," occurs the following:—" 'What, my old friend, Martha,' said I, 'still queen of the ocean, still industrious, and busy as ever; and how do you find yourself?'—'Well and hearty, thank God, Sir,' replied she, 'but rather hobbling. I don't bathe, because I a'nt so strong as I used to be, so I superintend on the beach, for I'm up before any of em; you may always find me and my pitcher, at one exact spot, every morning by six o'clock.'—'You wear vastly well, my old friend, pray what age may you be?'—'Only eighty-eight, Sir; in fact, eighty-nine come next Christmas pudding; aye, and though I've lost my teeth, I can mumble it with as good relish and hearty appetite as anybody.'—'I'm glad to hear it; Brighton would not look like itself without you, Martha,' said I.—'Oh, I don't know, it's like to do without me, some day,' answered she, 'but while I've health and life, I must be bustling amongst my old friends and benefactors; I think I ought to be proud, for I've as many bows from man, woman, and child, as the Prince hisself; aye, I do believe, the very dogs in the town know me.'—'And your son, how is he?' said I.—'Brave and charming, he lives in East Street; if your honour wants any prime pickled salmon, or oysters, there you have 'em.'—I promised her I'd be a customer; she made me a low curtsey, and I left her hobbling to the side of the London coach, to deliver cards from the repository of her poor withered, sea-freckled

* The Observant Pedestrian Mounted, or a Donkey Tour to Brighton, a Comic Sentimental Novel, in three volumes. London: W. Simpkin and R. Marshall, 1815.

bosom; for, like a woman of fashion, her bosom was her pocket."

The Prince of Wales had an unbounded propensity for gallantry, and his companions of broken fortunes about him ingratiated themselves in his favour by pandering to his evil propensities. The Pavilion of Brighton, therefore, being secluded, was chosen as his favourite resort, whereto were brought the mistresses of his passions; and such a notoriety did the building attain that it was commonly spoken of as "the residence having at one end a harem, and at the other a chapel." An incident of one of his early visits to Brighton will exhibit his irresistance of temptation. His Royal Highness, while walking on the beach, was struck with the beauty of a nymph who was reclining by one of the groynes. Her name was Charlotte Fortescue, an illiterate female, who counteracted her defective educational qualifications by artifice and intrigue, and by her art she threw such an air of simplicity and innocence over her actions as to hide the real nature of her character from the Prince, whose exalted position she soon discovered. Again and again he met her; and believed that he had gained her confidence. Tears suffused her cheeks as she spoke of a marriage to which she was about to be forced, that would take her from her native country. The Prince eventually proposed an elopement, and in order to give a romantic air to the affair, it was arranged that the dress of a footman was to be procured for his frail fugitive, and that His Royal Highness that evening should have his phæton in waiting a few miles on the London Road, to bear away his prize. However, while the Prince was dressing for dinner, Colonel Hanger, who had just commenced his life of profligacy, was announced. At dinner the Prince excused himself upon having to leave them early, as he had most important business to transact that night in the metropolis. Hanger spoke of having left there that morning in search of a girl for whom he had provided private apartments in London, and remarked, "The hussy takes it into her head every now and then to absent herself for a few days; and I have now been given to understand that she is carrying on some intrigue with a fellow at this place. Let me but catch him, and I will souse him over head and ears in the sea." A little explanation sufficed to convince them both that the runaway was none other than the female with whom the Prince was so smitten, and it was arranged, in order to outwit her, that Hanger should put on one of the coats in which she had been occasioned to see her Royal lover, and take his seat on the coach-box, instead of the Prince. That night Hanger bore off his mistress to London, much to her chagrin that the romantic elopement should have such an unexpected termination, as the manner in which His Royal Highness travelled, one horse before the others, the first ridden by a postilion, and himself managing the other two, prevented a recognition till the female footman descended from the "dicky," in London. The imposition terminated their intimacy.

To detail the numerous acts of gallantry of the Prince and his associates would in nowise add to the improvement and enlightenment of the present age; nor is it necessary to give a biographical sketch or even a list of all his companions. His connexion, however, with Mrs. Fitzherbert* demands some mention to be made of that excellent lady who received the most cordial kindness and formal honours from the first families of distinction in the land. The Royal Marriage Act, which passed soon after the commencement of the reign of George III., in consequence of the marriage of the Duke of Cumberland with Mrs. Horton, and the Duke of Gloucester with the Countess of Waldegrave, declared that the descendants of George II., except the offspring of such of the Princes, as were married to, or might marry foreign Princesses, were incapable of marrying till the age of five-and-twenty years, without His Majesty's consent previously obtained; or after the age of five-and-twenty, in the event of His Majesty's refusal, without the consent of both Houses of Parliament. The marriage, then, between the Prince of Wales and Mrs. Fitzherbert, which Horne Tooke declared did take place, inasmuch as he was acquainted with the English clergyman who performed the solemn ceremony on the 21st of December, 1785, was null and void. Mr. Fox, in the House of Commons, denied that there had been marriage; but his denial was an act of ex-

* Born Mary Anne Smythe (daughter of Walter Smythe, Esq., of Bambridge, in the county of Hants), she was first married to Edward Weld, Esq., of Lulworth Castle, Dorsetshire; secondly to Thomas Fitzherbert, Esq., of Swinnerton, Staffordshire. She was a second time a widow, living on a handsome jointure, and greatly admired in society on account of her beauty and accomplishments.

pediency, as, according to the Act of William III., the admitted marriage of the Prince of Wales would have prevented his taking upon himself the Regency of the country, as the people, from his having married a Papist, would have been absolved from their allegiance. Amongst the real friends of the Prince his connexion with Mrs. Fitzherbert was an event of much gratification; for irregular as might have been its nature, it preserved him from the vulgar propensities to which he had been previously prone. Dowers and legacies of two previous marriages qualified her to command all the elegancies of fashionable life, and to perform many noble acts of charity. A separation only took place in 1795, when the Prince was about to marry (for the payment of his debts), the unfortunate Caroline of Brunswick. In such high esteem was she held by the Royal Family that upon William the IV. ascending the throne, he, with his Royal Consort, Queen Adelaide, paid her numerous visits of courtesy. The remains of Mrs. Fitzherbert, upon her decease, 27th March, 1837, were deposited in a vault beneath the Roman Catholic Church, St. George's Road, where a handsome marble monument, by Carew, has been erected to her memory. Her age was eighty-one.

Some romantic notion gave forth the rumour that a subterranean communication existed between the Royal Pavilion and Mrs Fitzherbert's house, on the Steine. A greater fallacy never gained credence. All that she possessed, connected in any way with the estate, were the stables in the New Road, immediately north of the row of trees which bounds the Pavilion Grounds on the east. These stables—erected in 1806—are now used as the chief depôt of the Borough Fire Brigade, under Inspector Quartermain, They were immediately contiguous to the Burial Ground of the Society of Friends,—now the Corporation premises for depositing the Town Surveyor's materials,—and for a window in the stables that overlooked the ground Mrs. Fitzherbert paid one penny per month, as will appear by the following minute of the Committee of Friends:—

Brighton, 13th of 11th month, 1806.

Committee for the management and disposal of Lands at Brighton belonging to the quarterly meeting of Friends of Sussex.

This committee having taken into consideration the request of Maria Fitzherbert for permission to continue the window in the north side of her stables which looks into the premises belonging to Friends,

This committee, unwilling to pursue a conduct which may assume the appearance of acting otherwise than neighbourly (notwithstanding injury may arise to the said premises by complying with such request), consents to the window not being stopped up for the present, upon condition of Maria Fitzherbert's agreeing to pay one penny per month for such permission, and also undertaking to brick-up the same, at any time within one week after notice for that purpose from any of the trustees or committee for the said premises, and in default thereof that any of the Friends be authorized to brick-up the said window at the expense of the said Maria Fitzherbert, and that such agreement be prepared, signed and delivered to the said committee within two weeks from the date hereof, otherwise the foregoing proposals to be void.

William Tuppen is requested to take a copy of the above minute to Maria Fitzherbert, and obtain her sentiments thereon, and report the same to this committee.

Signed in and on behalf of the committee,

JNO. GLAISYER.

A subterranean passage is in existence from the Pavilion to the Stables, and was the medium by which, in disguise, the Prince and his friends went to and returned—comparatively in private—from their nocturnal rambles. Its immediate connexion with the royal suite of rooms was by means of a trap in the floor of one of the apartments, beneath which was an intricate staircase that gave him a means of ready exit; as, besides using it on occasions of fun and frolic, his constant fear of attempts upon his life from political motives,—as on the occasion of his being shot at with an air-gun, on his return from opening Parliament in 1817,—or in consequence of his numerous amorous peccadillos, rendered a means of escape desirable, and he was enabled also, in case of emergency, to attain with great facility the various galleries that ramified the roofs of the building.

The New Road—previously the garden of Mr Furner, the Prince's gardener,—was formed in 1805, by privates of the Royal Artillery; and on Monday, August 12th, — the anniversary of the birth-day of the Prince of Wales,—His Royal Highness gave the men employed on the work a guinea each. In 1807, there was a west entrance to the Pavilion Grounds, directly opposite the Theatre. On the 14th of August, that year, it happened that the Prince, purposing going out that way in the evening, found the gate shut and locked. His Royal Highness called out to his attendants to break the gate open,—an order which they attempted to obey, but found themselves unequal to the task. The Prince smiling, desired them to stand aside, as he had no doubt but his strength was sufficient to force the place, though their's had failed. In an instant he wrenched the gate from its hinges, and with his party passed on to the Theatre.

The trees in the New Road were not planted till 1812. The double row of elms immediately west formed the east range of Elm Grove, and in 1817 became the first resort of the rooks, which had been driven away from Preston Rookery by Mr. Stanford. These birds do not winter in Brighton, but come from Stanmer Park—whither they migrate,—annually towards the end of February.

The great additions to the Royal Pavilion, or rather its re-construction, so as to remain and adopt some portions of the original building, commenced in 1817, Nash being the architect. It is of no fixed style of architecture, but is a composite of the Moorish and Chinese. An Indian style was offered by Repton, who on the publication of it, upon its being rejected by the Prince, adopted the term "Pavillon," both in the plates and in the letter-press. The style selected is admired by some persons, but much ridiculed by critics. Sidney Smith said "the building looked as if the dome of St. Paul's, London, had come down to Brighton and pupped;" whilst William Cobbett observed that "a good idea of the building might be formed by placing the pointed half of a large turnip upon the middle of a board, with four smaller ones at the corners." The Pagoda towers, which form the north and south wings, are much admired for the beauty of their proportions, and for their in-version from the roof in a spheroidical elevation. They are covered with thin plates of iron, coated with mihl or mastic of great durability. The domes, and the minarets, which consist of open cupolas on tall pillars, have a similar covering of mastic.

In adapting the north pagoda to a concert room, every attention was paid by the architect to combine the harmony of the music in the perfect equilibrium of tone produced by each instrument. The Prince of Wales, who was a fine judge and promoter of music, made many suggestions to counteract the too great elevation of the ceiling, which somewhat destroyed the combination and vibration of sound, and under his accomplished taste the acme of scientific proportions of combination and sound was attained. The first time that this music room was used was about the middle of January, 1818, the performers being the Prince Regent's private band. The organ, by Mr Lincoln, was not erected till the end of that year. The organ previously used in the Pavilion was taken there on the 18th of November, 1805. The instrument now used in the room formerly stood in the Royal Chapel, and was the gift of her present Majesty to the town.

It is unnecessary to give a detailed description of the whole of the apartments of the Pavilion, or the furniture therein; it will suffice to say that with the exception of the Chinese Gallery, and the suite of rooms which forms the east front, there was not, while it remained Royal property, a room that would content any commoner of substance. The throne room, with its tawdry adjuncts, was vile in taste and of meagre proportions; wholly devoid of the grandeur and nobleness which should attach itself to Royalty. A casual observer of the present day would be led to suppose that the apartment was the lodge-room of some benefit society, or the smoking crib of George IV., the raised canopied dais being appointed for the chairman at Lodge Meetings, or for His Gracious Majesty when he presided over his Royal Pavilion midnight orgies. The whole of the King's Apartments, as they were designated, were of a like character; but they afforded him a contentment, inasmuch, as, from his bedroom,—by the secret stairs to which the bloated Marchioness of Conyngham descended from her chamber,—to the capacious marble bath where his Majesty laved, there was a seclusion to which in his later years he became habituated. The upper rooms of the Pavilion, are, for a Palace, low pitched, of very contracted dimensions, and from two windows alone, those in the large dome, is a sufficient view of the sea obtained to permit of the building being termed a Marine Pavilion. The furniture throughout the building was costly in the extreme, but incongruous. Huish, in his "Memoirs of George IV.," says:— "Nothing could exceed the indignation of the people, when the Civil List came before Parliament in May, 1816, and £50,000 were found to have been expended in furniture at Brighton, immediately after £534,000 had been voted for covering the excess of the Civil List, occasioned entirely by the reckless extravagance of the Prince Regent, whose morning levees were not attended by men of science and of genius, who could have instilled into his mind wholesome notions of practical economy; but the tailor, the upholsterer, the jeweller, and the shoemaker were the regular attendants of his morning recreations." On one of these occasions his servant entered his apartment at the Pavilion with the information, "*She* is come, your Royal Highness." "She!" exclaimed the Prince, "who is *she?*" "*She* is come," repeated the servant. "I ask," replied the Prince in an angry tone, "who is *she?*—where does *she* come from?" "It is *Shea* the tailor, from London, your Royal Highness." The Prince smiled, and the *Shea* was admitted immediately into the royal presence.

Irrespective of the great alterations and improvements at the Royal Pavilion marking an epoch for Brighton, in 1817, that year is also memorable in the town for the 5th of November riot, which then took place, referred to in in page 114, and thus satirised by Thomas Herbert*:—

THE CARD, OR POSTER.

'Twas t'other day a printed card,
A sort of petty war declared
  Against some little boys!
Three silly men, to say no worse,
Must needs pursue a foolish course
  To rob them of their joys!
This, being canvassed round and round,
At first produc'd a whispering sound
  Which soon grew into noise.

THE MORNING.

The morning lowers
And heavily in clouds brings on the day
Big with the fate of three deluded men.
A council, now, these three conven'd,
To see what mischief could be schem'd,
  Their victims to annoy;
This caus'd a dinner to be had,
Our heroes being very sad,
  To renovate their rage;
And at the dinner they got drunk—
Which soon produc'd a mighty funk,
  They wanted to engage.

---

* War at Brighton, or the Battle of The Tar Tub, a short November Tale. By Thomas Herbert. London: John Rowe, Cornhill.

THE DINNER*

The dinner's over and the table clear,
Each has a bumper of his favorite cheer,
Now up erect the company arise,
The Regent's health! the soaking hero† cries;—
The Regent's health! repeats the sable Knight,‡
We must him cheer or else it wont be right!
Most certainly repli'd the chief, half soaken,
With three times three 'twill be a loyal token;
For three times three, my boys, prepare your lips,
And you, dear sable, please to give the hips.
The glass pass'd round, with sentiment sublime,
Some choosing punch and some prefering wine;
Until at length, they growing pretty mellow,
'Tis said, their chief these words aloud did bellow:—
Stand by me, boys! I'll teach 'em such a story!
If you'll stand firm I'll lead you on to glory.
When having drank as long as they were able,
While some sat up and some lie under table,
I must go home exclaim'd the soaking chief—
Remember boys, you come to my relief!
And so must I—repli'd the sable hero,
And off they trudge like Beelzebub and Nero.

AT SOAKER'S DOOR.

Soaker to Black.—My dear friend Black I'm much afraid
There'll be a row—the soaking hero said.
Black.—I think so too, indeed, upon my word,
So I'll go home and sharpen up my sword.
Soaker.—That's right my boy, then shortly after tea
Come here again, I shall you want to see,
And as I fear this job will end in strife—
I'll just step in and reconcile my wife.
Black.—That's spoken well, and so my friend will I,
Then for the present you—I'll bid good by.
Soaker.—Good by my friend, good by—good by—good by.

AT BLACK'S.

Mrs. Black.—My husband, dear, what makes you look so white?
My heart forebodes 'twill be a shocking night.
Black.—Should it be so, pray don't you be alarm'd—
You know, my dear, I always go well arm'd.
Mrs. Black.—Alas, my dear, you look as almost dead—
A dreadful stone may smite you on the head.
Black.—Suppress these fears, with tears flush in his eyes,
Suppress these fears, the trembling *hero* cries;

* The dinner took place at the Dolphin, now the Queen's Hotel.

† Williams, of the Royal Baths, High Constable.

‡ White, Castle Square.

Should in the riot your dear husband fall,
The will he made conveys to you his all.
So one sweet kiss! and then, I go away,
'Tis duty calls, I must my love, obey.

Then for his sword the fear-struck hero cri'd—
The cause demands it, so, my dear, don't chide;
His sword is brought, and buckl'd round his waist,
With great precision, like a man of taste—
Away he swaggers, and his hands he rubs,
Looking, quite bold, like a new jack of clubs.

AT SOAKER'S.

Mrs. Soaker.—Oh, if, my dear, you must to night go out,
I pray, my love, mind what you are about.
Soaker.—My honor calls, indeed, my dearest wife!
My love, my joy, my only hope, my life!
And should the rebels your dear husband kill,
In yonder drawer you'll find his honest will.
I must away, my dear, 'tis growing late,
So kiss me love, and give me up to fate.

AT SOAKER'S DOOR.—BLACK AND SOAKER MEET.

Soaker.—At yonder corner when a man you place,
Bid him stand firm, and not our cause disgrace;
At that place, too, another must be fixed;
Likewise a third, the interval betwixt:
And the rear guard—as well as our van
Must all stand firm, ay, even to a man.

THE STEINE.

The signal made—the blazing foe appears—
Had you been there, you must have smelt their fears.
The scene was grand, illumining around,
You might have pick'd a sixpence from the ground;
The lookers on appearing at first glimpse,
Just like the Old One, and so many imps;
With heart-felt joy, and truly loyal shout,
'Tis now the boys the tar tub roll about;
Oh, 'twas a pity such a noble sight,
Should be the signal for a bloody fight.
The soaking hero runs amidst the crowd,
And in a rage vociferates aloud—
Patrole! d'ye hear! you're deaf upon my soul!
These villains take and lodge in the black hole!
The battle rages and the missile flies,
To fetch the troops the soaking hero hies;
He skulks away to the sage monster's* house
As much alarm'd, as e'er was cat-caught mouse.

* Serjeant Runnington, chairman of the Brighton Bench of Magistrates.

AT MONSTER'S HOUSE.

And when arriv'd at this great legal source,
He pli'd the knocker with uncommon force—
The door is open'd, in our hero goes,
And to the bear disgorges all his woes.
Assist us, sir, or else, this very night,
I and poor Sable shall be murder'd quite!
At this request the learned bear turns out,
And looks like one they, sometimes, lead about.
I'll pretty soon, he roars, the rabble clear,
I'll read the riot act, I've got it here!
Go get the troops, and then we need not fear!
How many troops? the soaking hero cri'd,
All that you can, the learned bear repli'd.

THE BARRACKS.

Now to the Barracks flies the soaking chief,
And calls for troops; assuming, bold and brief;
I want some troops, to sergeant he did say
At your peril dare to keep away!
The sergeant-major to the guard-house hies,
Turn out the piquet, there, he loudly cries,
The word is pass'd, the soldiers prompt obey,
And to the Steine that instant march away.

THE STEINE.

The troops arriv'd close to the learned bear,
He reads the proclamation in their rear,
And off he sculks half dead with dread and fear!
The soaking chief, like one bereav'd of wits,
And almost going into fainting fits,
Charge on, exclaimed, no mercy I'll afford!
Why don't you charge? You heard me give the word.
Charge! charge! charge! charge! the sable knight replies,
Charge! charge! again the soaking hero cries.
The charge is made, alas, poor luckless Rowles,
Thy life is gone, through these ambitious fools;
The battle's ended, and they look around,
When some are lying stretch'd upon the ground;
Some too with cuts and bruises there are found.
Just at the end of this disgusting scene,
A man of peace was walking on the Steine,
The soaking hero cri'd What brought you here?
Go home! go home! roar'd out the learned bear.
To these insults the man of peace replies,
With indignation beaming in his eyes,
Nothing I said, nor nothing have I done;
So when I please I, therefore, shall go home.
You won't go home, roar'd out the learned bear,
So mind to-morrow, from me you shall hear.

You look disdainful in my very face!
I'll bind you o'er to keep the public peace;
In this, believe me, though it seems absurd,
The learned monster strictly kept his word;
The peaceful man, however hard his fare,
Was bound, they say, next sessions to appear!
A frantic mother running on the Steine,
A poor man ask'd, have you my Billy seen?
The man repl'd, I havn't, on my soul;
You'd better ask, I think, at the Black Hole.
The wretched woman now borne down with grief,
Flies to that place in hopes to find relief,
Raps at the door, Who's there? with voice quite grim,
The night watch cried, we cannot take more in.
'Tis full of young and old, besides a quaker prim.

Woman.—Oh, pray sir, pray, relieve a mother's fear,
And tell me if you have my Billy here?

Watch.—Ay, that he is, I'm sure beyond a doubt,
And so to-morrow you may bail him out.

Woman.—She walks away, but still she sheds a tear—
And calls for imprecations on the bear.

Next day the learned bear flies to his station,
To be the judge of his own depredation;
'Tis now the foaming monster roars aloud,
With face as black as a November cloud.
Bring in your charge, but mind I say,
At your perils let him get away.
Now with a double guard there enters in
A child, but just escaped from leading string.
The monster with a dreadful stare, at large,
Against the pris'ner ask'd what was the charge;
The sable hero, with assurance ample,
'Tis dreadful, sir, exclaim'd, beyond example!
As I stood on the Steine with sword in hand,
I saw him brandish a huge fire brand.
Oh, fy, saith pris'ner, what a wicked fib,
'Twas but the paper of a discharg'd squib.
Pris'ner, your age? exclaim'd the learned bear,
While down his little face would steal a tear.
The truth, come tell me, or I'll commit you straight;
I am, saith pris'ner, somewhat turn'd of eight.
The monster roared, with truly savage grin,
Discharge the brat, and bring another in.

THE DEATH.

Alas, alas! poor lifeless Rowles,
It grieves me to relate—
Thy fam'ly lost its dearest friend
By thy untimely fate.

May Providence then guide the law,
Thy slaughter be avenged;
And may the halter catch the right,
For equity's just end.

Oh, may thy widow find support,
Thy family to rear;
And may she live to bring them up,
The living God to fear.

The visits of George IV. to Brighton were discontinued in 1824, in consequence of a deep resentment which His Majesty felt at some personal affront that was given by some of the inhabitants, to his then favourite mistress, the Marchioness of Conyngham, who was the Lady Steward of the Royal Household, and arrogated to herself the privilege of arranging the *entree* to the King, and of possessing control over the commonest domestics of the establishment. Her effrontery, however, was too intolerant for some of the towns-folk to brook; and, their virtuous indignation being aroused, they indulged in remarks upon her, and were so indifferent in courtesy towards her, that His Majesty considered the affront as almost given to himself. In fact, the extraordinary ascendency which the Marchioness had obtained over the royal mind, was then so apparent in all the King's actions that he was a Sovereign governed by one subject, and that subject more influential and powerful in her authority than the first minister of the State. Upon the retirement of the King from Brighton, the Princess Augusta was a frequent visitor to the town, her residence, by permission of her Royal Brother, being one of the private houses, to the west, just within the then southern entrance to the Pavilion Grounds.

The Royal Pavilion was a favourite autumn and winter residence of William IV. and Queen Adelaide, who made their first visit to Brighton on Monday, August 30th, 1830. Their Majesties effected many important alterations upon the Royal Property, causing the erection of the ivy-clad range of buildings known as the Dormitories, extending along the south margin of the western lawn, from Prince's Place to Carlisle House. A southern entrance to the Grounds was erected in 1831. It stood across the top of East Street, in a line with the north side of North Street; but upon the Royal Pavilion estate becoming the property of the Town of

Brighton, in 1850, the building was taken down; as, besides the structure being in nowise handsome, it was a screen that completely hid the Pavilion, and hemmed in the property now known as the Pavilion Buildings. The elegant northern entrance—a noble and faultless building, exhibiting every characteristic of boldness and stateliness,—was erected in 1832.

During the occupation of the Royal abode by William and Adelaide,—when it received the name of The Palace,—it was a continued scene of regal festivities, juvenile parties being very frequent. The present Duke, then Prince George of Cambridge, was a great favourite with Their Majesties, who specially humoured his fancies and frolics. Royalty, however, is very tenacious of its dignity; whereof the following is a proof: Upon occasions when the youthful aristocracy were invited to the Palace, it was invariably usual for the arrangements of the evening to be under the immediate superintendence of the celebrated *maitresse de danse,* Madame Michau, who, not unfrequently, was assisted in her duties by her son, now well-known as Mons. James Michau, and the arrangement graciously received the Royal sanction. With the Prince and his youthful associates the son of the dancing mistress was considered fair game for their sporting humour; they therefore resorted to practical joking upon him, well-knowing that difference in position forbad his making a retort. But it happened upon one occasion that either the Prince exceeded his usual indignities, or that young Michau was not in a philosophic placid temper, as he offered a remonstrance, which excited a blow from His Royal Highness, resulting in a bout of fisticuffs, from which the Prince came off second best. The indignity, thus justly administered, was forthwith resented, the Royal communication, through Mr. Gee, Her Majesty's page, being that Madame Michau's services would not again be required. A retributive incident shortly after occurred that entirely put an end to the Palace youthful gatherings. Prince George, for a diversion, had purchased a mechanical mouse, and, having wound it up, he placed it upon the floor, when it chanced to travel in the direction of the Queen. Her Majesty had not observed the toy until it closely approached her, when, feeling a sudden alarm, she rose hurriedly, uttering an ejaculation of fear, a procedure so undignifying to her exalted position that she immediately retired, and no other juvenile party at the Palace ever after took place.

Queen Victoria paid her first visit to Brighton, October 4th, 1837, and had a most enthusiastic reception. Her Majesty's second visit took place the following Autumn. In February, 1842, the Queen and Her Royal Consort, Prince Albert, made the stay of a month in Brighton; and on the 7th of September, the following year, Her Majesty and the Prince Consort landed from the Royal Yacht, at the Chain Pier, on their return from a visit to Louis Philippe, at Chateau d'Eu. The circumstance of their landing is commemorated by Mr. R. H. Nibbs, in a most exquisite painting which is placed amongst the local works of art that adorn the Borough Council Chamber, at the Town Hall. The Queen and Prince Albert embarked on the 12th for Ostend. In September, 1844, the last royal visit was made to the Pavilion, the Prince of Wales, the Princess Royal, and Prince Alfred being sent down for the benefit of their health. Their stay extended to a fortnight. Hopes were entertained that Her Majesty would again visit Brighton; but time passed on, and at length it was announced that the Queen had purchased an estate in the Isle of Wight, where she would have a marine residence, in the strictest sense of the word, easy of access, and so admirably situated that she could, with the greatest facility, indulge in her favourite pastime—a water excursion.

Gradually the Pavilion became despoiled of its costly furniture and fittings, many of the latter being ruthlessly torn down and destroyed. Eventually it was announced that the building was to be razed to the ground, the materials sold, and the land disposed of for building purposes. In November, 1848, it became known that the Royal Commissioners of the Woods and Forests intended to introduce a Bill the next Sessions of Parliament, for the sale of the property, to obtain funds for further improvements at Buckingham Palace. The Town Commissioners put in their claim for a restoration by the Crown of the road which formerly went through the Pavilion Grounds, from south to north from East Street. It was also pointed out that some portions of the ground that had been sold to the Prince Regent, had restrictions against building, which restrictions could not be removed without the consent of the Lords of the Manor.

The Bill for the disposal, however, passed, and on the 27th of July, 1849, a Vestry meeting of the rated inhabitants, determined upon purchasing the property for £53,000, the sum required for it by the Commissioners of the Woods and Forests. Another Bill had yet to be obtained to give the Town Commissioners power to purchase the estate. Such an opposition to the purchase in the meantime sprung up amongst some of the ratepayers, and at a Vestry meeting called to approve of the Bill, that, after two days' polling, the amendment, in effect "that the purchase be stopped," was only lost by a minority of 36, the numbers being: for the purchase, 1343; against it, 1307. The Bill was read in the House of Commons a second time, without opposition, on the 14th of February, 1850; and was read a third time in the House of Lords on the 2nd of May, 1850. The money for the purchase, and £7,000 for the expenses of obtaining the Bill, and to restore the building, amounting in the whole to £60,000, was borrowed of the Bank of England, and on the 13th of June, 1850, the Commissioners of the Woods and Forests were paid the sum required. The building is not yet wholly appropriated, but, immediately upon the completion of the purchase, the late Mr. Christopher Wren Vick was employed to effect the work of restoration, and he succeeded in obtaining the original blocks from which the former paper-hangings of the grand suite of rooms were printed, and also in engaging Mr. Lambelet,—who has since died in poverty—the artist who executed the original decorations. On the 21st of January, 1851, the Pavilion was re-opened with a grand ball of the inhabitants; since which time numerous balls, concerts, and meetings of scientific, benevolent, and other societies have taken place there, and it has now an excellent gallery for paintings, and several rooms have been set apart for the Brighton Museum, an institution that is well deserving of support. Paintings, by purchase and gifts, adorn many of the walls of the building, and in the Vestibule and Chinese Gallery are some excellent specimens of sculpture, principally by our local sculptor, Mr. Pepper. The most prominent is a full length statue by Noble, of the late Captain Pechell, son of the late member for Brighton, Sir G. R. B. Pechell, Bart. The gallant young officer fell during the Russian War, in the Crimea.

Besides the Pavilion and Grounds, the estate has many private houses, including the magnificent range called Pavilion Buildings. The debt consequent upon the purchase is being gradually reduced, and the opponents to the purchase not feeling the burthen which they dreaded, have the gratification of knowing, that, as a lung to their magnificent town, they have that which no other town in the kingdom possesses,—an extensive park of its own in its very centre.

CHAPTER XXVII.

ON AND ABOUT THE RACE-COURSE.

Royalty had scarcely taken up its abode in Brighton, when, according to the Racing Calendar, in 1783, racing commenced its career on the eastern down, better known as White Hawk Down, Brighton, The sports were principally amongst the officers of the Militia Regiments which were then quartered in the town, and they received the patronage of the Prince of Wales. Beyond the authority of the "Oldest Inhabitant," transmitted orally, there is no account of the extent, formation, or the tenure of the course. It is understood to have been about two miles in length, and to have occupied, as at present, the horse-shoe shaped ridge of the hill, and was defined, on sufferance, by the clearing away of the furze.

The Race Ground proper consists of 105 acres and 30 perches, over which the right of pasturage has become vested in the Marquis of Bristol, by purchase from Mr. Thomas Read Kemp, who bought it for £780, subject to public rights, as the erection thereon, by the inhabitants, of booths and stalls for the accommodation and recreation of the public during the races. The Course is two miles in length, and what is known as the New Course is one mile long. The counterpart of an alleged lease was in the possession of Mr. Thomas Attree, Queen's

Park, bearing date June 24th, 1796, purporting to be a demise of the Race Stand to various inhabitants,—all of whom are now deceased,—for 99 years, at the annual rent of one guinea. The counterpart came into the possession of Mr. Attree in 1822, many years prior to which no rent had been paid or demanded, and no lease could ever be discovered. On the 2nd July, 1846, a committee of the Town Commissioners were informed by Mr. Attree that he claimed the Stand for himself and others who had subscribed £400 for its erection, in eighteen shares, whereof he held nine, and that the sum still remained a charge upon the building; but he offered to sell the Stand for £400 to the Race Committee. The Committee considering that no valid lease was in existence,—inasmuch as in deeds, dated 1822, and to which Mr Attree was a party, whereby the Race Stand was specially granted, no allusion whatever was made to a lease or other incumbrance,—declined the offer. They furthermore considered that the debt alleged to be due and charged thereon ought long since to have been liquidated from the proceeds of the letting, and that the inhabitants beneficially interested therein were exonerated from such debt, charge, or encumbrance.

In 1849 a new Race Committee was formed, and their first step was to purchase the Stand, giving for it, to the surviving shareholders, Mr. T. Attree, Mr. H. Blackman, and Mr. Tamplin, the sum of £360, the London, Brighton, and South-Coast Railway Company liberally presenting to the Committee £100 towards the amount, independent of their annual subscription to the Race Fund of £200. The following six gentlemen also came forward as Trustees: Mr. Alderman Burrows, Mr. Alderman Martin, Mr. Robert Williams, Mr. H. F. Stocken, Mr. Lewis Slight, and Mr. Lewis Slight, jun., and the shabby wooden building, erected in 1798, gave place to the present commodious and handsome structure, the design of Mr. Allan Stickney, the Town Surveyor, at a cost of £5,000, the whole of which has been discharged by the Race Committee, who have likewise increased the public money from £350 given in 1848, to nearly £2,000 annually.

The old Race Stand, built in 1803, succeeded the first building, which was erected in 1788, and destroyed by fire on the 23rd of

August, 1796. The fire arose in consequence of the carelessness of the family who had been permitted to occupy the building. Notwithstanding the unfortunate occurrence took place about mid-day, it was distinctly seen at a distance of upwards of thirty miles. Many people from various parts of the county, some on horseback, and some on foot, entered the town during the succeeding night and day, to make enquiries respecting it, as apprehensions prevailed that the enemy had made a descent on that part of the coast, and was evincing his love for the natives by setting fire to their dwellings.

A singular incident occurred during the fire: An officer of the Prince's regiment, attracted to the spot by the volumes of flame and smoke, was reviewing the terrific encroachments of the devouring element, when a cat, dreadfully singed and terrified, sprung through the blaze, and alighted on his shoulders. The officer, somewhat surprised, at first endeavoured to shake her off; but poor puss, firmly fixing her claws in his jacket, was not so easily got rid of. Perceiving, then, her reluctance to leave him, he at length humanely determined, that as she had, in the moment of danger and fear, flown to him for protection, she should accompany him to the Barracks, where she was well taken care of by her new master and his comrades.

A curious circumstance took place on the morning of the Races, August 4th, 1805. The farmer who rented the race ground having explained to the Jockey Club that he had not received the usual compliment of the fourth of a pipe of wine for the previous season, threatened to plough up the course if he was not paid what he conceived to be his due. Accordingly, he set his plough to work, but a press-gang appearing in sight, his ploughman fled, and resigned the course to the gentlemen of the turf, the farmer the while declaring that he would not be jockeyed out of his wine, as he would have a sort of a race for it in Westminster Hall. The cause, however, never came off.

The support given to the Brighton Races by the Prince of Wales and those immediately about him, made the meeting amongst the nobility quite a national feature, as the *elite* of the turf were always in attendance, and a gaiety prevailed that no other place could boast of. The course was thronged with equestrians and the fashionable equipages of the day, barouches and four, driven by lords and baronets. Conspicuous amongst them was His Royal Highness on his German Waggon—as his barouche was called,—driving his six bays, with Townsend, of Bow Street, as his companion, as well to protect the Prince from insult as from robbery. But it was a position which gave His Royal Highness an opportunity to practise upon his guardian a somewhat unpleasant joke. Turning suddenly towards Townsend, just at the termination of a race, he exclaimed, "By Jove, Townsend, I've been robbed; I had with me some damson tarts, but they are now gone." "Gone?" said Townsend, rising, "impossible!" "Yes," rejoined the Prince, "and you are the purloiner," at the same time taking from the seat whereon the officer had been sitting, the crushed crust of the asserted missing tarts, and adding, "This is a sad blot upon your reputation as a vigilant officer." "Rather, say your Royal Highness, a sad stain upon my escutcheon," added Townsend, raising the gilt buttoned tails of his blue coat and exhibiting the fruit-stained seat of his nankeen inexpressibles.

The Brighton Races are now held on the Tuesday, Wednesday, and Thursday following the Goodwood meeting. Thursday is devoted to the racing of the Brighton Race Club, established in 1850. Formerly they were either on Saturday, Monday, and Tuesday, as shown by the calendar of the Brighton Races, July 28th, 30th, and 31st, 1804, now in the possession of Mr. Alderman Martin; or, as in 1810, on Friday, Saturday, and Monday, August 3rd, 4th, and 6th, when two races a-day took place, distinguished in their time of running by "Before Dinner," and "After Dinner." The arrangement of the days was to admit of a fair, termed "White Hawk Fair," being held on the east down on the intervening Sunday. It has now been abolished about forty years. The *Morning Herald*, Sunday, August 2nd, 1807, makes the following mention of this fair:—

> White Hawk Fair, as it is termed, has attracted much company to the Race Down to-day, though but few individuals of fashionable note were to be seen in the throng.

Connected with this Down is the

LEGEND OF THE WHITE HAWK LADY.

Less than half a century since, the remnant of a moss-covered unhewn stone marked the spot in Ovingdean churchyard, where, as gossips then said, were deposited the remains of Margaret Ladrone, probably a name conferred on her from the pilfering propensities of the gipsies, a tribe to which she belonged, though she was familiarly spoken of as "Mag Lade," a sybil or fortune-teller of her day, whose visits to Ovingdean were annual in the month of August, on the occasion of White Hawk Fair, a holiday gathering on White Hawk Down, at which the rustics were wont to learn their fate of the wise woman, as she was termed by the unmarried who would know the future through the vista of happiness; but the old crone or witch, by those whose stern thought attributed all the mishaps that befel either themselves or their substance to the influence of an evil one, with whom she was proclaimed to be in league. At other periods of the year she practised her vocation in various places throughout the county, so that she had a regular circuit, through the course of which the burning fervour of youth hailed her advent with earnest anticipations, equalled only by the dread entertained by mature age, that blight and murrain were her attendants. It happened on one occasion, the date whereof is immaterial, that Editha Elmore, the only daughter of the rich squire of Woodingdean, while intent on the palmistry of Mag,—whose hand she had crossed with a broad silver piece,—by chance cast her eyes upon the form of a dark young man of goodly mien, the very type of him whom the gipsey prophetess essayed to be her future husband. In the next country-dance he was her partner, and also the envy of one who, from their childhood, had been her companion, and was looked upon by the parents of each as her intended bridegroom. The festivities of the day closed; the dark stranger bade her adieu; the villagers returned to their homes; and ere the shades of night had gathered over the Downs, not a vestige was left of the scene which had been one of general festivity. Ralph Mascall, the son of the farmer at the Grange, Ovingdean, as had been his custom from a child, accompanied the fair Editha to Woodingdean, where he received the accustomed welcome of her parents; and, before midnight, he was on his way homewards somewhat disturbed in mind that he had a rival. His visits, however, to Squire Elmore's were not the less frequent; nor did the affection shown towards him by Editha in the least appear to wane. And so another year passed on, and the annual festival again arrived. There again was Mag, whom Editha sought once more, to learn her destiny. The Fates had not altered their decree; and there, as twelve months since he stood, was the dark comely stranger. The very type of previous years were the proceedings of the day; the same homely village simplicity, the jocund song, the rustic dance, the same potations of home-brewed and cider; the same greetings, the same partings. Somewhat later than was considered within the bounds of prudence, the handmaid of Editha, accompanied by Giles, her lover, approached the wicket that opened on the lawn before Squire Elmore's mansion, where she was met by the dark stranger of the Fair, who, tendering her a golden coin,—by way of hush money,—bade her convey to her young mistress a note of delicate proportions. Promise of secrecy was exacted; the parting kiss was exchanged between the blushing Abigail and Giles; and the latter accepting the companionship of the stranger, the two bent their steps to Rottingdean, where the honest rustic returned to his home. Where the stranger rested for the night has never transpired. Early the following morning Mag was at the mansion, the domestics of which, anxious to learn how they were ruled by the stars, parted freely with their silver pieces. The Abigail of the previous night's adventure was particularly anxious to learn her destiny; and the truth which was essayed of her Giles, his age, his complexion, his temper, and his prospects, gave full assurance of the marvellousness of Mag's divining skill, to which the fair Editha, with whom she also had an interview, gave implicit credence. Four-and-twenty hours, however, wrought a great change at the mansion, and likewise in the hamlet of Ovingdean. A more than usual oppression and sultriness pervaded the atmosphere throughout the day, and towards nightfall the war of elements commenced, the sharp flashes of lightning increasing in vividness, the artillery of the heavens roaring in awful solemnity, and the massive clouds discharging their drenching cataracts. Such a night had never been previously known in the neighbourhood; and every person anxiously waited the coming dawn to learn the havoc of the dreadful storm. The inmates of the mansion were early stirring, and, much sooner than usual, Mr. and Mrs. Elmore were at breakfast. But they had not been long seated when they were informed that Miss Editha could nowhere be found, and that by the appearance of her bed-chamber she had not retired to rest during the night. The note which had been delivered by the stranger, and was then lying on the dressing table, appointing a midnight interview upon the Downs, was all that could be found to account for her absence. The most diligent search of the premises and the plantation contiguous was immediately made, and a dispatch without delay was sent off to Ovingdean, in the hopes that tidings might be heard of her there; but all was fruitless. Previous, however, to the news reaching that village, upon passing by the church, the sexton discovered, in the south-west corner of the burial ground, the charred remains of a female, which, upon examination of the dress about them, were declared to be those of old Margaret Ladrone. At the place were they were found, there, in the course of the day, were they interred, without any funeral rites, and the stone, before referred to, was placed over them to mark the spot. The dark stranger was never afterwards seen.

The story continues, that, every stormy night after, the figure of a lady in white paced the White Hawk Down, and that always on the morning after the figure was seen, a foot-print, cloven like that of an ox, was found at the same particular spot. The *Morning Herald*, of July 17th, 1807, has the following:—"Brighton.—A few days ago were dug up upon the slope of the Downs to the north-east of this place, the bones of a woman, which, from their position, clearly evinced that they had been deposited there many years before, without ceremony. A singular rumour is now afloat of a young person having been ravished and murdered there, by a person of unsuspected character." It may be proper to add that since the finding of these bones the White Hawk Lady has not walked abroad. The Elmore and the Mascall families, after the mysterious disappearance of Editha, removed to Brighton; but it is a very singular fact that the name of Lade is now very common at Ovingdean, it being even that of the Sexton of the parish, who is a descendant of Sir John Lade, spoken of in the last Chapter. As, however, the church register dates back only as far as the year 1700, the genealogy of the family, even if it did come through Old Mag, cannot be more remotely traced.

The death of the Earl of Egremont, who was a great patron of the Brighton sports long after Royalty had abandoned contending on the course, was a severe blow to Brighton Races; added to which, the Duke of Richmond, a warm supporter of the turf, withdrew his influence in favour of Goodwood. Year by year the Races waned, with the prospect of an early dissolution, which, on the withdrawal of the Queen's Plate, in 1849, seemed inevitable. Persons, it is true, continued, as of yore, to journey in from the country to witness them, but there was a continual falling off in the attendance of the aristocracy, and a rage for gambling of a most pernicious character, in thimble-rig, roulette, Brunswick lottery, prick-in-the-garter, &c., having set in, the townspeople with-held the subscriptions which they had been accustomed to grant pretty freely to the races, as they found that instead of having an equivalent for their money in sport, they were only paying a premium for the encouragement and dissemination of vice. Eventually, legislation put a stop to the nefarious proceedings of the gamblers; and, in the very nick of time, the great modern civilizer, the railway, was inducted from London, to give an impetus to the prosperity of the town, which had perceptibly declined when the Queen gave a preference over Brighton to the Isle of Wight, for a marine retreat. The Railway was the turning medium for the resuscitation of the Brighton Races, and the new Race Committee promptly and successfully availed themselves of it, as it opened the prospect of a new class of supporters, in the inhabitants of the metropolis, who were by it within two hours' distance of the course.

At various periods since 1783, when troops were first stationed at Brighton,—in consequence of the Pavilion becoming a Royal residence,—reviews and sham fights of the military have taken place on the Downs contiguous to the Race Course, the spot being admirably adapted for army tactics. The troops upon such occasions have been generally of the line and the militia regiments quartered at the several Infantry Barracks in the town, and at the Cavalry Barracks on the Lewes Road, other regiments at Ringmer, Lewes, and East Blatchington marching in to take part in the evolutions.

The Cavalry Barracks were completed in 1795. In 1801 a range of stables was erected, for the reception of 400 horses, immediately in front of the main buildings, and abutting on the east boundary wall contiguous to the Lewes Road; but in 1818 these stables were removed, and the spacious grounds were thrown open to public view. The fives-court, between the wings, in the centre of the back court-yard, was erected in 1810, by the officers of the Prince of Wales's Regiment, the 10th Royal Hussars.

The modern grand military features of the Race Hill have been the sham fights of the Volunteers, and known as the Battle of Ovingdean, Easter Monday, April 1st, 1861, under Lord Ranelagh; and the Battle of White Hawk Down, Easter Monday, April 21st, 1862, under Lord Clyde; both great successes, and affording proofs of the valuable services and admirable efficiency of this noble auxiliary of England's military power. The force present on the first occasion numbered between 7,000 and 8,000 men, thus brigaded:—

ARTILLERY BRIGADE.—Colonel Estridge, commanding. 1st Battalion Brighton Artillery, 4th Cinque Ports, 2nd Hants, and 2nd Sussex.

FIRST BRIGADE RIFLE VOLUNTEERS.—Lieutenant Colonel Faunce, commanding; Captain Deedes, Brigade Major. 1st Battalion—Colonel M'Leod, 1st Middlesex Engineers; 32nd Middlesex (Guards). 2nd Battalion—Major Atherley, 2nd South Middlesex. 3rd Battalion—Capt. Ives, 11th Middlesex, (St. George's), 36th Middlesex (Paddington).

SECOND BRIGADE.—Lord Radstock, commanding; Captain Chitty, Brigade Major. 1st Battalion—9th West Middlesex, 2nd Middlesex (A.B.) 2nd Battalion—Colonel Money, 6th Tower Hamlets; 4th Tower Hamlets; 7th Middlesex (Islington). 3rd Battalion — Colonel Colville, 39th Middlesex (Finsbury); Kent Rifles, (Captain Jackson), 4th, 13th, 17th, 21st, and 34th.

THIRD BRIGADE.—Colonel Moorsom, commanding; Major Panton, Brigade Major. 1st Battalion—3rd Sussex (Administrative Battalion). 2nd Battalion—1st Cinque Ports. 3rd Battalion—2nd Sussex (Administrative Battalion).

FOURTH BRIGADE. — Colonel Vallancey, commanding; Major Deedes, Brigade Major. 1st Battalion—Colonel Couran, 1st Hants (Administrative Battalion), Winchester; 3rd Hants (Administrative Battalion); 6th Hants. 2nd Battalion—Major Roupell, 19th Surrey (Lambeth); 10th Surrey (Bermondsey). 3rd Battalion—Sir H. Fletcher, 2nd Surrey (Administrative Battalion); 20th Surrey (Norwood).

RESERVE.—3rd City of London; Brighton Cadets; 11th Tower Hamlets.

The troops were formed in battalions on the Level, from whence they marched by way of Marine Parade, and by the County Hospital to the summit of the hill on the right of the Race Course, along which, past the Grand Stand, they marched in review, before Major General Sir James Scarlett and his staff.

Upon the crown of this hill, during the wars with Napoleon, stood a signal-house and telegraph semaphore communicating along the coast with similar stations at Seaford and Shoreham, and forming a link in the important chain of signals which was in use between Portsmouth and Dover. There is very little doubt, that about that locality at a much earlier date than sporting records hand down to us, racing of some description took place, the Town Book having the following entry:—

> Memorandum, that on ye 7th of November, 1713, Henry May, Esq., paid us a half-penny acknowledgmt for carrying the Corpes of his father Sr Richard May, deceased, through the Laine, commonly called the Hilly Laine, from the place were formerly stood a Race post, to the town of Brighthelmston, it being noe high or Common Road. we Say red the Same for sufferance, Per us
>
> RICHARD MASTERS,
> SIMON WISDEN.
> JOHN GOLD.

The payment was doubtless exacted under the erroneous notion that the unobstructed conveyance of a corpse gave the public a right to the way or road along which the body was borne; and it is the generally received opinion that the right of road by the foot-path or bridle-way from Blatchington, by way of Watts's Laundry to the road on Church Hill, was obtained by a corpse having been conveyed from Blatchington for burial in the church-yard of St. Nicholas, Brighton.

The several corps engaged in the Review having passed up the Course took up heir first position on the ridge of heights overlooking Brighton, and afterwards formed an extended line on the crest of one of the hills running inland and parallel with the race-hill. This long line of about a mile in length was supported by four guns on the extreme left. At the time of commencing operations the furze on the side of the hill was, either by design or accident, set on fire. Huge volumes of smoke rose from the burning gorse, and as the line opened and kept up a heavy firing for some time, the imaginative spectators on the distant eminence might suppose that some quiet hamlet had been set on fire, either by the enemy or by the brave defenders of their hearths and homes. After some very heavy file-firing from right of companies, and two or three well-delivered volleys, the line fell back, protected in its retreat by the guns in position. The enemy was supposed to have followed them, but, like the Spanish fleet, they could not be seen, because they were not in sight. Lord Ranelagh's force was too small to admit of division into two forces; but even had it been larger, it is doubtful whether a Volunteer enemy would submit to be beaten according to orders, with so much cheerfulness, and with so much steadiness, as is the case with the regulars on the field-days of Aldershot and elsewhere. The retreating force next deployed towards the sea, the action became more general, and several battalions were moved up in support of the line. There were more rattles of musketry, and more volleys, and then, wearied out with the persistence of the enemy, two brigades, forming the right, charged down on the enemy's left and drove them over hill and dale. The unseen and flying enemy, however, got some imaginary reinforcements, and returned to the attack and retrieved their laurels. The gallant brigadiers led back their unwilling, but not disheartened men on the left wing; then the centre fell back, and the right, unable to stand alone, followed the example. Lord Ranelagh's eye instantly saw the cloud of dust which told of the approach of horsemen. Quick as lightning there went forth the command—"Form square to receive cavalry," and the order was promptly obeyed; and had there been any cavalry, they would no doubt have been very warmly and heartily received, in obedience to orders. The division took up a fresh position—again advanced—the Battle of Ovingdean was fought and won, and the well-known strains of the "National Anthem" told of the loyalty, as many courageous deeds had told of the valour, of the Volunteers.

At the second Easter Volunteer Field Day there were 19,000 of the following corps present:—

CAVALRY.—18th Hussars, Lieut.-Col. Knox. 1st Hants Light Horse, Capt. Bower.

ARTILLERY.—FIELD BATTERIES.—Lieut.-Col. Ormsby, R.A., commanding Staff: Capt. Tupper, R.A., Capt. Pitt, R.A., Capt. Ward, R.A., Capt. Blackwell, R.A. 1st and 2nd Batteries—Major Dalbiac, 1st Sussex. 3rd Battery—Capt. Darby, 2nd, 3rd, and 4th Sussex. 4th Battery—Major Harcourt, 4th Cinque Ports.

GARRISON BRIGADE.—Lieut.-Col. Estridge, commanding; Capt. Woodhead, 3rd Middlesex Militia, Aide-de-Camp; Capt. Wolf, R.A., Major of Brigade. 1st Battalion—Lieut.-Col. Sturdee, 1st Hants. 2nd Battalion—Lieut.-Col. Lord Truro, 3rd Middlesex. 3rd Battalion—Major Creed, 3rd Essex, 1 A Cinque Ports, 1st Middlesex, 2nd Middlesex, 1st Tower Hamlets.

INFANTRY. — FIRST DIVISION. — Major-General Crauford, commanding, Staff: Capt. Smith, Grenadier Guards; Lieut. Hon. J. C. Eliot, Grenadier Guards.

FIRST BRIGADE.—Lieut.-Col. the Duke of Wellington, K.G., commanding; Capt. Goff, 50th Foot, Major of Brigade. 1st Battalion—Lieut.-Col. Macleod, 1st Middlesex (Engineer), 1st Tower Hamlets (Engineer), and two companies 16th Middlesex. 2nd Battalion—Lieut.-Col. the Hon. C. Hugh Lindsay, 11th, 18th, and 36th Middlesex. 3rd Battalion—Lieut.-Col. G. Warde, 1st City of London. 4th Battalion—Major Whitehead, 1st Middlesex.

SECOND BRIGADE.—Lieut.-Col. the Marquis of Donegall, G.C.H., commanding; Major Mackenzie, Antrim Militia, Aide-de-Camp; Brevet-Major Shaw, R.A., Major of Brigade. 1st Battalion—Lieut.-Col. Jeakes, 4th and 37th Middlesex. 2nd Battalion—Major Vernon, 28th Middlesex, and 4th Bucks. 3rd Battalion—Lieut.-Col. Lord Enfield, 29th Middlesex. 4th Battalion—Lieut.-Col. Lord Bury, 21st, 30th, 38th, 42nd, 43rd, and 44th Middlesex.

THIRD BRIGADE.—Lieut.-Col. Viscount Ranelagh, commanding; Capt. Templar, Dorset R.V.C., Aide-de-Camp; Brevet-Major Deedes, 60th Foot, Major of Brigade. 1st Battalion — Major Atherly, South Middlesex. 2nd Battalion—Lieut.-Col. Somerset, 40th Middlesex. 3rd Battalion—Sir John Shelley, 46th Middlesex, 2nd City of London, and 4th City of London. 4th Battalion—Lieut.-Col. Bigge, 20th Middlesex.

FOURTH BRIGADE.—Brigadier-General Haines, C.B., commanding; Lieut. Arbuthnot, 10th Hussars, Aide-de-Camp; Capt. Wovell, 41st Foot, Major of Brigade. 1st Battalion—Major Beresford, 2nd, 7th, and 12th Surrey. 2nd Battalion—Capt. Trueman, Acting Major. 10th, 19th, 21st, and 23rd Surrey. 3rd Battalion—Major Farnell, 1st Administrative Battalion of Kent. 4th Battalion—Major Sir H. Fletcher, 5th, 13th, and 14th Surrey, and 2nd Administrative Battalion of Surrey.

FIFTH BRIGADE.—Major-General Taylor, commanding; Capt. Pemberton, Scots Fusilier Guards, Aide-de-Camp; Major the Hon. W. J. Colville, Rifle Brigade, Major of Brigade. 1st Battalion—Lieut.-Col. Capper, 5th and 9th Essex. 2nd Battalion—Lieut.-Col. Buxton, 1st Administrative Battalion of Tower Hamlets. 3rd Battalion—Lieut.-Col. Money, 4th and 6th Tower Hamlets. 4th Battalion—Lieut.-Col. Walker, 2nd, 8th, 9th, and 12th Tower Hamlets.

SECOND DIVISION.—Major-General Hon. A. Dalzell, commanding; Staff: Colonel Taylor, C.B., Colonel Walker, C.B., and Capt. Carleton, 21st Foot.

FIRST BRIGADE.—Lieut.-Col. Lord Radstock, commanding; Lieut. Peake, Aide-de-Camp; Major Gooch, unattached, Major of Brigade. 1st Battalion—Lieut.-Col. Wilkinson, 2nd Administrative Battalion, Middlesex. 2nd Battalion—Lieut.-Col. Bathurst, 19th Middlesex. 3rd Battalion—Lieut.-Col. Colvill, 39th Middlesex and 26th Kent. 4th Battalion—Capt. Fenton, 9th Middlesex.

SECOND BRIGADE.—Brigadier-General Brown, commanding; Lieut. Savery, 78th Foot, Aide-de-Camp; Capt. Morgan, 55th Foot, Major of Brigade. 1st

Battalion—Lieut.-Col. Grimston, 1st, 2nd, and 16th Hants. 2nd Battalion—Lieut.-Col. Conran, 3rd Administrative Battalion, Hants. 3rd Battalion—Lieut.-Col. Dunsmore, 1st Administrative Battalion, Isle of Wight. 4th Battalion—Lieut.-Col. Vallancy, 2nd Administrative Battalion, Hants.

THIRD BRIGADE.—Lieut.-Col. Moorsom, commanding; Lieut. Moorsom, Royal Artillery, Aide-de-Camp; Capt. Penton, 3rd Middlesex Militia, Major of Brigade. 1st Battalion—Acting-Major Meek, 3rd Sussex Administrative Battalion. 2nd Battalion—Sir Percy Burrell, Bart., M.P., 1st Sussex Administrative Battalion. 3rd Battalion—Lieut.-Col. Gage, 1st Cinque Ports Administrative Battalion and 17th Kent. 4th Battalion—Lieut.-Col. Barttelot, 2nd Sussex Administrative Battalion.

FOURTH BRIGADE.—Brigadier-General Garvock, commanding; Hon. Capt. Chetwynd, Aide-de-Camp; Capt. Jones, 20th Foot, Major of Brigade. 1st Battalion—Lieut.-Col. Lord Elcho, 15th Middlesex. 2nd Battalion—Lieut.-Col. Brewster, 23rd Middlesex. 3rd Battalion—Major Richards, 3rd City of London and 32nd Middlesex. 4th Battalion—Lieut.-Col. Lord Grosvenor, 22nd Middlesex, 1st Battalion. 5th Battalion—Lieut.-Col. Lord Gerald Fitzgerald. 22nd Middlesex, 2nd Battalion.

Upon the arrival of the various corps, they were marched to their several places of rendezvous, on the Level, St. Peter's Church and North Steine Enclosures, the Pavilion Grounds, and the Steine, where they partook of refreshments. At 11 o'clock the "assembly" was sounded, and very soon after the whole of the corps were on their march to the Race Hill, by way of the Marine Parade and Elm Grove, the Divisions meeting again in White Hawk Valley, whence they paraded down the Course and passed in Review opposite the Grand Stand, before Lord Clyde, the Earl of Chichester —Lord Lieutenant of the County,—and Lord Cardigan, passing out at the south end of the Course, and then descending to their original position in the Valley. The field evolutions took place principally on White Hawk Down, and were eminently successful, and the whole of the arrangements of the day, civil and military, were a practical demonstration of the facility with which troops might be moved towards a threatened point on the particular railway which would be most likely to be required for such a duty in an actual case of emergency. On the morning of the Review, 6,922 Volunteers were despatched from London Bridge in two hours and 41 minutes, and 5,170 from the Victoria Station in two hours and 20 minutes, without difficulty. They were conveyed in 16 trains, each composed of an engine and tender and 22 vehicles, and each carrying on an average 20 officers and 735 men; and they reached Brighton in an average of 2 hours and 28 minutes from the time of starting. The Brighton Company borrowed on this occasion 72 carriages from three neighbouring companies, and 79 carriages also brought Volunteers over their railway, from other lines; but they had to provide for their ordinary passenger-traffic on that day, as well as for the Easter Monday traffic to the Crystal Palace, which was very considerable, and to convey upwards of 2,000 Volunteers along the south coast from the several stations on their own line. Indeed, the total number of passengers who travelled upon the London, Brighton, and South-Coast Railway on that day was 132,202, including Volunteers and the holders of season and return tickets.

As a proof that the Queen takes a deep interest in the Volunteer movement, Her Majesty, several times during the day, telegraphed to be informed of every special incident in connexion with the military evolutions. Happily no accident happened to mar the general proceedings; but, to meet any casualty that might have arisen, Brigade Surgeon Burrows of the First Sussex Volunteer Artillery, issued a notice that every convenience for temporary hospital purposes was provided in a tent to the west of the Race Stand, in a tent at the south of the battle-field, and at the Industrial Schools.

The Industrial Schools are built upon what is known as the Warren Farm, which occupies an area of ten acres of arable land immediately north-east of the Race Course, aud was purchased for £2,000. The project of erecting these Schools for the purpose of training poor children to habits of industry and relieving them of the ban of pauperism, was first entertained by the Board of Guardians, in 1853, but no steps were taken to carry it out till it received the sanction of the Vestry in 1856; and even then, from time to time, numerous impediments arose, in the selection of plans and in borrowing the requisite money of Government, so that the first stone of the building was not laid till the 26th of March, 1859, the plans selected being those of Mr. George Maynard, the Parish Surveyor. Mr. John Fabian, of Brighton, was the builder, at a contract price of £8,223, the sum of £5,269 having previously been expended in forming roads, and necessary incidental work. On the 1st of

December, 1859, Mr. Fabian, as stipulated, completed his task, and delivered over the building to the Board of Guardians. Subsequently, Mr. Fabian erected the farm buildings at the cost of £1,514 16s, and Messrs. Patching and Son erected the boundary wall for £560.

An establishment to consist of more than 300 persons would of necessity require a good supply of one of the chief elements of existence, water; it therefore became a question with the Guardians how that supply was to be obtained, whether by sinking a well, and thus have their own source of the element, or by having pipes laid on from the Brighton Water Works. The Guardians decided upon the former course, as, having it in contemplation to erect a new Workhouse on a seven acre piece of land, which they had purchased for that purpose, between the Reservoir and the Race Hill, their own well would supply both establishments,—hence was projected the Warren Farm Well, the fame of which has spread to all parts of the civilized world.

This celebrated well was commenced on the 25th of March, 1858; but at the depth of 418 feet 3 inches, where a heading was driven laterally, a contract which had been entered into with Mr. North was abandoned, and the Board, after a consultation, determined to proceed with the work themselves, and commenced by driving another heading opposite the former, at a depth of 421 feet 9 inches, and from this a second perpendicular shaft, four feet in diameter, was dug, the superintendence of the labour being entrusted to Mr. Isaac Huggett, who persevered unremittingly with the work, and eventually, after surmounting innumerable difficulties, found on Sunday, the 16th March, 1862, at a depth of 1,285 feet, so abundant a supply of excellent water, that in a few days there were more than 200,000 gallons of that pure beverage in the well.

To celebrate the success of the undertaking, Mr. Henry Catt, a Guardian, entertained the whole of the members of the Board, with the Vicar, and their Officers, and likewise Mr. Huggett and his men, at a dinner at the Town Hall, 120 guests sitting down to the repast under the presidency of the delighted liberal donor, Mr. Churchwarden Marchant and Mr. Alderman Brigden occupying the vice-chairs. As a memento, also, of the happy event, Mr. Catt had silver medals struck by Mr. Norris, jeweller, West Street, one of which was given to each man who had worked in the Well. The medals bore the inscription: "By the blessing of God, on hard work, patience, and perseverance," and "Warren Farm Well, Brighton. Water found, March 16th, 1862." The medal presented to Mr. Huggett was of gold.

Immediately consequent upon finding water for the establishment, was the completion of the furnishing of the building, and obtaining the requisite staff of officers; and on Thursday, August 14th, 1862, the Institution being ready for occupation, the juvenile portion of the inmates of the Workhouse, 77 boys and 65 girls, were removed thither under the care of the Industrial Schools' Committee, many other of the Guardians and their friends taking part in the procession, which was headed by the Industrial School band. Mr. and Mrs. Sattin, the Governor and Matron of the Workhouse, also accompanied them to deliver over their youthful charge to Mr. and Mrs. Hales, the Superintendents of the Schools. The occupation of the Industrial Schools is at present the last public feature of the Race Hill and adjacent Downs.

Chapter XXVIII.

PAST AND PRESENT PASTIMES.

Fickleness in the habits of civilized nations is in no manner more clearly exemplified than in the pastimes of the people; for although many sports are characterised as national, and are of great antiquity, modernization has greatly destroyed their originality, and refinement has detracted from the natural enjoyment of them. Even in the rural districts of England, Harvest Home possesses but little of the rustic homeliness and jollity of yore, and the happy season of Christmas lacks the "Squires of Old," and the festivities and the freely dispensed bounties of the Baronial Halls. In towns, especially those which come under the denomination fashionable, there is a constant revolution in the "rounds of amusements." Brighton has been particularly prominent in this respect, a vast variety having run its course during the past century.

Without doubt the Toy Fair, now in a wretched state of decadence, was the earliest people's festival. It was formerly held on the Cliff, between Ship Street and Black-Lion Street; but the town increasing and the Fair assuming a corresponding magnitude, Belle Vue field, whereon now stands Regency Square, was its location. From thence it was translated to the Level, where, on the 4th of September, 1807, a Sheep Fair was first held, notification of the same having been in the *Brighton Herald*, and in the *Weekly Journal*, published at Lewes, as follows: —

The rapid strides which agriculture has made within the last ten years, in this country, and the extreme utility which has been the result of its present scientific mode of practice, has commanded the attention and admiration not only of all England, but of all civilised Europe. To those who are interested in the purchase of any particular breed of stock, it must be of extreme importance that their stock be *genuine* and uncontaminated.

To fix, therefore, a spot where a pure unmixed breed shall always be produced, and where the purchaser (who perhaps comes from a distance) shall be sure of unadulterated stock, appears to be a great desideratum. In no instance is it more so than in that useful and highly productive animal, the South Down Sheep. Those who possess this breed, true and genuine, have had much reason to lament that at fairs, where a great variety of sheep are brought to market, many are sold for South Down Sheep which have no pretensions to be so called; and which afterwards not answering the purpose of the buyers, bring unmerited disgrace on such as are really genuine. We, therefore, the undersigned breeders of true South Down Sheep, have come to a resolution to establish a Fair, to be holden on Brighton Level, the 4th of September, 1807. And we pledge ourselves to bring to it genuine South Down Tups, Stock Ewes, Ewe Lambs, and Wether Lambs; and moreover we will not, knowingly, either ourselves introduce, or suffer to be introduced to this Fair any but what shall be of the *genuine* and *true* South Down breed:

Alexander, W.
Blaker, N.
Beard, T.
Bull, J.
Boys, J.
Bine, —
Botting, J.
Beard, N.
Blaker, G.
Chatfield, J.
Croskey, S.
Dyer, R. L.
Elmes, W.
Fuller, H.
Falconer, W.
Gorring, W.
Geer, T.
Hardwick, J.
Hodson, W.
Hodson, T.

Hamshar, J.
Hamshar, R.
Hall, N.
Hart, R.
Hodson, A. W.
Hurley, R.
Ingram, J.
Lidbetter, T.
Murrell, W.
Marchant, J.
Noakes, W.
Newnham, —
Pilfold, J.
Poole, T.
Page, W.
Stanford, W.
Scrase, W.
Scrase. T.
Vallance J.
Verrall, R.
Wood, J.

About 20,000 prime South Down sheep of all denominations found a ready sale, buyers being plentiful. That year, on the same day, the general Fair was held on the Marlborough Steine, the southernmost of the present North Steine Enclosures, where gingerbread stalls, whirligigs, and roundabouts were in abundance. The next year the Sheep Fair was equally well attended; but notwithstanding the most strenuous exertions of its promoters, it had but an existence of four years. A Cattle Market was established on a piece of the Parish Ground on the Church Hill, adjoining the West Hill Estate, in 1831. Like the Sheep Fair, however, it had but a few years' duration, there being no meadows near for the accommodation of stock. The Corn Market, by sample, is held every Thursday, at the King and Queen Inn, in a spacious and commodious room. From the Level, where Gully and Cribb, on the 11th of August, 1807, in the presence of the Prince of Wales and his Royal Brothers, had a sparring match, the town authorities eventually ejected the Spring and Autumn pleasure Fair, which has since sought refuge upon any available spot contiguous. A few years more and it will be amongst the things of the past.

The Level has at various periods been the arena for the festivals in celebration of important national events, as on the 19th July, 1821, upon the occasion of the coronation of George IV., when two bullocks were roasted whole, and distributed hot, and four, previously dressed, were served out, the expenses being defrayed by a public subscription. The roasting of the two bullocks commenced on the preceding night, when partial fires were kindled to heat the carcasses through the thickest part. But about five o'clock in the morning the real roasting commenced. The grates were then piled high with blazing fuel, and a savoury vapour spread through the atmosphere. About six, one of the spits, a stout scaffold pole, gave way under its ponderous weight, but at the expense only of an additional spar, and a score or so of blistered fingers.

The work of carving commenced shortly after two o'clock, when Mr. Thomas Palmer, the King's cutler, in a waggon converted into a suitable platform for such a display, decorated with devices and waving streamers, and containing several hogsheads of ale, presented to Mr. John Vallance, the Chairman of the Managing Committee, a carving knife and fork, and a corkscrew, all of extensive dimensions, with the request that the coronation beef might be carved with the former, and the bungs extracted from the casks by the latter, and that they might be furthermore preserved by the local authorities, for use on similar occasions. The work of carving occupied about an hour, during which time many thousands of persons partook of the hot and the cold.

At this period there lived in a hut of very rude construction, consisting of but one room, on the southern incline of Round Hill, Corporal Staines, an old marine who served under Nelson at the siege of Copenhagen. He was very crippled, and obtained his living by exhibiting his miniature fortifications, constructed by himself of chalk, the soldiers and cannons which surmounted the battlements being likewise formed of chalk; as was also a very rude model of the gallant ship, the Victory, bearing, under a black canopy, a coffin containing the body of the Hero of Trafalgar. Upon great national anniversaries and festivities it was his custom to fire Royal salutes from four pistol barrels which he had formed as a battery, and every day he was accustomed to fire the sun-set gun. While the feast was being made off the roasted oxen, the old corporal fired a Royal salute, for which he was rewarded with a good substantial dinner and a compliment of money, besides presents which were made him by the holiday folk. Corporal Staines first took up his abode at Brighton in a cavern hewn in the Church Hill chalk-pit, the site—filled up,—of the east end of Upper North Street.

Agreeing with his residence in the chalk-pit is the following entry in the Vestry book:—

> October 2nd, 1809.—That Corporal Staines be allowed a blanket and a great coat during the winter.

Staines removed from the chalk pit to a hut constructed by himself, immediately east of the Manor Pound, then at the back of the Parish Church, on the spot now occupied by the entrance of the northern Burial Ground, contiguous to which were the Parish Stocks, that were afterwards removed to the Market Place, in the Bartholomews. Upon the re-building of the Market, the Stocks were placed against its southern wall at the back of the Thatched House Inn, where, after remaining a few years as a relic of a barbarous age, they went to decay. In 1824, the Pound was removed to the north-west corner of the Workhouse grounds, on the Dyke Road. In course of time, however, it became obsolete for the impounding of cattle, and in 1853 it was purchased by the parish of the Lord of the Manor, for £100. For some years after his removal from Church Hill, the old marine took up his abode in the east bank of the pond at the junction of the old Shoreham and Ditchling Roads, on Rose Hill; but when the ground adjacent was enclosed by Mr. Colbatch, he translated himself to just without its eastern boundary wall, on the incline of the hill which commands an uninterrupted view of the Level and the Steine in general. He ended his days in Brighton Workhouse.

The earliest town record of the Proclamation of a Sovereign is a minute of Vestry, date, March 19th, 1701, which runs thus:—

> Israel Paine, Constable, being accompanyed with the chief Inhabitants of the town (after open proclamation made by the Cryer) did in the mercat place about Eleven of the clock in the forenoon, solemnly proclaim our Gratious Sovereign Lady QUEEN ANNE, Queen off England, Scotland, France, and Ireland; upon which there followed great shoutings and acclamations of all the people. Saying, GOD SAVE QUEEN ANNE.

The coronation of Her present Majesty was celebrated on the Level, June 28th, 1838, in a similar manner to that of George IV. The last occasion of public rejoicing there was to commemorate the Peace with Russia in 1855. The great Peace Festival, consequent upon the overthrow of the sovereignty of Napoleon Bonaparte, on his retiring to Elba, took place on the 12th of August, 1814, on the

Prince Regent's Cricket Ground, which occupied the extreme north of the Level, immediately in front of the Peircy Alms Houses, Lewes Road. The animated scene which the Cricket Ground presented on the memorable occasion was, in the highest degree, interesting. Seventy-five double rows of tables were formed, each in an oblong square, open at the bottom only, and each adapted for the accommodation of one hundred and twenty-two persons. These were furnished in a plentiful manner, with true old English fare of roast beef and plum puddings, garnished with a suitable number of hogsheads of ale and brown stout, at convenient distances, giving an air of hospitable importance to the whole. At each table a president was appointed, with six assistants, under the denomination of stewards; the former wearing white sashes, with the inscription, "Brighton Festival," and the latter purple and white favours, bearing the number of the table at which they were to officiate, affixed at the left breast. Flags of blue silk, lettered in gold, "Peace," "Wellington," "Blucher," &c., waved at the head of the various tables, where were seated upwards of 7,000 persons.

At two o'clock a bugle sounded from No. 1 table, at which presided the Rev. J. Carr (Vicar), who rose and pronounced the following benediction:—

O Thou who art the great God of Nations, Thou hast filled our hearts with joy by the restoration of Peace and the prospect of Plenty: we meet under the canopy of Heaven as members of Thy family. May this Festival be crowned with Thy blessing, and may our lives express the gratitude which Thy goodness inspires, for the sake of Jesus Christ our Lord. Amen.

This was repeated by Mr. Robert Ackerson (High Constable) at the lower table, and by the Presidents of the other tables severally, and then the busy scene of feasting commenced in the presence of some thousands of spectators, who, in carriages, waggons, carts, and caravans, took up their positions just without the boundary rails.

The sound of the second bugle having announced the dinner at an end, the Vicar rose and thus returned thanks:—

Merciful Father, our grateful hearts acknowledge Thy goodness; may Charity ever assist the poor, and the poor confess their infinite obligations unto Thee, as the Bountiful Giver of all their blessings, through Jesus Christ our Lord. Amen.

The following toasts and airs then succeeded, the Band of the 3rd Buffs being in attendance and adding to the pleasures of the fete :—

Our Good Old King.—"God Save the King."
The Prince Regent.—"Rule Britannia."
The Queen and Royal Family.—"The Brunswick March."
The Duke of Wellington.—"See the Conquering Hero comes."
The Allied Sovereigns.—"The March to Paris."
Louis XVIII.—"Henri Quatre."
May Peace produce Plenty and Plenty Gratitude.—"Speed the Plough."
Prosperity and Unanimity to the Town of Brighton.—"Tight little Island."

The after part of the day was devoted to dancing, blind-man's-buff, jingling matches, foot-racing, stool-ball, kiss-in-the-ring, jumping in sacks, &c.; and the happy throng concluded the day by joining hands and forming long chains of human beings, and thus in high glee they "threaded the tailor's needle" to Castle Square, where, after singing "God Save the King," they, in the most orderly manner, dispersed, and made for their several homes.

Cricket was a favourite pastime with the Prince of Wales, who was frequently engaged in the manly game with the noblemen and gentlemen of his suite, on the Royal Ground, which had been granted for his use by Mr. Thomas Reed Kemp, the Lord of the Manor. His Royal Highness, however, upon coming to the throne, retired from cricket, and hence the Ground was given up. Mr. Kemp then made the grant of a portion of it to the Town for the recreation of the inhabitants, and the road to the north of the Level was formed.

In 1822, an enterprising townsman, Mr. James Ireland, became the purchaser of ten acres of the land immediately north of the road, and in the following year, Ireland's Gardens and Cricket Ground were opened to the public. The original entrance was at the south-west corner, where was a neat lodge that conducted to the cricket ground, and an excellent bowling green, with raised banks, and a billiard room with colonnade and rustic seats in front. At the lower or east end was the tavern department, the Hanover Arms Inn, where, also, was an excellent fives' court. The Gardens were approached either by crossing the Cricket Ground, or by a separate road that skirted the property.

Mr. Ireland was the successor of Mr. Daniel Constable, who, with his brother William as shopman, commenced May 29th, 1802, the drapery business, now the well-known establishment of Messrs. Hannington and Son, at No. 3, North Street. Mr. Ireland became the purchaser of the business in 1806, and it passed from him to the late Mr. Hannington, the successor also, at No. 4, of Mr. William Diplock, who, in the summer of 1819, when Brighton churchyard was despoiled of its dead, announced himself as sole agent for the sale of patent metallic coffins, of the security of which he assured the public, every person would be satisfied. Previous to the formation of the Hanover Grounds, Mr. Ireland carried on the business of woollen draper and undertaker at No. 10, North Street.

A noble and conspicuous building, comprising reading, refreshment, and dressing rooms on the basement, and an elegant promenade room, eighty feet by thirty feet, over them, formed the junction of the Cricket Ground with the Gardens, just within the entrance of which was the ladies' bowling green, surrounded by a beautiful lawn and tea arbours. There were likewise, adjacent, an aviary and a grotto. A Gothic tower and gateway approached by a bridge that spanned a piece of water at the north end of the main central avenue, was the entrance to a Maze, in the centre of which was a Merlin swing. From the want of that support from the public which was due to Mr. Ireland, for the spirit he evinced in so zealously catering for their entertainment, the thousands which he expended were entirely lost to him, and he retired from that which ought to have been a benefit to the town and himself, a ruined man.

During the time that he held possession, a public declaration was made by the town crier that a man would fly from the top of the assembly room to the extreme north of the Grounds. All Brighton was tickled by the announcement, and hours previous to the time stated for the intended flight, throngs of people were wending their way northward, and taking up their position, where they imagined they could obtain the best view of the sight. The Round Hill was covered with one mass of human beings, whose eyes were concentrated upon a slight scaffold that was erected on the roof of the building. From the top of this structure a stout cable was stretched to the foot of the bridge at the maze, affording sufficient evidence that no hoax was intended. Expectation, therefore, was on tip-toe; and after patience had undergone a long endurance, a slightly-built man, in light fleshings, with Zephyr-like wings, was seen to ascend the scaffold, causing an universal clapping of hands, and the firing of the guns at Staines's mimic fort. About a couple of minutes sufficed for the performer to make the necessary adjustments for his flight, and then, amidst loud huzzas, he, waving a flag in each hand, gracefully glided down, head foremost, beneath the cable, along which revolved an arrangement of wheels, to which he was attached longitudinally. Those who had a gratis view of the exploit smiled, and contented themselves with the satisfaction that the sight had cost them nothing; but those who went into the Gardens and paid, to see whatever could be seen, felt sorely vexed, and some were so excited as to attempt a castigation of the exhibitor. His friends, however, quickly liberated him from his machinery, and he took a flight through the maze that enabled him to elude his pursuers.

The "Flying Man" was Mr. William Constable, who, on the disposal by his brother of his business to Mr. Ireland, accompanied Daniel to America, where they devoted themselves to scientific pursuits. His flying freak, on his return, was as well for a scientific purpose as to benefit Mr. Ireland, and the principle has been since applied in saving human life in cases of fire and shipwreck. In 1841 he introduced the art of photography, then called Daguerrectype, into Brighton, his "blue room" being a very attractive feature on the Marine Parade, near Atlingworth Street. He died on Sunday, December 22nd, 1861.

Other speculators from time to time, with but little better success than Mr. Ireland, tried their luck upon the estate. Year by year showed the gradual decay which neglect engenders; the buildings became dilapidated and unsafe for occupation, the flower-beds were transformed into a wilderness of weeds; and at length, after having been made even the asylum for wild beasts, and the arena for the dissoluteness of pleasure fairs, the Gardens, that might have continued one of the chief prides of Brighton, and the Cricket Ground—the fame of which is perpetuated by Mason's celebrated print of the renowned players of Sussex and Kent, and their supporters,—the envy, as it was, of other cricketing counties, were sacrificed to the spirit of building, from the want of foresight in the inhabitants, who now universally admit that both should have been preserved to the town, as they were an establishment for the people's amusement and recreation, with which nothing of the kind in the county could compete. The present, the Royal Brunswick Cricket Ground, kept by the veteran Box, is capacious and well-formed; but it lacks the picturesqueness, and the spectators have not the shelter from wind and rain, and the shade from the trees which gave so vast a superiority to the Hanover Ground. Previous to the formation of Ireland's Gardens, some tea-gardens were in existence on the Marine Parade, about the locality now occupied by Eaton Place. They were merely a summer retreat for a cup of tea during an afternoon stroll, and a place of call in winter for a glass of hot elderberry wine.

In the "good old times" the people's entertainments differed much from the sports of the present race, as the following copy of a handbill will show:—

COCKING.

To be fought at the Cock Pit,

WHITE LION,

NORTH STREET, BRIGHTON,

ON

THURSDAY,

THE 18TH APRIL, 1811,

A Main of Cocks for TWENTY GUINEAS a Battle, and FIFTY GUINEAS the Main; between the Gentlemen of the Isle of Wight and the Gentlemen of Sussex.

Feeders { Pollard, Isle of Wight,
Holden, Sussex.

N.B.—A pair of Cocks to be on the Pit at Eleven o'clock.

[RUDDUCK, Printer, Brighton Place, Brighton.

On Easter Monday, April 23rd, 1810, the holiday folks, in all their Sunday finery, assembled in great numbers, as was their custom, at the Bear public house, Lewes road, on the ground contiguous to which they were entertained with the polished diversions of cock fighting and the baiting of a badger. On the following day, Easter Tuesday, according to annual custom, a bull-bait came off at Hove; when, during the proceedings, the bull unexpectedly broke from the stake, and in an instant charged upon and routed the compact phalanx of gazers, happily without inflicting material injury on any one. The incident caused a postponement of the bait till June 11th. The hand-bill announced:

A BULL BAIT AT HOVE,
ON
MONDAY,
JUNE 11TH, 1810.
A DINNER will be provided, and on Table at
Two o'clock.

The dinner took place at the Ship Inn, Hove, in the field belonging to which,—that whereon the Coast Guard Station is erected, at the bottom of Hove Street,—the baiting took place.

The vicinity of Brighton is admirably adapted for Hunting, a sport which received considerable impetus from the Prince of Wales having an excellent pack of harriers kennelled at the Prince's Dairy, a suburban retreat on the London Road, which His Royal Highness purchased of Mr. William Stanford, in October, 1805. In October, 1821, some of the dogs exhibited symptoms of hydrophobia; the whole pack was in consequence destroyed by poison, and the carcasses were conveyed away in a waggon and buried in a pit, purposely dug to receive them, in the south part of Streeter's garden, just within the gateway, to the right of the church path, opposite North Street Brewery. The Duke of Richmond at that period hunted his fox hounds in the neighbourhood of Brighton, The present packs are supported by subscription, and consist of the Southdown Fox Hounds, and the Brighton and the Brookside Harriers.

About forty years since "hobby horse" exercise was a very favourite diversion with the gentry. These "hobbies" were the original velocipedes, now worked by a crank action; but they then consisted only of a fore and a hind wheel, with a slight saddle rail between, upon which the rider sat, holding on by a handle that guided the front wheel, and then, by striking out his feet with a walking action, the machine became propelled, its speed being regulated by the ability of the horseman. Much practice and great judgment were required to make a proficient rider. Many extraordinary feats of pedestrianism were performed with these machines; but the most arduous were the competing with the stage coaches to and from London. The earliest account we have of stage coaches at Brighton is in 1798, when the Princess of Wales pair-horse or post-coach was put on the road to London by way of Steyning and Horsham, the same route by which the eight-horse fly-waggons had previously travelled. Pack-horses were the only mode of performing the journey prior to the fly-waggons, and the lanes and bye-ways then being very narrow, recesses in the hedge-rows were made in certain places to permit of the laden animals standing aside that they might be passed, as their packs, which extended considerably on each side of the animals, would otherwise, frequently come in unpleasant contact with the fair sex, who on pillions occupied similar positions to merchandize when on horseback. In 1801, two pair-horse coaches ran between London and Brighton on alternate days, one up, the other down, and they were driven by Messrs. Crossweller and Hine. The progress of these coaches was amusing. The one from London left the Blossoms Inn, Lawrence Lane, at 7 a.m.; the passengers breaking their fast at the Cock, Sutton, at 9. The next stoppage for the purpose of refreshment was at the Tangier—Banstead Downs,—a rural little spot, famous for its elderberry wine, which used to be brought from the cottage "roking hot," and, on a cold wintry morning, few refused to partake of it. George the Fourth invariably stopped here and took a glass from the hand of Miss Jeal, as he sat in his carriage. The important business of luncheon took place at Reigate, where sufficient time was allowed the passengers to view the Barons' Cave, where it is said the Barons assembled the night previous to their meeting King John at Runnymeade. The grand halt, for dinner, was made at Staplefield Common, celebrated for its famous black cherry trees, under the branches of which, when the fruit was ripe, the coaches were allowed to draw up and the passengers to partake of its tempting produce. The hostess of the hostelry here was famed for her rabbit puddings, which, hot, were always waiting the arrival of the coach, and to which the travellers never failed to do such ample justice that ordinarily they found it quite impossible to leave at the hour appointed; so grogs, pipes and ale were ordered in, and, to use the language of the fraternity, "not a wheel wagged" for two hours. Handcross was the next resting place, celebrated for its "neat" liquors, the landlord of the inn standing bottle-in-hand at the door. He and several other Bonifaces, at Friar's Oak, &c., had the reputation of being on pretty good terms with the smugglers who carried on their operations with such audacity along the Sussex Coast. After walking up Clayton Hill a cup of tea was sometimes found to be necessary at Patcham; after which Brighton was safely reached at 7 p.m. It must be understood that it was the custom for the passengers to walk up all the hills, and even sometimes, in heavy weather, give a push behind to assist the jaded horses.

About 1809, a great revolution took place in coach travelling. Some gentlemen,—at the head of whom was the late Mr. William Bradford, or, as he was then styled, "Miller" Bradford,—12 in number, formed a capital by shares of £100 each, and established two four-horse coaches. The cattle were cast-horses of the Inniskilling Dragoons, then stationed at Brighton. In 1815, another vehicle of the same class, the "Bellerophon," a huge concern, built with two compartments, one carrying six, the other four inside, and with several out, was driven by Mr. Hine. This coach received its name from the ship in which Bonaparte, after his defeat at Waterloo, was conveyed to exile at St. Helena. The "Bellerophon" was soon found to be too heavy for the improving speed, and was abandoned for lighter vehicles, until travelling attained its perfection on the Brighton road, the time taken in the transit having diminished from twelve hours to five, and on one occasion the "Quicksilver," with a "King's speech" of William IV., made the journey down in three hours and forty minutes! From the year 1822, at different periods of the year, not less than sixty coaches were on the road,—thirty each way.

On a moderate calculation, Hine must have brought into the town more than one hundred thousand persons, and that without an accident; a circumstance which, in its day, was as beneficial to Brighton as is now the proverbially high character for safety, convenience, and civility of the London and Brighton Railway. Amongst the celebrities of the day whom Hine was accustomed to bring down, were Mathews, in his "prime and bang-up," who used invariably to borrow the huge box-coat of seven capes; Munden; Lieutenant or Jack Bannister; Quick, another famous actor; "Squire" Thornton, of Clapham; Rev. Rowland Hill; and many noblemen of the Court of George IV. Most of these men are, of course, like Hine himself, "dead and past away." Some few passengers, however, who have travelled by the "Union" and "Alert," and who have "booked" in East Street by Miss Hine,—the honest old coachman's daughter and sister of Mr. H. G. Hine, the artist whose works adorn much of the illustrated literature of the present day,—still survive; others must have had the name made familiar to them by hearing their fathers and grandfathers talking of the famous coaches and coachmen of Brighton.

In the height of Brighton coaching times, Castle Square upon the departure and arrival of the coaches,—but more especially at noon, when from the "Blue," the "Red." "Snow's," and the "Age" offices, the "crack" whips, the *elite* of passengers, and the best "blood" on the road, started at the striking of the Pavilion clock,—was thronged with company to witness a most animating and animated scene. Of coaching nothing now remains at Brighton but the parcels' booking office of the Railway Company, originally the "Red" and subsequently the "Blue" coach office.

By a singular inadvertence the word "Company" was omitted in the original Act of the Brighton Railway, so that the Directors of it were of the London and Brighton Railway, and not Railway Company. The amalgamation of the Eastern and Western branches, under more recent Acts, has constituted the whole scheme in connexion with the main line, the London, Brighton, and South-Coast Railway Company.

As early as 1825 the construction of a railway between Brighton and London was contemplated; but it was not till 1835 that the subject was entertained with earnestness. Five schemes were then propounded, known by the names of the different engineers who projected them, namely: Stephenson's, Rennie's, Gibbs's, and Cundy's; and the South-Eastern. The first scheme was most favourably received; and in September of that year, at a public meeting of the inhabitants of Brighton, a resolution was passed requesting the Borough Members to support its adoption in Parliament. Upon reconsideration, the inhabitants were impressed with the idea that they had been too precipitate; as the Terminus of Stephenson's line, being immediately to the west of Brighton, would only favour that special district, instead of being beneficial to the town in general; they therefore reversed their decision in favour of Rennie's, or the Direct Line. The public mind being thus fickle, the other competitors anticipating that there was yet a chance for them, pressed forward their suit, resulting in a severe contest, which gave promise of a great expenditure of money, with no line at all; as, protracted by the accumulation of oppositions, the Session of Parliament for 1837, was about to terminate without its sanction to either project. The interposition of Government determined the business; a military engineer, Captain Alderton, was deputed to investigate and report upon the merits of the several lines, and his conclusion was, "That the Direct Line is the best line between London and Brighton." That line, then, was accordingly adopted, and on the 8th July, 1837, the Bill for its construction received the Royal assent, with this clause attached, "That the total capital of £1,800,000 be raised by the subscribers to the several lines in the following proportions:—The Direct line—Rennie's,—£550,000; Stephenson's, £550,000; Cundy's, £100,000; South-Eastern, £330,000; and Gibbs's, £70,000." The various contracts for the formation of the line were soon entered into, and on the 4th of February, 1839, Mr. Alfred Morris laid the first permanent rail of the line, at Hassock's Gate, Mr. Samuel Thornton being the contractor, and Mr. T. H. Statham the resident engineer.

On the 11th of May, 1840, the first six miles of the western branch, to Shoreham, was opened; on the 25th of March, 1841, the main-line from London to Hayward's Heath, within fifteen miles of Brighton, was opened; and on Tuesday, September 21st, 1841, the whole of the line of railway from Brighton to London, was opened with some little ceremony and great rejoicing, the first trip—from Brighton to London—being performed in two hours and a quarter; leaving Brighton at 6.45 and arriving at London Bridge Terminus about 9. From time to time other additions, as branches from the main trunk, have been added, affording facilities for travelling to most parts of the kingdom south of the metropolis.

The handsome building of Italian style, which constitutes the Brighton Terminus, is the design of Mr. Mocatta; and the original sheds attached to the Terminus were designed by Mr. Rastrick, whose remains, under a massive granite monument, are deposited in the Extra-Mural Cemetery, Lewes Road. The Railway is considered a passenger and pleasure line, and, during the Summer season, excursion trains make important items in the traffic returns, as the line is in the direct route from London to Paris, *via* Newhaven and Dieppe, and at the various stations throughout the line villa residences are the retreats of the families of the London merchants who diurnally travel to and from their places of business.

Hobby Horse racing round the Level formed an attraction to the fashionable company that, daily, on horseback and in good old-fashioned and aristocatic hammerclothed coach-box and powder-bewigged coachmen and footmened family carriages, thronged Morris's Royal Repository: for that great toy-mart and favourite lounge really had regal patronage, especially from William and Adelaide, who were frequently extensive purchasers. His Majesty, upon one occasion, when Duke of Clarence, was struck, while there, with the entrance of three ladies in the garb of Quakers; and as the two eldest were looking over some articles of peculiar attraction, His Royal Highness addressed himself to the youngest, who was about fourteen, and said, "So, I see that thou art not above the vanities of this gay world." The fair young Friend said nothing; but the matron, under whose care she was, gave a look more expressive than words. The Duke felt it; and immediately purchasing a handsome work-basket, respectfully asked the eldest lady's permission to present it to her daughter. The answer was mild, but laconic. "She will receive it, and thank thee, friend." The basket was accordingly taken, with the same courtesy as given; and thus the matter ended.

During the prosperity of the Repository, which had a fame for the bows and arrows which it supplied, archery was much in vogue, the Archery Club having their rendezvous in the Queen's Park, which is situate on the south-west acclivity of the Race Hill, and is approached by an entrance that abruptly terminates Park Street, contiguous to the German Spa. This Park, which is between sixty and seventy acres in extent, was formed in 1825, by Mr. Thomas Attree, whose Italian villa, designed by the late Sir Charles Barry, crowns its northern summit.

Various as have been the attractions offered for the entertainment of visitors, the meed of their success and duration has preponderated in favour of those projected in the vicinity of the sea, which is the main feature of attraction to Brighton, that commands an uninterrupted marine drive and promenade along its whole three miles' frontage. The promenade was of small dimensions at its commencement, and originated with the owners of property between Cannon Place and Preston Street, Mr. Pocock, coal merchant, at its east extreme, and Mr. Robison, of Regency House, at the west end,—the promoters of the undertaking,—superintending its construction. Its position was in about the middle of the present carriage-way, which from time to time has been widened to accommodate the increased traffic. The original seats upon the Esplanade—for so from its commencement has the walk been called,—bore the names of the houses in front of which they were erected; but the Commissioners of the Town, in the plenitude of their wisdom, perceiving the improvement which would be effected by extending the walk, took the control of it into their own hands; and earth from the excavations made for the erection of the Places, Squares, and Streets adjacent, being abundant, in a very short space of time the promenade was continued to the extreme point of the parish, much to the discomfiture of the owners of boats and bathing machines, who were accustomed, for safety, to haul up their property upon the Wharf that stood, protected by a strongly-built brick wall to the south, immediately off the bottom of Regency Square, whereon, when it was known as Belle-Vue Field, stood a large capstan, that was used by means of a small tunnel under the road—through which a hawser passed,—to haul up vessels upon the Deals, ship-ways that were fixed there for repairing moderately sized craft.

Not unfrequent sights at this spot were severed capacious boats of slight build, which had been captured from smugglers, who had

had the temerity to try a cargo there; as forty years since, and even more recently, contraband ventures were of very common occurrence. The last successful "run" in broad daylight took place about 3 o'clock in the afternoon, July 19th, 1821, at the bottom of Ship Street, while the Custom House Officers were attracted to the Level to witness the Coronation sports. The working party had assembled in the Old Ship Yard, and at a signal given, by way of the Gap 300 kegs of Hollands were slung and off before the few persons present, who remained in the town, could comprehend the scene. Most of the cargo was, as usual, conveyed inland, where the readiest means were offered for its concealment and disposal. Captured smugglers were, at that period, put on board the Hound revenue cutter, Captain Butler commander, which was stationed off Brighton, and a smuggler chase by her was frequently a very exciting scene from the shore. Men who embarked in the hazardous enterprise were frequently missing; but whether their lives were sacrificed or they had been captured and shipped off in the Royal Navy, upon foreign service, a considerable lapse of time and a combination of circumstances only determined. One of the most desperate of a noted gang in the neighbourhood of Brighton was David Scales, who, on the night of November 7th, 1796, while going, with many more, over the hill to Patcham, heavily laden, was overtaken by excise officers and soldiers. The smugglers fled in all directions; a riding officer, as such persons were called, gave chase to Scales, who was likewise on horseback, and called upon him to surrender his booty, which he refused to do. The officer knew that Scales was too good a man for him, they having tried it before; so he shot Daniel through the head.

A monument to his memory was erected in Patcham churchyard, with the following inscription, now obliterated by time:—

Sacred to the Memory
of
DANIEL SCALES,
Who was unfortunately shot, on Tuesday evening,
Nov. 7, 1796.

Alas! swift flew the fatal lead,
Which pierced through the young man's head
He instant fell, resigned his breath,
And closed his languid eyes in death.

All you who to this stone draw near,
Oh! pray let fall the pitying tear:
From this sad instance may we all
Prepare to meet Jehovah's call.*

On the 24th of April, 1806, an encounter took place off Brighton, between the revenue cutter, Leopard, and a smuggler, when Aldridge, the commander of the contraband vessel, was killed in the action, and one of his crew, named Morris, was so desperately wounded in the chest that he died a few days afterwards.

As a more immediate than a sidelong marine walk, the Chain Pier was projected, agreeable to the annexed prospectus:—

The utility of a Pier at Brighton, carried a sufficient distance beyond high-water mark, so as to enable Steam Packets and boats to lay alongside, and embark or land their passengers, is universally admitted; and the proposition has excited greater interest since the resolution has been formed of establishing a Steam Packet Company to France, because it is reasonably anticipated that the two concerns, although not intended to be incorporated, must be essentially beneficial to each other.

In a national point of view it is certainly most desirable, that the intercourse between the two countries should be facilitated and extended; and there can be no measure adopted which could more effectually promote this end and increase the prosperity of this great and flourishing town, than the proposed Pier.

When so many advantages are evidently comprehended, both to the individuals who may be concerned in the undertaking, and the public generally, it becomes a subject of deeper solicitude, that there should be no fallacy in the principle, no imperfection in the constitution, which would endanger its future security, and frustrate the important object.

First, with regard to the durability of the materials, it should be observed, that it is intended to construct the Pier, wholly of iron, with the exception of the platform. The oxedale of cast Iron is so incorruptible that its effects can scarcely be brought within the scope of calculation; and wrought iron, with common attention to cleaning and painting, may be considered as almost imperishable. But even if the time should arrive (which must be exceedingly remote) to render it necessary to renew it, every bar can be taken out and the whole replaced in detail, without any interruption to the passage of the Pier, so that the capital invested in the concern is not chargeable with more than commmon interest. The planking of the gangway will require to be renewed perhaps once in ten or fifteen years, and this expense is accounted for under the head of charges.

With regard to its strength, when there are so many conspicuous examples of the powers of piles to resist the sea in the most exposed situations, any theoretical illustration would be superfluous. But before notice is taken of the works which have preceded and given rise to the proposed plan, a few instances may be

* Contiguous was a headstone, whereon was the epitaph:—

She in affliction bore a son,
The milk forsook her breast,
Her legs they mortified and run,
But hope she's now at rest.

stated, such as the Sheers, the Whittaker, the Gun Fleet, and other beacons on the North Coast; and coming nearer to the point itself, the iron beacon on the Black Rock, near Leith, which is about two miles S.E. from the Trinity Pier, has stood alone for years; North Yarmouth jetty, and the Pier at Ostend, on the opposite coast, remain firm, opposed to the sea from the S.E. and N.W. and require no repair but what arises from the decay of the timber; and at Cronstadt, in the Gulph of Finland, there are batteries erected on piles like so many islands, which have remained there from the time of Peter the Great.

It may now be noticed, without entering into so wide a field, that the Trinity Pier, which (although on the same principle) is in all respects a more slender and inferior structure to the proposed Pier for Brighton, was erected during the stormy season of the equinox; and even in its unfinished state, while it was of course less capable of resisting the shock of the sea, it suffered no injury; and since its completion, the following reports will show that its strength and security are beyond all question, and what is of as much importance, its utility has surpassed the most sanguine expectations.

Copy of a Report from the Directors of the Trinity Pier Company, dated Leith, Sept. 20, 1821:—

"These are to certify, that the Trinity Pier was loaded with 118 Pigs of iron ballast, or upwards of 20 Tons, the same that were sent out by Mr. Crichton for proving the said Pier, and that the above ballast was loaded between the piers regularly placed. And we also certify that there was no interruption to the passengers to and from the Steam Boats that were laying alongside at the time it was so loaded. And we further certify, that under all the circumstances of the case, that the said Pier has undergone a more severe trial or proof than was specified in the agreement with Captain Brown; and that the said Pier is in all respects perfect, and in good order.

"Given under our hands at Leith, this 20th day of Sept. 1821.

(Signed) "ALEXANDER SCOTT,
"ALEXANDER STEVENSON, } Directors of the Trinity Pier."

Copy of the second Report from the Directors of the Trinity Pier Company, dated Leith, the 16th November, 1821:—

"Leith, Nov. 16, 1821.

"CAPTAIN SAMUEL BROWN, R.N.

"Sir—In compliance with your wish to hear how the new Pier of Suspension, at Trinity, has stood the late violent easterly gales, to which it is very much exposed, we feel very great pleasure in informing you that it has not received the most trifling damage; and that since the pier-head has been lengthened to 70 feet, the Steam Boats are able to lay on the lee-side of it with perfect security in the strongest gales we have had, the violence of the sea being exhausted in passing through the different ranges of the piles.

"So little is the vibration of the chains and platform, that we have never known the least alarm to be expressed by passengers going along it; and great numbers frequent it even in this inclement season, merely for the purpose of taking a walk along it.

"We are, Sir,
"Your obedient Servants.

(Signed) "ALEXANDER SCOTT,
"ALEXANDER STEVENSON, } Directors of Trinity Pier Company.
"GEORGE CRICHTON, Treasurer."

As there will be plans upon an extended scale, laid before a general meeting, or a committee of management, it is unnecessary to advert to them at present: it may, however, be satisfactory to state, the extent, from high-water-mark to the end of the Pier, 1,000 feet, and the width ten feet: each of the inverted arches will be 251 feet span, and the outer Pier-head will form an area of about 4,500 feet, and an elevation of 10 feet above the highest spring-tides. The expense of erecting a Pier and constructing a floating Break-water, which will be essential, as a protection from ships or vessels running foul of it, and at the same time afford additional facility and convenience for ships putting to sea from the beach, will be £27,000*. It is proposed that a Company should be constituted and incorporated, under the denomination of the Brighton Pier Company, and that the sum of £27,000, forming the joint stock of the Company, be raised by subscriptions of £100 each.—The affairs of the Company to be conducted and managed by a Committee, consisting of a Treasurer and 10 Members, who are to be chosen by a majority of votes of the Proprietors, at a General Meeting; and that five of the said Committee are also to be chosen by a majority of votes to act as Directors or Managers of the Company; and that the Committee of Management and the Directors collectively, shall have the power of appointing a Pier Master, and other persons, whose services or avocations may be required for the general benefit and advantage of the Company. All other rules relative to the reciprocity of interest and the financial branches of the Company, are to be fully set forth and explained in a separate instrument, to be drawn up in a proper legal form by a Solicitor.

The situation in all respects most suitable both for the convenience of the public and the interest of the Brighton Pier Company, is opposite the East Parade of the Old Steyne, and as T. R. Kemp, Esq., and C. S. Dickens, Esq., have, in the most liberal and handsome manner, which must lay, not only the proprietors of the Pier, but the whole community, under lasting obligations, granted a sufficient space of ground for forming the Pier, and relinquished all their manorial rights, it will not be necessary to apply for an Act of Parliament for authority to levy and collect a toll, or pontage in the Pier, because the beach is free for landing and embarking in boats as heretofore, and it becomes perfectly voluntary or optional to enter upon and pay for the accommodation of the Pier.

It is intended that the platform shall be horizontal with the East Parade, and extend in the same direction out to sea—as there can be no doubt that the Pier would become a place of fashionable resort, great emoluments would be derived from this source alone,—independent of this, would be the specific revenue secured by a lease to be paid by the Proprietors of the Steam-Packets, and as it is one of the objects of the Pier to permit the shipment of carriages and horses, under certain regulations consistent with the convenience of visitors, a considerable sum will be raised by this means.

It is not intended that Merchant's ships should load or discharge their cargoes at the Pier, and no fish to be landed unless under particular circumstances to be judged by the Pier-Master;—but as great advantages must be derived to the Town, and Proprietors of the Pier, from the traffic in fruit, eggs, &c. &c. with France, small-craft and boats are to be permitted to come alongside, by

* If the ships should discontinue to run on the beach, and go into Shoreham Harbour or Newhaven, the Breakwater may be dispensed with, which will save £3,000.

paying certain dues for the vessels, and a certain rate upon their goods, the amount of which will be fixed by the Committee of Management; pleasure-boats, and boats hired for pleasure, are to pay certain dues for laying alongside the Pier, and a further rate for the company landing from or embarking on board them, and the shore boats belonging to the Town of Brighton and others, which are in the constant practice of using the beach, whether owned in the town or not, are to be permitted to land passengers, who are to pay the usual rate for landing on the Pier; but the boats before-mentioned are to be exempted from paying any dues for *coming* alongside, and the crew are to be allowed to land without any charge being made: but such boats are not to continue at the Pier longer than is necessary to land or take on board passengers or pleasure parties, and are to be subject to the orders of the Pier-Master, in regard to the length of time to be allowed for this purpose, and this permission alluded to is not to be considered as an abandonment of the right of the Pier Company to charge boats of the above description the usual Pier dues, but as a favor and preference given to the fishermen and boatmen belonging to the Town of Brighton and its dependencies.

There is no circumstance connected with this establishment of a Pier at Brighton, which will be viewed with more satisfaction, either by the Proprietors or the Public, than the ready means it will afford of dispatching boats to the assistance of vessels in distress—however well disposed the fishermen or pilots may be to venture to sea in a heavy gale to their relief, their utmost skill and hardihood are unavailable to launch their boats through the serf at low water; and even at the height of the tide it is frequently impracticable; it is therefore intended either to construct a slip or inclined plane in the centre of the outward Pier, to contain a boat of the largest class, and provide anchors and cables for her, and appoint her in all respects ready to launch off in the heaviest gale at a moment's notice,—or to erect Davits on each side of the Pier to support boats, which will always be ready to lower down.—There are no description of vessels better calculated for this service than what are termed the Brighton hog-boats,—when they are fairly clear of the beach and breakers, (which the boat would be the moment it was launched,) they work off the coast in the most surprising manner.

As it will at all events be necessary to have a boat's crew of at least four active able bodied men, belonging to the Pier, those men, in order to be available for the duty alluded to, must be Pilots for Shoreham or Newhaven, and when the large boat is to be sent to sea there can be no difficulty in engaging three or four men to complete the compliment. That in the course of time many ships and vessels may receive assistance, and be saved from shipwreck by this means, is the most reasonable of all hypotheses—and as the vessel and other smaller boats would be part of the property of the Company, and maintained by it, they would be entitled to salvage or to a remuneration in proportion to the extent of services rendered, as usual in such cases.

But the sources from whence the revenue of the Pier is to be derived, which will yield a large interest to the Proprietors agreeable to the sum which they may have respectively invested, will be so satisfactorily shewn in the following statement, that it is not necessary to reckon on any profits arising from such contingencies, however plausible and flattering the prospect may be.

REVENUE:

	£	s	d.
Pier dues from 4 Steam-boats, each £100 yearly	400	0	0
" 25,000 passengers to and from France, per Steam-vessels, in the course of the year, at 2s	2500	0	0
" Luggage, packages, &c. &c	500	0	0
" French vessels to pay 1s per ton, and the crew to be exempted from dues, viz.—200 vessels averaging 20 tons each, 1s..	200	0	0
" Goods, packages, &c., from French vessels	300	0	0
" 100 carriages to and from France, 20s	100	0	0
" 200 horses ditto ditto, 10s	100	0	0
" Pleasure Yachts, crews exempted, supposed	50	0	0
" Company embarking and landing, 2s	100	0	0
" Parties of pleasure in the Brighton shore boats	50	0	0
" Ship boats landing and embarking passengers 5s for the use of the Pier, which will exempt the crew	50	0	0
" Produce of the Pier as a promenade, at £10 per day	3650	0	0
	£8000	0	0

CHARGES:

	£	s	d.
Pier Master, yearly	200	0	0
Boat's crew, 4 men, yearly	150	0	0
Two Toll-keepers	104	0	0
Wear and tear of ropes, &c	40	0	0
Painting Pier twice a year	40	0	0
Wear and tear of gangway of Pier	30	0	0
Lighting of Pier	20	0	0
Night watchman	38	0	0
Secretary, office, &c	300	0	0
	£922	0	0

	£	s	d.
	£922	0	0
Net produce yearly, or 25 per Cent. on amount of capital	£7078	0	0

The merits of the plan are here brought to a very narrow compass, and it is confidently believed that there will appear no disposition to overrate the advantages, or to excite any undue bias in the public mind that might ultimately lead to disappointment.

Subscriptions will be received at Messrs. HALL, WEST, and BORRER; Messrs. WIGNEY, STANFORD and Co., Brighton; and Messrs. WILLIS, PERCIVAL and Co., London.

It is much doubted whether the expectations of either the projectors or the shareholders have ever been realized, except as regards outlay and charges. The structure was commenced in October, 1822, and completed in twelve months. On the 25th of November, 1823, it was opened by the skilful projector, Sir Samuel Brown,

R.N. The Pier, which projects 1,150 feet, is approached by an Esplanade 1,250 feet in length. The foundation consists of four clumps of iron shod and nail-mailed piles strongly bound by cross and wale pieces of great substance. The clumps are 250 feet apart, and are crowned with cast-iron towers, over which pass the main suspension chains that emerge from the cliff, into which they are carried fifty-four feet, and are there fastened to a mass of iron, three tons in weight, firmly embedded in masonry. The south ends of the chains pass down a casing of wood to the rock, into which and the massive piles of the extreme platform they are bolted and keyed.

Just one year after the completion of the Pier, namely, on the 23rd November, 1824, the structure underwent a severe trial, but it nobly stood a storm which devastated the southern coast of England, some portion of the wooden platform and the ornamental iron-work alone receiving slight damage. Two dolphins, however, to the west of the Pier in an angular position, consisting of small clusters of piles, over the crown of which to the Pier-head large chains were stretched to fend-off any vessels that might be driven in by a south-west gale, were completely washed away. The havock to property along the sea-front of the town was tremendous.

On the 15th of October, 1833, the structure received some injury from lightning, and on the 22nd of November following a dreadful gale of wind, after causing the platform to writhe like the action of a serpent, heaved-up the chains, twisting the pendant rods into fantastical shapes, discharging the wooden roadway into the raging surf, and wrenching one of the towers from its perpendicular. The inhabitants, looking upon the injury done as a calamity to the town, immediately set a subscription on foot, and in a very short time, £1,200 was raised to effect the restoration of the edifice, which was further secured by a chain cable beneath the platforms, attached to each clump of piles, to check all future oscillation and heaving.

For many years the arrival and departure of steam packets, employed in the passenger intercourse between Brighton and Dieppe, formed a great attraction for visitors to the Pier. The first steamer employed in the station was the Swift, of eighty-horse power. A packet service by sailing vessels, previously existed, during the times of peace, dating as far back as 1792, when the Prince of Wales, a schooner, Captain Burton; the Princess Royal, a schooner, Captain Chapman; and the Speedwell, a cutter, Captain Lind, were the vessels employed. These were succeeded by the Nancy, Captain Blaber, which was run down in mid-channel; Ann and Elizabeth, Captain Daniels; Nautilus, Captain Wingfield, who is still alive and vends pork in Brighton Market; Elizabeth, Captain Lind; Lord Wellington, Captain Cheesman, who was afterwards, for years, in the General Steam Navigation Company's service, on the same route; Prince Regent, Captain Bulbeck; Neptune, Captain Wallis; and the Thomas, Captain Clear. This vessel was instrumental in saving the life of Mr. Charles Green, the celebrated aeronaut, on the occasion of his ascent from the Gas Works, at Black Rock, October 1st, 1821, with his Coronation balloon. The Thomas had left some of her passengers and the Captain at Eastbourne, and was just off Beachy Head, in charge of the Mate, Francis Cheesman, who bore down upon the balloon, then unmanageable upon the water, and driving the vessel's bowsprit into the silk of the aerial machine soon liberated the gas, and rescued Mr. Green from his frail wicker-work car.

At various periods the Chain Pier has been the medium and focus of special entertainments in the separate and combined attractions of fire and water. The structure on the evening of its inauguration was illuminated on both sides throughout its whole extent, in coloured lamps forming "God Save the Queen, and the House of Brunswick." More recently exhibitions of fireworks have taken place upon it. The most memorable event by way of pastime was the Brighton and Hove Regatta, which took place on Thursday and Saturday, July 21st and 23rd, 1853, when public money to the extent of £364, was competed for, prizes of £120, £105, and £52 10s, by yachts, and other prizes varying from £20 downwards, to the number of fourteen by sailing and rowing boats. The weather for several days previous to the Regatta—which had been arranged to extend through three days,—was most unfavourable, a strong wind from the south-west preventing the arrival of yachts which had just contended in the Yarmouth Regatta. Several however, of heavy tonnage were in the matches, the first of which was gained by the Alarm, 248 tons, J. Welds, Esq., in a contest with the Sveridge, 280 tons, T. Bartlett, Esq., which was declared by yachting men unparalleled in the superior nautical tactics which were displayed. The Hotel-Keepers' Prize of 50 guineas, with 50 guineas added, was won by the Arrow, 102 tons, T. Chamberlayne, Esq., four competed. The Ship-Owners' Prize of 50 guineas was gained by the Phantom, 25 tons, S. Lane, Esq., beating the Thought, 25 tons, G. Coope, Esq. The First Class Pleasure Boat match, £20, was won by the Skylark, Mr. A. T. Mills; and in the Second Class Pleasure Boat contest for 10 guineas, the Royal Frederick, Mr. B. Kent, successfully contended against three others. In the four-oared Galley contest for £15, the Arrow, Mr. J. Nottidge succeeded against six others. Friday, the intervening day of the matches, was an entire blank; a dense fog with a drizzling rain prevailing from sun-rise to sun-set. On the evening of Saturday, there was a grand display of fireworks on the Chain Pier.

The Regatta was of simple origin. A few of the principal tradesmen who were accustomed to meet of an evening in conviviality at the New Ship Hotel, chanced in the early part of March, 1853, to have in their company Captain Moore, connected with several yachting clubs. He spoke of the admirable position of Brighton for yachting matches, and the attraction they would be to the inhabitants and visitors. A communication was forthwith made to the Commodores of the various Royal Yacht Clubs, and the idea being favourably entertained by them, a committee was formed, with Mr. H. P. Tamplin, the High Constable, as their Chairman, and the author of this book as their Honorary Secretary. Subscriptions came in bountifully, the whole of the town being most favourable to the project. The Railway Directors presented 50 guineas; the Hotel Keepers gave a prize of 37 guineas; the inhabitants of Cliftonville 50 guineas; the Ship-Owners 50 guineas; and Chain Pier Company 18 guineas. The Theatre was placed at the service of the Committee, and the proceeds of an amateur performance under the management of Mr. D. H. Greenin, aided the funds, as did also a fete at the Swiss Gardens, Shoreham, and a concert at the Royal Pavilion. So anxious and energetic, in fact, was the public in general for the Regatta to be a great success, that at its termination the sum of £148 remained in the hands of the Treasurer, arising principally from the weather preventing the whole of the programme being gone through.

As an Englishman's conclusion to a popular enterprise, a dinner took place at the Old Ship Hotel; and then, at the New Ship, where the Committee held their meetings, the Committee—of which Mr. Charles Sprake, the landlord, was a member,—gave an invitation dinner to the Honorary Secretary, who was presented, at the hands of the High Constable, with a most gratifying testimonial, thus inscribed,—surmounted with the Brighton Arms,—upon a silver-mounted portemonnie :—"Brighton and Hove Regatta, 1853. Presented to Mr. J. A. Erredge, with a Complimentary Sum, by the Committee, for his Valuable Services, as their Honorary Secretary." As a feature of and to commemorate the Regatta, Mr. John Smith, King's Road, who fitted-out several of the Committee in nautical attire, had an appropriate gilt button struck, of neat design.

Amongst the matches not contended for in the Regatta, was that for the Cliftonville Prize, which remained in abeyance till the Autumn of 1856, when fresh subscriptions and the interest of the money in hand, accumulating the Fund to £304, a second Regatta was arranged, which came off on the 26th of August, when Prizes to the amount of £207 were awarded. A grand display of fireworks and the discharge of incidental expenses cleared off the balance.

A great attraction to the Chain Pier, after the packets ceased running to and from Dieppe, was a band of music that entertained the company who promenaded the Pier-head. The Military Concerts at the Pavilion, however, are at present the musical feature for visitors, who every Wednesday and Saturday afternoon throng the suite of Assembly Rooms; and, when the season and weather are favourable, the eastern lawn, where also, for nine years past the Brighton and Sussex Horticultural and Floricultural Society have held their Summer and Autumn Shows, which annually increase in attraction and importance. The Museum and Picture Galleries that occupy upper portions of the Pavilion, likewise afford visitors many an hour's agreeable ramble amongst the works of art and other rarities which are daily accumulating. An annual exhibition in connexion with the Brighton and Sussex School of Art, with an

Art Union attached, takes place in the Galleries; and there is also an apartment appropriated to the School of Art. In the height of the season, grand concerts by *artistes* of celebrity take place in the Music Room, which, being easier of approach than the Town Hall, has superseded the large room there, where on the occasion of Jenny Lind—the Swedish Nightingale,—singing on the 23rd of August, 1847, the receipts were £1,200.

A species of diversion, termed a soirée, has of recent years been very popular, the intellectual being by it agreeably blended with the recreative; science and the fine arts gracefully admitting a sisterhip with Terpsichore, the active votaries of which goddess in their sundry modern gyrations of polka and schottische, contrasting strangely with "Lady Montgomery's Reel," led off in the same Pavilion, August 13th, 1805, by the Honourable Miss Seymour and a son of the Duke of Clarence, "with suitable ease, spirit, and vivacity," and in a country-dance to the tune "Murphy Delaney," the Prince of Wales and the Duke of Clarence "taking an active part in the wholesome exercise." There was as great a diversity then in dance music as at the present time, passing events suggesting new ideas to composers and musicians, Upon one occasion, Mr. Kramer, the leader of the Prince's private band, being in the Telemachus Room of the Old Ship Hotel, arranging the music for a ball which was to take place in the evening at the Royal Pavilion, had his attention attracted by the voice of a noted character from Lewes, Jemmy Gosney, who with a peculiar nasal twang was announcing in Ship Street that he had for sale "Book almanack, new almanack, Moore's Almanack." To the surprise of the vendor of *Vox Stellarum,* he heard his words repeated at a window opposite, where, on his clarionet, Kramer so imitated the old man's voice, that, in the evening, he availed himself of the incident to introduce it as a novelty, in the course of a dance, much to the delight of His Royal Highness and the company in general.

During the sojourn of William and Adelaide in Brighton, in 1834, Sir Andrew Barnard, at the request of his Majesty, enquired of Mr. Gutteridge, the organist of the Royal Chapel, if there was anything to be obtained in the way of singing amongst the townsfolk. Mr. Gutteridge recommended the members of the Brighton Madrigal Society, with whom, for eight guineas the evening, an engagement was effected, but at so short a notice that the singers were perplexed to procure the appropriate dress for the occasion, namely, black coats and white vests. At the suggestion of a friend, however, a second-hand clothes' shop in the Lanes was visited, and there they found all that was required; but one of the party, who was desirous of the loan of a coat for the night,—for which loan a half-crown was asked,—not having the cash about him for the deposit that was required to ensure its safe return, was necessitated to go out and obtain a well-known hair-dresser in Ship Street as his bond. The performance of the Madrigals took place in the Royal Music Room, in the presence of their Majesties and party, amongst whom was Lady Kennedy Erskine, the King's daughter, an excellent judge of music, who highly complimented them on the efficient manner in which they had acquitted themselves. After the singing, they withdrew and partook of supper, at which they were attended by two footmen in the Royal livery, to one of whom the leader of the party—who had a black ribbon pinned in his waistcoat pocket to simulate that he wore a watch, and who was unaccustomed to a servant in waiting,—said, "Hulloa, old fellow, don't bother yourself about us, sit down and have some with us." The servant smiled, but declined, and only forgot his position as attendant by taking, when urgently pressed, a glass of wine all round with the guests.

In 1834, when Madame Sala, the mother of Mr. F. A. Sala, the novelist, was in the zenith of her profession as a songstress, and also as a teacher of singing, a placard on a board was placed at Eber's Library, now Dutton and Thorowgood's shoe warehouse, Castle Square, announcing a concert at the Town Hall, for her benefit; when some person,—it was supposed envious of her fame,—two evenings previous to that announced for her concert, disfigured the placard by cutting out some of the letters of her name, making it to read thus:—MAD SAL, which, coming to her knowledge, caused Madame to abandon the concert from fear of further insult. Her patrons recompensed her, but could not erase from her recollection the unmerited malignity.

Only a few years since, Brighton was greatly infested with street music from organs, hurdy-gurdies, and pianettes; a crusade, however, of the peace authorities drove them from the town, to which they have not since been allowed to return. Itinerant bands of wind instrument players yet remain, greatly to the annoyance of the inhabitants, of whom the performers most importunately ask remuneration for the woful discord they discourse. An accredited Town Band of no mean talent is in existence, supported by voluntary contributions and subscriptions; but it struggled for some years before it could attain a position, intruders upon their presumed rights frequently drafting off, by offers of superior engagements, their best performers. German bands were at one time very prevalent, but they remained only the novelty of a few seasons; pilferings by their leaders, petty quarrels and jealousies amongst themselves, and the non-appreciation by the public of what by some persons might be termed their talent, causing most of them to leave the town, if not the kingdom. The most respectable of them formed the nucleus of the Town Band, whose most general place of performance is on the lower western Esplanade, contiguous to the principal pleasure-boat station, where parties for a sail or row, or fishing excursion meet with everything they desire for a nautical pastime.

Persons who are desirous of witnessing deep-sea fishing can also be gratified by making arrangements with owners of the regular fishing boats; and as the various kinds of fish, the habits, manners, customs, and costumes of the fishers, and the mode of fishing off this coast have not undergone any change by time, the graphic description of the Brighton Fishery by the Welsh Zoologist, Thomas Pennant, who died in 1798, is here most apposite:—

"The fish-market, both wholesale and retail, is kept on the beach, a little beyond the baths; the boats used in the fisheries are from ten to fifteen tons, made remarkably strong to secure them against the storms in their winter adventure. The mackarel boats are navigated by three or four men and a boy; there are about forty-five for the mackarel fishery, and twenty-five for the trawling; they set sail generally in the evening, go eight or ten leagues to sea, and return the next day. The fishing is always carried on in the night. The crew are provided with tea, coffee, water, and a small quantity of spirits, for at sea they are remarkably temperate; their indulgence is only on shore. They only take with them bread, beef, and greens, which, and sometimes fish, they often eat with their tea and coffee. They are a hardy race, and very healthy; yet, during the Summer season, they have very small interval from labour. They get a good meal, and a very short repose by lying themslves on a bed during the few hours in the day on which they come on shore. They bring their fish in baskets to the beach, fling them in vast heaps, and instantly a ring of people is formed round, an auction* is begun, and the heap immediately disposed of; the price is uncertain, according to the success of the night. Mackarel in the year 1793, were sold from £1 to £7 a hundred; they have been sold as high as £15 a hundred.† Mackarel and soles are the great staples of the place, nine or ten thousand have been taken at one shooting of the net. Mackarel swim deep in calms, and rise to the surface in gales, when the largest fish and the greatest quantity are taken.‡

"The nets consist of a number of parts, each of which is from thirty-six to fifty yards long and deep, and are kept buoyant by corks. These united form a chain of nets a mile and a half long. Before they are used in the Spring, they are taken from the store-houses and spread upon the Steine; a privilege, time immemorial, granted to the fishermen. The boats are drawn on shore at the latter end of the Winter, and placed in ranges on the lower part of the

* The sale is by "Dutch Auction,"—doubtless introduced by the Flemings, —the salesman offering his several lots at whatever price he chooses, reducing it till a buyer says "have 'em," when the name of the purchaser, and the price, are entered in the salesman's book, and the fish are immediately transferred, but the payment is made after the business of selling is over. No sales are allowed to take place before six o'clock in the morning, when the market is opened by the ringing of a bell.

† In "Yarrell's History of British Fishes," mention is made that in May, 1807, the first Brighton boat-load of mackarel sold at Billingsgate for forty guineas per hundred—7s. each, reckoning six score to the hundred; the highest price ever known in that market.

‡ The Lord of the Manor of Brighthelmston, by his reeve, is entitled to the claim of the six finest mackarel from each boat, on its landing. A few years since some of the fishermen disputed this right, but the Magistrates, on the appeal of the reeve, Mr James Henry Mills, acknowledged and enforced the right.

Steyne, and other places near to the sea. The interval from labour is very small, for numbers of the boats are in the early Spring hired out to dredge for oysters, to supply the beds in the Medway and other places.

"The greater part of the fish is sent to London, packed in baskets, usually weighing about three quarters of a hundred in each; they are put into small light carts, which go post, carry from fifteen to thirty baskets each, and reach our capital in eight or ten hours.

"The mackarel are supposed to come from the Bay of Biscay. In the early Spring they are taken off Dieppe; they next appear off Mount's Bay, where they are caught in seines, and sent by land to London in small baskets; the shooting of nets has not been found to answer off the Cornish shore. They arrive in the channel off Brighthelmston in the middle of April, and continue to the middle of July, after which they will not mesh, but are caught with hooks, and are at that season nearly unfit for eating. In June they are observed to approach nearer the shore; they continue in the channel till the cold season commences, when they go progressively north or east. The fry is seen of very small size in October and November.

"The herring fishery begins in October; those fish appear in great quantities along shore, and reach Hastings in November. The fishery is very considerable, and adventurers from every country engage in it. A boat has ten last of ten thousand each. The fish which are not sent to London fresh, are salted or cured as red herrings. The nets resemble those used in the mackarel fishery, only the meshes are smaller: they are about twenty feet deep, and are left to sink of themselves. The congenerous pilchards are sometimes taken here in the mackarel nets, but in very small quantities.

"Soles, the other staple fish, are taken in trawls in great numbers. The fishery begins in April, and continues all the Summer: in April, 1794, the weight of two tons was caught in one night. I saw in the same month a heap of soles on the market beach none of which were less than nineteen inches long. The other congenerous fishes were turbots, generally very indifferent; brills or pearl; smear dabs; plaice, and flounders.

"Various kinds of rays are taken here; such as the skate, the fuller, the thornback, the sand-ray, which has sharp slender spines on the edges, opposite to the eyes; minute spines along the edges of the fins, and upon the fins like the fuller; the back and tail shagreened, marked with round black spots; the teeth sharp and slender. A ray, not uncommon on the Flintshire coasts, is twenty-one inches long, of which the tail is eleven; the nose is pointed, and semi-transparent; two spines above each eye, and three placed in a row on the back; three rows on the tail, of which the middle runs far up the back edges of the body from the nose to the anal fin, rough, with rows of minute spines; back quite smooth, of a fine pale brown, regularly marked with circular black spots; teeth quite flat and smooth.

"Of the shark genus, the angel-fish is not uncommon. The smooth sharks, or topes, are very numerous; they grow to the length of four feet. I saw opened several of this species, and can vouch for the truth of the young entering the mouth of the parent in time of danger, and taking refuge in the stomach. I have seen from twelve to twenty taken out of a single tope, each eleven or twelve inches long. This species is split, salted, and eaten.

"I here met with the corbeagle of Mr. Jago. The length was three feet nine inches, the thickest circumference two feet one inch. It is a rare species, allied to the Beaumaris shark. The greater and lesser spotted dog-fish are very numerous.

"The common angler is frequently caught here, and sometimes of an enormous size; from the vast width of the mouth it is called here the kettle-man. The launce, and two species or weevers, are very common; the greater grows to the length of sixteen inches, is two inches deep, the weight of two pounds, and is a firm well-tasted fish. The fishermen have a great dread of the spines, and cut them off as soon as taken.

"The cod fish tribe are rather scarce, except the whitings, which are sometimes caught in mackarel nets, but chiefly with hooks. They are taken in April; but the best season is in October. I saw here the common cod, the whiting-pout, the coal-fish, and the five-bearded cod.

"The doree is frequently taken here: I saw one of fifteen pounds weight, and the length of three quarters of a yard. I saw here the lunated gilthead, and ancient wrasse, the basse, and red or striped surmullet: the last small. The red and the grey gurnards were common.

"Salmons are unknown here, which I am told is the case on all chalky coasts. The gar or needle-fish are often seen here, and of great lengths. I shall digress improperly in saying that the razor bills and guillemots, inhabitants of Beachy Head, are frequently caught in the mackarel nets, unwarily diving in the pursuit of the fish. Prawns are in their season taken in vast abundance near the shores, which wanting rocks to give shelter to the lobsters and crabs, those delicacies are brought from the more distant parts of the coast."

A very general pastime with the low caste of the seafarers, when the weather is too boisterous for their fishing and boating operations, is sea-roaming, watching the margin of the turbulent waves upon the beach, to pick up the trifles which the surge may chance to throw up. Some years since,—before steam vessels were in use,—when weather-bound ships were unable to get out of the bay, of which Brighton forms the northern boundary, wrecks of richly laden crafts frequently afforded rare prizes for the roamers, who now, more than from the spoils, *via jetsam et flotsam,* pick up from strangers whom they may chance to meet on their stroll, many a silver coin, fictitious tales of their losses, bad voyages, and their starving large families, rarely failing to exact a coin of the realm, hence they are known amongst the better class of the nautical fraternity by the name of cadgers. On the faith, too, that "early birds pick up the worms," not to be despised a living is obtained by frequenting at day-break the vicinity of houses where parties have been held the previous night, in search of jewellery, trinkets, or money that by any casualty may have been dropped. For many years this mode of life has been a monopoly by a man named Simmonds, who, also, throughout the livelong day pursues with a keen eye and a raking stick the business of gutter hunter.

Chapter XXVIII.

THE HISTORICAL STREET OF THE TOWN.

For historical lore, few continuous ranges of buildings in the kingdom are connected with so many national and local incidents as West Street, Brighton, which was formerly approached from the west, at the south end, by a hill, that ranged with Kent Street, which originally terminated due south to the West Cliff. The hill was of an altitude that, upon its removal, to make the roadway level between Russell Street and West Street, the front doors of the houses were one story above the pathway, compelling the construction of flights of steps in the fore-courts, commencing from east to west half the distance up, where a landing was formed, from whence another flight set off northward to the door-ways. The Cliff there at that time, was known as The Bank, a provincial term still used for it by most of the aborigines. The incline of the Gap went from the east corner of the street, direct south to the sea, which washed it in stormy weather, when, for safety, the bathing-machines and the boats stationed thereabouts, were hauled into the street as high up as Duke Street.

Upon the first house in the street, that at the south corner of Kent Street, for many years, just beneath the parapet which surmounted the front wall, was a Latin inscription in raised Roman capitals, which at various periods, as some of the letters became obliterated by their great exposure to the weather, and from their restoration not being effected with promptitude, underwent several changes, as, EXCITAT ACTA ROBUR, strength awakens action, i.e., the consciousness of power arouses men to acts; EXCITAS ACTIS RODUR, thou awakest strength by deeds; EXCITAT ACTIS ROBUR, he arouses to strength by acts; EXCITAS ACTA, ROBUR, thou wakest or excitest to deeds or actions, O strength. Its last appearance, EXCITUS ACTA ROPAT,—which defied all efforts of translation,—being the cause of much ridicule, the letters were entirely removed. Immediately opposite this house, suspended from the Cliff, was the town fire-cage, constructed of iron hoops, wherein, at night, a fire of strombolum—collected along the sea shore,—and common coal, was generally kindled, as a guide to the fishermen on their return to shore.

On New Year's Day, 1810, a horrid act of brutal violence was committed in connexion with this land-mark: Two men, named Rolfe and Barton, who were engaged to attend to the fire, having some words in the course of the evening, Rolfe determined to arrange the beacon by himself, and therefore procured a new iron frame and suspended it accordingly. This, however, he had no sooner done than Barton attempted to cut the fastenings and let it over the Cliff, and as Rolfe endeavoured to prevent his carrying his ill-natured design into effect, Barton thrust a knife into his abdomen, and literally let out some of his bowels. Barton escaped, but a reward of £20 being offered through the Town Crier, he was captured, but only suffered a short imprisonment, as Rolfe, after having endured great pain, eventually recovered.

The events connected with the King's Head have been detailed in Chapter XVIII. The low, stone-coloured, brick building immediately opposite this hostelry, was the favourite residence of Mrs. Thrale, the wife of the wealthy owner of the London Brewery, now known as "Barclay and Perkins's Brewery." Amongst the general visitors to Mrs. Thrale were Dr. Samuel Johnson and Madame D'Arblay—Fanny Burney—the authoress of Evelena, who in one of her letters—Madame d'Arblay's Diary—describes the residence as being at the court end of the town, and exactly opposite the inn where Charles II. lay hid previous to leaving the kingdom. "So I fail not," she adds, "to look at it with loyal satisfaction, and His black-wigged Majesty has from the time of its restoration been its sign." Mrs. Thrale, who upon her second marriage was Madame Piozzi, the mother of Mrs. Mostyn, who died recently at Sillwood House, has her name thus recorded in the parish book:—

February 16th, 1791.—On application of Mrs Thrale, it is ordered that a poor boy proposed by her be received into the Poor House, during the pleasure of the officers, on being paid by the said Mrs Thrale 4s weekly for his board.

It happened upon one occasion that while Dr. Johnson was visiting the Thrales, he accompanied them to the Baths,—those on the site where Brill's Ladies' Swimming Bath now stands,—at which public lounge he met the Vicar, the Rev. Henry Michell, with whom, drawing their chairs close to the fire in the ante-room, he soon got into conversation. For some time their manner was calm and their language subdued; but at length some strong difference arising in their arguments, the Vicar seized the poker, and the Doctor the tongs, with which, upon the grate they suited "their action to the word" with the utmost energy. The general company present, who were enjoying a country dance, suddenly ceased their evolutions, which could not be resumed till the Master of the Ceremonies, Wade, with his proverbial politeness, pacified the heated debaters.

The water from a wooden pump at Thrale's house, was supposed to be endowed with peculiar medicinal properties, from the circumstance that after his too potent night indulgences in wine, Dr. Johnson was accustomed early the following morning—before the family were about,—to slip down stairs in his dressing gown, and doffing his wig, require of the female domestic to pump freely on his over-heated bald head. Mr. Hargraves, apothecary, who afterwards occupied the premises, being aware of the Doctor's infallible restorative after his potations, strongly, in the way of business, prescribed the marvellous liquid to customers who had been too devout at the shrine of Bacchus.

Foote, the comedian, one day, dining at the house, with Johnson and others, finding nothing to his liking, for some time sat in expectation of something better. A neck of mutton being the last thing, he refused it, as he had the others. As the servant was taking it away, however, understanding that there was nothing more, Foote called out to him, "Holloa! John, bring that back again, for I find it's neck or nothing."

Prior to 1794, a low public house, called the Half-Moon, stood out prominently and fronted down the street immediately below Bunker's Hill. It was the general resort of gipsies and beggars, who so continued to throng the house during the Summer months, that on their taking their leave at the termination of the previous Autumn, the owner, Mr. Patching, demolished the old premises and constructed the present building, known as the Brighton Sauce Warehouse, to afford the wandering customers better accommodation upon their return. The Winter of 1793-4 was very severe; to facilitate, then, the progress of the building during the frost, the boulders of which the front is principally composed, were heated at the malt-kiln of the West Street Brewery, the men employed in the work being principally the soldiers of the militia regiments quartered in the West Street Barracks. The new building proved to be a great mistake; as the migratory tribes, on their return in the Summer, thinking that extra charges would be made upon them to assist in defraying the expenses of the new erection, betook themselves to other quarters, and hence, from lack of custom, the license was transferred to a smaller house, the present Half-Moon, at the corner of Boyce's Street, just below which, in Ashby Court, lived an old matchman, a well-known character of the town.

Although "Lucifers" have almost rendered null and void the flint, steel, and tinder-box, yet in villages the brimstone-tipped bunches of flat matches are even now extant, and age picks up a scant existence in vending them from door to door, to dames who pride themselves upon their antiquated notions and doing what their good mothers did before them; their almost sacred observance being always to have hot embers on their social hearth, from which by means of a common match, a light may always be obtained.

In Brighton, the most celebrated of the match-vending craft, was John Standing, familiary known as "Old Rosemary Lane," from the following song which he incessantly uttered while pursuing his daily avocation: —

> There was an old 'oman
> In Rosemary Lane,
> She cuts 'em and dips 'em
> And I do the same.
>
> Come, buy my fine matches
> Come, buy 'em of me,
> They are the best matches
> 'Most ever you see.
>
> For lighting your candle
> Or kindling your fire
> They are the best matches
> As you can desire.

Standing was a native of Hurstperpoint, where for some years he followed the occupation of a bricklayer, and was considered a good workman; but having had the misfortune to fall from a scaffold when about 30 years old, he was disabled from his usual employment, as he by the accident received a severe injury to the spine, which ever after prevented him from assuming an erect posture; and one of his eyes was knocked out, his thumb was broken and reversed, and he was otherwise much mutilated.

At first his business circuit with matches was through the villages under the hill, where he was very well known; but other venders, of the gipsey tribe, combining to drive him off their ground by underselling him, he moved on to Brighton, where his injured bodily condition and the novelty of his ditty obtained him a good trade, and in a very short time many regular customers. In fact, to the outward world his prospects appeared so thriving, that many persons asserted he was, miser-like, accumulating a fortune; for although he never asked alms, his lame, blind, and aged condition excited sympathy amongst strangers, who rather gave to him than purchased of him.

John was married; but his wife, who was also aged, was not without her share of misfortunes. She was the manufacturer of the establishment, and being exposed to hard work and the rigour of a severe winter, the cold so affected her limbs that it was found necessary to amputate one of her legs, and, also remove nearly all the toes from the other foot, from their becoming frostbitten; added to which, she by an accident lost an eye. In January, 1833, Standen was taken suddenly ill in East Street, during one of his morning perambulations, and in a few days, on the 9th of February, he terminated his life, after having for nearly 40 years traversed the town, singing his unvaried song, day by day, through all weathers. His wife survived him but three days, the shock, occasioned by his death, being too severe for her shattered constitution to withstand. They were borne together to their grave in the Old Churchyard, by some kind neighbours, their coffins having been provided by the parish.

The house, the Albany Tavern, at the top of Duke Street, commanding the view of the sea, down West Street, was for many seasons during the abode of George IV. in Brighton, the residence in lodgings, of Johnny Townsend, the noted Bow Street Runner, who was in constant attendance for a long series of years, upon the Royal Personage when he was Prince of Wales and King. West Street at that period was a place of fashionable resort, especially for equestrians, Royal blood daily frequenting it, and often paying a visit to Townsend, with whom they frequently essayed to luncheon, the viands for the occasion being sent up from the Royal Pavilion. Townsend was a shrewd but illiterate man, a staunch politician of the Tory school, kind-hearted, generous, and charitable, an agreeable companion with his equals, a man who commanded the respect of his superiors and his inferiors; but he was a sore terror of refractory boys and girls.

In the house immediately above Duke Street, and directly opposite Cranbourne Street, lived, on his retirement from business, Mr. Beach Roberts, a Brighton celebrity, who, at the commencement of the present century was a tinman, carrying on a respectable and lucrative business upon the premises now occupied by Mr. B. Lewis, silversmith, Ship Street. In his latter days he was termed the "Walking Newspaper," inasmuch as he was acquainted with all—and sometimes more than all, of the news of the day. On the 13th March, 1810, some person, by way of a hoax, inserted in the London papers, the following:—"Died, yesterday, Beach Roberts, Esq.,—a gentleman who had enjoyed a wider sphere of connexion in the County of Sussex than most men, who had been elected to the office of High Constable of this Parish seven different times; for the last twelve years been foreman of the Grand Jury at the Quarter Sessions at Lewes; and who has left one hundred thousand pounds; ten thousand of which are to be applied to charitable purposes within the limits of the town; one thousand towards the support of the Magdalen Hospital, and the remainder to be equally divided between his son and daughter." The hoax became the current topic of the day, and subjected Mr. Roberts to several congratulatory addresses from his friends; as he was at the time about forty-five years of age, in the enjoyment of good health, and of a promising constitution. It may be added that he never served the office of High Constable, and that he had no children.

In the house next above that wherein Mr. Roberts lived, for some little time resided—carrying on the business of a butcher,—James Ings, who on the 23rd of February, 1820, was, on the information of a confederate, apprehended with eight others, in a hay-loft, in Cato Street, Paddington, for being concerned in a plot to destroy the Ministers of the King, while at a cabinet dinner that evening in Grosvenor Square, London, at the residence of the Earl of Harrowby, the President of the Council. The plot is known as the Cato Street Conspiracy, wherein Ings took so conspicuous a part that it was arranged that on their leader, Arthur Thistlewood, presenting a parcel at the door of Lord Harrowby's house, he should head the rest of the conspirators, rush in where the company were assembled, and massacre the whole of them indiscriminately. Just previous to their apprehension Ings prepared himself for the desperate enterprise, by putting a black belt round his waist and another over his shoulders; he also put on two bags like haversacks, and placed a pair of pistols in his belt. Then looking at himself with an air of exultation he exclaimed, uttering an oath, "I'm not complete now; I have forgot my steel;" whereupon he seized a large knife, about twelve inches long, and, brandishing it about, swore he would bring away two heads in his bags, and one of Lord Castlereagh's hands, which he would preserve in brine, as it might be thought a good deal of hereafter. The whole of the conspirators were found guilty of High Treason, and on the morning of the first of May, Thistlewood, Ings, and three others were hanged and decapitated at Newgate; the rest of the traitors were transported.

The executioner of these misguided men was James Botting, a native of Brighton, and son of Jemmy Botting, the possessor of some small property at the back of West Field Lodge, immediately to the west of the bottom of Cannon Place, and known as Botting's Rookery, from its being the resort of tramps of the lowest order, Botting also, on the 30th of November, 1824, at Newgate, carried out the last penalty of the law upon Henry Fauntleroy, the banker, who formerly had his residence at the west end of Codrington Place, Western Road, and was found guilty of uttering a forged deed with intent to defraud Frances Young of £5,000 Stock, and a power of attorney to defraud the firm of Marsh, Stacey, Fauntleroy, and Graham, Bankers, Berner's Street, London, of which house he was the acting partner.

For several years previous to his decease, which took place at Brighton, October 1st, 1837, Botting, in consequence of paralysis, retired from his situation as public hangman, the latter days of his existence being eked out by a pension of five shillings a week, granted by the Court of Aldermen of the City of London, for whom, in the course of his duties, he had deprived 175 "parties" —as he termed them—of their lives; as during his career executions at Newgate were very common, the offences for which life was forfeited being so numerous that in one week thirteen persons, namely, eight on Wednesday, November 23rd, and five on the Tuesday following, November 29th, 1821, suffered, none of the crimes for which they were executed—thanks to the enlightenment of our legislators,—now exacting as a penalty the life of a fellow creature. Botting, in his latter days, was a well known character about Brighton, the streets of which he was accustomed to traverse by means of a chair, which he alternately used as a species of crutch, and as a seat, but he always appeared isolated from the world, as no grade of society seemed ambitious of the acquaintance of Jack Ketch.

The most commodious and commanding family mansions of the Old Town are in West Street, wherein have resided, during the past forty years, several of the magistrates and the clergy, and many members of the medical profession of Brighton. At the present time several of the houses are occupied by opulent families: and the lanes and courts which formerly on its west side detracted from the general respectability of the street, having been demolished, the property thereabouts has become considerably enhanced in value, and is much sought after.

Chapter XXIX.

THE PUBLIC INSTITUTIONS, CHARITIES, AND ENDOWMENTS.

It is the pride of the inhabitants that no town in the kingdom possesses so many Public Institutions for the general well-being of the community, as Brighton.

Foremost amongst these, though a National Institution and but co-equal with similar other branches to complete its general working throughout the kingdom, is the Post Office, which, in all probability, originally formed a part of the General Postal systems as established in 1657 and 1660.' We have no authority as to the primitive mode of conveyance of letters, but doubtless it was on horseback, and afterwards by mail cart, as "A Description of Brighthelmston"* mentions:—"During Summer the post sets out from Brighthelmston for London every morning (excepting Saturday) at nine o'clock; and arrives there every evening (excepting Monday) about seven. In the Winter season the post goes out at eleven o'clock at night on Mondays, Tuesdays, Thursdays, and Saturdays; and returns from London about eight on Thursday and Saturday mornings." The Post Office was then at Widgett's, afterwards Crawford's, and then Fisher's Library, Old Steine, the present premises of Mr. Shaw, confectioner, from whence, upon the throwing of the Promenade Grove into the Royal Domain, in 1803, it was removed to premises constructed in the Grove gateway at the top of Prince's Place, when Mr. J. Redifer was appointed the Post Master. During the time that Crawford was Post Master, his son, one of the present Members of Parliament for the city of London, was the only letter-carrier in Brighton. Mail coaches between London and Brighton were not put on the road till 1807. On the 22nd September, 1822, the Post Office was removed to 67, East Street, where it continued till June, 1827, when the premises, 149, North Street, were appropriated for the business. From thence, on the 23rd of September, 1831, it was removed to the house immediately south of the Unitarian Chapel, New Road, Mr Ferguson being the Post Master.

The uniform charge for letters of one penny per half ounce,—introduced in 1840, by Mr. Rowland Hill,—and afterwards the abolition of the newspaper duty, when the postage of the public journals, and subsequently and now all printed works passing at the rate of one penny for four ounces, rendering the premises in the New Road inadequate to the increase of business, the Post Office,

* London: Printed for Fielding and Walker, Paternoster Row; E. Widgett, Brighthelmston; and W. Lee, Printer, Lewes, 1779.

on the 26th of March, 1849, was removed to the present site, opposite Trinity Chapel, in Ship Street. The premises there were very narrow and contracted, till August, 1858, when the present commodious structure was erected. Mr. Charles Whiting, the present Post Master, entered upon his duties in October, 1850. Previous to the postage reduction, letters in the out districts of Brighton were collected every evening by bellmen, who, for one penny, conveyed letters to the General Office. Branch offices superseded the bellmen, or collectors; and now, pillar-boxes, placed with great discretion in all parts of the town, have rendered the branch offices in some localities wholly unnecessary. The first pillar letter-box in the kingdom was erected at the corner of Fleet Street and Farringdon Street, London, in March, 1855. The Post Office Savings Bank opened at Brighton on the 10th of March, 1862.

The first Bank in Brighton—the Old Bank,—immediately opposite the premises subsequently and now the Union Bank, was established in 1787, under the firm, Messrs. Shergold, Michell, Rice, and Mills. It withstood the panic of 1825; but a few years after transferred its declining business. The New Bank was the next established, the firm being Messrs. Wigney, Rickman, Stanford, and Vallance. Wigney, who was also a brewer, happening one day to meet the builder of the sea wall of the Junction Road, Mr Bennett, upon whom Dame Fortune rather frowned than smiled, said, "Why, Bennett, surely, if I remember right, you also, were once a brewer?" "Yes," said Bennett, "but I made a sad mistake, Wigney; I turned at the same time a builder instead of, as you did, a banker; thus I have always continued a needy man, from not having other people's money to speculate with." The rejoinder was very significant, as the sequel proved. The Bank was at first in Steine Lane, with a second public entrance by the side way to the Pavilion Shades; from whence, in 1819, it was transferred to the apartments, now the coffee room of the Pavilion Hotel, Mr. Edmund Savage, who had obtained the license in 1816, having arranged with the bankers that they should rebuild the house in the Castle Square front, so that they might have the Bank on the ground-floor of the new building, and give up the rooms in Steine Lane, in exchange. The room where the banking business had been transacted, Mr. Savage then appropriated to a smoking-room, and converted the clerks' room into a Gin-shop. But as Mrs. Fitzherbert was then living immediately opposite, in Steine Lane, he was fearful of offending her by placing any writing on the house; the thought, however, struck him, that, inasmuch as the height of Mrs Fitzherbert's house, to the south of him, prevented the *sun* from *shining* upon his house, he would adopt the word "Shades," and place it over the door, where had before been written "Bank,' that being the only word used to publish the place. An immense trade was soon carried on in that little room, where three young men found full employment in serving at the counter, and two as porters were engaged besides. The extensive trade thus obtained soon induced other publicans to adopt the word "Shades" to their bars; and at the present time there is scarcely a public-house in the kingdom but uses the term. The only place previously where the word "Shades" was adopted was at a Vault near Old London Bridge, where nothing was sold but wine measured from the wood.

When known as Wigney's Bank, from the other partners having withdrawn from the firm, the banking business was carried on at the premises which occupied the western entrance of the Avenue in East Street. Mr. Isaac Newton Wigney, M.P., who was then sole proprietor, to the dismay and ruin of many of the inhabitants, stopped payment on the 4th of March, 1842. The chief clerk of the New Bank, as it was originally constituted, was Mr. Thomas West, who, on the 1st of August, 1805, with Messrs. Browne, Hall, and Lashmar, founded the Union Bank, their neighbour, Mr. Daniel Constable, being the first person to open an account with them; Messrs. Hall, Lloyd, Bevan, and West constitute the present firm. Mr. Lashmar left the Union Bank, and, in conjunction with Mr. Mugridge, opened the Sussex Bank, in St. James's Street, which closed its doors on the pressure of the panic of 1825.

The panic was also the death-blow to the County Bank, at the south-east corner of Castle Square, which a few years previous had been opened by Messrs. Tamplin, Creasy, and Gregory, the latter, —who was the manager of the concern,—being the noted Barnard Gregory, who alternately was a banker's clerk—at Masterman's,

London, and Wigney's, Brighton,—wine merchant, chemist and druggist, editor of the *Brighton Gazette*, chapel building speculator, theatrical performer, manager of the Sussex and Brighthelmston Fire Insurance Company, and finally, as a public man, proprietor and editor of an infamous London newspaper, the *Satirist*, for a frightful calumny published in which, on the ex-Duke of Brunswick, he was incarcerated one year in Newgate. Later in a life which has but recently terminated, he speculated on a second wife, an elderly maiden lady, the daughter of Mr. Thompson, a wealthy public-house broker, of the Priory, Hampstead. The circumstance of his marriage with this poor lady is an illustration of the character of the man. He was passing the evening with some friends, when the facility of getting a wife became the topic of conversation. Gregory spoke with his usual confidence: he could get a wife whenever he pleased—at a day's notice. Being rallied on his vanity, he offered to lay a wager that he would be married, and to a woman of reputation, before the next night. The wager was accepted—the stakes deposited. Gregory was the winner. Before the next day was over he had proposed, was accepted, had a wife, and, in compliance with the conditions of the wager, had brought her to Brighton from London, where the marriage was solemnised, before the close of the twenty-four hours.

The London and County Bank, Pavilion Buildings, a branch of the London and County Joint-Stock Banking Company, Lombard Street, London, first opened in Brighton, at the south-east corner of Prince's Place, in 1838. It removed to the present premises in 1853. Mr. John Geddes Cockburn is the Manager.

The Brighton Savings' Bank was established in Duke Street, at the top of Middle Street, in 1817, with Mr. George Sawyer as Actuary. His successor, Richard Buckoll, became a defaulter, and absconded. Mr. William Hatton is the present Actuary, and the business is carried on in the New Road, upon premises erected by Mr. John Fabian, to the plan of Mr. Baxter, architect, on the site of the Royal Pavilion ice-well. Upon its removal from Duke Street, the Bank occupied a portion of the property on the east side of Prince's Place.

No other Banks are now in existence in Brighton. The Unity

Joint-Stock Mutual Banking Association, about four years since, had a branch of their establishment at the north-east corner of North Street, but its business was so limited that it soon closed its doors. The National Savings' Bank Association (limited), 1, Pavilion Buildings, had for a time a puny existence, and then, on becoming amalgamated with a like institution, was lost to public notice. The Bank of Deposit,—branches of which were in all parts of the kingdom, and the Parent Office in Pall Mall, London,—on premises next to the London and County Bank, held a position in public confidence for some years; but in 1861, in consequence of Peter Morrison, the Manager, becoming a defaulter and a bankrupt, and eventually absconding, many hundreds of depositors were irretrievably ruined. The District Savings' Bank, contiguous to the Odd Fellows' Hall, Queen's Road, after enjoying an unenviable notoriety, and involving many small capitalists in pecuniary difficulties, in 1861 abruptly closed. Bill discounters and usurious money-lenders abound in the town, their business being principally amongst those whose bills and promissory notes are not recognised by the regular bankers, who abstain from transactions that afford a probability of proceedings in the County Court; hence exorbitant bonuses and interest—which no fair trading can meet—are exacted, and the non-fulfilment of payment becomes the precursor of ruin.

The Fourth Estate of the Kingdom, the Press, is, for independence of principles, well represented in Brighton. The oldest locally established of this important institution is the *Brighton Herald*, first published in September, 1806, the proprietors being Mr. Matthew Phillips and Mr. H. R. Attree, at 9, Middle Street, under the editorship of Mr. Robert Sicklemore. Its price was seven pence, and such was the size of the sheet—upon each of which there was a stamp of three pence half-penny, besides a duty of three shillings and six pence upon every advertisement,—that it did not contain more than a quarter the matter now sold for two pence. From Middle Street the publishing office was removed to 13, North Street, from whence, after between two and three years, it was removed to premises on the site now occupied by 114, in the same street, immediately opposite the North Street Brewery. Since March 25th, 1810, the *Brighton Herald* has been printed and published in Prince's Place, by Mr. William Fleet, who, about twenty years since was joined by his son, Mr. Charles Fleet.

The first number of the *Brighton Gazette* was printed and published on premises beneath Donaldson's Library, Old Steine, on the 22nd of February, 1821, by Mr. Edward Hill Creasy. In November of the same year the business was removed to the premises, 168, North Street, where it has ever since continued to be published. On January 22nd, 1824, Mr. John Baker became part proprietor, and on the 26th of February, 1835, it was first printed in Church Street, at the office adjoining the National Schools. The last publication of the *Brighton Gazette* with the name of Mr. Creasy attached thereto, was on the 18th of July, 1844, only a few months prior to his decease. On the 28th of December, 1848, the paper first bore the name of the present publisher, Mr. Charles Curtis, and in the Autumn of 1852, the printing office was removed to the Pavilion Dormitories. In professed opposition to the *Brighton Gazette*, the *Brighton Chronicle* was published on Wednesday, the 6th of June, 1821, at 3, Prince's place, by Mr. Cummins; its career, however, was very short.

The *Brighton Guardian* made its first appearance under the management and editorship of Mr. Levi Emanuel Cohen, on the 31st of January, 1827. It was enlarged on the 30th of November, 1830, and, on the 1st of January, 1851, it appeared as an eight page—small size—publication. In its present size it was first published on the 3rd of October, 1853. From the day of its first issue to the present time, the printing and publication have taken place on the same premises, 34, North Street. For some years prior to the decease of Mr. Cohen, which took place on the 17th of November, 1860, the *Brighton Guardian* was his sole property. His brother, Mr. Nathan Cohen, is the present proprietor. Strong party feeling, some few years since, started the *Brighton Patriot*, in opposition to the *Guardian*; but its existence was very ephemeral.

The *Brighton Examiner*, which since its first issue, January 18th, 1853, has continued the property of Mr. J. F. Eyles, was originally published at 33, Western Road; from whence it was removed to its present printing and publishing office, in North Street, opposite the Queen's Road.

Consequent upon the abolition of the newspaper duty, the *Brighton Observer*—the original of the local cheap press,—made its appearance at 54, West Street, on the 28th of November, 1856. It was first enlarged on the 27th of November, 1857. On the 28th of December, 1858, the printing and publication of the *Brighton Observer*, the property of Mr. Ebenezer Lewis, took place at 16, King Street, where, on the 30th of September, 1859, it was again enlarged; and on the 25th of July, 1862, the office was removed to the premises where it is at present printed and published, 53a, North Street, the building which was originally the first Theatre in Brighton, and, then, in 1790, the printing-office of Messrs. William and Arthur Lee.

The only other local newspaper now in existence is the *Brighton Times*, printed and published by Mr. William Pearce, Bartholomews; established the 28th of April, 1860. From time to time, since the repeal of the stamp duty, speculators have started the *Sussex Mercury*, *Brighton Chronicle*, &c., but only as errors consequent upon the lack of experience, and upon the parade of great professions.

The Alms-Houses, those termed the Percy Alms-Houses, six in number, immediately north of Hanover Crescent, and bearing along their façade "These Alms-Houses were erected and endowed at the request of the late Philadelphia and Dorothy Percy, 1796," were built by Mrs. Mary Marriott, for the reception of a similar number of poor widows, of the Church of England, who have received no parochial relief, agreeably to the testamentary instructions of Mrs. Philadelphia and Mrs. Dorothy Percy, —daughters of the Duke of Northumberland,—who endowed them with the sum of £48 per annum, which amount was doubled upon the demise of Mrs. Mary Marriott. Two gowns and a bonnet are also allowed to each widow every year, and a Duffield cloak once in three years. By a bequest of Mr. James Charles Michell, in 1833, the sum of £1 16s. is added to the endowment; and there is also £300 invested by Mr. Skinner, for repairs of vaults, and the surplus in coals. Attached to the Percy Alms-Houses are other similar dwellings, the two to the north and three nearest the south having been erected by Mr. John Fabian, for Miss Wagner, the sister of our much respected Vicar, conjointly with whom was built that which bears on its face the following inscription: "1861. In pious remembrance of the late Marquis of Bristol. M. A. W.—H. M. W." pleasingly expressive of the purport of its erection.

In unison with this grateful memento, the annexed address of condolence was presented to the present Marquis :—

The Rev. the Vicar of Brighton, to the Marquis of Bristol,

Brighton Vicarage, February 24, 1859.

My dear Lord,

Enclosed is an address of condolence on the part of the Brighton Clergy. I make myself responsible for the signature of Mr. Henry Elliott, now on the Continent, because I know his deep feeling of affectionate gratitude to your venerated Father, from whom he, like myself, received countless benefits.

I have the honour to remain, my dear Lord,

Your Lordship's ever faithful servant,

H. M. WAGNER.

TO THE MARQUIS OF BRISTOL,

ADDRESS OF CONDOLENCE ON THE PART OF THE CLERGY OF BRIGHTON.

Through a long period of time we have been connected with your Father by so many holy and endearing associations, that we hope you will allow us the privilege of a fellowship with you even in the deep affliction which it has pleased God now to send upon you. We know that sympathy belongs indeed to One, and we earnestly pray that He, who only can, will make all grace and comfort abound to your own heart, and to the hearts of all your family, under your present bereavement.

But while we thus feel how little worth is all human consolation in our hours of deepest sorrow, we nevertheless trust that it may not be unacceptable to you at this time to receive, as certainly it is most pleasant to us to render, the united tribute of our respectful gratitude to the memory of your venerated father. Associated as he was with us for so many years as a parishioner, friend, and a benefactor, there are few who can appreciate, as we can, the extent and the self-forgetfulness and the humility of his singular benevolence.

It would be very difficult for us to give adequate expression to our sense of the devotedness with which he used his high station, his property, and his influence for the promotion of those holiest interests of religion and charity, of which we are in some measure the guardians and representatives in this Parish. There are very few of us who have not personally experienced, in some good word or work, the great kindliness of your father's character. To the poor, his whole life copied Him who "went about doing good." Very many are there of the humblest and most indigent, who would be the first to testify that they ever found in the Marquis of Bristol a brother's love. While the monuments of his munificence which stand forth amongst us, the record to many generations of his pious care for the souls, and bodies of his fellow men, are, we believe, well nigh unparalleled in any parish, the Sussex County Hospital, with its commodious

Chapel, the Church of St. Mark, our Parish Church in its restored beauty, and our two Cemeteries, with many other noble or sacred Institutions scarcely less than these,—all associated with his name,—bear witness, not only to his vast beneficence, but to the wisdom also with which he selected the channels in which that beneficence should flow. And over all he threw such a suavity of manner and beautiful simplicity, that it was only when the action had passed that we woke up to the discovery of its greatness, which the grace of his presence had forbidden us to see.

Accept, then, at our hands the assurance of the sorrowing affection, not of ourselves alone, but of a whole parish, which feels itself, like you, bereaved; and permit us to add the prayer, that your father's God may pour upon you, and upon your children, and upon your children's children, the rich inheritance of that father's spirit of universal love.

H. M. Wagner, Vicar of Brighton.
Thomas Cooke, Perpetual Curate of St. Peter's.
C. E. Douglass, Curate of Brighton.
John Ellerton, Curate of Brighton.
W. Mitchell, Curate of Brighton.
James Vaughan, Perpetual Curate of Christ Church.
Thomas Trocke, Perpetual Curate of the Chapel Royal.
C. D. Maitland, Perpetual Curate of St. James's.
H. V. Elliott, Perpetual Curate of St. Mary's.
Edward B. Elliott, Perpetual Curate of St. Mark's.
Spencer R. Drummond, Perpetual Curate of St. John the Evangelist.
Joseph Hurlock, Chaplain of the Sussex County Hospital.
A. D. Wagner, Perpetual Curate of St. Paul's Church.
J. H. North, Perpetual Curate of St. George's.
Randolph Payne, Assistant Curate of St. Paul's Church.
Charles Beanlands, Assistant Curate of St. Paul's Church.
Thomas Scott, Assistant Curate of All Souls' Church.
J. Chalmers, Perpetual Curate of St. Stephen's.
H. H. Wyatt, Perpetual Curate of Trinity Chapel.
Frederic A. Stapley, Assistant Curate of St. John the Evangelist.
Alexander Poole, St. Mark's Church.
Henry G. Cutler, Assistant Curate of Christ Church.
Thomas Coombe, Perpetual Curate of All Saints'.
W. Fleming, Assistant Curate of All Souls'.
John Allen, Chaplain Brighton Workhouse.
R. S. Smith, Perpetual Curate of All Souls' Church.

What may be very appropriately termed the Wagner Alms-Houses—which are without endowment,—are for the benefit of unmarried women,—spinsters,—above the age of fifty, and who possess, or are ensured the yearly income of £15 at the least.

Howell's Alms-Houses, which are not yet endowed, are situated in an open space of ground approached by iron gates on the west side of George Street. They are eight in number, and in the centre of the block of buildings, surmounted by a dial, is the following inscription :—

HOWELL'S ALMS HOUSES,

Erected 1859.

Supported by voluntary Contributions, for the reception of reduced Inhabitants of Brighton and Hove, under the regulation of a Committee of Management.

The inmates of these houses are elected by the donors and subscribers, and all persons not under 60 years of age, who have resided in Brighton or Hove at least ten years previous to the time of election, and have not received parochial relief during such period, are eligible.

These were built by Charles Howell, Esq., Dial House, Hove, upon ground valued at £1,000. It was the original intention of this philanthropic gentleman to have bequeathed the ground and the money for the erection of the houses, by will; but with the very laudable desire of seeing his benevolent intention realized during his life time, Mr. Howell preferred perfecting his work himself, and he has vested the property in the following Trustees:—Henry Michell Wagner, Vicar of Brighton; Charles Wellington Howell, Robert Upperton, jun., John Pankhurst, and Piercy George Pankhurst. He has also conveyed to the above named trustees two houses in George Street, the rents of which, about £26 a-year, are charged, first with the repairs of the Alms-Houses, and then for the general purposes of the Charity.

The original plan provides for five more houses; for the erection of which and the endowment of the whole thirteen the co-operation of the public is solicited. May the anxious wish of Mr. Howell that the whole of the buildings be completed and permanently endowed, before it pleases the Almighty to remove him from this sphere of his benevolent acts, be speedily realised.

For mutual benevolence no institution has a firmer basis than the Manchester Unity, I.O.O.F., whose Hall for the Brighton district, forms a prominent feature of the Queen's Road, where the first stone of the building was laid on the 27th of June, 1853, by Mr. Tamplin, the then High Constable of Brighton. Mr. John Fabian was the builder of the edifice, upon a piece of ground which was purchased for £500 of the Rev. James Edwards. The building proceeded without interruption until the 27th of August, when a Bill in Chancery, to restrain the erection, was filed by Mr. Alderman Patching, who possessed property and resided immediately opposite the Hall. The building was thus delayed; but, on the 4th of November, an appearance was put in on behalf of the Building Committee, when the case, Patching *v.* Dubbins, came on for hearing before Vice Chancellor Sir Page Wood. The plaintiff's plea was, that in the covenant under which he bought the ground upon which his premises stood, it was stipulated that no building, except monuments or headstones, should be erected on the plot of land opposite, which was an unburied-in portion of the Hanover Burial Ground. Defendant's counsel argued the fact that plaintiff had permitted the erection of the Dispensary on a portion of the same ground, and had allowed two months to expire since the building was commenced before he filed his injunction; and further, that the building was not opposite, but a foot or two to the north of being opposite. The case was argued at length, and the Vice Chancellor gave a verdict for defendant, with costs.

The building then proceeded; was formally opened on the 26th of June, 1854; and its opening was shortly after celebrated with a public banquet, at which the Mayor of Brighton, Lieut.-Colonel Fawcett, presided. The total cost of the ground, building, fittings, furniture, &c., was £3,000. Four Lodges of the Order hold their meetings weekly in the Hall, and endeavours are being made to establish Schools upon the premises for the education, at a reasonable cost, of the children and orphans of members. Five other Lodges meet in various parts of Brighton and Hove. The first Lodge, 118, one of the oldest belonging to the Unity, was established in Brighton, in 1822. The Widows and Orphans' Fund, in connexion with the District, has been in existence twenty-one years, having been established in 1841, and its members, with very few exceptions, include the whole of the members in the Brighton District. It has an accumulated capital of over £6,000, chiefly invested in debentures on the rates of the town.

Lodges of the Brighton, London, and Nottingham Unities of Odd Fellows, are held in various parts of the Borough, as are also Lodges and Courts of the several Orders of Druids and Foresters.

The Free and Accepted Masons hold the Royal Clarence Lodge, No. 394; the Royal Brunswick Lodge, 1,034; the Lennox Chapter Lodge, No. 338; and the Royal Sussex Chapter Lodge, No. 1,034, at the Old Ship Hotel, where also the Lodge of Instruction is held.

The Brighthelmston Dispensary, now known as the Brighton and Hove Dispensary, from a branch being established in the latter parish, was founded under the patronage of the Prince of Wales, November 27th, 1809. The Institution was opened on January 1st, 1810, on premises in Nile Street, contiguous to the Old Vicarage, or, as it was then called, the Parsonage House. In July 1811, it was removed to North Street, at the corner of Salmon Court, opposite Ship Street, where in November, 1812, was added the Sussex General Infirmary. Early in 1819, the joint establishments were removed into Middle Street, the premises now occupied by the Young Men's Christian Association, the purchase of which property was completed the following year. The present noble building of the Institution,—which is entirely supported by voluntary contributions,—was built by Messrs. Cheesman,—Mr. Herbert Williams, architect,—and was completed and occupied in 1849, a committee of gentlemen, amongst whom Mr. Gavin E. Pocock, surgeon, was most zealous, having with untiring energy raised the means of entirely freeing the edifice from any debt.

At a meeting of the Governors and Subscribers of the Dispensary, at the Old Ship Tavern, on the 10th of February, 1813, it having been announced that the Right Honourable the Earl of Egremont, the Vice-President, had offered to contribute £1,000 towards the erection of a County Hospital, the building of that Institution for the reception of sixty patients was determined upon, and contributions from other noblemen and gentlemen to the extent of another £1,000 were at once made. It was not, however, till the 11th of December, 1824, that the erection of the building was fully determined upon; and then the subscription of the noble Earl amounted to £2,000—afterwards increased to £3,000,—and that of Thomas Read Kemp, Esq., £1,000 and the ground whereon the building stands. The foundation stone of the main building was laid on the 16th of March, 1826, by the Earl of Egremont, Sir Charles Barry being the architect. The Adelaide wing, to the east, Mr. Herbert

Williams, architect, and the Victoria wing to the west, Mr. William Hallett, architect, have since been added. The Institution is supported by legacies, benefactions, dividends of stocks, and general voluntary contributions.

The Sussex and Brighton Infirmary for Diseases of the Eye was formed at a public meeting of the inhabitants of Brighton and the vicinity, held at the Bedford Hotel, August 27th, 1832, Dr. Jenks being the physician, and Mr. (now Dr.) Pickford and Mr. Seabrook, the surgeons. On the 12th of January, 1837, a resolution was passed by the Governors of the Institution that severe cases and those for operation should have admission into the house, then in Boyce's Street.

The first stone of the present building, in the Queen's Road, was laid on the 29th of June, 1846, by the Right Reverend Father in God, Ashurst Turner, Lord Bishop of Chichester, from a design after the temple of Theseus, from plans and specifications prepared by Mr. Thomas Cooper, architect, the builders being Messrs. Wisden and Anscombe. The cost of the site was £480, and of the structure £1,273 7s., and the business of the Institution was transferred from Boyce's Street to the new building on the 10th of November, 1846. At the annual meeting of the Governors, on the 14th of January, 1847, resolutions were passed:—

That the Silver Trowel, with which was laid, 29th June, 1846, by the Lord Bishop of the Diocese, the first stone of the building, erected for the purposes of the Charity, be presented to

JAMES H. PICKFORD. Esq., M.D., M.R.I.A.

In acknowledgment of his successful efforts as the original promoter of the Charity, of his unceasing exertions for the general interests of the Institution, and in testimony of his talent and ability as a Medical Officer.

That the foregoing resolution be engraved on the trowel.

Dr. Pickford was, on the resignation of Dr. Jenks, appointed physician, April 4th, 1853, and Mr. George Lowdell was then elected surgeon. Upon the resignation of Dr. Pickford and Mr. Seabrook, January 27th, 1859, the former was elected a Vice-President, and the latter was appointed Consulting-Surgeon to the Institution, which is supported by voluntary contributions.

The Blind Asylum at Brighton had its origin in 1839, when Mr. Moon the eminent teacher and printer for the Blind, becoming deprived of his sight, devoted his attention to the learning of embossed reading; and such was his progress that he soon, with the benevolent assistance of a lady, advanced sufficiently to assist others in learning also, first at their own homes, and then in a small class at his residence. At length, the number becoming large, it was considered advisable to establish a daily public school for the Blind in Brighton; and the use of a portion of St. James's Sunday School-room was obtained for that purpose. This School, in which were also a few Deaf and Dumb children, was opened on the 22nd of October, 1839. In the following Summer, a Committee of Ladies made an effort to raise the means for opening an Asylum to receive as many of the Blind and Deaf and Dumb of the number thus brought together, as were desirous of partaking of the benefits which such an Institution might afford. In the Summer of 1841, it was deemed expedient to separate the Blind from the Deaf and Dumb, which latter were retained in the Institution, but the Blind pupils were re-formed into a daily school.

In 1842, the scholars were assembled for instruction in a class-room of the Central National School; and eventually the Rev. H. M. Wagner—the Vicar,—raised sufficient funds to build premises contiguous, in Jubilee Street, for the reception of twelve pupils, who were admitted to the Asylum, as it was then termed, early in January, 1846. Year by year the number of pupils increased, till at length, the accommodation on the premises being wholly inadequate to the demand, the Rev. H. V. Elliott, in the Summer of 1860, kindly gave the present site near the County Hospital, for the erection of the New Asylum, to the building fund of which the Rev. G. Oldham generously contributed the munificent donation of £2,000, while the proceeds of a Bazaar amounted to £1,000 more. The opening ceremony took place on Tuesday, 22nd October, 1861.

Mr. G. Somers Clarke is the architect of the structure, which is Italian Gothic, of Venetian character, and is built entirely of brickwork with stone dressings. The front is very fine. It has an elevation of four stories, and by a somewhat liberal use of stonework an almost palatial aspect has been imparted. The entrance is double, and in a finely sculptured medallion over the door is an Angel of Mercy teaching the Blind. The apex of the doorway arch is continued into a bracket whereon is placed a stone group of Charity Relieving the Blind. In the adjacent carving are introduced the emblems of Faith, Hope, and Charity—the two latter being personified in the anchor and the pelican feeding its young from its own body. The different stories are shown by graceful mouldings on which rest the stonework of the windows. Those belonging to the two middle stories are very massive, the elegant proportioning of the columns dividing the four lights being especially noticeable. The harmony of the whole work is extremely good.

Mr. Moon, who, for his invention of a plan for teaching the blind to read, has obtained a justly deserved world-wide fame, continues his indefatigable exertions to ameliorate the condition of his fellow-sufferers. Not only has he been enabled to emboss the whole of the Bible in the English language, but portions of it also in fifty more; and he is daily receiving testimony from various parts of the world of the high appreciation of his system, and of the rich consolations of many of the blind who are thus enabled to read the Word of God for themselves.

The Brighton Institution for the Deaf and Dumb,—established in 1840,—first located at 12, Egremont Place, in 1842, and from thence, in 1848, it was removed to the present building, in the Eastern Road, Messrs. Cheesman and Son being the architects and builders. The new wing was added in 1854, Messrs. Wisden and Anscombe being the builders.

Like the Blind Asylum, this Institution is supported by voluntary contributions. It has received several small benefactions, amongst them £300 as a tribute of respect to the memory of the late Mr. George Gainsford, by his son and daughter, "in dutiful remembrance of their father." To perpetuate also, the memory of Miss Mohun, who was deeply attached to the Institution, and unwearily devoted her useful life aud benevolent exertions in its behalf, the "Hester Mohun Fund" has been commenced expressly to aid in educating or apprenticing a few poor deaf and dumb children.

The Asylum for Poor Female Orphans, instituted in 1822, and established in the Western Road, near the corner of Crown Street, for some years occupied the garden whereon now stands the north side of Glo'ster Street. It was removed to its present situation in the Eastern Road,—where so many monuments to Benevolence are reared,—in 1853. The first stone of the building was laid on the 16th of June. The design of the Asylum is to save innocent and unprotected Female Orphans from the too frequent misery attendant on idleness and poverty, to instruct them in such branches of household employment and needlework as may qualify them to become useful servants, while care is taken that their instruction and employment shall be such as it is hoped may render them honest and industrious members of Society.

The Provident and Self-Supporting Dispensary was established at 32, Middle Street, in 1837. Its object is to promote a feeling of laudable independence among the working classes, that they may help themselves, and so be prevented from seeking charitable assistance from others; to encourage habits of provident frugality; and to enable those to obtain immediate relief who are not able to pay for it in the usual way, but are not in circumstances so indigent as to justify an application to the gratuitous Dispensary.

The Brighton and Hove Lying-in-Institution and Dispensary established in High Street, in 1831, has appropriate premises at 76, West Street, and by the means of subscriptions and donations affords the requisite assistance and comfort to poor women at a time when the evils of poverty are most keenly felt.

The Dollar Society, instituted in November, 1813, is so called from every annual subscription to that amount entitling the subscriber to recommend one person yearly to become a partaker of the fund, such recipient not to be a person deriving assistance from parochial resources. The Society extends its kindness to the chamber of sickness and the abode of unforeseen calamity, and particularly to deserving persons bending beneath the pressure of years.

The Maternal Society, formed 28th July, 1813, provides child-bed linen and other suitable articles of clothing, with nourishment for poor lying-in married women, and such attentions and comforts as their condition may require.

The Brighton Auxiliary Town Missionary and Scripture Readers' Society meet weekly at 25, Middle Street, with the view to extend the knowledge of the Gospel amongst the poor of the town, without regard to denominational distinctions.

The Society for Promoting Christian Knowledge is a district Committee for the Deanery of Lewes, and was established in 1815, under the sanction of the Bishop of the Diocese, to promote the diffusion of the Scriptures and Religious Tracts amongst the lower orders of society. The parent Society, in London, was formed by members of the Church of England, in 1669.

The Provident and District Society, established in 1824, under most admirable arrangements, gives direct charitable assistance; encourages the poor to make deposits, which are returned to them in winter in useful articles, with the amount increased by a premium; and prevents mendicity by having an office, 108, Church street, where beggars may be referred and have their cases examined into. The Society has the town divided into districts, for the purpose of visiting and inquiring into cases of distress. The Benevolent Loan Fund, at the same office, grants pecuniary assistance to those who, by misfortune, require temporary aid; re-payments being arranged by easy instalments, and not subjecting the borrowers to the usury of trading money-lenders.

The Brighton and Sussex Mutual Provident Society, Prince Albert Street, commenced its operations in January, 1847. Its rules and tables provide weekly allowances and medical aid in sickness; sums at death; endowments; and immediate and deferred annuities; it is the only local institution of the kind.

Bowen, in his "Complete System of Geography,"* says, "There are two considerable charity schools here, one for 50 boys, who are taught arithmetic and navigation, and 20 girls, who are put out to apprenticeship or services." These were termed Free Schools, and that for boys was founded within the precincts of the Bartholomews, in 1725, by the Rev. Anthony Springett, who, in addition to an annual subscription of 8s., in the year 1740 gave the further sum of £25 per annum, for the education of twenty poor boys belonging to the parish. In 1735, Mr. George Beach left the interest of £59 1s. 6d., and in 1781, the Right Honourable the

* Two volumes, folio, London, 1747.

Countess of Gower gave the interest of £234 12s. to the same charity. The money, however, having been laid out in the short annuities, the funds were not available to the intentions of the founder, the school-house, therefore, and a small parcel of land adjoining, were sold for £400, and in February, 1818, another school, established upon its foundation, in the Lanes immediately north of Black Lion Street, was opened, under the denomination "National School for Boys," the premises being sufficiently commodious to contain 300 youths, for education in reading, writing, and arithmetic, and in the principles of the Established Church.

Another Free School was founded by Mr. William Grimmett, for twenty boys, the children of parishioners, to be clothed, and instructed in reading, writing, arithmetic, merchants' accounts, navigation, and the principles of the Established Church of England. Mr. Grimmett had been instructed in the Free School founded by Mr. Springett; and having afterwards been bred to the sea, he realized by his industry above £10,000, nearly £2,000 of which—now accumulated to £2,330 11s. 6d., producing an income of £69 18s. 4d.,—he bequeathed for the endowment of his School. Some informality in his Will gave his heirs-at-law an opportunity of contesting the legality of the bequest; but his widow generously maintained against them a suit in Chancery, and the validity of the Will was confirmed. But from the nature of the bequest, and the disagreement that afterwards arose amongst the appointed Trustees, the school was not established before 1769. It is now managed according to the directions of the devisor, by sixteen Trustees, namely, the Vicar and three Churchwardens of the Parish, and twelve other inhabitants of the town, chosen at a Vestry meeting, among whom every vacancy by death, resignation, or removal from the town, is in like manner to be always supplied by public election of the majority of the parishioners, convened at a Vestry meeting the 1st day of May annually; and every vacancy in the School is supplied by the election of the Trustees, or the greater part of them, by ballot, at a public Vestry, of which notice shall be given on a Sunday at the Parish Church, ten days at least before such meeting; no boy to be received into the school under the age of eight, nor permitted to remain there after the age of fifteen years. Forty boys are now educated on this foundation, at the National School, in which it is merged.

The most remarkable man in connexion with the Free School, as founded by Mr. Springett, was Mr. John Grover, under whose care for instruction the inhabitants obtained signal benefit. He was born of poor parents in Brighton, about the year 1648, and passed his infancy and early youth in the lowest drudgeries of a country life, and it was while tending a flock on the hills adjoining the town that his youthful mind was often employed in exploring the power and relations of numbers; and when he was of sufficient strength for the more laborious employments of agriculture, the moments of his leisure were still dedicated to study. On his spade and shovel, with a lump of chalk, he worked his problems, and calculated the motions of the tides and stars. The early acquirements of this self-taught philosopher soon attracted public wonder and investigation; indeed, his intellectual powers and industry could not pass without some notice and patronage; and there is no doubt he was chiefly assisted by the Scrase family, upon whose farm he was employed, and the Rev. Mr. Falkner, the Vicar. Books, paper, and time, were the only things his indefatigable genius seemed to require; and with such aid he soon became one of the best penmen and mathematicians of his time. Not long after he had thus established his fame for useful and abstruse science, he was appointed master of the school, and his unambitious breast aspired to no higher distinction, as he was enabled to apply the enthusiasm of his genius to the cultivation of his favourite studies. This mode of instruction, being that suggested by reason, not the initiative pedantry of schools, facilitated the attainment of the several branches he taught. Navigation being the most necessary and profitable science to the inhabitants of Brighthelmston, he taught it with singular conciseness and precision. Mr. Grimmett was amongst the last of his pupils, as he died, universally respected, soon after the commencement of the present century.

In 1788, in an apartment of the old Town Hall, a School of Industry for Girls was established, under the patronage of Mrs. Nathaniel Kemp and other ladies. It consisted of 150 girls, 70 of whom were clothed in green, educated, and carefully initiated in the sentiments and practice of religion and industry. This School is that known as the National School, the central or head building of which Institution, erected in 1829 by Messrs. Stroud and Mew, and subsequently enlarged by Messrs. Cheesman, is in Church Street. The Gothic style of architecture is preserved throughout. There is a shield with a scroll over the arched doorway of the principal entrance containing the Arms of the Town and the inscription "National Schools." Entering by the grand door of the vestibule, three tiers of balconies present themselves, having staircases leading to them and conducting to the several suites of rooms. The hall, 50ft. high, is terminated by a groined roof. The Boys' School is approached by an elegant flight of stone steps, the room is 75ft long, 35ft wide, and 20ft high, well lighted from the west, and has also an entrance in Regent Street. The Girls' School-room, which is of similar dimensions to the Boys', and immediately above it, is approached by two additional flights of stone stairs. It has a branch in Warwick Street, built by Mr. Ackerson. The Infant Schools, in connection with the National Schools, are in Upper Gardner Street, Kent's Court, and Warwick Street.

Swan Downer's School was founded in 1819, under the will of Mr. Swan Downer, who in 1811 left the sum of £10,106 15s. 3d., for paying the expenses of providing a proper School-house for the instruction of 20 poor girls of the parish in needle-work, reading, and writing, and completely clothing them twice in every year, each of such girls to have two suits of clothes at or on their election or entrance. On the foundation of the said school he also provided that out of the interest and produce of the trust funds—£303 4s—a salary of £40 per annum should be paid to a competent schoolmistress, and the surplus applied to the education and clothing of fifty girls, which has, since 1859, been carried on in a large room temporarily rented by the Trustees in Windsor Street. The first school was in Gardner Street, taken by the then Trustees at an annual rent of £30, and at a loss of something like £400 in appropriating the premises. A site for the erection of a New School-house has been approved by the Trustees. It is situated in North Street, adjoining Messrs. Smithers and Son's Brewery, and has a frontage to the street of 33ft., and a depth of more than 60ft.

The situation thus selected combines two essentials, proximity to the Parish Church, with which the founder connected the charity, and a central position, so important to a day-school for the children of the poor. The Union Schools, in Middle Street, were founded by Mr. Edward Goff, of Scotland Yard, London; that for girls by a donation of £400, in 1807, and that for boys by a legacy of £200 the following year. These schools, which are supported by voluntary contributions, were re-erected in 1837. The other National Charity Schools, independent of Sunday Schools, are: British Schools (Boys' and Girls'), North Lane; Ragged School, Dorset Street; Ragged Schools, Spa Street and Essex Street; St. John's Schools, Carlton Hill; St. Nicholas' Church Memorial School, Frederick Street; St. Stephen's School; Bethel Arch, on the Beach, for Fishermen's children; Wesleyan Schools, Nelson Row; St. Mark's Church of England Schools, Rock Street; St. Paul's, West Street.

There are several public educational establishments in the town; the principal of which is the College. It was established January, 1847, at the top of Portland Place, on the premises now occupied by J. Jardine, Esq., LL.D., and known as Portland House Boarding School. The foundation stone of the present building, in Eastern Road, was laid on the 27th of June, 1848, by the Right Rev. Ashurst Turner Gilbert, D.D., Lord Bishop of Chichester, assisted by the architect, Mr. G. G. Scott, of London, and the builders, Messrs. Wisden and Anscombe. A bottle was deposited under the stone containing various papers connected with the College, and a copy of the *Times* of that day. An elegant trowel, having a richly carved ivory handle, and enclosed in a handsome mahogany case, was presented to and used by the Lord Bishop on the occasion. At first the principal front, which afforded accommodation for 300 pupils, only was erected, since which has been built the Chapel and other additions. The College is divided into two departments —the senior and the junior. The pupils in the senior department wear an academical dress. Students are admitted into the two departments after nine and fifteen years of age respectively. The education is of the very highest order, and will bear a favourable comparison with that of any other Institution in England.

Patron, the Bishop of Chichester: Principal, the Rev. John Griffith.

A short distance to the east is St. Mary's Hall, an institution for educating the daughters of poor clergymen, established in 1836. To the benevolence of the late Marquis of Bristol the building of this institution is principally attributable. His benefactions were not few nor small; they were, from first to last, every one of them, the unsolicited spontaneous effusion of his noble heart.

His Lordship's first gift was £500,—to purchase a site for the building, which was originally designed to look east and west, with only frontage for the present lodge and the carriage-drive to the Hall. On the land so bought St. Mary's Hall stands. But before the excavations for the first design were finished, it was judged best to turn the building, so as to look north and south, and to purchase the additional frontage to the south. The piece of land at the back was given by Mr. Enos Durant. These together cost £1,100, in addition to the munificent gift of £500 from the Marquis, which was given before a sod was turned. In September, 1849, his Lordship gave to St. Mary's Hall its drilling room, which before had been a painting room, as a free gift; and, moreover, sold to St. Mary's Hall, for £500 (about half its cost), No. 6, Hervey Terrace, which had been connected with the drilling room. In 1842-3, he gave a donation of £200, to mitigate the loss which fell on the Institution, in consequence of a secret and outstanding mortgage on the play-garden and kitchen-garden, which had been purchased for £500. The Trustees were obliged to pay £700 more to reclaim the land, after it had been walled-in and stocked. The last gift of his Lordship was a cottage and half an acre of land at the north-west extremity of the premises, together with his share of right in the road leading to it. This gift was fully worth £400, and was intended as an encouragement for the establishment of an Infant St. Mary's Hall, which has not yet been carried out. President, Lord Bishop of Chichester; Secretary and Treasurer, Rev. H. Venn Elliott.

Chapter XXX.

THE CHURCHES AND CHAPELS.

Immediately in connexion with St. Mary's Hall, is St. Mark's Church, Kemp Town. This is another instance of the benevolence of the late Marquis of Bristol. In 1838-9, he conveyed to the Trustees of St. Mary's Hall the land on which the Church now stands. After the conveyance thereof, and when the land was no longer his own, such was his zeal to hasten the erection of St. Mark's, that, at the expense of some £2,000, he actually built the carcase of the Church, roofed it in, and glazed its windows. If the Church Commissioners would have sanctioned it, he originally designed entirely to build and complete the Church himself. Baffled in that desire, and feeling at his age the uncertainty of life, he made over the property to the Trustees of St. Mary's Hall, in the confidence that the interests of that Institution would induce them, sooner or later, to complete his purpose. After eight years of ineffectual effort and negociation, St. Mark's Church was at last finished, and consecrated on St. Matthew's Day, September 21st, 1849; and for some years his Lordship was a worshipper in that house of prayer. The cost of its completion and of the endowment, in addition to his Lordship's free gift of the site and the carcase, was not far short of £5,000. For this expense one of the Trustees became personally responsible, on account of the immense value of the Church, and its gratuitous accommodation to St. Mary's Hall. The subscriptions and collections entrusted to him amounted to £4,832 5s. 8d., of which sum Lord Bristol contributed a benefaction of £500.

In grateful remembrance of his Lordship, a splendid Memorial Window and Monumental Tablet were erected to his memory, in the Church, in 1860. The expense of the Window was defrayed by subscriptions, chiefly by the members of the congregation, and that of the Tablet by the Rev. E. B. Elliott and Lawrence Peel, Esq.

The Memorial Window is an elaborate work of art in the Gothic style, the subjects of the paintings being well selected fro sacred history. The centre compartment has two divisions. In the upper division is the ascending Saviour, with His arms stretched out in the act of blessing His Disciples. The lower division represents the figure of St. Mark, writing the concluding verses of his Gospel. In the north compartment, the subject is the Lord descending, after the Paschal Supper with His Disciples, from Jerusalem towards Gethsamane; the Disciples are sorrowing at the thoughts of His speedy departure from them, and He is comforting them with the hope of His going to prepare for their re-union in Heaven. The south compartment contains a group of Disciples looking towards the ascending Saviour, in the upper central window, whilst two angels address them—as recorded in Acts I., ch. ii.

The Monumental Tablet is of Caen stone, bearing the following inscription in Latin:—

FENESTRA
ORIENTALIS TRIPARTITA HUJUS ECCLESIÆ
A QUIBUSDAM AMICIS HIC SACRA COLENTIBUS
ALIISQUE OPPIDI HUJUSCE CIVIBUS,
GRATO ANIMO POSITA EST

In Memoriam

FREDERICI GULIELMI, PRIMI MARCHIONIS DE BRISTOL.

NOBILITATE INSIGNIS, MUNIFICENTIA INSIGNIOR,
DIVITIIS NON SIBIMET, SED ALIIS, UTI DELECTATUS EST.
ECCLESIAM HANC,
PROPRIIS SUIS SUMPTIBUS QUOAD MUROS EXTRUCTAM,
CULTUI DIVINO DEDICANDAM IN ALIORUM MANUS TRANSTULIT.
AULÆ SANCTÆ MARIÆ, PROXIME ADJACENTI,
AGRUM PRETIOSUM PRO SITU DONAVIT.
HOSPITALI BRIGHTONENSI SACELLUM ADDIDIT.
CŒMETERIUM PAROCHIALE TRANS COLLEM LARGE AMPLIFICAVIT.
USQUE AD EXTREMAM SENECTUTEM VITA PROTENSA,
FACULTATIBUS MENTIS VIX LANGUIDIORIBUS
CORDIS BENEVOLENTIA, UTI PRIUS, MINIME IMMINUTA FRUEBATUR.
TANDEM, MORBO LETHALI CORREPTUS,
RELIGIONIS CONSOLATIONIBUS
SACRAQUE COMMUNIONE, NANU FILII IPSIUS MINISTRATA, REFECTUS,
PLACIDE, FAMILIA SUA CIRCUMSTANTE, IN FIDE CHRISTI OBDORMIVIT.
QUOD ILLIUS MORTALE ERAT
IN CRYPTA FAMILIARI SUBTER ECCLESIAM ICKWORTHIENSEM SEPULTUM
JACET.
IBI, UT SPERAMUS, BEATAM RESURRECTIONEM EXPECTAT,
QUANDO QUI OLIM ASCENDIT
RURSUS, SECUNDUM PROMISSUM, GLORIOSE DESCENDET;
SUOS SIBI UNDIQUE ET MORTUOS COACTURUS.
JESUS HOMINUM SALVATOR.

The base of the Tablet bears the Escutcheon of the House of

Bristol. On a brass plate, that extends under the whole window, is the following Latin inscription :—

In Memoriam
HONORARISSIMAM FREDERICI GULIELMI,
PRIMI MARCHIONIS DE BRISTOL.
FUNDATORIS HUJUS ECCLESIÆ.
NATI, A.D. 1769; MORTII, XV. MAR. 1859.

The present Marquis of Bristol bore the expense of the enclosure of the Chancel and the painting of the walls in a style accordant with the new ornamental window, thus completing the work.

The Chapel in Prince's Place, subsequently named by special Act of Parliament the Chapel Royal, was projected originally for the accommodation of the increasing number of visitors, and especially to lull an outcry prevailing at the time in consequence of the non-attendance of the heir apparent at any place of worship during his periodical residence in Brighton. The corner stone was laid with masonic honours by H.R.H. George, Prince of Wales, K.G., G.M., &c., on the 25th November, 1793. Divine service was performed in the building, which was unconsecrated until the year 1803, by various clergymen connected with the Court, and only during the season. Among them may be named Archbishop Moore, Bishop Horsley, and Bishop Horne, the latter of whom preached his celebrated published sermon there, on the text, "The sea is His, and He made it." The Prince regularly attended, and the chapel was thronged with the nobility and gentry. A story is told that H.R.H finally took umbrage at some very personal remarks spoken at him from the pulpit by the Rev. W. Brooke, who had taken for his text the words, "Thou art the man." Mr. B. was then Curate of Brighton, and had been suddenly requested to take the duty in consequence of the indisposition of the appointed clergyman. The Prince never again entered the chapel, and curiously enough Mr. Brooke soon after quitted the established church and officiated for some years in a building, erected by certain of his followers, in Church Street. The last occupant of the Royal Closet was H.R.H. the late amiable Princess Augusta, who died in London in 1840. This chapel was the last place of public worship in which H.R.H. was enabled to appear. In 1803, during the incumbency of the Rev. T. Hudson, it was thought desirable by him, as Vicar of Brighton, to secure the building as a Chapel of Ease to the Parish Church, St. Nicholas. He held the freehold, and obtained an Act, 43rd Geo. III., cap. 91, constituting the Church a perpetual curacy, and reserving to himself and his successors in the Vicarage the right of nomination. The incumbent is subject solely to the jurisdiction of the Bishop of Chichester, "as if the curacy of the said chapel were a presentative Vicarage." It may be mentioned that under the special Act, the perpetual Curate is required to solemnize baptisms and churchings (marriages are exempted), and empowered to demand double the fees usually received at the Parish Church for the like duties. After Mr. Hudson's removal from Brighton, the lay property of the chapel passed, by purchase, to his successor (Rev. Dr. R. J. Carr) and others. The present proprietors are R. Sedly Tilstone, Esq., of Alverstoke and Moulse-coombe, R. C. Cox, Esq., of Taunton, and Rev. Thomas Trocke, M.A., the present Incumbent. The building externally is very plain, having none other decoration than a fine cast of the Royal Arms in patent stone, on the pediment over the central window in front. The interior, however, is somewhat elegant. The Royal Closet still remains, and the Pulpit, Desk, and Altar arrangements are very handsome. Over the latter, there is a valuable Painting of "The Crucifixion," by Van Een, a pupil of Vandyke. The organ has two sets of manuels. There are sittings for about 800 persons, of which 150 are thrown open to the public.

St. Peter's Church was commenced in 1824, the first stone being laid the 8th of May. It is a beautiful Gothic structure of Portland stone, embellished with various decorations, and from its combined elegance and situation forms one of the most striking features of the town. The interior is divided into three aisles, the principal of which runs through the body of the Church, leading from the chief entrance to the altar, over which there is a magnificent stained glass window representing the Evangelists and the Apostles, which was presented by the Vicar, the Rev. H. M. Wagner. The Church was designed by the late Sir Charles Barry, built by Mr.

Ranger, and consecrated 27th January, 1828. Incumbent, Rev. Thomas Cooke, M.A.

The following are the names of the trees planted in St. Peter's Church-yard, with their symbolical description:—

Cedar of Labanon—being the tree selected by Solomon for building the Temple of Jerusalem; *Weeping Willow*—a native of Babylon, and the tree on which the unhappy Israelites hung their harps when they bemoaned the loss of Jerusalem; *Sycamore*—the tree on which Zaccheus climbed to see Christ pass on His way to Jerusalem; *Thorn*—to remind us of the Crown of Thorns; *Aspen*—it being the tree of which the Cross is said to have been formed; *Lime*—the principal papyraceous tree of the ancients, and on the bark of which the Scriptures were probably first written; *Ash*—esteemed a sacred tree in ancient times, and one to which the Serpent is said to have a strong antipathy; *Plane*—the favourite tree of the Greeks, and under whose shade the Athenian philosophers retired to study; *Birch*—the tree from which the Lictors made their fasces; *Elm*—the funeral tree of the Romans, and the coffin timber of Britons; *Cypress*—the funeral tree of all Eastern nations; *Yew*—the funeral Yew so famed in war, and a tree consecrated and dedicated to the grave; *Arbor Vitæ*—although the tree of life, it shows that immortality is not the lot of anything terrestrial; *Holly*—as being used in the decorations of churches at sacred festivals; *Box*—the plant formerly used in the feast of the Purification of the Blessed Virgin; *Poplar*—a plant held sacred by the Romans, and the tree used to mark the boundaries of their lands; *Maple*—the tree of which the bowl of hospitality was formed in days of yore; *Pine*—"And the tall pines for future navies,"—*Dant utile lignum Navigus Pinus*, (the useful pine for ships,) "To thee I consecrate the pine:"—in Pagan days it was consecrated to Diana; *Bay*—the "Laurus Nobilis" of the ancient warriors, the crown of our Poet Laureates, a supposed protection from lightning, and a purifier of pestilential air; *Laurel*—as an honourable badge for those who bravely defend their country and their laws; *Oak*—once the refuge of a British Monarch, and ever the best bulwark of our Church and State.

Of all the places of worship in the town not one has a more

interesting history attached to it than the Countess of Huntingdon's Chapel—commonly known as North Street Chapel,—facing the New Road.

Before entering into the particulars of this Chapel the following anecdote may not be deemed uninteresting, as it is somewhat connected with the subsequent motives of Lady Huntingdon* building a religious edifice in the town:—In the year 1755, the illness of the youngest son of the Countess induced her ladyship to come to Brighton for the benefit of sea-bathing. About this time the following singular circumstance occurred, which Lady Huntingdon related to the Rev. A. M. Toplady, and which is extracted from the manuscript in the Posthumous Works of that gentleman, published by the executors in 1780:—"A gentlewoman who lived a little way out of Brighthelmston dreamt that a tall lady dressed in a particular manner would come to that town, and be an instrument of doing much good. It was about three years after this dream that Lady Huntingdon came to Brighton. A few days after her Ladyship's arrival, the above gentlewoman met her in the street, and, making a full stop, exclaimed 'Oh! Madam, you are come.' Lady H., surprised at the singularity of such an address from an entire stranger, thought the woman was bereft of her senses. 'What do you know of me?' asked the Countess. 'Madam' replied the gentlewoman, 'I saw you in a dream three years ago, dressed just as you are now,' and proceeded in the relation of her dream to the Countess. This person was, in consequence of her acquaintance with Lady H., converted in a few weeks, and died in the triumph of faith about a year after.

About three months after her Ladyship's arrival she visited a poor soldier's wife who had just been delivered of twins, and administered to her temporal and spiritual wants. It happened that next to that room was an oven belonging to a baker's shop, thither the people flocked for bread. Overhearing the pious conversation, some of the poor women sought and obtained admission, and from time to time they met there and conversed on religious topics. The news of the religious labours of a person of rank

* Lady Selina Shirley, born 1717, married to Theophilus Earl of Huntingdon, 3rd June, 1738, and died in 1799, aged 82.

was soon scattered through the town, and the people began to be anxious of doing more good than was yet accomplished. The Countess sent for her Chaplain, the Rev. George Whitefield. He came, and preached his first sermon in a field at the back of the White Lion Inn, North Street. A little society was formed in consequence, and after a time there was a growing anxiety for a place wherein they might hold their meetings. The Countess would have been glad to have provided a house of meeting, but at that time her funds were exhausted, she having already given some hundred thousand pounds to the cause of God. She, however, devised a plan for raising the necessary means; she sent for her jeweller, opened her casket of jewels, and disposed of them, the following account of which cannot fail to interest:—

	£	s.	d.
Two 13 X drops	400	0	0
Twenty-eight 13 X 3 drops	90	0	0
Thirty-seven pearls, at £4 15s each	175	15	0
Seed pearls	10	0	0
Gold Box	23	0	0
	£698	15	0

Her Ladyship at that time lived in a house which formed a part of North street,—the business of the town then being transacted in the Lanes,—and built a little Chapel with these funds at the back of her private house, on the site of the present chapel, which was opened in the Autumn of 1761, the Rev. Matthew Madden preaching the opening sermon. It had only been opened six years when it was found to be too small for its congregation, and, in February, 1767, it was enlarged and re-opened by the Rev. M. Madden and the Rev. G. Whitefield. In 1774 it was taken down and rebuilt, this time at the expense of Miss Norton, a friend of the Countess, who lived in an adjoining house. In 1775 it was re-opened, for the third time, by the Rev. W. Romaine, the then Rector of St. Ann's, Blackfriars. In 1810, a further enlargement was found to be necessary, and it was then made capable of accommodating 1,000 persons.* In 1821 another considerable enlargement took place,

* An interesting circumstance was recorded in the census of 1851; it was said there, concerning North Street Chapel, that it was a building capable of holding a thousand people, but there were present on the morning of the census eleven hundred.

making it capable of holding 1,500 persons. It was again enlarged in 1842,—when the chapel-house was thrown into the body of the place,—to its present condition.

Among the celebrated Ministers who have preached there, besides those already mentioned, may be named, Revs. A. M. Toplady, Berridge, Jones, Fletcher, Henry Venn, Dr. Rawes,—the founder of the London Missionary Society,—and the late lamented Pastor, the Rev. Joseph Sortain. The Rev. J. B. Figgis is the present Pastor.

Union Street Chapel was erected, after the repeal of the Non-Conformist Act, in 1698, and for upwards of one hundred years continued in the hands of the Presbyterians. It now belongs to a congregation of Dissenters of the Independent denomination. In 1810 it was considerably enlarged, under the Pastorate of the Rev. Dr. Styles. In 1823, the Rev. J. N. Goulty, at the earnest request of the congregation, accepted the Pastorate. At that time there was a debt of £1,000 on the Chapel, only about half of which had been provided for before he took the office. The attendance so increased, especially at evening services, that it was found desirable, in the Summer of 1825, to have it taken down and entirely re-built. The expenses of this alteration were immediately subscribed by the congregation, except about £500, which was lent upon debentures, to be taken up in five years, which were ultimately satisfactorily settled. It is now capable of seating nearly 1,000 persons. In January, 1862, after 38 years' indefatigable labour, the Rev. J. N. Goulty resigned the Pastorate, and was succeeded by the Rev. R. Vaughan Pryce, M.A., LL.B.

Trinity Chapel is situated in Ship Street, and was built in 1817, by Messrs. Wilds, at the sole expense of Thomas Read Kemp, Esq., M.P., who officiated personally until 1825, when it was purchased by the Rev. Robert Anderson. It has undergone several alterations, and is at present used as a Chapel of Ease to the Church of England. The interior is extremely handsome. In the centre of the ceiling rises a small dome, partly covered with glass, which adds to the light, and gives a free ventilation of air. The Rev. Henry Herbert Wyatt, M.A., is the present Incumbent.

Wesleyan Chapel, Dorset Gardens, was erected in 1808, and

is capable of accommodating 700 persons. There is no settled Pastor to the congregation, but it is supplied with ministers appointed by the Conference. In connexion with this Chapel are the Windsor Street and Upper Bedford Street (Zion) Wesleyan Chapels.

St. James's Chapel, on the north side of St. James's Street, was built in 1810. The Duke of Marlborough, on being apprized that the scheme for the erection of this Chapel was on foot, and that the expences attending it would be covered by voluntary contributions, with that liberality which so distinguished him during his residence in Grove House, instantly subscribed £100, and expressed a hope, on doing so, that—to use his own words—"the playhouse method of receiving shillings for admission, as at the Chapel Royal, would not be adopted when the building was completed." His Lordship's hopes were fully realized, and the Chapel, being built by shares, was called a Free Chapel. Some few years after its erection, in consequence of the congregation dissenting from the Established Church, it was taken by the late Nathaniel Kemp, Esq., of Ovingdean, who purchased all the shares, became sole-proprietor, and had it duly consecrated. The property has now passed into the hands of his widow and children. The Rev. C. D. Maitland, the present Incumbent, was nominated in February, 1828. In 1836 the school-room was built adjoining the Chapel, wherein about 250 children of both sexes have been religiously instructed every Sunday since that time, and 130 girls have been daily receiving an useful education.

St. Margaret's Chapel is situated in St. Margaret's Place, on the west side of Cannon Place. It was built, in 1825, as a Chapel of Ease. This Chapel is "proprietary," though consecrated under special Act of Parliament. The Rev. Edmund Clay, B.A., who was appointed in February, 1856, pays a rental of £375 per annum, and all expenses of repairs and others incidental to the due performance of Divine Worship: averaging over £200 per annum. In connexion with this Chapel are the Industrial Girls' School, built by the Rev. E. Clay, in 1856, at a cost of £1,600; the Youths' Evening School, in Cannon Street, and an Infant Nursery, in Regency Square.

St. George's Chapel, built, in 1825, under a special Act of Parliament, in St. George's Road, and directly opposite the

Hospital, at the sole expense of Thomas Read Kemp, Esq., is capable of holding about 1,200 people. The Rev. J. S. M. Anderson, Chaplain to the Queen and Queen Dowager, officiated for a number of years, and was very popular. He was succeeded by the present Incumbent, the Rev. J. H. North, M.A.

St. Mary's Chapel, St. James's Street, was erected in 1827. This Chapel is built after a model of the Temple of Nemesis, at Athens. Incumbent and Patron, Rev. H. V. Elliott, M.A.

St. John's (the Evangelist) Chapel, Carlton Hill, was built in 1840, by Messrs. Cheesman, upon a site most unfortunately selected, and without any architectural advice. There are four Schools in connexion with this Chapel, under the clerical management of the Perpetual Curate, upon the principles of self-support, which are calculated to exercise a powerful influence for good in this, the very poorest portion of the town, the building being made over for ever to the National Society for the Education of the Poor in the principles of the Established Church, and placed under trust of the Archdeacon of Lewes. Rev. A. A. Morgan, M.A., is the present Incumbent.

Christ Church, Montpelier Road, was consecrated on 26th April, 1838, and built by Mr. G. Cheesman. There was no public laying of the foundation stone. It is capable of holding about 1,200 people, 700 of the sittings being free. The Rev. James Vaughan, M.A., has been Incumbent from the opening. Adjoining this Church, in Bedford Place, are Educational Schools for middle classes, erected, in 1843, by Messrs. Wisden and Anscombe. Besides these there is an Infant School, connected with the Church, in Clarence Gardens.

St. Paul's Church, West Street, is a large and handsome building, built, in 1848, by Messrs. Cheesman, from a design by Mr. Carpenter, architect. It is built of cut flints with stone coignes, and is intended to be finished with a lofty spire. It is in the decorated English style. The Church is entered by a covered way or cloister. The interior is highly decorated in the mediæval style. The roof of the nave is of timber, and that of the chancel is painted blue with gold stars; several of the windows are of stained glass. It contains a nave, north and south aisles, and chancel, and has a fine toned organ; a peal of bells, the largest in the town, have been hung in the unfinished tower. It was consecrated on St. Luke's Day, 1849. The Rev. A. D. Wagner is the Incumbent.

Hanover Chapel, situated at the top of Church Street, in the rear of the Odd Fellows' Hall, was opened for public worship on the 30th of August, 1825, and belongs to the Presbyterian denomination. It was erected at the sole expense (£4,000) of the Rev. M. Edwards, of Petworth, who, with the assistance of some of the most popular preachers of the day, also supplied its pulpit. It is calculated to seat 1,200 persons.

Salem Chapel, Bond Street, was erected in 1787; was enlarged in 1825, and rebuilt in 1861. It is now a very handsome building, belonging to the Particular Baptists. The Rev. George Isaacs is Minister.

All Saints' Church, Clifton Road, is a fine specimen of early English architecture. It was built in 1852 by Messrs. Cheesman, It has a nave, side aisles, and chancel, and contains a fine toned organ. Its spire remains as yet unfinished. The Rev. Thomas Coombe, B.A., is Incumbent and Surrogate.

All Souls' Church, in Eastern Road, was erected by subscription in 1833, by Messrs. Mew, for the accommodation of the poor and working classes; the seats are nearly all free. The benefice is a Perpetual Curacy. The Rev. Richard Snowden Smith, M.A., is Incumbent.

St. Andrew's Chapel, Waterloo Street, in the parish of Hove, is a neat building, and contains several handsome marble tablets. It was completed in 1828, and will contain 600 people. The Rev. W. H. Rooper is the present Patron and Incumbent, assisted by the Right Rev. Bishop Trower.

Providence Chapel, Church Street, is of the Calvanistic persuasion, and was built in 1805. Minister, Rev. Thomas Bayfield. The other Calvanistic Chapel in Brighton (Jireh Chapel) is in Robert Street, Glo'ster Lane, of which the Rev. Thomas Dray is the Minister.

Ebenezer Chapel, Richmond Street, was the second Place of Worship erected in Brighton for the Particular Baptists. It was opened in 1825. Rev. Israel Atkinson, Minister.

The other Baptist Chapels in the town are Queen's Square—Rev. Joseph Wilkins; Tabernacle Chapel, West Street—Rev. John Grace; Bethsaida Hall Chapel, Windsor Street—Rev. Thomas Stringer.

St. James's Church, Cambridge Road, is a noble edifice, of Kentish rag and Bath stone, in the early decorative English style. It has a lofty nave, chancel, two aisles, and chapels, and for external beauty is one of the most imposing churches in Brighton. It was erected in 1858, at the sole expense of the Rev. Thomas O'Brien, D.D., who is now Patron and Incumbent.

Christ Church, New Road, originally known as the Unitarian Chapel, was built from a design of Mr. Wilds. It has a light and elegant fluted Doric portico, and is built after the style of the Temple of Theseus. Since the appointment of the Rev. Robert Ainslie great improvements have been made in the interior arrangements, and the comfort of the congregation thereby much enhanced.

There are three Roman Catholic Chapels in Brighton: St. John the Baptist's, Bristol Road; St. Mary Magdalene, 51, Upper North Street; and West Cliff Catholic Chapel, Sillwood Lodge. The first chapel of this denomination was in High Street. In 1833, the number of Roman Catholic visitors increased so rapidly that it was deemed expedient to build a larger one, and in 1837, St. John the Baptist's was opened, and the one in High Street abandoned. The old Chapel is now used as a printing office, by Mrs. Sickelmore. The interior of the Chapel in Bristol Road is very airy, and commodious, but its external appearance is heavy, the Corinthian pilasters being disproportionately large. The officiating Priests there at the present time are the Very Rev. Canon Reardon, the Very Rev. Canon Rymer, and the Rev. William Stone. St. Mary Magdalene's was erected in 1861-2, by Messrs. Cheesman, from a design by Mr. Rodley, and opened in February, 1862. It is in the Gothic style. The Rev. G. A. Oldham is the priest. Of West Cliff Chapel, the Rev. E. J. Clery is the priest.

The following is a list of the places of worship in Brighton, with the officiating clergymen, in addition to those already enumerated:—London Road Chapel, Ann Street, Rev. R. Hamilton; Queen's

Square Independent Chapel, Rev. E. Paxton Hood; Circus Street Chapel, various; Pavilion Chapel (Independent), Rev. J. A. Wallinger; Bible Christians, Cavendish Street, Rev. Paul Foskett; Friends' Meeting House, Ship Street, various; Jews' Synagogue, 38, Devonshire Place, Reader, M. S. Nuremberg; Primitive Methodist, Sussex Street, various; Catholic Apostolic Church, Grand Parade, various; St. Michæl and All Angel's, Victoria Road, Rev. C. Beanlands, M.A., ; Temporary Church of St. Mary Magdalene, Bread Street,—a branch of St. Paul's Church, West Street, which supplies the Ministers; Huntingtonian Chapel, Union Street, Mr. Christopher Sharp; Swedenborgian Church, Odd Fellows' Hall, Queen's Road, various; St. Ann's Church, Burlington Street, is now in course of erection by Messrs. Cheesman, from a design by Mr. Terry, Architect.

Chapter XXXI.

HOVE AND CLIFTONVILLE.

Adjoining Brighton on the west, is the parish of Hove, which still retains nearly its ancient name, being written in the Doomsday Book *Hov.* It covers a large area of ground, and, for the most part, is laid out in fine open streets, and houses of noble elevation. Palmeira Square and Adelaide Crescent, projected by the late Baron Goldsmid, and now completed, is the most magnificent range of buildings in the parish. In 1801, the population of Hove was only 101, in 1811 it increased to 312, and in 1831 to 1,360, in 1851 to 4,104, in 1861 to 9,818. This great increase in population during the last ten years is to be attributed to the building of Cliftonville, forming quite a new town in the centre of the parish. The houses generally are semi-detached villas and private residences, many of which display much architectural beauty. The parish church (St. Peter) is a flint and stone building in the Norman style, and was restored in 1834 from the ruins of one which was formerly considered a structure of great beauty and grandeur, the tower of which fell down in 1801. After the falling of the tower, a wooden pigeon-house steeple was erected, and the centre aisle sufficiently accomodated the congregation up to the time of its restoration. The accommodation afforded by Hove parish church, owing to the rapid rise of Cliftonville, was soon found to be inadequate to the requirements of the community,—as in certain seasons of the year the influx of visitors is so great that the population is considered not less than 12,000; and in 1852, another church was erected at the west end of the Western Road, and dedicated to St. John the Baptist, and even now the church accommodation is insufficient. In 1855 a Town Hall was built by the Commissioners. This was necessitated in consequence of Brighton having obtained a Charter of Incorporation, and consequently criminal cases arising in Hove and villages in its neighbourhood could no longer be adjudicated on by the Brighton Bench. The County Magistrates are C. Carpenter, Esq., John Borrer, Esq., W. Furner, Esq., R. Henty, Esq., Colonel Paine, M. D. Scott, Esq., F. S. Hurlock, Esq., J. H. Pickford, Esq., W. F. Smithe, Esq., Sir G. A. Westphal, and P. Salomons, Esq. The police force is very effective, there being one constable to every 500 inhabitants. The fire brigade is made up from the police force, and is organised under the direction of Superintendent Breach. Building operations still continue in Hove to a large extent, a new road (Cambridge Road) being just completed, and a new street having recently been laid out to the west of the Sussex Hotel, in Cliftonville. The houses there are being built by Mr. Jabez Reynolds, of Brighton, on a large scale, and bids fair to form one of the finest streets in the parish.

CHRONOLOGICAL TABLE OF LOCAL EVENTS.

693.—Bishop Brighthelm slain above Brighthelmston.

913.—First constable of Brighton appointed by Edward I. (the Elder), by the statute of Winchester.

1008.—Ulnoth, the Lord of the Manor of Brighthelmston, ordered by Ethelred II. to equip and command the fleet sent by the county of Sussex to oppose the Danes.

1014.—September 28th, a great sea-flood on this eve, that of St. Michæl, which spread over the land.

1046.—Earl Godwin dispossessed of Brighton by Edward the Confessor.

1053.—April 17th, Earl Godwin, son of Ulnoth, died suddenly while dining with the King, Edward the Confessor, at Winchester, where the Court then resided. His death was no doubt from apoplexy; but the monkish writers attributed it to a stroke of divine vengeance for the murder of Alfred the son of Ethelred, in the monastery of Ely.

1066.—October 14th, the battle of Hastings fought.

1080.—Convent of mendicant friars, dedicated to St. Bartholomew, founded by William de Warren and his wife, Gundred.

1081.—The survey of Sussex taken, by order of William the Conqueror. The *gablum* or rent of the manor of Brighthelmston-Lewes was worth £12 a-year.

1313.—Charter for holding a market every Thursday obtained for the town by the Earl of Warren, of Edward III.

1377.—Brighton pillaged by the French.

1513.—The town pillaged and burnt by a French fleet, under Admiral Primauget.

1535.—Ecclesiastical valuation of the town made, by order of Henry VIII., a thus:

"DEANERY OF LEWES; PRIORY OF LEWES.

"BRIGHTHELMYSTON.

"Farm of the Rectory there, with all first fruits and advantages, and various things, let to Mr. Richard Nicolle, for a term of years, and the rent thence by the year £16,"

"PRIORY OF MICHELHAM,

Whence,

BRIGHTHELMYSTON.

"Farm of certain land and tenements there in the occupation of John Smyth, otherwise Waterman, returning thence by the year, 100s.

1538.—The Parish Church register of baptisms and burials commenced.

1545.—July 18th, the town attacked, pillaged, and burnt by the French, under Admiral D'Annehault.

1555.—Deryk Carver, a brewer, of Brighton, burnt at the stake, at Lewes, for his resistance of Popery.

1558.—The Block-house and fortifications of the town erected.

—— In July, about the end, the Spanish Armada passed off Brighton, pursued by the English navy.

1584.—The Bartholomews purchased by the town, of William Midwinter, a mariner.

1597.—Warlike materials, for the defence of the town against the Spaniards, were sent from Lewes to Brighton.

1651.—October 14th, Charles II. escaped from Brighton to the continent.

1670.—Captain Tettersel appointed High Constable of the Hundred.

1703.—November 27th, a great storm, which did much damage to the town and the vessels belonging to it.

1705.—August 11th, a terrific storm.

1713.—Mr. Henry May paid to the parish one halfpenny for permission to convey the corpse of his father through Hilly Lane, from the Race Hill to the town, there being no high road.

1727.—The Town Well, on the Knab, finished.

1749.—January, the Block-house partially destroyed by an extraordinay high tide.

1750.—Dr. Richard Russell took up his residence in Brighton.

1754.—Russell Street (so named from Dr. Russell, the founder of the fame of Brighton) built.

1761.—Battery erected at the bottom of East Street.

—— Lady Huntingdon's Chapel first erected.

1768.—The first baths in Brighton constructed, on the site of Brill's Ladies' Swimming Bath.

1771.—A small brass figure dug up in the Vicarage garden, supposed to be a votive offering of some person who had escaped the horrors of a shipwreck.

1772.—First Local Act obtained.

1774.—Lady Huntingdon's Chapel re-built.

—— The Theatre built in North Street.

1777.—The peal of bells placed in the tower of St. Nicholas' Church.

1782.—The Prince of Wales first visited Brighton. The master gunner on the occasion lost both of his arms while firing the Royal salute from the battery at the bottom of East Street.

1784.—Royal Pavilion commenced.

1786.—November 17th, battery at the bottom of East Street washed down by a storm.

—— Theatre in Duke Street opened.

1787.—Salem Chapel built.

1788.—First Race Stand erected.

—— On December the 22nd, in consequence of the severity of the frost, on the receding of the tide, the water within the sand bar was frozen over.

1790.—January 13th, Mr. William Attree, at a public Vestry meeting at the Old Ship, was appointed Vestry Clerk, at 10 guineas per annum.

1792.—September 20th, by order of the Duke of York, an ox was roasted whole.

—— Streeter's mill (the mill on the Dyke Road, above Preston Drove), was removed by 86 oxen, from Bellevue field, now Regency square.

1792.—October 22nd, thirty-seven nuns, in the habit of their Order, landed at Shoreham, and afterwards proceeded to Brussels.

1793.—Brighton Camp is formed in the fields to the west of Brighton.

—— April 26th, Rooke and Howell executed for robbing the mail.

—— The east and west batteries erected

—— November 25th, the corner stone of the Chapel Royal laid, by his Royal Highness the Prince Regent.

1794.—February 10th, Dr. Henderson at a Vestry meeting, held at the Unicorn Inn, was presented with a pint silver cup, for his care and attention to the Parish.

—— April 16th, Howell's stables, in the Bartholomews, burnt down, and nine troop horses consumed.

—— Cannons planted on the east and west batteries.

—— General inoculation, 2,113 persons, including 250 from the neighbourhood, were inoculated for small pox.

—— An encampment of 7,000 men at the west part of the town. It was broken up in November.

1795.—Great flood and 18 weeks' frost.

—— June 12th (Saturday), Edward Cooke and Henry Parrish, shot at Goldstone Bottom, for mutiny.

—— Cavalry Barracks on the Lewes Road completed.

1796.—By order of Vestry all vagrants and beggars were to be apprehended by the Crier, who was to receive a shilling a-head for their capture.

—— The Percy Alms Houses, Lewes Road, built.

1798.—The Royal Crescent commenced by Otto, who built three houses at each end and then bolted, leaving his creditors in the lurch.

1799.—November 20th, several of the Brighton fishermen taken out of their boats whilst fishing off Seaford, by two French lugger privateers, and carried to France.

—— There lived at 3, Artillery Place, Mr. Nathan Smith, inventor, patentee, and operator of an Air-pump for extracting the gout, &c.

1800.—The Pavilion property purchased by the Prince of Wales.

—— The high-road from East Street to Marlborough Place closed.

—— The New Road opened from North Street to Church Street.

—— March 31st, Thomas Waring appointed parish beadle and town crier.

1802.—The two wings added to the Royal Pavilion.

—— October 26th, Capt. William Codlin executed at Newgate, for sinking his ship, the "Adventure," off Brighton, in August.

1803.—April 15th, the Churchwardens and Overseers accept Dr. Bankhead's offer to attend the poor gratuitously.

—— August 23rd, Race Stand destroyed by fire.

—— The trees in the New Road planted.

—— A sewer constructed from Pavilion Parade to the back of Williams's Baths, at the expense of the Prince of Wales and the Duke of Marlborough,

—— Chapel Royal consecrated, and an Act of Parliament procured, securing it as a Chapel of Ease to the Parish Church.

1805.—April 18th, the Vestry Clerk's salary increased to £30 per annum.

—— July 29th, a boy killed on the Race Hill, by being thrown out of a swing whereby his back was broken.

1805.—September 23rd, grand review near Rottingdean of the Inniskilling (Queen's) Dragoons, Artillery, and South Gloucester, Dorset, Monmouth, Brecon, and South Hants Militia, under General Paget.

— October, the organ at the Pavilion erected.

— October, the Prince of Wales purchased the Dairy at Preston, of Mr. W. Stanford.

— November 6th, at 40 minutes after 3 o'clock this afternoon, an express arrived at the Royal Pavilion to announce to the Prince of Wales the glorious defeat of the enemy's fleet at Trafalgar, and the death of the brave and victorious Nelson.

— December 26th, the Royal Stables, Church Street, completed.

1806.—March 12th, A heavy snow-storm, in which Neville, a well-known inhabitant of Brighton was lost in a drift about the spot where the Adur Inn now stands, at Aldrington.

— March 13th, the subject of a Charter of Incorporation mooted at a Public Vestry Meeting.

— July 25th, the Earl of Barrymore and Mr. Howarth fought a duel at Black-rock Bottom in consequence of a dispute at cards the previous night at the Castle Tavern.

— August 12th, mock invasion of the town.

— Sept. 1st, Williams's Baths opened.

— Sept. 12th, Lord Thurlow died at his residence, West Cliff.

— Sept. 25th, Mr. Brunton, sen., laid the Foundation Stone of Theatre, in the New Road.

— *Brighton Herald* first published.

1807.—Zion Chapel, Bedford Street, erected.

— May 28th, the great county election contest terminated :—

Wyndham	4,333
Fuller	2,530
Sergison	2,473

— Theatre in New road opened.

— Sept. 3rd, the Sheep and Lamb Fair on the Level was well attended.

— October 1st, Masked ball at Old Ship.

— October 22nd, three brigs, two colliers, and a vessel laden with corn, were wrecked in front of the town.

1808.—Wesleyan Chapel erected in Dorset Gardens.

— April 27th, Mr. Jonathan Grenville appointed poor-rate collector at a compensation of 3d. in the £ on all monies collected; the appointment to be discretionary in the "Breast" of the parish officers.

— Mr. Forth succeeds Mr. Wade as Master of the Ceremonies.

1809.—August 9th, neither a house nor lodgings to be got for love or money.

— March 21st, a meeting held at the Old Ship Tavern to inspect and consider a plan for the consideration of a harbour at Brighton.

— Brighton Dispensary founded.

— July 7th, Mr. Tilt, proprietor of the Castle Tavern and Subscription Rooms, died.

1810.—St. James's Chapel built. The Duke of Marlborough contributed £100.

— Lady Huntingdon's Chapel enlarged.

— The Town Act of 1773 repealed, and a new Act passed.

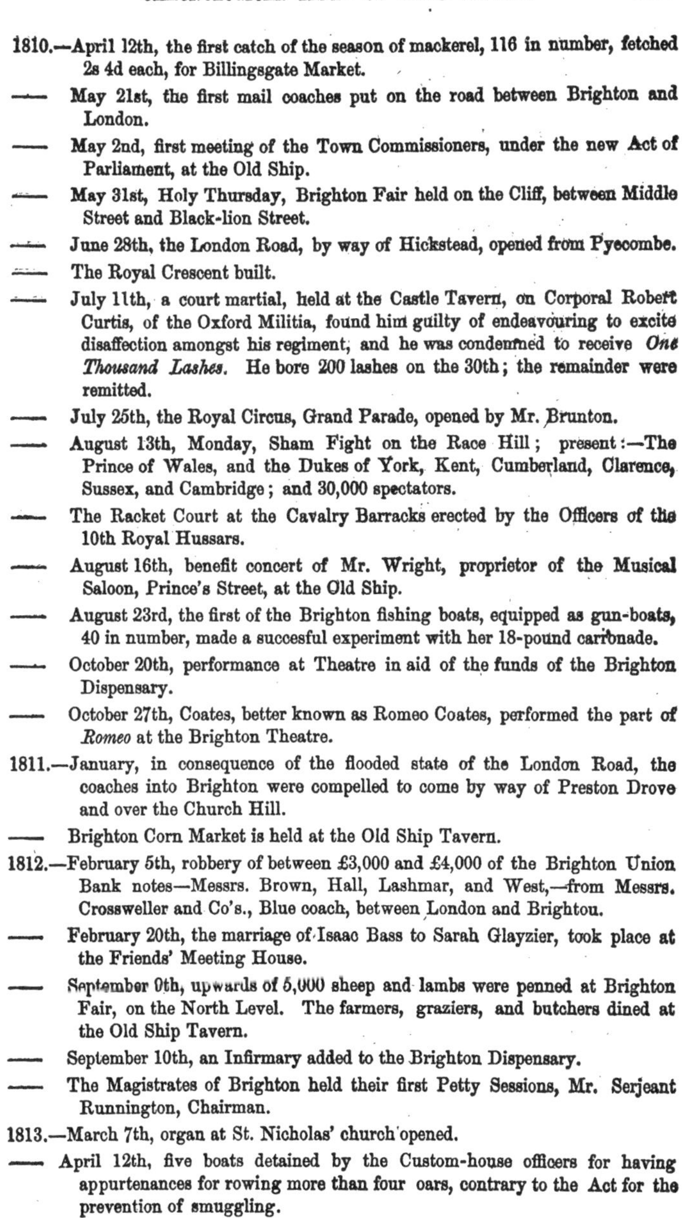

1810.—April 12th, the first catch of the season of mackerel, 116 in number, fetched 2s 4d each, for Billingsgate Market.

—— May 21st, the first mail coaches put on the road between Brighton and London.

—— May 2nd, first meeting of the Town Commissioners, under the new Act of Parliament, at the Old Ship.

—— May 31st, Holy Thursday, Brighton Fair held on the Cliff, between Middle Street and Black-lion Street.

—— June 28th, the London Road, by way of Hickstead, opened from Pyecombe.

—— The Royal Crescent built.

—— July 11th, a court martial, held at the Castle Tavern, on Corporal Robert Curtis, of the Oxford Militia, found him guilty of endeavouring to excite disaffection amongst his regiment, and he was condemned to receive *One Thousand Lashes.* He bore 200 lashes on the 30th; the remainder were remitted.

—— July 25th, the Royal Circus, Grand Parade, opened by Mr. Brunton.

—— August 13th, Monday, Sham Fight on the Race Hill; present:—The Prince of Wales, and the Dukes of York, Kent, Cumberland, Clarence, Sussex, and Cambridge; and 30,000 spectators.

—— The Racket Court at the Cavalry Barracks erected by the Officers of the 10th Royal Hussars.

—— August 16th, benefit concert of Mr. Wright, proprietor of the Musical Saloon, Prince's Street, at the Old Ship.

—— August 23rd, the first of the Brighton fishing boats, equipped as gun-boats, 40 in number, made a succesful experiment with her 18-pound carronade.

—— October 20th, performance at Theatre in aid of the funds of the Brighton Dispensary.

—— October 27th, Coates, better known as Romeo Coates, performed the part of *Romeo* at the Brighton Theatre.

1811.—January, in consequence of the flooded state of the London Road, the coaches into Brighton were compelled to come by way of Preston Drove and over the Church Hill.

—— Brighton Corn Market is held at the Old Ship Tavern.

1812.—February 5th, robbery of between £3,000 and £4,000 of the Brighton Union Bank notes—Messrs. Brown, Hall, Lashmar, and West,—from Messrs. Crossweller and Co's., Blue coach, between London and Brightou.

—— February 20th, the marriage of Isaac Bass to Sarah Glayzier, took place at the Friends' Meeting House.

—— September 9th, upwards of 5,000 sheep and lambs were penned at Brighton Fair, on the North Level. The farmers, graziers, and butchers dined at the Old Ship Tavern.

—— September 10th, an Infirmary added to the Brighton Dispensary.

—— The Magistrates of Brighton held their first Petty Sessions, Mr. Serjeant Runnington, Chairman.

1813.—March 7th, organ at St. Nicholas' church opened.

—— April 12th, five boats detained by the Custom-house officers for having appurtenances for rowing more than four oars, contrary to the Act for the prevention of smuggling.

—— April 15th, the salary of Mr Battcock, parish surgeon, raised from £80 to £100 per annum.

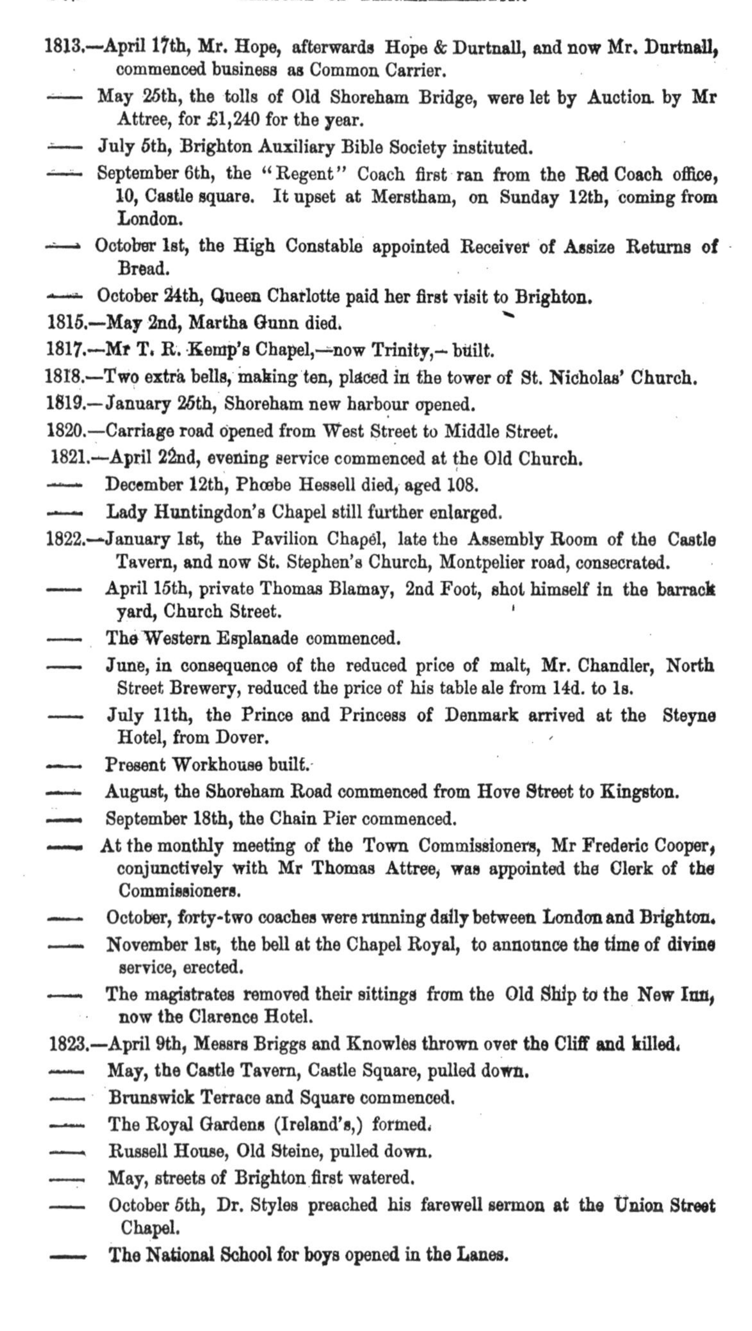

1813.—April 17th, Mr. Hope, afterwards Hope & Durtnall, and now Mr. Durtnall, commenced business as Common Carrier.

—— May 25th, the tolls of Old Shoreham Bridge, were let by Auction by Mr Attree, for £1,240 for the year.

—— July 5th, Brighton Auxiliary Bible Society instituted.

—— September 6th, the "Regent" Coach first ran from the Red Coach office, 10, Castle square. It upset at Merstham, on Sunday 12th, coming from London.

—— October 1st, the High Constable appointed Receiver of Assize Returns of Bread.

—— October 24th, Queen Charlotte paid her first visit to Brighton.

1815.—May 2nd, Martha Gunn died.

1817.—Mr T. R. Kemp's Chapel,—now Trinity,— built.

1818.—Two extra bells, making ten, placed in the tower of St. Nicholas' Church.

1819.—January 25th, Shoreham new harbour opened.

1820.—Carriage road opened from West Street to Middle Street.

1821.—April 22nd, evening service commenced at the Old Church.

—— December 12th, Phœbe Hessell died, aged 108.

—— Lady Huntingdon's Chapel still further enlarged.

1822.—January 1st, the Pavilion Chapel, late the Assembly Room of the Castle Tavern, and now St. Stephen's Church, Montpelier road, consecrated.

—— April 15th, private Thomas Blamay, 2nd Foot, shot himself in the barrack yard, Church Street.

—— The Western Esplanade commenced.

—— June, in consequence of the reduced price of malt, Mr. Chandler, North Street Brewery, reduced the price of his table ale from 14d. to 1s.

—— July 11th, the Prince and Princess of Denmark arrived at the Steyne Hotel, from Dover.

—— Present Workhouse built.

—— August, the Shoreham Road commenced from Hove Street to Kingston.

—— September 18th, the Chain Pier commenced.

—— At the monthly meeting of the Town Commissioners, Mr Frederic Cooper, conjunctively with Mr Thomas Attree, was appointed the Clerk of the Commissioners.

—— October, forty-two coaches were running daily between London and Brighton.

—— November 1st, the bell at the Chapel Royal, to announce the time of divine service, erected.

—— The magistrates removed their sittings from the Old Ship to the New Inn, now the Clarence Hotel.

1823.—April 9th, Messrs Briggs and Knowles thrown over the Cliff and killed.

—— May, the Castle Tavern, Castle Square, pulled down.

—— Brunswick Terrace and Square commenced.

—— The Royal Gardens (Ireland's,) formed.

—— Russell House, Old Steine, pulled down.

—— May, streets of Brighton first watered.

—— October 5th, Dr. Styles preached his farewell sermon at the Union Street Chapel.

—— The National School for boys opened in the Lanes.

1823.—Brighton Savings' Bank opened in Middle Street.
—— June 3rd, Mr. T. Furner appointed Town Surveyor.
—— September 8th, Old Steine enclosed.
—— September 22nd, Post Office opened in East Street.
—— November, Chain Pier opened.
—— Infant Schools first established in Brighton.
1824.—Saturday, May 8th, first stone of St. Peter's Church laid by Dr. Carr, Vicar.
—— Queen's Park and German Spa, Brighton, formed by Mr. Armstrong.
—— May 1st, Ireland's Gardens, Lewes Road, opened.
—— May 11th, Brighton Royal Catch and Glee Club (from the Golden Cross Inn,) meet at Old Ship for the first time.
—— May 3rd, Old Steine first lighted with gas.
—— First steam packet to Dieppe, the *Swift*, 80 horse power, put on.
—— June 1st, Rev. J. N. Goulty appointed to Union Street Chapel.
—— Brighton first lighted with gas.
—— August 1st, Rev. H. M. Wagner entered on his duties as Vicar.
—— November 24th, violent storm, which did great damage to Chain Pier.
—— December 11th, first meeting (at Old Ship,) for establishing the County Hospital.
—— December 26th, St. Margaret's Chapel opened.
1825.—February 7th, at a meeting at the Old Ship a resolution was passed to construct an iron railway between Brighton and Shoreham.
—— Ebenezer Chapel opened.
—— June 22nd, Brighton Improvement Act passed.
—— September 27th, Mr. Amon Wilds elected Town Surveyor.
—— December 18th, Trinity Chapel opened by the Rev. R. Anderson.
—— St. Margaret's Chapel built.
—— German Spa, Queen's Park, established.
—— St. George's Chapel built.
—— Hanover Chapel built. Opened August 30th.
—— Salem Chapel, Bond Street, enlarged.
1826.—Road in front of York Hotel formed.
—— Foundation stone of County Hospital laid, March 16th.
—— Western Esplanade, opposite Regency square, formed.
—— The name, King's Road, applied to the Cliff roadway from East Street to the extreme west of the town.
—— April 21st, Trinity Chapel consecrated.
1827.—January 18th, St. Mary's Chapel consecrated.
—— April 5th, Mr. N. Cooke, organist of the Parish Church, died.
1828.—January 25th, St. Peter's Church consecrated.
—— June 12th, County Hospital opened.
—— October 11th, the statue of George IV., by Chantry, erected on the Old Steyne.
—— October 29th, Musical festival at St. Peter's Church.
1829.—June 27th, Bethel Chapel (site of the present St. Paul's) West Street, opened.

1829.—August 16th, Mr. W. Crossweller, coach proprietor, died.
— November 20th, St. Peter's clock erected.
1830.—The Battery on the King's road rebuilt further to the south.
— April, corner stone of Town Hall laid.
— April 12th, Mr. Somers Clarke appointed Vestry Clerk.
— April 15th, Brighton Police Force established, under Chief-Officer Pilbeam.
— August 30th, William IV. and his Queen (Adelaide) first visit Brighton.
— National Schools opened.
— First stone of the Town Hall laid by T. R. Kemp, Esq.
1831.—Easter Monday, Road across the Steine opened.
— July 16th, Celia Holloway murdered.
— September 23rd, Post Office opened in the New Road.
— October 20th, first stone of New Shoreham Bridge laid.
— December 5th, Body of Hannah Hobbs found.
— December 10th, Holloway executed at Horsham.
1832.—Cattle Market opened on Church Hill.
— August 6th, Sand Cause decision.
— December 11th, First Brighton Election, Wigney and Faithfull returned.
1833.—May 12th, Fire at Wisden's, Western Road.
— September 30th, the Antheum, Hove, fell.
— October 15th, the Chain Pier partially destroyed during a terrific gale.
— Carriage road opened across the Steyne from Castle Square to St. James's Street.
— Rev. T. Trocke appointed to Chapel Royal.
1836.—November 29th, Great storm, which destroyed much of the platform of the Chain Pier.
— St. Mary's Hall, Eastern road, erected.
1837.—(5,598) Jews' Synagogue in Devonshire Place erected.
— October 1st, James Botting, the Old Bailey Executioner, died at Brighton, his native place.
— October 4th, Her Majesty's first visit to Brighton.
— December 25th, Great Snow storm.
1838.—January 15th, the Northern sewer commenced.
— March 19th, London and Brighton Railway commenced.
— April 26th, Christ Church consecrated.
— May 28th, Swiss Gardens opened.
1839.—February 4th, first permanent rail on the London and Brighton Railway laid at Hassock's Gate, by Mr. Alfred Morris.
1840.—February 18th, Upfold, stage coachman killed.
— May 11th, Railway to Shoreham opened.
— June 9th, Rev. J. Allen appointed chaplain of the Workhouse.
— July 14th, Court of Requests opened.
— August 1st, Crim. Con. trial, Heaviside *v.* Lardner, at Lewes, damages £8,000.
— Court Martial at Cavalry Barracks, on Capt. R. A. Reynolds, 11th Hussars, who was cashiered.
1841.—June 30th, Pechell and Wigney elected.

1841.—July 5th, line opened to Hayward's Heath.

— September 21st, Railway opened from Brighton to London.

1842.—May 5th, Lord Alfred Hervey first elected for Brighton.

1844.—February 1st, experiment of Bude Light on the Old Steine.

— March 13th, Mr. Solomon, Chief-Officer of Police murdered.

— Lawrence executed for the murder of Mr. Solomon.

1845.—The Level planted with trees.

— May 17th, first stone of the Viaduct over the London Road laid.

— November 24th, Railway opened to Worthing.

1846.—May 25th, Fountain on the Steine opened.

— King's Road widened from West street to the Battery.

— June 8th, Railway opened to Chichester.

— June 8th, Railway opened to Lewes.

— June 27th, Railway opened to Hastings.

— July 12th, last Lewes coach ran.

— August 23rd, Jenny Lind, sung at Brighton.

— November 10th, Eye Infirmary opened.

1847.—March 5th, Mr. Maynard appointed Parish Assessor.

— General fast, on account of the famine.

— April 16th, first County Court held.

— June 14th, Line opened to Portsmouth.

— July 31st, Pechell and Harvey re-elected.

— December 6th, Railway opened to Newhaven.

1848.—June 27th, the first stone of Brighton College laid by Dr. Gilbert, Lord Bishop of Chichester.

— July 1st, the clock is removed from the clock tower of the Pavilion.

— The new Post Office in Ship Stıeet erected.

— October 18th, St. Paul's opened by license.

— October 23rd, Mechanics' Institution inaugurated.

1849.—February 7th, Mr Griffith murdered.

— July 28th, Race Stand purchased.

— August 10th, Mr. Hatton appointed Actuary of the Savings' Bank.

— September 21st, St. Mark's Church consecrated.

— November 3rd, Mr. F. Slight appointed Secretary to the London, Brighton, and South-Coast Railway Company.

— Royal Pavilion property purchased by the town for £53,000.

— Post Office opened in Ship Street.

1850.—June 19th, the Town took possession of the Pavilion.

— June 23rd, Sunday labour discontinued at the Post Office.

— June 28th, Pavilion Grounds first opened to the public.

— July 17th, great storm, Pool Valley, &c., flooded.

— November 27th, first interment in the Extra Mural Cemetery.

— November 19th, violent storm. Two houses blown down near the Wick.

— December 30th, first Pavilion rate made.

1851.—January 21st, opening Ball at the Pavilion.

— May 15th, south portion of the Pavilion property sold for £1722.

1851.—Electric Telegraph opened to Brighton.

— August 11th, first fête of the Mechanics' Institution at the Swiss Gardens, Shoreham.

— August 14th, consecration of the Brighton Extra Mural Cemetry, by the Bishop of Chichester.

— The Mantellian Academy of Science opened.

1852.—September 4th, fire at P. Salomons, Esq., Brunswick Terrace.

— September 29th, fire at Bickford's King's Road.

— November 8th, Mr. Furse's shop, North Street, robbed of £400 worth of jewellery, &c.

1853.—February 3rd, burglar shot at Shoreham.

— March 6th, Caroline Sherwood murdered her child, at Hove.

— March 17th, explosion at the Railway Terminus, three men killed.

— April 1st, Messrs. Black and Foakes appointed Assessors.

— May 16th, First stone of Female Orphan Asylum laid.

— August 14th, Rev. F. W. Robertson died.

— December 21st, Mr. George White appointed Chief-Officer of Police.

1854.—April 3rd, Charter of Incorporation obtained.

— April 8th, Parish Church restored and re-opened.

— June 7th, Major Fawcett elected first Mayor of Brighton.

— August 28th, Mr. and Mrs. Passmore appointed Governor and Matron of the Workhouse.

— November 1st, Preston toll-gate removed.

1855.—July 9th, East Grinstead line opened.

— July 10th, Gregory's house, North Street, fell.

— July 19th, Mr. Lewis Slight, jun., elected Borough Accountant.

— July 22nd, Mr. Hannington died, in his 71st year.

1856.—March 28th, Brighton Protestant Association formed.

— June 4th, Peace Demonstration at Brighton.

— July 29th, fire at Stubbs's, Trafalgar Street.

— September, fire at Funnell's, chemist, Upper North Street.

— December 2nd, Tractarian defeat at the Town Hall.

1857.—April 7th, Dodson and Pevensey returned for East Sussex.

— June 25th, Brown, the Sussex cricketer, died.

— October 7th, Day of Humiliation for the Massacres in India.

— October 8th, Wreck of the "Pilgrim."

— November 3rd, Music Hall, Edward street, destroyed by fire, second time.

— November 18th, Anti-Tractarian Demonstration and Riots at Lewes.

— Mr. Isaac Tester died, aged 54.

— December 22nd, consecration of the Parochial Burial Ground.

1860.—Sir G. B. Pechell, M.P. for Brighton, died.

— Great storm, wreck of the "Transit" and "Atlantique" off Brighton.

— Mr. James White returned as a Member for Brighton.

1861 Easter Monday, Volunteer Review on the Downs, under Lord Ranelagh.

— August 25th, frightful railway collision in Clayton Tunnel, twenty-one persons killed.

1862.—Easter Monday, Volunteer Review on the Race Hill, under Lord Clyde.

1862.—John O'Dea, a private of the 18th Hussars, shot in the Barrack yard, Church Street, by Private John Flood, of the same regiment. Flood was tried at the County Assizes and condemned to be hanged, but the capital sentence was ultimately commuted to penal servitude for life.

—— Water found in the Warren Farm Well.

—— Temporary Church of St. Mary Magdalene erected and opened in Bread street.

—— October, Police Station built on the Level.

—— November 5th, the author of this work died suddenly in his 52nd year.

—— November 27th, first Brighton and Sussex Fat-Stock Show held.

—— December 12th, Mr. Lewis Slight, jun., Borough Accountant, committed suicide by hanging.

Index

OPINIONS OF THE PRESS.

"In a town with such an unchequered existence as Brighton has had the publication of its history is an event in itself. And when the work has been undertaken by a townsman, who seems to have brought to bear on his task much industry and research, the event is all the more noticeable. Possibly in deference to the general wish for small outgoings in connexion with literary expenses, Mr. Erredge is publishing in monthly parts, and thus, as only one-twelfth part of the whole work is before us, a decided opinion as to its merits can hardly be pronounced. Already, however, as we have intimated, industry and research are evolved in the composition. This specimen part is very interesting, especially to all who take the least pleasure in local archæology, in which it is peculiarly rich. The situation, soil, geology, and climate, are, further, spoken of, the best authorities extant being quoted on each subject. Altogether, the work gives good promise. It is well got up."—*Brighton Guardian*, Dec. 18th, 1861.

The chapter "on and about the Race Course" is not so replete with interest as many of its predecessors, but the reason for this is simple—it speaks generally of matters of too recent occurrence. But though this is a disadvantage now, with what pleasure will a future generation turn to the pages preserved by their predecessors and read of the heroic deeds performed on the Downs by the Volunteers of 1861-62. Also what a record will be presented to their minds of indomitable perseverance, resulting in obtaining water in the Warren Farm Well, even at a depth of 1,285 feet. The chapter "On past and present pastimes," speaks of Brighton in the "good old times when George the Third was King," his son acting as Regent. Interesting details, including the original prospectus are introduced concerning the Chain Pier. How glorious the prospectus still looks on paper—how sad the realization to the unlucky ones induced to invest their capital in shares.—*Brighton Gazette*, Oct. 23rd, 1862. (Tenth notice.)

This emanation from the lately active brain of one who has now been laid in the cold grave, has an interest tinged with sadness. The work, of which this is almost the final instalment, will soon be brought to its completion, and will then remain a kind of monument to the skill and industry of the departed. The portion before us gives the conclusion of the Chapter on "Past and Present Pastimes," followed bo a very interesting Chapter on "The Historical Street of the Town," to wit, West street, and by an account of the Brighton Public Institutions, Charities, and Endowments.—*Brighton Times*, Nov. 15th, 1862. (Ninth nctice.)

A melancholy interest attaches to this the 11th number of the *History of Brighthelmston* from the sudden death of the author, Mr Erredge, last week, just as he had arrived at the completion of his labours as a chronicler, of the fortunes and celebrities of his native town. One more number will complete the work. In this part, as in the previous ones, there is much curious matter connected with the past days of Brighton, and West street is made to figure in it as "the historical street of the town." Here, we know, is the King's Head, of Charles the Second celebrity; and here Mr Thrale had a house, at which Dr. Johnson was a sojourner; and in connection with this street some other personages, who figure in history in not an over-reputable fashion, are brought upon the stage again by Mr Erredge.—*Brighton Herald*, Nov. 15th, 1862. (Sixth notice.)

No. 10.—Mr Erredge's "History" is progressing capitally, and will form, when complete, a very excellent book of reference for facts in connection with the ancient and modern history of the "Queen of Watering Places." The "Past and Present Pastimes" of Brighton, the history of the formation of our railway lines, of the Chain Pier, the Warren Farm Well, and other matters of lively interest, form the principal contents of the October number.—*Brighton Examiner*, Oct 21st, 1862. (Tenth notice.)

ERREDGE'S HISTORY OF BRIGHTHELMSTON.—The third number of this history has reached us, and we have read it with very great interest; indeed, we have given one or two extraets therefrom. Although, as we have said before, Brighton is not surrounded by much historical interest, nevertheless, Mr Erredge manages to make his work amusing; and we are reminded that the events of the present century have an historical interest which is quite refreshing, without going into the musty records of the Saxon and Norman days. The writer appears not to let anything of the slightest value pass by; and in preserving, both the little and great matters associated with the history of Brighton, he makes the work alike useful and amusing.—*West Sussex Gazette*, March 6th, 1862. (Second Notice)

The further Mr. Erredge proceeds in producing a complete history of Brighton, the more are we surprised that it had never been accomplished before. That it was not for lack of matter is evident, for we scarcely remember any local history in which so many valuable facts and occurrences could be evolved to make up a work of such general and thrilling interest. In the ninth number now before us we are introduced to that ex-domain of Royalty, the Marine Pavilion, in connection with which ample scope is afforded for the display of the versatile ability of the author. The anecdotes and incidents related in connection with the Prince of Wales and his voluptuous associates have about them a raciness which recommends them to the notice, not only of those more immediately interested in local events, but to all the subjects of Her Majesty's dominions. Though not quite up to the "sensational" standard of the Reynold's school, some portions of the work are somewhat exciting, and would serve as capital *materiel* for romancists.—*The News*, Sept. 6th, 1862. (Third notice.)

ORIGIN OF THE BRIGHTHELMSTON "FLY."—Everybody who has gone to Brighton must have wondered why it is that cabs are there systematically called "Flys." Mr J. A. Erredge, in his admirable *History of Brighthelmston*, offers the explanation.—*Twice a Week*, for May.